lonely planet

Bolivia

Alexis Averbuck, Michael Grosberg, Brian Kleupfel, Vesna Maric, Joe Sills, Ryan Ver Berkmoes

CONTENTS

Gateway of the Sun, Tiwanaku (p71)

FROM LEFT: MARTIN DOCAR/SHUTTERSTOCK, MIROSLAV SR.../SHUTTERSTOCK

Andean Flamingo, Laguna Colorada (p168)

SASIPA MUENNUCH/GETTY IMAGES

La Paz (p50)

BOLIVIA

THE JOURNEY BEGINS HERE

Walking through La Paz's Plaza San Francisco one day, I saw a *curandero* (Aymara healer) taking small pieces of paper from a woman, blowing on them and chanting, and burning each, piece by piece. This small act of ancient faith, juxtaposed with the massive Catholic icon which they were leaning against, says everything about Bolivia: indigenous systems overlaid, but never quite replaced by, the colonists.

Brian Kluepfel

Brian is an author on travel, sport and music, and lives on the banks of the mighty Hudson River. He's co-authored more than 20 Lonely Planet guides and coffee-table books, including three about Bolivia.

@briankluepfel

My favorite experience would have to be **paragliding over La Paz's rugged outskirts** (p79). I am terrified of heights, but I had to do it – and I'll never forget it, either.

WHO GOES WHERE

Our writers and experts choose the places which, for them, define Bolivia.

SL-PHOTOGRAPHY/SHUTTERSTOCK

I felt genuinely honored to be assigned the Uyuni section of this guide book. The salt flats have been on my personal bucket list for a decade. In hindsight, I find myself daydreaming of a place I'd never heard of before traveling to Bolivia for this book – **Isla del Sol** (p96; pictured). While Uyuni is indescribably beautiful, Isla del Sol feels endlessly interesting. I long to return and renew my days of research, wandering through its ruins without an itinerary.

Joe Sills

@JoeSills

Joe is a Memphis-based freelance writer and photographer covering travel, conservation efforts and climate research around the globe. He wrote the Lake Titicaca and Southern Altiplano chapters.

JOSE ARCOS AGUILAR/SHUTTERSTOCK

In all of my years of travel I have never encountered anything quite like arriving from hours of driving through Chiquitania's rain-bright forest to **San Xavier** (p280; pictured), my first of the UNESCO-listed Jesuit missions. Parrots flew through the treetops on the broad square and the soft cream façade and pillars of the church blew my mind...traced all over with soft sienna patterns, like henna. The massive carved spiraling interior columns created a procession to the fascinating, hand-carved gilded altar within.

Alexis Averbuck

alexisaverbuck.com

Alexis paints and writes about her adventures – from living in Antarctica for a year to crossing the Pacific by sailboat – for Lonely Planet, National Geographic UK and other international outlets. Alexis wrote the Santa Cruz & Gran Chiquitania chapter.

There's no easier place to imagine the age of the dinosaur than **Torotoro National Park** (p194; pictured). The number and quality of the footprints and the scale of the tectonic uplift, like a diagram in a geology textbook, make it appear you're tromping through a primordial scene. Which makes it even more startling to see school-age kids on their way home along cliffside pathways at 3600m.

Michael Grosberg

likelocal.io

Michael is a longtime travel guidebook writer and co-founder of travel startup LikeLocal. He wrote the Central Highlands and History chapters.

LARISSA CHILANTI/SHUTTERSTOCK

Sorata (p138; pictured) sits on the edge between the lush Yungas and the high-altitude wilds of the Andes. I love getting far above the treeline, where the mists part to reveal peaks looming overhead that shrink you right down to size and where trails were trod by Inca llama trains in centuries past.

Ryan Ver Berkmoes

bluesky: @ryanvb

Ryan has traveled the world for Lonely Planet, always ready to go around just one more bend in the road. Ryan wrote The Cordilleras & Yungas chapter.

FELIPE DUENAS/SHUTTERSTOCK

ADAMSPENCER/SHUTTERSTOCK

Being on a rainforest walk is unlike anything I have ever experienced in my life – the sheer amount of life unfolding around me was just sublime. I must add to that the priceless feeling of safety of being led through the forest by a professional guide indigenous to the area. Their knowledge revealed the many magical aspects of the surrounding flora and fauna. I don't think anything will match up to being inside the incredible environment of the **Amazon** (p293; pictured).

Vesna Maric

@vesnamarx

Vesna writes literary fiction and non fiction, and essays. She wrote the Amazon Basin and Bolivia Wildlife chapters.

CONTRIBUTING WRITER

Maria Silvia Trigo

@MariaSTrigo

Maria is a freelance journalist based in Bolivia. Before setting up in a place to raise her two children, she has traveled to 29 countries and more than 90 cities and towns. What does she want most in life? To have the chance to hold her family and backpacks up and go around the world the way she loves: going slow, disconnected and with no fixed plans.

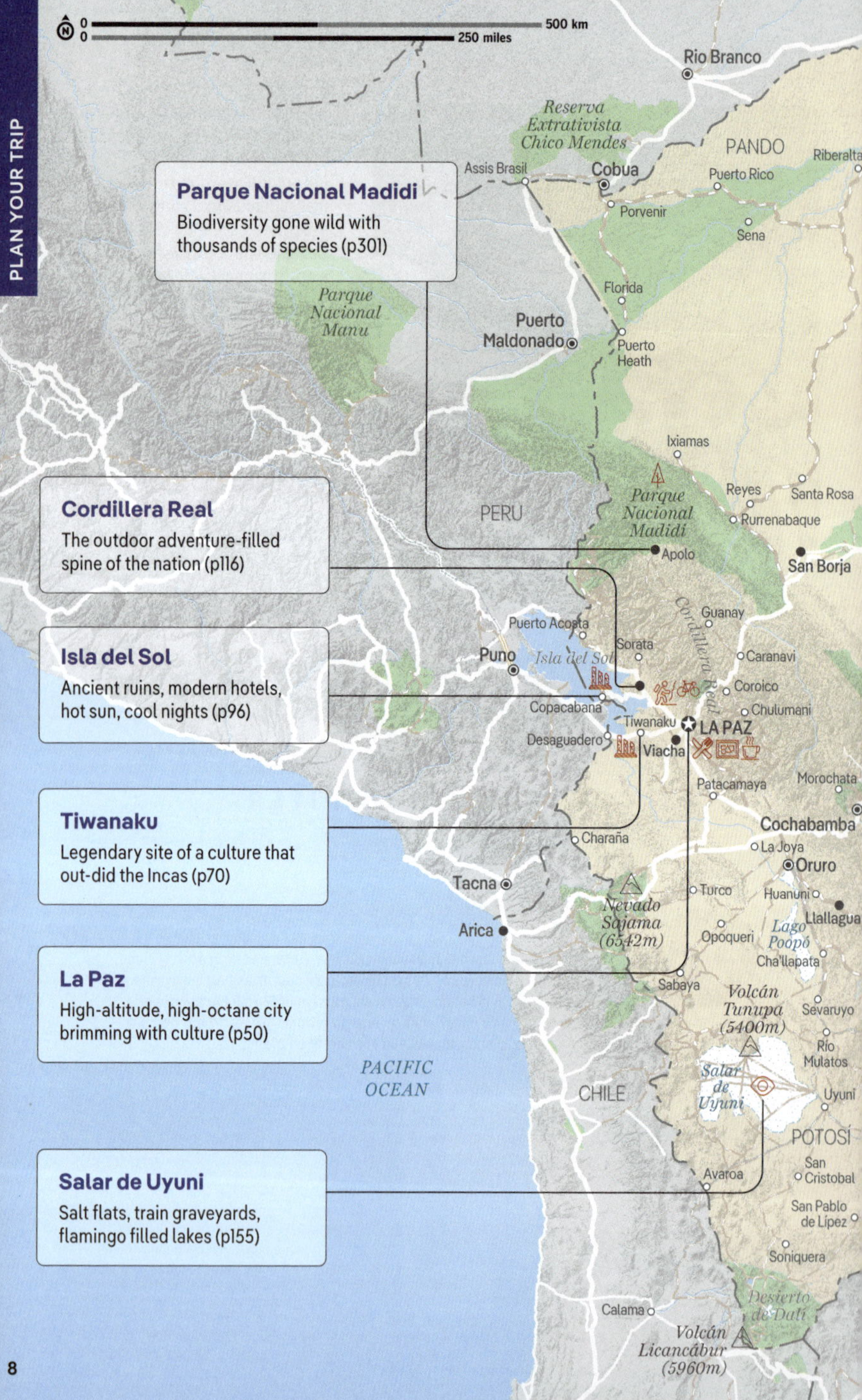

0 500 km
0 250 miles
Parque Nacional Madidi
Biodiversity gone wild with thousands of species (p301)
Cordillera Real
The outdoor adventure-filled spine of the nation (p116)
Isla del Sol
Ancient ruins, modern hotels, hot sun, cool nights (p96)
Tiwanaku
Legendary site of a culture that out-did the Incas (p70)
La Paz
High-altitude, high-octane city brimming with culture (p50)
Salar de Uyuni
Salt flats, train graveyards, flamingo filled lakes (p155)
Rio Branco
Reserva Extrativista Chico Mendes
PANDO
Riberalta
Assis Brasil
Cobua
Puerto Rico
Porvenir
Sena
Parque Nacional Manu
Florida
Puerto Maldonado
Puerto Heath
Ixiamas
Reyes
Santa Rosa
Parque Nacional Madidi
Rurrenabaque
PERU
Apolo
San Borja
Cordillera Real
Guanay
Puerto Acosta
Sorata
Caranavi
Puno
Isla del Sol
Coroico
Copacabana
Chulumani
Tiwanaku
LA PAZ
Desaguadero
Viacha
Patacamaya
Morochata
Cochabamba
Charaña
La Joya
Oruro
Tacna
Turco
Huanuni
Nevado Sajama (6542m)
Llallagua
Arica
Opoqueri
Lago Poopó
Cha'llapata
Sabaya
Volcán Tunupa (5400m)
Sevaruyo
Río Mulatos
PACIFIC OCEAN
Salar de Uyuni
CHILE
Uyuni
POTOSÍ
Avaroa
San Cristobal
San Pablo de Lípez
Soniquera
Desierto de Dalí
Calama
Volcán Licancábur (5960m)

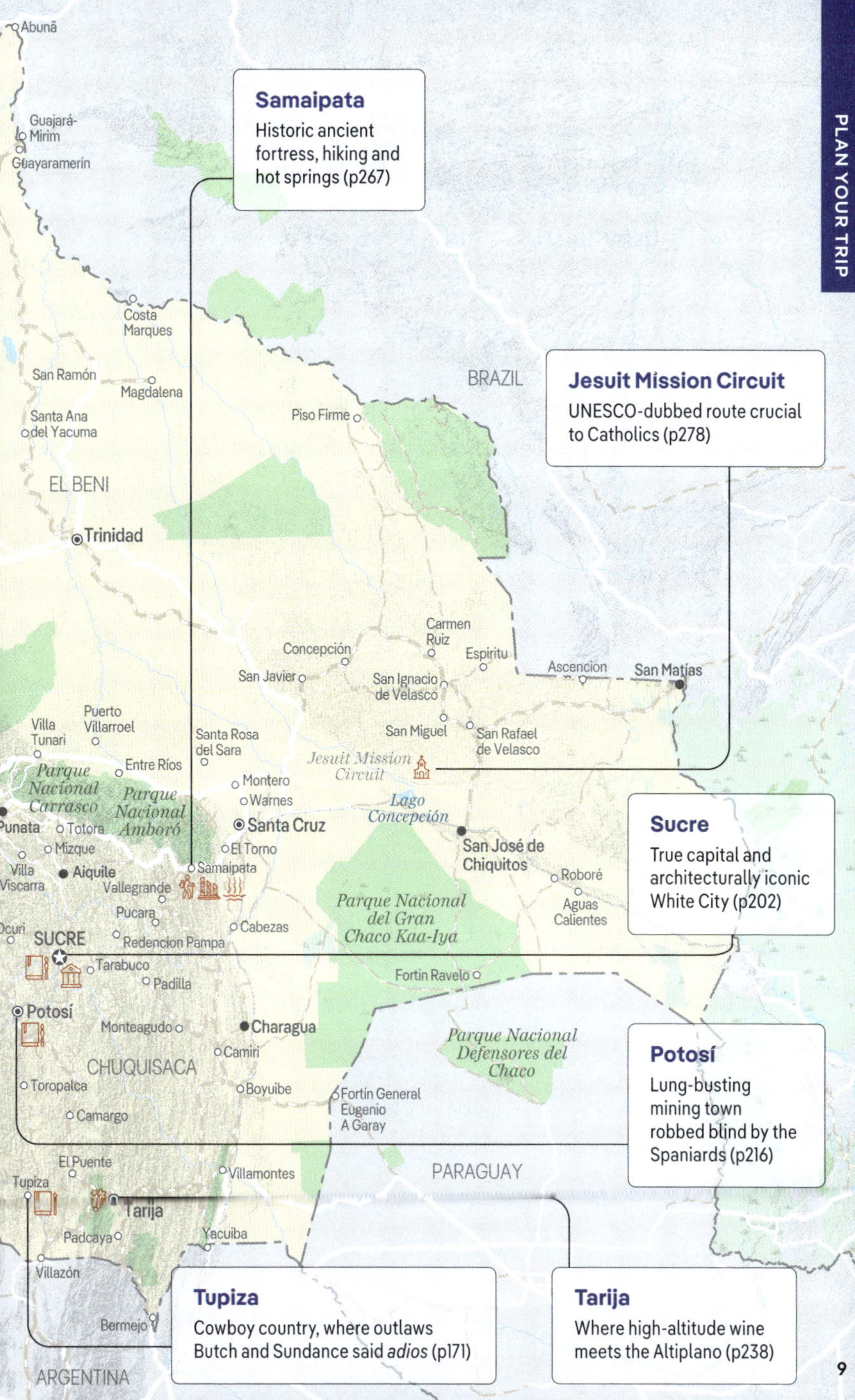
Samaipata
Historic ancient fortress, hiking and hot springs (p267)
Jesuit Mission Circuit
UNESCO-dubbed route crucial to Catholics (p278)
Sucre
True capital and architecturally iconic White City (p202)
Potosí
Lung-busting mining town robbed blind by the Spaniards (p216)
Tupiza
Cowboy country, where outlaws Butch and Sundance said *adios* (p171)
Tarija
Where high-altitude wine meets the Altiplano (p238)
Abunã
Guajará-Mirim
Guayaramerín
Costa Marques
San Ramón
Magdalena
Santa Ana del Yacuma
EL BENI
Trinidad
BRAZIL
Piso Firme
Carmen Ruiz
Concepción
Espiritu
San Javier
San Ignacio de Velasco
Ascencion
San Matías
San Miguel
San Rafael de Velasco
Puerto Villarroel
Villa Tunari
Santa Rosa del Sara
Jesuit Mission Circuit
Entre Ríos
Parque Nacional Carrasco
Parque Nacional Amboró
Montero
Warnes
Lago Concepción
Punata
Totora
Santa Cruz
San José de Chiquitos
Mizque
El Torno
Villa Viscarra
Aiquile
Samaipata
Roboré
Vallegrande
Parque Nacional del Gran Chaco Kaa-Iya
Aguas Calientes
Pucara
Ocuri
SUCRE
Redencion Pampa
Cabezas
Tarabuco
Padilla
Fortin Ravelo
Potosí
Monteagudo
Charagua
Parque Nacional Defensores del Chaco
Camiri
CHUQUISACA
Toropalca
Boyuibe
Fortín General Eugenio A Garay
Camargo
El Puente
Villamontes
PARAGUAY
Tupiza
Tarija
Padcaya
Yacuiba
Villazón
Bermejo
ARGENTINA

ARTISTIC VISIONS

Bolivia is a nation proud of its artistic and cultural heritage, and this is obvious in galleries large and small throughout the country. Each region seems to have its own favored artist or artists, and more active galleries (and even coffee houses) have rotating shows. From political and social themes to indigenous and nature-inspired creations, take the time to appreciate the range of artwork at your fingertips.

The Mural Majority

The buildings of Bolivia are absolutely covered in artwork. Murals may be based on wildlife, respected or defected politicians, cultural traditions, or even food.

The Personal is Political

One window into Bolivia's soul is through artists like **Walter Solón** (p78) and **Gastón Ugalde** (p78), whose works express equal amounts of outrage and admiration.

Gallery Walks

High-flying La Paz has two neighborhoods worth your while, with art walks in Sopocachi and Downtown getting you some exercise while you take in the culture.

Sucre (p202)

BEST ARTISTIC EXPERIENCES

Dig the modernist and classic at ❶ **Museo Nacional de Arte** (p62), a colonial-era gem of a building with rotating modern art and a classy permanent collection.

Weave a tale of wonder in Sucre at ❷ **Museo de Arte Indígena** (p202), which focuses on the weavings of the Jalq'a and Tarabuco people of Chuquisaca.

Explore floor upon floor of international art and photography exhibitions in the ❸ **Manzana Uno Espacio de Arte** (p261) in Santa Cruz.

Raise your fist at ❹ **Casa/Museo Solón** (p78), an encapsulation of Bolivia's political and social struggles, featuring Don Quixote.

Get a taste of Guaraní culture at Santa Cruz's ❺ **Museo Guaraní** (p264), where you'll find indigenous art, ceremonial dress and artisanal goods.

ARTISAN CRAFTS

Whether you fancy pottery, weaving, painting, or jewelry, you're sure to find it among the street vendors, galleries, and custom goods shops of Bolivia's towns and cities. You'll find ample opportunity to see a variety of hand-crafted goods, support local artisans, and bring a unique keepsake home to adorn your living room, art collection, or personal wardrobe. Local markets are among the places to browse.

FROM LEFT: GRAYSONSTOCK/SHUTTERSTOCK, SL-PHOTOGRAPHY/SHUTTERSTOCK, LOUIELEA/SHUTTERSTOCK

Gone to Pot

The incredible craft of indigenous Bolivian pottery tells a cultural-historic tale. You'll find examples at Alma de Monte's stores in Tarija, La Paz and Cochabamba.

Wondrous Weaving

Woven blankets, shawls, hats and other colorful pieces make durable mementoes of your trip; find great handmade examples in Sucre's **Sunday Market** (p211).

Handbags & Jewels

Necklaces of quality and other accessories can be found at **Inca Pallay** (p209) in Sucre and **Mistura** in La Paz.

Traditional totora reed boats, Lake Titicaca (p85)

BEST ARTS & CRAFTS EXPERIENCES

Enchant yourself with a purchase at La Paz's famed ❶ **Mercado de las Brujas** (p65), which has ponchos, hats, and a whole array of woven and worked goods.

Watch in wonder as the craftspeople at ❷ **Lake Titicaca** (p85) weave boats and other items from the totora reeds plucked from the lakeside.

Stop and stare at the ❸ **Precious Metals Museum of La Paz** (p62), appreciating centuries-old handiwork.

Worship at the temples of ❹ **Tiwanaku** (p89) while taking in the spectacular array of pottery created by this Pre-Incan civilization.

Take a tour in the Amazon to meet indigenous artisans from the ❺ **Tsimané** (p311) communities and observe them at work.

PARKS, PLANTS & GARDENS

Variety in topography and ecosystems means that Bolivia has a bonanza of plant life, in bloom and on display at its lovely nature parks and botanical gardens. From prickly cactus displays to hummingbird-catching roses, the nation's Amazon forest, *cerrado* (savanna) and *bosque seco* (dry forest), and other vegetation types can be found at these public parks. A nice respite from the bustle of their home cities, full of fascinating flora.

FROM LEFT: MANAMANA/SHUTTERSTOCK, MAPIMARF/SHUTTERSTOCK, ESKYSTUDIO/SHUTTERSTOCK

Into the Unknown Biome

Bolivia was only recently catalogued botanically, so there's still a lot of discovery happening. Imagine trying to take it all in.

A Botanist's Wonderland

While categorization has been slow, botanical exploration began long ago. Since 1600, Swedish, German, Hungarian and American botanists have visited.

Flora & Fauna

Bolivia's botanical gardens double as habitats for some of the country's extraordinarily diverse wildlife – besides the flora you'll see everything from llamas to rare birds to butterflies.

Butterfly at Biocentro Güembé (p265)

BEST PARK & GARDEN EXPERIENCES

Commune with tortoises and sloths at Santa Cruz's ❶ **Jardín Botánico** (p264), 200 hectares outside the city limits with a cactarium and viewing platform.

Relax in extravagant gardens surrounding a mining magnate's Versaille-inspired mansion at the ❷ **Palacio Portales** (p191).

Play on a butterfly farm, examine orchid exhibitions, or cool off in 15 natural pools at ❸ **Biocentro Güembé** (p265).

Stroll around 4 hectares of exotic plants at ❹ **El Picacho** (p238), the hacienda residence of a former president.

Wander among mausoleums that dwarf most Sucre residents' homes at the city's ❺ **Cementerio Municipal** (p207).

Salar de Uyuni (p155)

NATURAL WONDERS

From the jagged snow-topped Andean range to the odd stalactite-like spires of Valle de la Luna and Valle de las Ánimas; endless salt flats with shimmering lakes, splendid jungle roads carved out of hillsides, and canyons echoing with the cry of condors. Bolivia practically screams 'the great outdoors;' it's for you to measure.

National Parks

Bolivia has 14 national parks and integrated natural management areas, from massive Madidi to (relatively) tiny Torotoro. Spanning eight departments, you'll find something in every corner.

Climb Every Mountain

Twelve Bolivian peaks are higher than 6000m, and three top 6400m: **Sajama** (p150), **Illimani** (p123), and **Ancohuma** (p122). Daunting, but doable: many tour companies offer excursions.

BEST NATURAL WONDER EXPERIENCES

Share the space of ❶ **Parque Nacional Amboró** (p272) with more than 900 avian species, ocelots, jaguars and rare spectacled bears.

Adjust your eyes to ❷ **Salar de Uyuni's** (p155) stunning salt flat, the world's largest. Lose yourself in the endless horizon and gasp at a train graveyard.

Take it to the edge at ❸ **Pilaya Canyon** (p250) between Chuquisaca and Tarija, where you'll come to the brink of the world's sixth-deepest canyon, dotted with cacti, condors soaring above.

Tickle yourself pink at ❹ **Laguna Colorada** (p168) of Eduardo Avaroa National Reserve, a high-altitude lake that's home to 60,000 flamingos.

Scale the heights at ❺ **Huayna Potosí** (p118), the closest mountain to La Paz: at 6000m it is both stunning and a challenge to climbers.

INTO THE WILD

More than 2000 bird species, including many endemic to Bolivia; cud-chewing camelids sauntering the high plains in collective tranquility; jungles of jaguars and riverine pink dolphins. Plant life ranging from unimaginable orchids to dozens of spiny cacti species. From mountaintop to jungle floor, you'll view a natural abundance that defies expectations.

FROM LEFT: ADALBERT DRAGON/SHUTTERSTOCK, DANNY YE/SHUTTERSTOCK

Mad for Madidi

Parque Nacional Madidi (p296) is one of the world's most precious wilderness gems. From lowland rainforests to Andean peaks; it contains 44% of all mammal species in the Americas.

For the Birds

Wildlife conservation organization **Asociación Armonía** (p277) administers seven wildlife areas, protecting their colorful rare birds and rarities like the giant anteater, while also supporting indigenous communities.

The Camelids

Llamas, alpacas, vicuñas, guanacos...can you tell the difference? You'll see all these traditional Andean beasts of burden at high-altitude locations, free to roam.

❶ ❺ ❸ ❷ ❹

BEST WILDLIFE EXPERIENCES

Hike to ❶ **Reserva Barba Azul** (p324), the blue-throated macaw reserve, where an experiment in eco-ranching is saving trees and the world's rarest macaw.

See red at ❷ **Eduardo Avaroa National Reserve's** (p166) Laguna Colorada, where 60,000 flamingos nest on alabaster islands of borax.

Show your colors at ❸ **Reserva Paraba Frente Roja** (p277), home to a welcoming community effort to save these raucous parrots from the pet trade.

Get elevated at ❹ **Reserva Biológica Cordillera de Sama** (p249) and **Pilaya Canyon** (p250), Tarija with families of llamas dodging cacti, and Andean condors soaring above the canyon.

Make a splash on boat rides through ❺ **Rurrenabaque and Trinidad**, where you'll spot the oddity of the Amazon, the strangely beautiful **pink river dolphin** (p312).

URBAN DELIGHTS

A nation of only 11 million souls still vibes with city life: Santa Cruz, a mini-Miami, is closer culturally to neighboring Brazil in many aspects; rival La Paz features colonial plazas, cable cars in the sky, and the country's tallest building. Sucre and Cochabamba are smaller, yet still bustling: in Bolivia, city folk will do just fine.

Cafe Culture

Santa Cruz and La Paz are host to an amazing **cafe culture** (p60) (including coffee tastings) buoyed by growing pride in tasty beans from Bolivia's humid valleys.

Museum Tours

In La Paz's **museums** (p62) you can take in a lot of art, history and cultural factoids while getting a break from the weather.

Murals and Public Art

La Paz is not shy about expressing itself through colorful graffiti or murals; the **Chualluma** (p74) barrio of El Alto has been completely adorned by local artists.

FROM LEFT: GRAYSONSTOCK/SHUTTERSTOCK, DCSTOCKPHOTOGRAPHY/SHUTTERSTOCK, WOODVILLAGE/SHUTTERSTOCK

Parade in La Paz (p50)

BEST URBAN EXPERIENCES

❶ **Love a parade** (p56) down the Prado in La Paz, participants decked out in full folkloric costume. Don't be shy: you may be asked to join!

Ride the skyways of La Paz or Cochabamba via the wondrous ❷ **teleférico** (p58; aerial cable car) system: built for commuters, loved by tourists.

Shout your lungs out at a ❸ **soccer match** (p66) at the stadia of Santa Cruz, Potosi, Cochabamba, or La Paz. Gol! Face-painting optional.

Karaoke or dance the night away in a ❹ **bohemian pub-crawl** (p192) in Cochabamba in one of its popular bars or discotecas.

Take a gander from ❺ **Tarija's two hilltop lookouts** (p245), one Christian-themed, and one wineglass-shaped.

FOLK CULTURE

A startling range of cultures inhabit the aptly-named Plurinational State of Bolivia. Their dances, culinary arts and festivals are well preserved – from the Aymara of the highlands to the Guaraní of the Paraguayan border and the Afro-Bolivian population just outside of La Paz. Musical traditions also live on in the Jesuit missions near Santa Cruz.

BEST FOLKLORIC EXPERIENCES

Find true religion at ❶ **Misiones de Chiquitos Baroque Music Festival** (p284), a weeklong festival celebrating the Jesuit musical legacy in Moxos and Chiquitos.

Hail queens of many colors at ❷ **Carnaval parades in Santa Cruz** (p286), a ribald celebration of the onset of Lent celebrated for a month in advance.

Show school spirit at ❸ **Parade of El Gran Poder** (p56) as university students in traditional costumes step to centuries-old dances.

Think big at ❹ **Las Alasitas** (p63), the fair of 'little things' overseen by the lord of abundance, a tradition dating back to Aymara priests.

Enjoy a night out of folkloric dance, song and a bit of llama steak at one of ❺ **La Paz's historic peñas** (p66).

FROM LEFT: CONNECT IMAGES/BEN PIPE PHOTOGRAPHY/GETTY IMAGES, MINDSTORM/SHUTTERSTOCK

Virgin of the Lake

February and August, the **Fiesta de la Virgen de la Candelaria** (p88) rocks the streets of Copacabana, where Andean and Catholic traditions blend.

A Nation of Music

Cacharpaya (p243) hosts not only bands from the south of the country, but from every corner of Bolivia.

The Charango

Originally crafted from armadillo shells, these finely carved mandolin-like instruments provide rhythmic drive to Andean music. Some of the best are sold in **Cochabamba** (p186).

MAPIMARF/SHUTTERSTOCK

Puma Punku Ruins, Tiwanaku (p71)

BEST ARCHAEOLOGICAL EXPERIENCES

Examine the awe-invoking building blocks and mystifying stone stelas of ❶ **Tiwanaku** (p89), a site as iconic and mysterious as Easter Island or Stonehenge.

Dissemble and discuss at ❷ **Tarija's Paleontology Museum** (p242), a truly underrated collection of reconstructed fossils, haunting in their completeness.

Stand tall at ❸ **El Fuerte** (p269) of Samaipata, which overlooks Santa Cruz, predates the Incas, and includes Chané, Inca and Spanish cultural remnants.

Pay your respects to *las momias* in ❹ **Coqueza's** (p161) Cave of the Mummies in **Uyuni** (p161).

Gaze at the ❺ **burial towers of Rio Lauca** (p149) in Parque Nacional Sajama. Prehistoric *chullpas* (burial towers) of the Aymara are along the banks of the river, painted in pigmented mud.

OLD BONES, OLD BUILDINGS

Mysteries are still being unearthed in Bolivia, from the enigmatic ruins of Tiwanaku and other Altiplano sites (unfortunately somewhat ravaged by earlier 'investigations') to the amazingly complete dinosaur fossils discovered in the sere valleys outside of Sucre and Tarija. Feel the power as you walk in the footsteps of legendary cultures and extinct giants.

Stolen Goods

While **Tiwanaku** (p89) remains a marvel, some wonder what it truly was before Spaniards did their best to destroy it and others looted the site.

False Fossils

You may be hailed on the streets of Bolivia by ambulant vendors hawking *fosiles* (fossils). These are undoubtedly fake; caveat emptor.

EMBRACE THE HOLY

Bolivia is largely a Catholic nation but don't let the exterior images fool you; deep-rooted indigenous religious customs often exist side-by-side with the more recent Christian settlers' belief system. Churches are often a place where these parallel faiths work out their differences in practice or artwork. Aymara and other gods co-exist comfortably with icons of the Virgin Mary and Jesus Christ; it is a fascinating exercise in non-competition.

Seasonal Spirituality

In **Tiwanaku** (p70), the **Isla del Sol** (p96) and the Plaza near Pujzara outside of Tarija, the Aymara New Year is a cultural touchstone of utmost significance.

Catholic Churches

Iglesia San Francisco in La Paz is beautiful Baroque; the San Roque church in Tarija hosts a **celebration** (p246) of national import.

Best Spiritual Experiences

Embrace the sun on the Aymara New Year, the solstice of June 21, at Tiwanaku's **Puerta del Sol** (p71).

RADOSLAW CZAJKOWSKI/SHUTTERSTOCK, R.M. NUNES/SHUTTERSTOCK, FAVIO ANTEZANA/SHUTTERSTOCK

San Roque procession, Tarija (p246)

BEST SPIRITUAL EXPERIENCES

Embrace the sun on the Aymara New Year, the solstice of June 21, at Tiwanaku's ❶ **Puerta del Sol** (p71).

Honor the queen when the ❷ **Fiesta de la Virgen de Urkupiña** (p205) is celebrated outside Cochabamba in August.

Hail from on high at Tarija's ❸ **San Roque Festival** (p246), at the bright-white church on a hill dedicated to their patron saint.

Step into a slice of Christian history at ❹ **Iglesia de San Xavier** (p280), a highlight of the Jesuit Mission Circuit.

Delve into a world of fine art and religious history at ❺ **Museo y Convento de San Francisco** (p222), Bolivia's oldest monastery.

EPIC ROAD TRIPS

Hardly touched by trains, and with airplane service just between major transit points, Bolivia offers the open road to the adventurous traveler, sometimes still on routes unpaved and unmarked on any map. Here, more than most places, the truly open road still beckons.

FROM LEFT: ELZBIETA SEKOWSKA/SHUTTERSTOCK, FERNANDO CUELLAR ROSSEL/WIKIMEDIA/CC BY-SA 4.0, JULIUSBLAUENFELDT/SHUTTERSTOCK

Cruising the Amazon

Road trips aren't always on land – you can also hop on a **riverboat cruise** (p304) of the Amazon from Rurrenabaque for some aquatic diversion.

Tarija's Frightening Angosto

If the Death Road experience didn't get you, riding or **walking these 'narrows'** (p253), with 400m drops and no guardrails, should.

The (Scary) Road to Chulumani

So what if the Death Road doesn't run motorized traffic anymore? **Take a bus** (p137) from La Paz to Chulumani in Los Yungas for a real, um, thrill.

World's Most Dangerous Road (p128)

BEST ROAD TRIP EXPERIENCES

Drive the ❶ **Jesuit Mission Circuit** (p281), hitting seven towns and churches of historic and cultural import.

Explore the crystal lakes of the Altiplano on a ❷ **Tupiza 'Triathlon' tour** (p172), including 4WD, hiking, and horseback rides through the canyons and hot springs.

Follow the trail of legendary revolutionary Che Guevara's final days on the ❸ **Vallegrande** circuit (p277) marking his ultimate end in Bolivia.

Embark on an ❹ **epic mountain biking journey** (p141) from Sorata to Mapiri and through Bolivia's remote and challenging regions to the Amazon.

Hold onto your handlebars as you plunge from above La Paz to sweltering valleys on the ❺ **infamous Death Road bicycle challenge** (p127).

REGIONS & CITIES

Find the places that tick all your boxes.

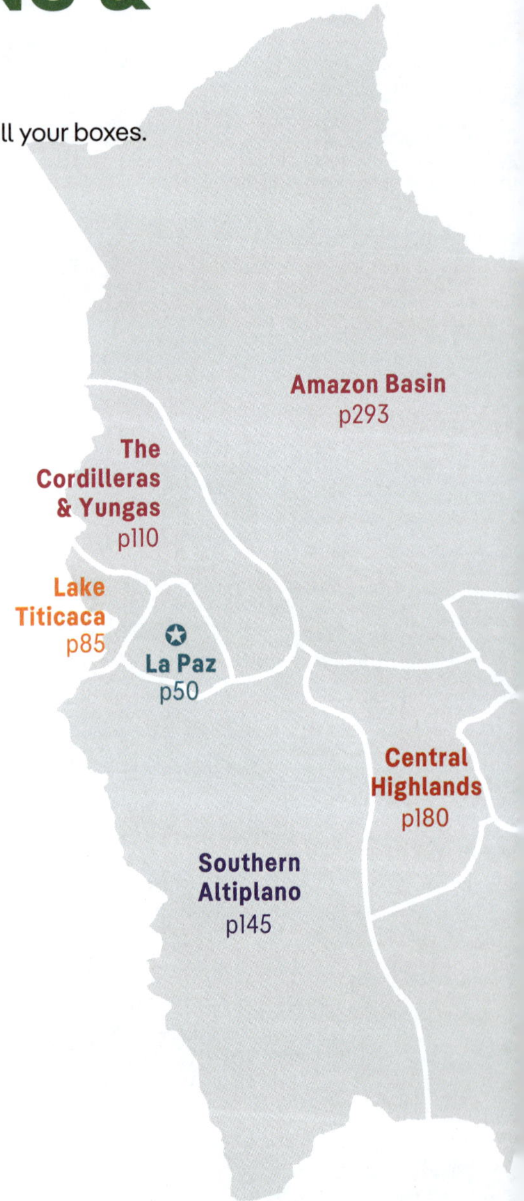

The Cordilleras & Yungas

INCA TRAILS, UPHILL CLIMBS, DOWNHILL THRILLS

Bike the notorious World's Most Dangerous Road down to these steamy valleys outside of La Paz and you'll be tempted to stay a while; waterfalls cascade over hiking trails and monkeys and parrots chatter in the trees; coffee comes fresh from the surrounding hills.

Lake Titicaca

ANCIENT HEART OF ANDEAN CULTURE

Feel like you're walking on water on the totora-reed islands of the world's highest navigable lake; spend a night on the Island of the Sun, appreciate ancient Incan treasures on Island of the Moon; tour the lake in a genuine totora-reed boat and feast on grilled trout straight from the lake.

Southern Altiplano

OTHERWORLDLY ADVENTURES AT EXTREME ALTITUDE

Devils dance and delight at Oruro's incredible carnaval celebrations. Uyuni's train graveyard is a foreshadowing of the world's largest salt flat where you can cavort on 4WDs in the mirrored, lithium-rich surfaces. Camelids of every stripe – llamas, vicunas, alpacas – stroll this near-empty paradise and flamingos flock to saline *lagunas*.

La Paz

BOLIVIA'S URBAN SOUL AND CULTURAL EPICENTER

An urban epicenter of culture and cafe life, but with enough of a natural edge to explore your wild side through hiking, biking, and even *parapente* (paragliding). Its fascinating museums, riotous markets awash with color and thriving food scene will have you coming back for more.

Amazon Basin

ENTER THE RAUCOUS REIGN OF THE RAINFOREST

Disconnect from your social media reality in a land of caimans, capybaras, pink dolphins and anacondas. Dive into the world's most biodiverse park, Madidi, and revel in the acai-berry harvest in the communities near Riberalta. Jump on the back of a taxi-scooter for a ride to dinner in Rurrenabaque.

Central Highlands

HISTORIC CITIES AND ALPINE SCENERY

The nation's colonial past dominates the impassive mines and narrow streets of Potosí, while its geologic past comes to life in the dinosaur footprints of Parque Nacional Torotoro. Charming Cochabamba's climate is near-perfect and Sucre's whitewashed walls adorn the official and sometimes under-appreciated capital.

Santa Cruz & Gran Chiquitania p256

South Central Bolivia & the Chaco p233

Santa Cruz & Gran Chiquitania

ABUNDANT LOWLANDS STEEPEDIN HISTORY

Contrast Bolivia's most modern city – a gastronome's dream – with placid tours of the forested Jesuit Missions of days of yore. Trek the revolutionary Che Guevara's trail, challenge the rivers and cloud-forested volcanoes of Amboró National Park in 'the elbow of the Andes.' Dig in at Samaipata's historic fortress.

South Central Bolivia & the Chaco

HIGH TIMES, WINE AND ALTIPLANO ADVENTURES

While vintage vines dominate the conversation, proximity to the altiplano promises endless vistas and near-bottomless canyons with soaring condors and wandering llamas. In the torrid Chaco, bike and hike to historical lookouts and indigenous villages.

T A MCKAY/SHUTTERSTOCK

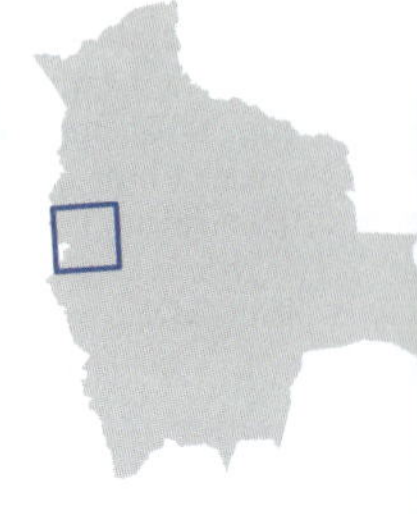

Llamas, Isla del Sol (p96)

ITINERARIES

Adventuring from La Paz

Allow: 10 days **Distance:** 100 miles

Radiating out from the fascinating, intense Altiplano city of La Paz, adventures of all sorts await. From the shores of glistening Lake Titicaca and the ruins of Tiwanaku to the the eco-diverse areas around the Yungas and in the Cordillera Real, hike, climb and bike to your heart's content.

1

LA PAZ 1 DAY

Start with a day of acclimatization in **La Paz** (p50), wandering from stall to stall at the markets, so disjointed, colorful and fascinating. Explore the city's museums and galleries and zip up in the ***teleférico*** (p58) to see the unusual architecture of the neighborhood of **El Alto** (p68), then dine at La Paz's excellent restaurants and visit a *peña* (folk-music venue) in the **Casco Viejo** (p261) neighborhood.

3½-hour drive

2

LAKE TITICACA 2 DAYS

Continue acclimatizing to the altitude at **Copacabana** (p90) for a day or two of beachfront fun on Lake Titicaca. Ferry to **Isla del Sol** (p96) – stopping at **Isla de la Luna** (p97) for an afternoon – then roam the impressive **Chincana ruins** (p100), a 700-year-old stone labyrinth. As you watch the sun set across the lake, you'll realize it'd be easy to stay longer, trekking to lost valleys and small villages.

3½-hour drive

3

SORATA 2 DAYS

The laidback, cool-air, Andean town of **Sorata** (p138) is a prime gateway for shorter walks on the edges of the **Cordillera Real** (p116). Or opt for longer **four- to 14-day treks** (p114) with climbs into the glaciated wilderness of the mountains. They're no small undertaking, but it will be worth every drop of sweat and every blister as you connect with Pachamama (Mother Earth) deep within her potent realm.

4-hour drive

FROM LEFT: LEONID ANDRONOV/SHUTTERSTOCK, MATYAS REHAK/SHUTTERSTOCK, DREAMART123/SHUTTERSTOCK

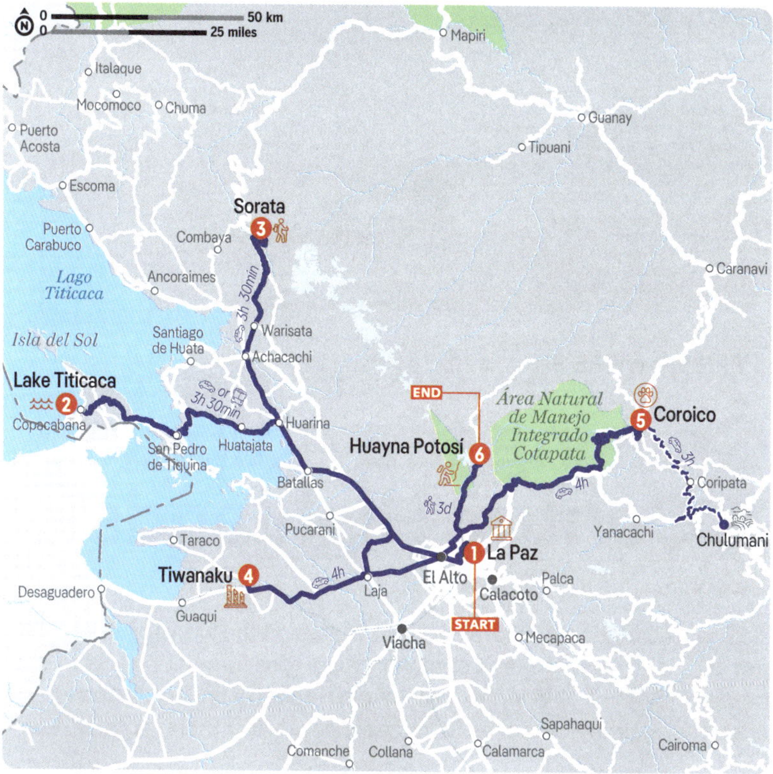

4

TIWANAKU 1 DAY

Bolivia's hallmark archaeological site, the enigmatic ruins of **Tiwanaku** (p70), sets your imagination on fire. Wander the monumental remains where you'll find mysterious carved monoliths, archways and arcades. A massive celebration is held on the solstices, and the on-site museum provides a thought-provoking glimpse into life in this religious and astronomical center. It's usually visited as an easy day tour from La Paz.

4-hour drive

5

COROICO 1 DAY

Dive into the Yungas on a adrenaline-rushing daylong mountain-bike ride down the so-called **World's Most Dangerous Road** (p128). At the end, you can kick back in the pleasant village of **Coroico** (p125) which also offers plenty of hikes, swims, a **wildlife sanctuary** (p132) and a laidback vibe. *3-hour drive back to La Paz*

***Detour:** Custom-build trips from Coroico to waterfalls, canyons or the chilled-out villages of **Chulumani** (p136) and **Tocaña** (p136).*

3-hour drive

6

HUAYNA POTOSÍ CLIMB 3 DAYS

Strap on crampons, swing an ice axe and bag a 6000m peak. The 3-day **Huayna Potosí** (p118) ascent allows newer climbers to properly acclimatize and learn the ropes before hitting higher sections. For safety, only go on a guided trip, usually from La Paz. While most come to climb, you can also stay at a mountain lodge and do day hikes or go mountain biking.

STEFAN ZIEMENDORFF/SHUTTERSTOCK, ALBERTOGONZALEZ/SHUTTERSTOCK, CARLOSLIMA/SHUTTERSTOCK

MARIAN DREHER/SHUTTERSTOCK

Salar de Uyuni (p155)

ITINERARIES

Cruising the Altiplano & Central Highlands

Allow: 11 days **Distance:** 290 miles

Bolivia's Altiplano is austere and vast. Marvel at the world's largest salt flat, the Salar de Uyuni, and spot whimsical rock formations and wild herds of llamas and vicuñas. Then circle through a series of colonial-era cities, jumping off points to volcanic peaks and Technicolor lakes.

1 PARQUE NACIONAL SAJAMA 1 DAY

Most people cruise straight from La Paz to Uyuni, but adventurous spirits can stop first at **Tomarapi** (p176), 5½ hours from La Paz, and explore the high-plains wonderland of **Parque Nacional Sajama** (p150), where hot springs and wildlife watching await. You'll hike through geyser fields and bathe in natural hot springs, and seek out the rare wildlife that inhabits this northern extension of the Atacama Desert.

7½-hour drive

2 SALAR DE UYUNI 3 DAYS

If you're pressed for time, fly directly to **Salar de Uyuni** (p155) from La Paz, then pick up a three-day jeep tour of the world's largest *salar* (salt desert). The shimmering crystalline perfection of the salt flat – and flamingoes! – could quite possibly be the defining experience of your Bolivian experience. *3½-hour drive*

***Detour:** Go mountain biking in **Tupiza** (p171), the former territory of Butch Cassidy, then sip wines around warmer-weather **Tarija** (p238).*

3 POTOSÍ 1 DAY

Swing up to **Potosí** (p216), a starkly beautiful UNESCO World Heritage city, said to be the world's highest city at 4070m. It once sat upon lodes of silver that funded the Spanish empire for centuries. See remnants of the wealthy past in the ornate colonial-era buildings, wonderfully preserved churches, and at the **Casa Nacional de la Moneda** (p216), once Bolivia's national mint. *3-hour drive*

FROM LEFT: JEF WODNIACK/SHUTTERSTOCK, JULIAN PETERS PHOTOGRAPHY/SHUTTERSTOCK, NORADOA/SHUTTERSTOCK

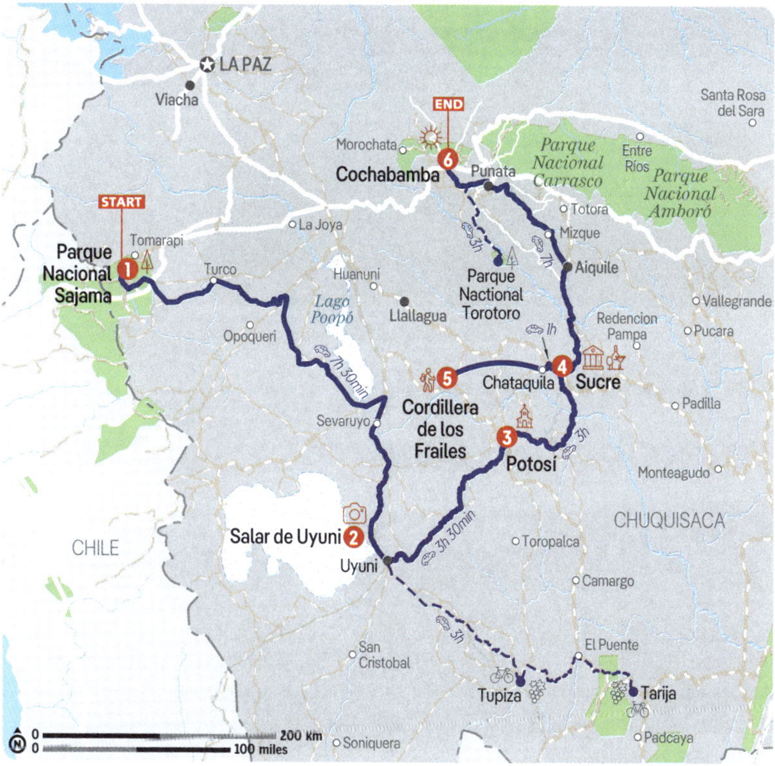

LA PAZ
Viacha
END
Morochata
Cochabamba 6
Punata
Parque Nacional Carrasco
Santa Rosa del Sara
Entre Ríos
Parque Nacional Amboró
Totora
Mizque
Aiquile
7h
3h
START
Tomarapi
Parque Nacional Sajama 1
Turco
La Joya
Huanuni
Lago Poopó
Llallagua
Parque Nacional Torotoro
Opoqueri
Redencion Pampa
Vallegrande
Pucara
1h
7h 30min
5 Cordillera de los Frailes
Chataquila
4 Sucre
Padilla
Sevaruyo
3 Potosí
3h
Monteagudo
CHUQUISACA
3h 30min
Salar de Uyuni 2
Uyuni
CHILE
Toropalca
Camargo
3h
San Cristobal
El Puente
Tupiza
Tarija
Padcaya
Soniquera
0 200 km
0 100 miles

4

SUCRE 2 DAYS

The white walls and red-tile roofs of the Bolivian capital of **Sucre** (p202) glisten in the Andean sun. The birthplace of the nation occupies a lush valley, surrounded by mountains, and is an eclectic mix of the old and the new. While away your days perusing historic buildings and museums and strolling grand plazas, and spend your nights enjoying the city's famous nightlife.

1-hour drive to Chataquila (an entry point to Cordillera de los Frailes)

5

CORDILLERA DE LOS FRAILES 1 DAY

Lace up your boots for hikes through the **Cordillera de los Frailes** (p213), serrated mountains rising between Sucre and Potosi. You'll get well into the lands of the Jal'qa people where you'll be stunned by **colorful rock formations, craters and rock paintings** (p213) and, for the best of hikers, plenty of steep inclines. Go on your own or with a Sucre guide.

7-hour drive from Chataquila to Cochabamba

6

COCHABAMBA 1 DAY

Busy, buzzy **Cochabamba** (p186) is one of Bolivia's boom cities and has a distinct vitality that perhaps owes something to its clement climate. *Cochabambinos* (Cochabamba residents) say their year-round spring-like weather makes it the ideal place to live.

***Detour:** Spend a day in one of Bolivia's most memorable national parks, **Parque Nacional Torotoro** (p194), where awe-inspiring geography, fossils and dinosaur footprints surround tranquil colonial village Torotoro.*

3-hour drive to Torotoro

JESS KRAFT/SHUTTERSTOCK, ABLANDIN/SHUTTERSTOCK, STREETFLASH/SHUTTERSTOCK

JEF WODNIACK/SHUTTERSTOCK

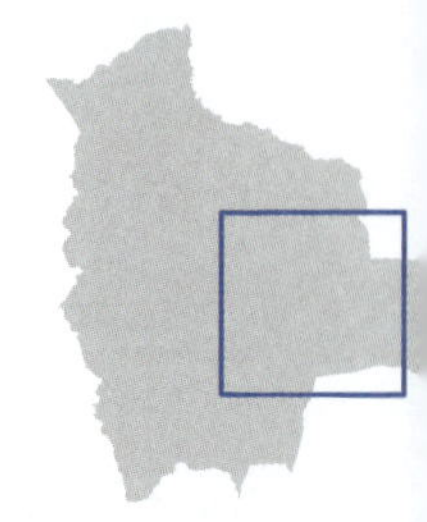

Parque Nacional & Área de Uso Múltiple Amboró (p272)

ITINERARIES

Unexpected Charms: Southeast & the Jesuit Mission Circuit

Allow: 7 days **Distance:** 185 miles

This route lures you away from the main tourist track and into Bolivia's warm southern comforts. Discover booming Santa Cruz and one of the country's most surprising highlights: the beautiful missions of the Jesuit Mission Circuit. Unwind in Samaipata with its ancient ruins, and go hiking and birdwatching in the national park of Amboró.

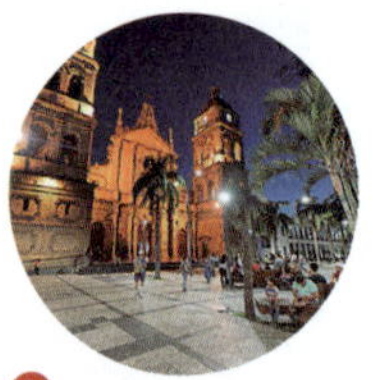

1

SANTA CRUZ DE LA SIERRA

1 DAY

You can fly directly to **Santa Cruz** (p260), a sophisticated and cosmopolitan city with a dreamy (sometimes steamy) climate and tropical atmosphere. It's great fun just wandering around the streets as you soak up *camba* (lowland) culture, eat at some of the country's most diverse restaurants and kick back on the **central plaza** (p260) while the kids play, couples flirt and old-school gamers play (chess).

4½-hour drive

2

JESUIT MISSION CIRCUIT

2 DAYS

Traveling around the **Jesuit Mission Circuit** (p281) has become more accessible with newly paved roads, so don't miss out on the elaborate 18th-century Jesuit churches that are the centerpieces of the mission villages along the route. Lovingly restored, they offer a glimpse of their former glory, and the complicated missionary history in the region, home to the Guaraní people.

2-hour drive (from San José de Chiquitos to Santiago de Chiquitos)

3

SANTIAGO DE CHIQUITOS

1 DAY

Make the jaunt to **Santiago de Chiquitos** (p289), dominated by a *mirador* (great sunset views) and surrounded by temperate-climate walks to rock pools, waterfalls and cave paintings (p289). The hilly location makes for a good respite from the lowland heat. On the way back west to Samaipata, you'll likely choose to overnight in Santa Cruz, to break up the journey.

7-hour drive to Santa Cruz

3-hour drive to Samaipata

FROM LEFT: POSZTOS/SHUTTERSTOCK, NORADOA/SHUTTERSTOCK, HELMDYCK/SHUTTERSTOCK

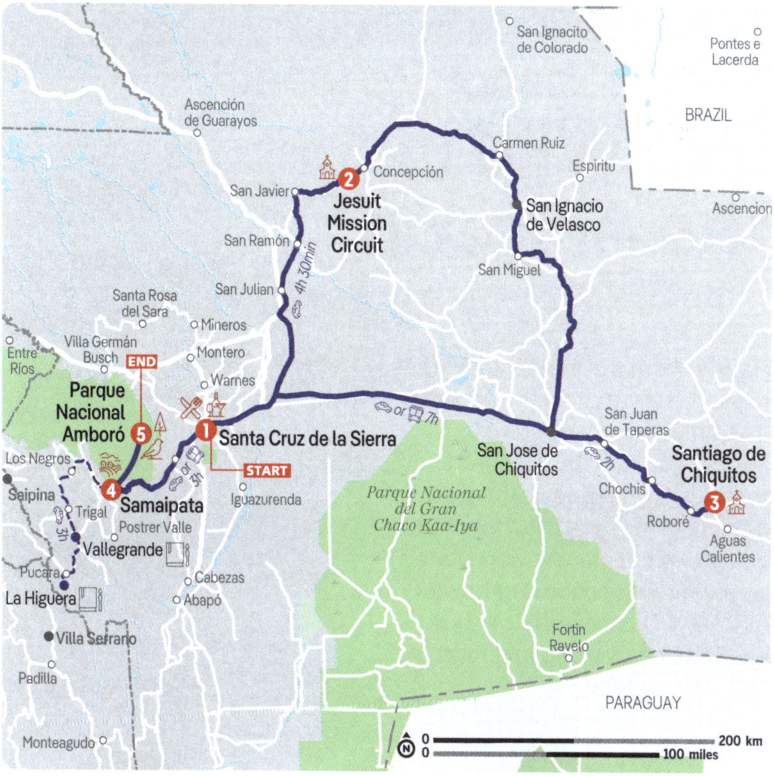

San Ignacio de Colorado
Pontes e Lacerda
BRAZIL
Ascención de Guarayos
Carmen Ruiz
Espiritu
Concepción
2 Jesuit Mission Circuit
San Javier
San Ignacio de Velasco
Ascencion
San Ramón
4h 30min
San Miguel
Santa Rosa del Sara
San Julian
Mineros
Entre Ríos
Villa Germán Busch
END
Montero
Warnes
Parque Nacional Amboró 5
or 7h
1 Santa Cruz de la Sierra
San Juan de Taperas
San Jose de Chiquitos
Santiago de Chiquitos
Los Negros
2h
START
or 3h
Chochis
Seipina
4 Samaipata
Iguazurenda
Parque Nacional del Gran Chaco Kaa-Iya
3
Trigal
Roboré
3h
Postrer Valle
Aguas Calientes
Vallegrande
Pucara
Cabezas
La Higuera
Abapó
Villa Serrano
Fortin Ravelo
Padilla
PARAGUAY
0 200 km
0 100 miles
Monteagudo

4

SAMAIPATA 1 DAY

Boho village **Samaipata** (p267) retains the air of a relaxing mountain village, despite becoming an increasingly unmissable stop on the tourist trail. But it's not just the rolling valley views, pleasant climate, great-value accommodations and interesting restaurants that bring in the visitors. Samaipata's proximity to the **El Fuerte ruins** (p269), ancient petroglyphs and day trips to Amboró mean that many stay longer than they planned. *3-hour drive*

Detour: *Che Guevara fans make a beeline for* ***Vallegrande*** *(p277) and La Higuera, where the revolutionary's life came to an end.*

3-hour drive

5

PARQUE NACIONAL & ÁREA DE USO MÚLTIPLE AMBORÓ 1 DAY

The 430,000-hectare **Parque Nacional & Área de Uso Múltiple Amboró** (p272) lies in a unique geographical position at the confluence of three ecosystems: the Andes, the Amazon Basin and the Chaco. You can make trips, usually on guided tours, into the park from Samaipata and look for both highland and lowland species: elusive spectacled bears, jaguars, tapirs, peccaries and monkeys, plus more than 800 bird species.

Parque Nacional & Área de Uso Múltiple Amboró is visited via tours

ITINERARIES

Get Wild in the Amazon

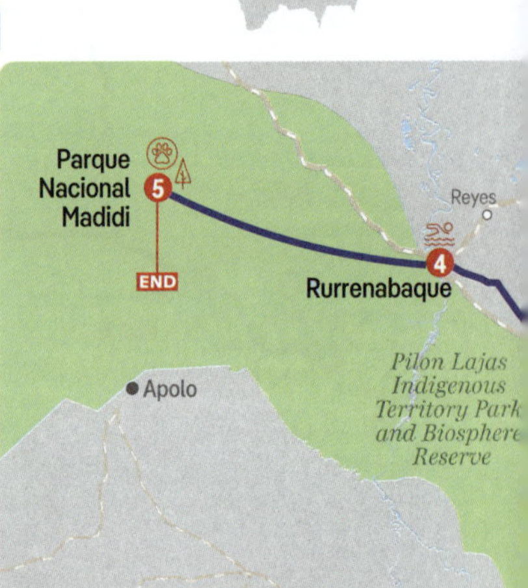

Allow: 7 days **Distance:** 70 miles

Hands down the most biodiverse region on the planet, the Amazon has almost mythical status among ecotourists, who are tempted by the possibility of a fleeting glimpse of a jaguar or the world's rarest macaw, and wooed by the morning chorus of howler monkeys. Progress is slow, but you will be rewarded mightily.

1

TRINIDAD 1 DAY

From Santa Cruz, fly or catch the overnight bus to **Trinidad** (p313), a central hub for Amazon adventures further afield. While in town, tuck into a local fish meal, rent a motorcycle for a spin or have a much-needed siesta – it gets hot. If you have more time, take a one or two-day boat trip on the **Río Ibare** (p312) to see the unique pink river dolphins.

3-hour drive

2

SAN IGNACIO DE MOXOS 1 DAY

San Ignacio de Moxos (p298) is a friendly, tranquil village with an ambience quite distinct from any other Bolivian town. The people speak an indigenous dialect known as *ignaciano*, and their lifestyle, traditions and food are unique – a mixture of the Moxos culture and colonial Christian Jesuit influences. If possible, plan your trip around the town's colorful **Fiesta de Moxos** (p305) at the end of July.

3-hour drive

3

RESERVA DE LA BIOSFERA Y ESTACIÓN BIOLÓGICA DEL BENI 1 DAY

San Borja (p309) is the jumping off point for wildlife watchers heading into **Reserva de la Biosfera y Estación Biológica del Beni** (p309), the historic home to the Tsimané people (p311). In the park, the trained eye can spot up to 412 unique species of birds, including a cornucopia of herons and egrets. There are around 100 different mammals in the reserve, from bats to pumas.

3-hour drive

4

RURRENABAQUE 1 DAY

Rurrenabaque (p298) is hammock country, a chance to rest after some hard travel, eat well and do some lighter day trips, like a swim at the **El Chorro waterfall** (p300). With enough time, one of the 'Rurre' highlights is setting out for a couple of days on a **jungle or pampas tour** (p304). Depending on your schedule and budget you can reach Rurrenabaque by land, air or boat.

 *3-hour drive*

5

PARQUE NACIONAL MADIDI 3 DAYS

Whatever you do, don't miss a trip to **Parque Nacional Madidi** (p301). Bolivia's best-known national park and one of the largest protected areas in the world, it offers adventures over 1.8 million hectares encompassing a spellbinding range of habitats, from Andean mountains to steamy lowland rainforests. It's home to an astonishing array of wildlife, and the park's remarkable biodiversity – the most in the world – is best enjoyed at a slow pace – so leave time to stay in one of the highly regarded, community-run **ecolodges** (p302).

Parque Nacional Madidi is visited via tours

MIROSLAV SRB/SHUTTERSTOCK (2)

WHEN TO GO

Shoulder season between August and November is the best time to go, avoiding winter's crowds and summer's rainy months.

From May to October, you'll have the sunniest skies and warmest weather, if a bit cool in the Altiplano. The rainforests of the Beni receive their least rainfall in June and July; these are also the coolest times in towns like Riberalta. This makes outdoor activities and transit more reliable, but overall costs run a bit higher. In Santa Cruz, the occasional *surazos* (winds from Argentina) can chill things considerably on summer days.

In October and November, it's less crowded as North American and European students have returned to their studies; by November and December it turns rainy and you risk getting washed out of some activities; roads become less certain, even dangerous. Climbing activities take on more of a risk, and biking and hiking in the rain, or hail, are just a bummer. You're more likely to see Salar de Uyuni's mirror effect during the wetter months of December to March; the drier months of April to November make for easier traveling here.

I LIVE HERE

WINTER AROMAS OF LOS YUNGAS

Erika Palacios is a social researcher and budding writer in La Paz's Calacoto neighborhood. *@erikapwrites*

Most people from La Paz know the northern region of the department, Los Yungas, but few visit during winter – my favorite season. Here, no snow falls. Instead, mandarins drop from the trees, filling the air with a rich, bittersweet fragrance. Alongside rushing rivers, lush green landscapes and glimpses of wild animals, what truly makes this land special is the lingering scent of mandarins.

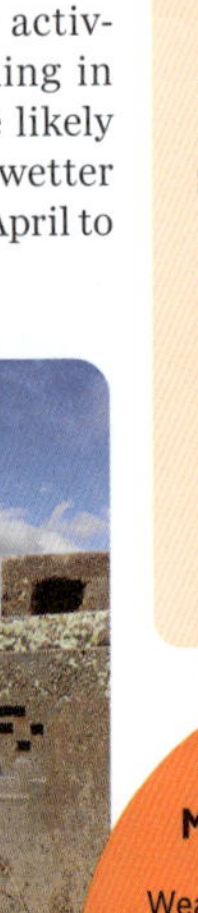

Tiwanaku (p70)

FROM LEFT: DANIELA SIERRA LOZANO/SHUTTERSTOCK, JREMES84/SHUTTERSTOCK

MOUNTAIN WEATHER

Weather in the mountains comes up on you fast: one moment you're taking a selfie at Tiwanaku and the next minute you're running from driving rain. You could be blinded by sunshine, drenched by rain and pelted by hail, all within a half hour.

Weather through the Year in La Paz

JANUARY	**FEBRUARY**	**MARCH**	**APRIL**	**MAY**	**JUNE**
Avg daytime max: **13°C**	Avg daytime max: **13°C**	Avg daytime max: **13°C**	Avg daytime max: **12°C**	Avg daytime max: **10°C**	Avg daytime max: **11°C**
Days of rainfall: 21	Days of rainfall: 15	Days of rainfall: 9	Days of rainfall: 4	Days of rainfall: 2	Days of rainfall: 2

SNOWFALL

Global warming has lowered the snowcap on some Andean mountains, but you still might be surprised by the occasional snowstorm. Around La Paz they may cause traffic chaos and sometimes halt transport in and out of the city for a day; be flexible.

Christian Festivals

Dia de los Reyes Magos As in many Latin American countries the 'kings' day' marks the visit of the three magi to newly born Jesus Christ. Big in the Beni and rural areas. **January**

Fiesta de la Virgen de Candelaria/Socavon This week-long party (p153-4) kicks off carnaval and is particularly big in Oruro, where a 45m statue to the virgin stands. **February/March**

Semana Santa Holy week (p88) is especially holy at Copacabana on Lake Titicaca, where hundreds make the pilgrimage on foot. **March/April**

Fiesta de San Roque Tarija commemorates the end of the plague and reveling *chunchos* (lepers) twirl in colorful costume in this eight-day extravaganza (p246). **August**

Fiesta de la Virgen de Urkupiña Outside Cochabamba, crowds gather to celebrate the legend of the appearance of the Virgin to a local shepherdess (p205). **August 15**

Other Festivals

Las Alasitas (p63) Who doesn't love the fair of 'little things,' when you ask the ubiquitous Ekeko (a chubby little pipe-smoking icon) to bring you something based on a small-scale model (eg a car). **January/February**

Carnaval The biggest party in Latin America gets no short shrift in Bolivia, and the onset of Lent is celebrated in style in Oruru (p153-4) and Santa Cruz, notably. **February**

Pujllay Tarabucans bust out the *chicha* (corn liquor) to commemorate the defeat of the dastardly Spaniards in 1816. A Quechua mass is attended by more than 60 local communities. **March**

Aymara New Year Indigenous and others hail the **Solstice** (p72) and the Aymara New Year; particular persuasive celebrations occur at **Tiwanaku** (p89) in an overnight gathering. **June**

Independence Day (p89) August 6, when Alto Peru became Bolivia in 1825, is celebrated throughout the nation with all manner of parades. **August**

I LIVE HERE

THE MIRACLE OF MIGRATION

Tjalle Boorsma is the conservation manager for wildlife NGO Asociación Armonía, based in Santa Cruz with reserves around Bolivia. *@tjalleboorsma*

For me, seasons are marked by the birds. One of Bolivia's most sublime regions is the Beni Savanna, where Armonía created the Barba Azul Nature Reserve to protect the critically endangered blue-throated macaw. Each September, it becomes a temporary home to thousands of Arctic-breeding buff-breasted sandpipers, arriving to feed. Their arrival is exciting as it confirms we're successfully managing the habitat they depend on.

Blue-throated macaw

RAIN: THE PROS & CONS

Rain washes out roads and brings more mosquitoes in the lowlands; in the rainy season floods can cut transport links and greatly increase travel times. The upside is lusher vegetation and blooming flowers, but be prepared for severe delays.

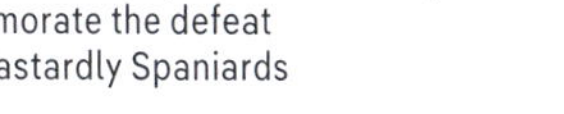

JULY	AUGUST	SEPTEMBER	OCTOBER	NOVEMBER	DECEMBER
Avg daytime max: **10°C**	Avg daytime max: **11°C**	Avg daytime max: **12°C**	Avg daytime max: **13°C**	Avg daytime max: **14°C**	Avg daytime max: **14°C**
Days of rainfall: 4	Days of rainfall: 7	Days of rainfall: 7	Days of rainfall: 11	Days of rainfall: 11	Days of rainfall: 16

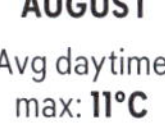

FROM LEFT: FABIO LAMANNA/SHUTTERSTOCK, MARTIN SILVA/AFP VIA GETTY IMAGES

Inca trails, Isla del Sol (p96)

GET PREPARED FOR BOLIVIA

Useful things to load in your bag, your ears and your brain.

Clothes

Layers With everything from the Andes to the Amazon, and a few deserts thrown in, the climate in Bolivia is varied and changes quickly. Versatility is key – bring plenty of light layers so you can adapt.

Rain gear On the high plains and in the jungle, rains can appear out of nowhere, so a lightweight waterproof jacket is essential.

Boots and sneakers You'll probably spend a lot of time in the great outdoors, so pack a pair of impermeable hiking boots – and if you plan on going rafting or caving, bring an old pair of sneakers you don't mind getting wet.

Manners

Bolivians are formal in their manners. When greeting someone for the first time, use the formal *'usted'* instead of *'tu'* if your Spanish conjugation skills are flexible enough. In a restaurant, a hearty *'buen provecho'* (good appetite!) to your fellow diners will earn you a smile. Timekeeping is not of the essence; if your coffee date is 15 or 30 minutes late, don't make a big deal of it.

Hats, gloves, and sunglasses Weather on the Altiplano can get intensely cold at night or in shadow, and also unbelievably bright, so pack warm gear and eye protection.

READ

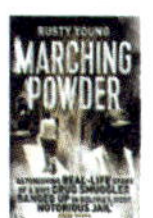

Marching Powder (Rusty Young; 2007) An Australian traveler pairs up with an English convict in a La Paz prison where bribes get you anything, and almost anywhere.

The Devil's Agent (Peter McFarren; 2013) How did notorious Nazi war criminal Klaus Barbie hide in plain sight for years in Bolivia? Answers here.

Turing's Delirium (Edmundo Paz Soldán; 2007) A cyberpunk political thriller set in the future involving 'hactivists' and antiglobalists; magical realism for the 21st century.

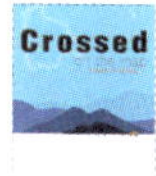

Crossed off the Map: Travels in Bolivia (Shafik Meghji; 2022). Journalist and travel writer Meghji explores the country's history through a contemporary lens.

Words

'Hola' Hello.
'Ciao ciao' A very Bolivian way of saying 'goodbye.'
'Que tal?' 'What's up?'.
'Buenos días/buenas tardes' Good morning/ good afternoon.
'Lo mismo or **igualmente'** 'The same to you.'
'No hay' 'There isn't any.' Sometimes modified by a noun: *'no hay pollo'* means 'there isn't any chicken,' often accompanied by a nonchalant hand-flip.
'Por favor' Please; it can be used at the beginning or the end of a request.
'Gracias' Thank you.
'Con (mucho) gusto' 'With (much) pleasure;' the equivalent of 'you're welcome.'
'Listo' Technically means 'ready' but can also be used to signal approval or at the end of a sentence to convert it into a question.
'Donde está' Used to ask the location of something; it translates as 'where is.'
'Entonces' One of the most common words you'll hear; it means 'so' and fills pauses in conversation, but is also used as an informal greeting.
'Pues' Utilitarian word normally used to begin a response similar to 'well'.
'Chevere' Ubiquitous around the country and means 'excellent' but can also be used to refer to a likable or amusing person.
'Ayuda' 'Help'; can be used in any situation where you need assistance.

WATCH

Cholitas (Jaime Murciego, Pablo Iraburu; 2019; pictured) Follows a quintet of Aymara women in traditional dress as they brave Bolivia's highest peaks.

Utama (Alejandro Loayza Grisi; 2022) This tale of an aging Aymará couple gained international acclaim.

Amargo mar (Antonio Eguino; 1987) Probes the nation's deepest psychological wound: the loss of sea access in the War of the Pacific.

Boliviana (Mariano Agudo; 2015) The true stories of four modern women convey the rugged reality for women in 21st-century Bolivia.

El gran movimiento (Kiro Russo; 2019) A miner marches to La Paz to recover his job, and his health, with the aid of an elderly woman and a witch doctor.

LISTEN

Cuecas de Siempre (Alfredo Coca; 2004) Traditional Spanish dances adapted to the *charango*, the 10-stringed Bolivian mandolin, executed by one of its masters.

0 km (Jade Bolivia; 2000) The ska-inspired track *Viernes por la Noche* is a highlight of this Cochabambino rock band's debut album.

Ningún Vals (Efecto Mandarina; 2014) A modern jazz-fusion combo featuring tasty piano accompanying a note-perfect vocalist.

Aires Indios (Piraí Vaca; 2010) Vaca is Bolivia's contribution to the classical guitar canon and puts on a deft display in this tribute to the Chiquitana region.

MARK GREEN/SHUTTERSTOCK

Food stall, Potosí (p216)

THE FOOD SCENE

Besides the hearty traditional fare, Bolivian chefs are winning international awards for their flair with local ingredients from the Altiplano to the Amazon.

Food may not be the reason most visitors come to Bolivia, but many will leave surprised at the variety and richness. Potatoes and root crops may dominate the Altiplano, but the Amazon provides a wealth of fruits that are readily available around the country as side dishes, juices, or even in yummy smoothies or ice creams. The Yungas just outside of La Paz is growing in reputation for its coffee worldwide, and the full bodied Tannats of Tarija and Sucre delight wine-lovers. There you'll also find the country's famous hams and cheeses in abundance.

La Paz and other cities and towns are dotted with markets offering all manner of rich, fresh produce and meats, and hip restauranteurs are offering up New Bolivian cuisine in increasing numbers. Bolivian chefs have risen in the rankings of South America to award-winning status. Pride in local ingredients and recipes over the past decade have resulted in amazing 11-course tasting menus as well as small-plate specialties – a veritable explosion of creativity and taste.

Magical Markets

The lively and colorful markets of most any Bolivian town or city will truly keep your finger on the pulse of the regional culture: finding out what locals eat and drink or sitting down alongside them for a meal, there's hardly a better way to get to know a place.

Bolivian markets are a jumble of noise, color and action. While you'll be tempted to take a photo, take a moment to bask in the tumult, and take the opportunity to sit cheek-to-jowl with your fellow shoppers, eating at one of the market's small stands or tables.

Cochabamba's sprawling La Cancha market sells absolutely everything under the sun, from large furniture to rows of stalls dedicated to every natural herb and supplement.

Santa Cruz and San Ignacio de Velasco are profound in their selections, selling everything from fruits and veggies to deep-fried empanadas and *cuñapés* (cheese puffs).

Best Bolivian Dishes

SOPA DE MANI
Peanut soup, popular nationally with good reason.

PIQUE A LO MACHO
Beef and rice stew, a great hangover remedy.

CHAIRO
Altiplano soup made with meat and *chuño* (freeze-dried potato).

CHANCHO AL PALO
Roasted pig – a big weekend feast food.

El Torno, on the way to Samaipata, has a huge weekend fruit and vegetable market featuring foods that are grown in that area.

La Paz's markets are legion, from downtown to El Alto, you'd need an entire weekend to see them all. Indeed, weekends are the most animated market days, but you'll find a bit of adventure on any given day. Fruits from the jungle, potatoes from the altiplano, cheese and honey from nearby goat farms and apiaries, maybe some fish from Lago Titicaca: it's a culinary adventure from start to finish.

Street Food

Street snacks are ubiquitous: *pipoco* (popcorn) is sold by the bag, *salteñas* and *tucumanas* offer empanada varieties both baked and fried, rich with chicken or beef, egg, and a sticky-textured, ineffable liquid filling. *Anticuchos* (beef hearts) are seasoned with salt, vinegar and other spices, then grilled up and served on a skewer with a potato; especially favored among late-night drinking friends (sellers will gather conveniently outside of bars on the weekend).

Api morada (purple corn) is a lovely, thick, cinnamon-laced warm-up drink served alongside a fried dough *buñuelo* (doughnut) for cold Altiplanos mornings. Potosí is known for its goat cheese and hearty miners' meals and sweet empanadas of *lacayote*, a pumpkin relative.

Vegetarian Dining

Vegetarians and vegans will do well here. Numerous restaurants, health-food stores and cafes offer an array of options to enjoy.

CHATHAM172/SHUTTERSTOCK

Majadito

When in doubt, a stop at a local market can provide a quick snack like a banana or passion fruit. Antioxidant-rich acai berries come fresh from the jungle, as does rich cacao, from there and other warm-weather terrains.

Santa Cruz offers exotic and nutritious fruits like *lúcuma* (a creamy orange-colored favorite for making ice cream), *tarumã* (a fleshy, sweet, cherry-like fruit, nice blended with milk), *carambola* (star fruit), and vitamin-C-rich *copoazú*. *Achachairú* (a citrus-like version of the mangosteen) has gained traction in foreign markets outside of its native Santa Cruz cultivations.

In Sucre and other market towns, rows of juice stalls, all selling the same varieties, are cheap, delicious and healthy.

ILDI PAPP/SHUTTERSTOCK

Salteñas

FOOD & DRINK FESTIVALS

Vendimia Chapaca Celebrating the best of the region's wine and dance, 27km outside of Tarija in Uriondo province in February/March.

Fiesta de la Uva Tarija In March, celebrating the grape (uva), this one held in the city proper.

Sabalito Fest In April, Villamontes celebrates the popular sport fish with much involvement from the local indigenous community.

Festival de la Salteña In La Paz every April or May, 50-plus contestants compete for the title of 'Best Salteña' – the audience wins big.

Festival de Anticucho In a neighborhood famed for this skewered delight, Sopocachi hosts 30 cooks of the street meal in October.

LOCRO
Soup with *charque* (beef jerky).

MAJADITO
Rice, *charque*, plantain and a fried egg.

PESCADO EN DUNUCABI
Amazonian fish wrapped in rainforest leaf, baked over a wood fire.

MONDONGO CHUQUISAQUEÑO
Sucre specialty of spicy pork stew on top of a large-kernel corn.

Specialities

Bolivian Street Food

Salteñas A baked empanada filled with chicken or beef, usually.
Tucumanas A fried empanada often sold alongside salteñas as a crunchier alternative.
Anticuchos Street meat on a skewer (usually beef heart) with a roasted potato and peanut sauce.
Chicha Fermented, sometimes not, corn or other grain drink.
Api A lovely purple corn drink often served piping hot.
Papas rellenas Baked potato stuffed with meat and cheese.

Enjoy with a Hot Drink

Buñuelo Bolivian *buñuelos* are crispy, fried doughnut shaped sweetbreads popular around Christmas time.
Cuñapes Cheese-filled soft pastries, nice with coffee.
Tawa-tawas Potosino rectangular-shaped dough fritters, covered in honey and powdered sugar.
Jawitas Another soft empanada, from Los Yungas, filled with soft cheese or sometimes a spicier alternative.

Buñuelos

THE ART OF PICS/SHUTTERSTOCK

The Adventurous Gourmet

Caldo de Cardán Bull's penis soup; an aphrodisiac and hangover cure.
Patasca Soup using pig's head and/or cow's tongue.
Cola de caiman and chicharrón de lagarto Alligator tail cooked simply with salt and herbs – 'tastes like fish!'
Llama brains/tongue High in protein and low in grease.
Charque Dried meat of *guanaco*, similar to jerky.

MEALS OF A LIFETIME

Casa de Campo (p300) Doña Aldela's homemade pastries and 'tropical breakfasts' are to die for at this low-key Rurrenabaque cafe.
Proyecto Nativa (p207) High profile, innovative chef-driven 10-course tasting menu (a la carte also available) using only Bolivian ingredients in Sucre.
El Solar (p207) Seven-course tasting menu inspired by regional Bolivian specialties like cured fish with Amazonian fruit juices. The capital's finest food.
Francois (p247) An immersive wine-and-dine experience in Tarija featuring tasting courses, French specialities, and *singani* (grape brandy)- and wine-infused omelettes and desserts.

THE YEAR IN FOOD

JANUARY–MARCH

January brings *plato paceño*, a dish of pork, potato, peas, choclo, fried cheese and salsa. During Carnaval *puchero* is popular, with beef, rice, beans, potato and hot pepper sauce. Easter is celebrated with 14 dishes – one for each Station of the Cross.

APRIL–JUNE

June and July bring ripe mandarins and oranges. La Paz's foundation is celebrated with *anticucho*, *sucumbe* (warm singani, milk, cinnamon) and other hot alcoholic drinks.

JULY–SEPTEMBER

For August's independence day and the 'fiestas patrias' each family makes their own recipes of dishes like *fricasé* (soup) and *picante surtido* (aka *picante mixto*), which has wide-ranging variations including different kinds of meat, vegetables and peppers.

OCTOBER–DECEMBER

For Dia de los Muertos, *tawa tawas* are prepared. When Christmas rolls around, it's time for *picana* (Christmas soup), each family recipe unique (often three different meats with a touch of wine).

FROM LEFT: ALEX ARIEL TORRICO SOTO/SHUTTERSTOCK, JHON PERCY TICONA MAMANI/SHUTTERSTOCK, GRAYSONSTOCK/SHUTTERSTOCK, BEATA KROLIKIEWICZ/SHUTTERSTOCK

FABIO LAMANNA/SHUTTERSTOCK

Mate de Coca

HOW TO... Handle High-Altitude Sickness

Coming into La Paz, Potosí or any other high-elevation Bolivian destination may involve an uncomfortable reality: altitude sickness, or *soroche* in the local idiom. *Soroche* is the body's reaction to dealing with a lot less oxygen, and its effects can include headaches, nausea, shortness of breath, difficulty sleeping and lack of appetite. The condition respects neither age nor physical condition: in recent years, even very young travelers in their 20s have died from the malady, while hiking in Peru.

Dealing with Altitude Sickness: Dos and Don'ts

Here are few tips to combat the effects of *soroche*:

Do take it easy on your first day at high altitude. Give yourself a day to adjust to the sea level, if possible.

Don't overdo it if you're compelled to sightsee: limit yourself to gentle walking.

Do try folk remedies – coca tea and tri-mate (a blend of three different herbal teas) often have a calming effect on the *soroche* sufferer; many hotels will serve it upon arrival.

Do ask your hotel or accomodations for help. If breathing becomes a real burden, some high-end hotels have oxygen tanks on offer.

Do ingest coca leaves – the ancient energy lift of the Aymara – as these may also help. Stuff some leaves in your cheek and avoid chewing; this may lead to a big wad of liquid in your mouth.

Do use prescription medicines if you can. There are a handful of these that can help deal with *soroche* (consult with your doctor, too, of course). Diamox (Acetazolamide) is a common one, but it has been known to have side effects ranging from tingling in the hands to diarrhea.

Do keep track of the altitude. There's a rough formula for how much acclimatization you should prepare for: for every 1000 ft above 8000 you ascend, you should take one day of rest. If possible, 'ramp up' on your trip, starting at lower altitudes (eg go from Santa Cruz, to Cochabamba to La Paz).

Do limit your alcohol consumption in the mountains – it may only add to your headache later on.

Do drink lots of water in order to remain hydrated.

Don't smoke cigarettes and consume tobacco.

TYPES OF ALTITUDE SICKNESS

The Cleveland Clinic defines three types of altitude sickness: Acute Mountain Sickness (AMS), High Altitude Pulmonary Edema (HAPE) and High Altitude Cerebral Edema (HACE). In HAPE, your lungs begin to fill with fluid; with HACE, your brain begins swelling. Both HACE and HAPE can lead to death, and symptoms like chest tightness, slurring of words, shortness of breath or clumsiness can be indicators of these conditions.

FROM LEFT: EVGENY SUBBOTSKY/SHUTTERSTOCK, JOAOSALES/SHUTTERSTOCK

Huayna Potosí (p118)

THE OUTDOORS

No ocean? No problem. Bolivia's diverse topography and ecosystems challenge the most ardent outdoors person. There's a smattering of options for anyone who loves wide open spaces.

Gifted with a vast range in its climate and geography, from towering mountains to sweltering jungle, Bolivia is an outdoor-lovers dream. You can plan everything from the soul-soothing to adrenaline-pumping action. The Andes has plenty of high-altitude climbs apt for both expert mountaineers and novices, and the rivers are calm enough in places for tubing, raging enough elsewhere for white-water rafting. Dramatic shifts in altitude mean challenging biking and hiking, much of it on centuries-old trails. Nature lovers and photographers alike will marvel at the plant, mammal and bird life.

Mountaineering

Crampons and ice-picks ready? Bolivia has dozens of mountains of 5000m or more. The Andes loom within a short drive of La Paz, and whether you're doing a day trip to Chacaltaya, or you're up for a bigger challenge of one or more days on Huayna Potosí, Condoriri Massif, Illimani or Chachacomani, these majestic peaks will challenge and thrill you. Be prepared. Sajama (6542m) and Ancohuma (6427m) offer higher summits and degrees of difficulty, while Pico Austria (5100m) and Pyramid Blanca (5230m) are less taxing. The Cordillera Quimsa Cruz, also near La Paz, is a relatively recent discovery among climbers

HANG-GLIDING
Soaring above the valleys of La Paz or Cochabamba is truly an otherworldly experience but not for the faint of heart.

RAFTING/TUBING
The Pilcomayo between Sucre and Villamontes gets a bit testy (III-IV class rapids) but at either end you can find your Zen spot in a inner tube.

BOATING THE AMAZON OR LAKE TITICACA
Catamarans and smaller vessels ply the world's highest navigable lake; passenger vessels and others work the Amazon's winding waterways.

FAMILY ADVENTURES

Short hikes The valleys just outside of Zona Sur (p80) in La Paz offer 45-minute and even 15-minute options, with cacti and zany rock formations.

Nature and birding The country's national parks are a haven to favored camelids like llamas and vicuñas; Amazon tours float by pink river dolphins (p312); and birding promises a treasure trove of life-listers.

Cycling Good opportunities for learning and riding outside of Tarija (p250) and Villamontes (p254); experienced and conditioned families with older children can also consider exploring the Death Road by bike.

Ziplining Outside of Coiroco (p133) and Rurrenabaque, glide through the treetops on ziplines or go at your own pace on a canopy tour, communing with toucans and monkeys.

and offers high-altitude lakeside camping. Asociacion de Guias Montanas (the Association of Mountain Guides) has a list of accredited, professional guides: this is one area where you don't want to skimp.

Hiking & Trekking

In Bolivia you can follow in the footsteps of indigenous predecessors around the country, scaling ancient footpaths of the Inca and other peoples. National parks like Amboro and Sajama are incredible, while locally in La Paz you can clamber around Valle de la Luna or Valle de las Animas in half-day hikes a short bus ride from town. Sucre's Cordillera de los Frailes and Samaipata's Refugio de los Volcanes offer history and hot springs in one fell swoop; Tarija's Sama park offers endless altiplano vistas, shimmering lakes and a connection with the Inca Trail, which you can also pick up in Takesi's two-day hike. Sorata, in the La Paz valleys, has both easy and difficult options. Hiking around Isla del Sol and/or Isla de Luna on Lake Titicaca rewards the trekker with historic sites and inspiring sights.

ACTION AREAS

For the best outdoor spots and routes, see the map on p46.

Cyclist on the World's Most Dangerous Road (p128)

Mountain Biking

The parks just outside La Paz, Valle de las Animas and Valle de la Luna, are host to wickedly fun dirt trails that can be combined with *parapente* (hang-gliding) adventures. The unforgettable 'World's Most Dangerous Road' adventure begins high above La Paz at La Cumbre, and is easy asphalt until you hit the Death Road itself, where it gets a bit bumpy (but still not too hard). Chacaltaya, accessible with tour groups from La Paz, is the starting point of a 60km mountain-biking adventure with some steep descents (up to 410m) down to Zongo. Sorata is known for its variety of trails of varying experience levels.

ROCK CLIMBING
On the wild edges of Sucre and La Paz, test your inner and outer strength on ancient formations while appreciating the surrounding beauty.

KAYAK/CANOE
You can raft or kayak the Río Coroico in Los Yungas, as well as the Río Espiritu Santo in the Chapare.

ZIPLINING/ CANOPY WALKS
Tour the Amazon's treetops and other forested locales - slowly on steel walkways, or speedily, hanging onto a cable for dear life!

4WD-ING
The rugged terrain of the altiplano and the salt flats of Uyuni offer various 4WD-ing opportunities.

ACTION AREAS

Where to find Bolivia's best outdoor activities.

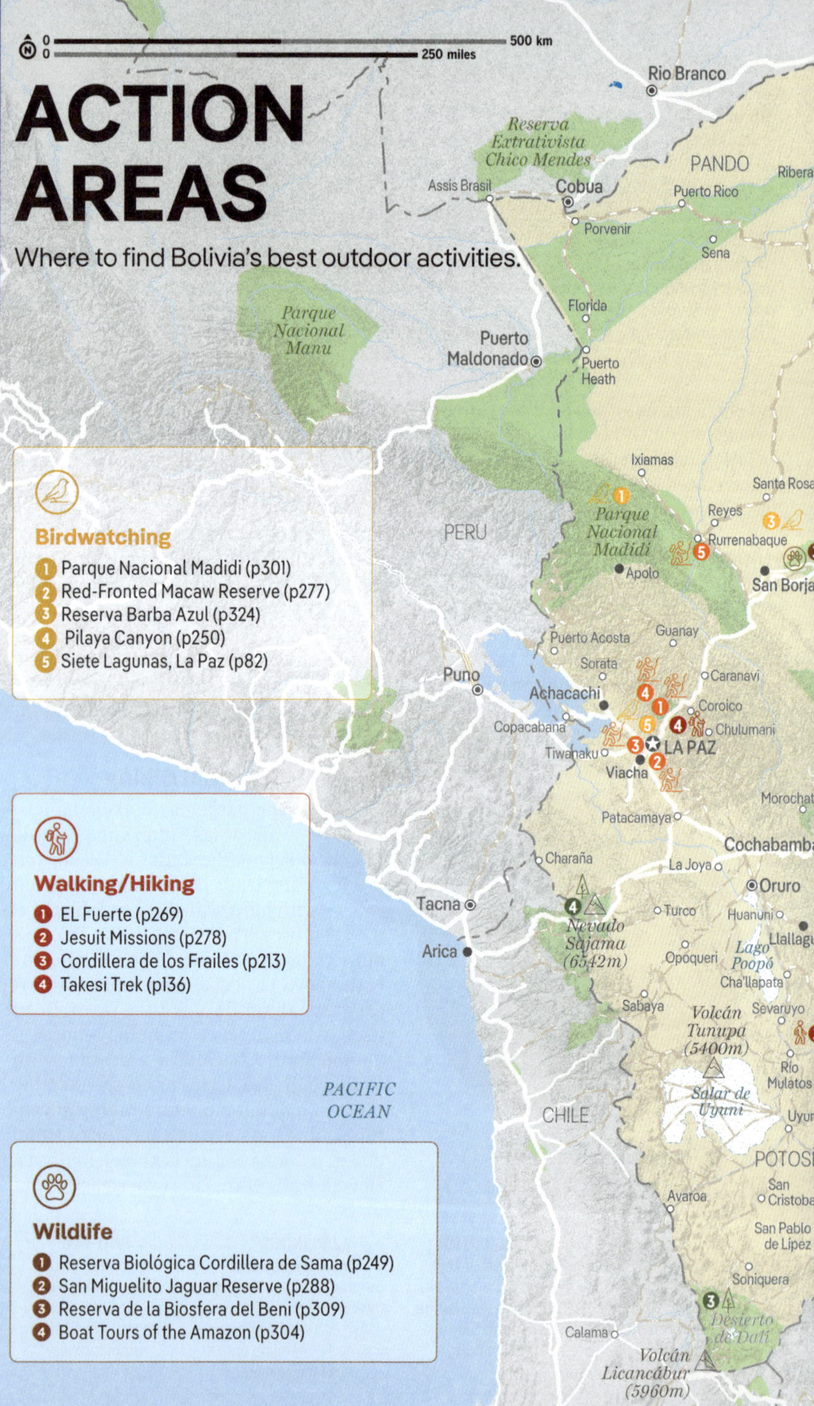

Birdwatching

1. Parque Nacional Madidi (p301)
2. Red-Fronted Macaw Reserve (p277)
3. Reserva Barba Azul (p324)
4. Pilaya Canyon (p250)
5. Siete Lagunas, La Paz (p82)

Walking/Hiking

1. EL Fuerte (p269)
2. Jesuit Missions (p278)
3. Cordillera de los Frailes (p213)
4. Takesi Trek (p136)

Wildlife

1. Reserva Biológica Cordillera de Sama (p249)
2. San Miguelito Jaguar Reserve (p288)
3. Reserva de la Biosfera del Beni (p309)
4. Boat Tours of the Amazon (p304)

National Parks
1 Parque Nacional Amboro (p272)
2 Reserva Biológica Cordillera de Sama (p249)
3 Reserve Nacional de Fauna Andina Eduardo Avaroa (p166)
4 Parque Nacional Sajama (p150)
5 Parque Nacional Torotoro (p194)
Extreme Adventures
1 Death Road Bicycle Trip (p128)
2 Parapente, La Paz (p79)
3 Rock Climbing in La Paz (p55)
4 Climbing Huayna Potosi (p118)
5 Ziplining Rurrenabaque
Abunã
Guajará-Mirim
Guayaramerín
BRAZIL
Costa Marques
San Ramón
Magdalena
Santa Ana del Yacuma
Piso Firme
EL BENI
Trinidad
Carmen Ruiz
Concepción
Espiritu
San Javier
San Ignacio de Velasco
Ascencion
San Matías
Puerto Villarroel
Villa Tunari
Santa Rosa del Sara
San Miguel
San Rafael de Velasco
The Pantanal
Parque Nacional Carrasco
Entre Ríos
Montero
Warnes
Lago Concepción
Punata
Totora
Parque Nacional Amboró
Santa Cruz
Mizque
El Torno
San José de Chiquitos
Villa Viscarra
Aiquile
Samaipata
Roboré
Aguas Calientes
Pucara
Vallegrande
Parque Nacional del Gran Chaco Kaa-Iya
Ocuri
SUCRE
Redencion Pampa
Cabezas
Tarabuco
Padilla
Fortin Ravelo
Potosí
Monteagudo
Charagua
Camiri
Parque Nacional Defensores del Chaco
Toropalca
CHUQUISACA
Boyuibe
Fortín General Eugenio A Garay
Camargo
El Puente
Villamontes
Tupiza
Tarija
PARAGUAY
Padcaya
Yacuiba
Villazón
Bermejo
ARGENTINA

BOLIVIA

THE GUIDE

The Cordilleras & Yungas p110

Amazon Basin p293

Lake Titicaca p85

La Paz p50

Central Highlands p180

Santa Cruz & Gran Chiquitania p256

Southern Altiplano p145

South Central Bolivia & the Chaco p233

Chapters in this section are organized by hubs and their surrounding areas. We see the hub as your base in the destination, where you'll find unique experiences, local insights, insider tips and expert recommendations. It's also your gateway to the surrounding area, where you'll see what and how much you can do from there.

Valle de la Luna (p81)

IN GREEN/SHUTTERSTOCK

Researched by
Brian Kluepfel

La Paz

BOLIVIA'S URBAN SOUL AND CULTURAL EPICENTER

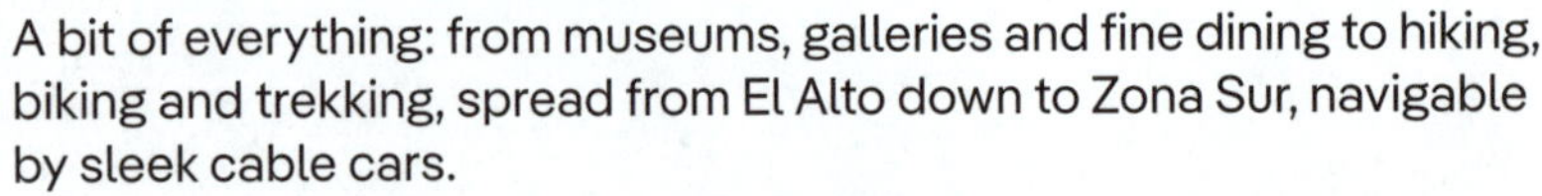

A bit of everything: from museums, galleries and fine dining to hiking, biking and trekking, spread from El Alto down to Zona Sur, navigable by sleek cable cars.

La Paz is a mad carnival, a sensory whirlwind settled into a montane bowl 2 miles above sea level. Like a three-tiered upside-down cake, its poorest inhabitants live up high, in El Alto, while the wealthy class abides in the warmer, oxygen-rich suburbs like Zona Sur. The rest fare in between, in the dizzying rabbit warren of cobblestone streets, some pitched so steeply you're at risk of slipping and falling without a bit of rehearsal. Lung-busting ascents lead to claustrophobic alleys populated with merchants, opening out at intervals into open-air markets bursting with a kaleidoscope of patterned cloth, fruits, and vegetables, all monitored by watchful *cholita* (indigenous) hawkers.

It's not the capital city of Bolivia, but proud *paceñas* (La Paz locals) point to the seat of government and former president Evo Morales' 29-story modernistic monstrosity, Casa Grande del Pueblo, as proof that the most important action happens here. Ironically, for a city whose name translates to 'the peace,' this is often the heart of strife when the nation has paralyzing protests, citizens cramming the streets holding placards and, sometimes, projectiles.

La Paz is rich in history and culture: the city's museums and art galleries are testament to such. Resplendent with murals representing everything from Aymara iconography to the natural world, and spattered with graffiti denouncing the latest sins of the ruling class, there's always an eyeful to behold. Feel the energy as you flow with the human traffic down El Prado; let your mind wander and wonder from great vistas to the sacred mountain of Illimani, always present.

A hub of national and international transportation, you'll likely pass through La Paz while traveling in Bolivia. And charmed by its incessant action, people-watching plazas and comfy cafes, both bohemian and business-like, not to mention a passel of restaurants and bars to fill anyone's evening, you'll be tempted to stay. From soccer matches to live music and the nation's best selection of art galleries and museums, La Paz will leave you wanting more, and glad you decided to stick around.

THE MAIN AREAS

DOWNTOWN & EL PRADO
Business La Paz meets museum district. **p56**

EL ALTO
Gritty high-altitude Aymara stronghold. **p68**

SOPOCACHI
The city's soulful, bohemian light. **p75**

ZONA SUR
Suburban edge with a refined touch. **p80**

For places to stay in La Paz, see p83

TR.-S.-DIEZ/SHUTTERSTOCK

Left: Valle de la Luna (p81); Right: Calle Sagarnaga, leading to Mercado de las Brujas (p65)

Find Your Way

La Paz is bustling. There seems to be nonstop human and vehicular traffic night and day. Taxis are expensive, yet reliable, shared *trufis* (minibuses) are cheap and let you get up close and personal with Bolivians. But the third 'T,' the *teleférico* (cable car), lets you fly above the crowds at minimal cost.

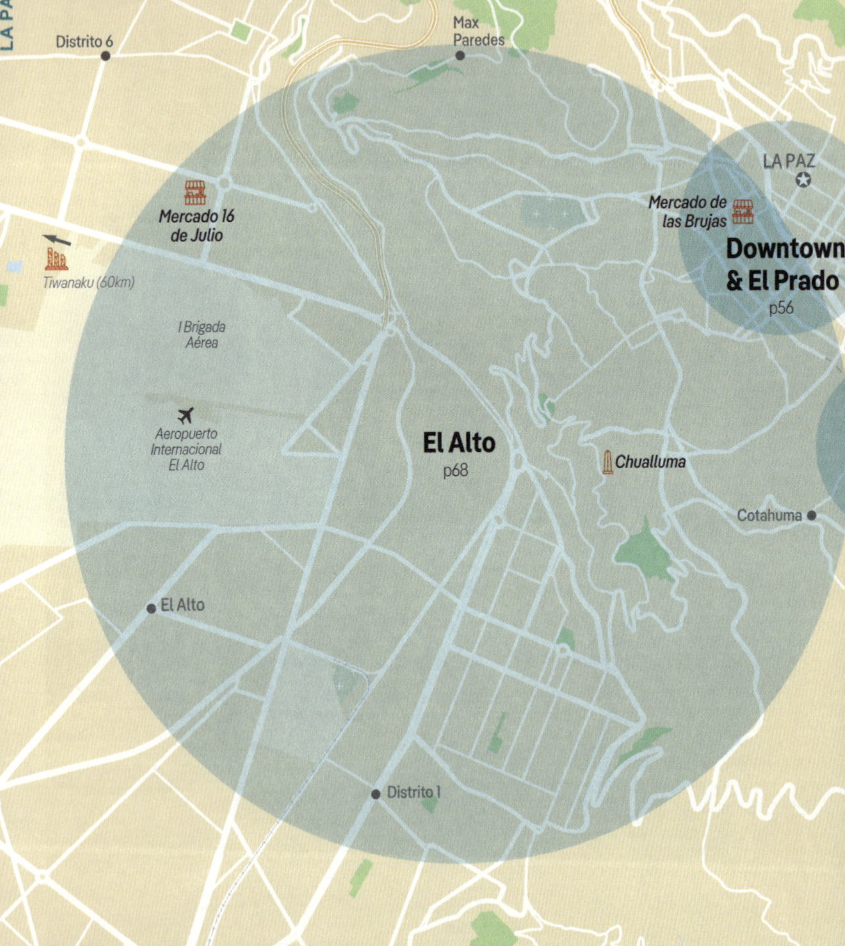

TRUFI

These shared vans are notable for their window placards advertising their destinations; if you're not sure the *voceros* (shouters) will let you know where they're headed. Cheap and chummy, you'll pay the least for a ride around town. Check your change, if you're counting *centavos*.

TELEFÉRICO

Ah, the coolest transit around. Eleven different lines of these aerial cable cars curl around the city from El Alto to Zona Sur, at B$3 for a single-line ticket and B$5 for a transfer to another line on the system. The *teleférico* runs until 10pm.

TAXI

Taxi: often the most convenient mode, also the most expensive; best to hail an official taxi with a meter, or ask your hotel or restaurant to get one for you. Get to know your prices; *taxistas* have been known to overcharge tourists a bit.

FROM THE AIRPORT

Taxis are the easiest option, and at some times of the night, the only option, at around B$80-90 for the half-hour trip to downtown. *Trufis* run services downtown, but if you catch one make sure you know where to get off.

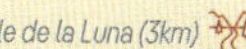

Plan Your Days

Jump-start your morning with a *marraqueta* (crunchy bread roll) and a piping cup of Bolivian brew before hitting the cobblestones of La Paz for an action-packed day and evening.

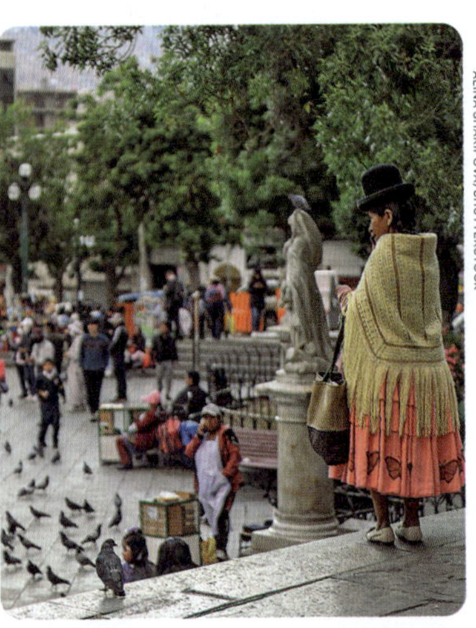

ALINA SHARIPOVA/SHUTTERSTOCK

Plaza Murillo (p67)

Day 1

Morning

Begin at **Plaza San Francisco** (p59) and its eponymous church. Head up Sagarnaga and turn down to the **Mercado de las Brujas** (p65). Cross the Prado and head for **Plaza Murillo** (p67) to begin the Museum walking tour at the **Museo Nacional de Arte** (p62).

Afternoon

Midday, lunch in one of **Calle Jaén's** (p62) cafes. Then take Sopocachi from the top, viewing the city from **Plaza España** (p77) and the scenic Monticulo. Do the Sopocachi Gallery tour, beginning on Avenida 20 de Octubre and finishing at **Museo Casa Solón** (p78).

Evening

In the evening hop on the **teleférico's** (p58) Yellow/Green line down to Zona Sur for dinner in one of its swank eateries.

You'll Also Want To...

Dive into different food experiences and cultural choices – how about ice cream and a movie? You also might have time for some shopping or a concert.

CHECK OUT SOME TRADITIONAL MUSIC

Hit up one of the **peñas** (p66) or try the **national theater** near Calle Jaén for scheduled shows.

DO SOME HIGH-END SHOPPING

The malls and boutiques of Zona Sur comprise a mini-Miami of ***fashionista*** offerings, in a barrio dominated by the **Green Tower** (p80).

HAVE AN ICE CREAM

La Paz is famous for its ice cream (p81). Check out the legendary **Helados Splendid** or **Frigo** (both have been around for decades), or lovely gelato at **Gigibonta**.

Day 2

Morning

Dedicate day two to some adrenaline-pumping action. The ***Parapente*** (p79) experience can involve some preflight biking, and you can also do some **rock climbing** in the same area.

Afternoon

Stick around the outskirts of town for a hike around **Valle de la Luna** (p81) or the Valle de las Ánimas and their otherworldly cacti and stalactite-like formations.

Evening

Head over to the **Green Tower** (p80; Torre Verde) in Calacoto for a drink or dinner on the 38th floor and some of the city's coolest views.

Day 3

Morning

Tour the city by **Mi Teleférico** (p58). Take the Purple line up to El Alto, appreciate the views from **Mirador Virgen Blanca** and **La Tea**.

Afternoon

Transfer to the Blue line to view the *cholets* (new Andean mansions; p68), take the Red Line to Chualluma and its murals (p74). If it's Thursday or Sunday, take in **Mercado 16 de Julio** (p73) and then hit the Cholita Wrestling (p69).

Evening

Jump on the Red Line downtown and enjoy a bag of popcorn at **Plaza Murillo** (p67) while locals feed its legion of pigeons. Or, hit **Calle Jaén's** (p62) cafes one last time.

BROWSE FOR BOOKS

The **Alianza Francesa** (p78) has a wonderful collection of books, CDs, in French, Spanish, and English. The **Alquimista** in San Miguel is rather comprehensive in its selection.

VISIT ANCIENT ALTIPLANO TEMPLES

A short 72km from La Paz are the ruins of **Tiwanaku** (p70), crucial remants of a once-dominant civilization centered around Lake Titicaca featuring incredible stone masonry.

MEDITATE ON HIGHER GROUND

Escape the bustle of downtown and enter the baroque wonder of **Iglesia de San Francisco** (p59), a 400-year-old stone monument to the city's Catholic founders.

PEOPLE WATCH IN PLAZAS

The city's ample plazas, from the ghosts of government past in **Plaza Murillo** (p67) (and its pigeons) to **Plaza San Francisco** (p59) and **Plaza Avaroa** (p77), offer close-up views of ordinary *paceño* life.

Downtown & El Prado

BUSINESS LA PAZ MEETS MUSEUM DISTRICT

GETTING AROUND

Trufi, taxi, or *teleférico (single ticket/transfer B$3/5)* remain the choices, not necessarily in that order. Downtown is a good walking spot if you're not in a rush. The uphill climbs on either side of the Prado, up Sagarnaga Street, or to Plaza Murillo and the museum district, can be challenging aerobically. *Teleférico* stations are the Obelisk (Purple/Morada line) and El Prado (White/Blanca line).

TOP TIP

While wandering downtown La Paz, go with the flow. The human traffic can seem overwhelming, but anticipate sudden stops, bumps, and changes in direction as you ping-pong up the Prado, and you'll be fine. When you can, take the calmer center pedestrian walkway of El Prado and admire the statues.

Feel the urban hustle of this bustling district, beginning at the Plaza de Estudiante and bisected by the famed 'El Prado' (Avenida 16 de Julio) with streets ramping up from Plaza San Francisco to the Witches' Market, Sagarnaga, and the cemetery on one side and to Plaza Murillo and the museum district on the other.

The hulking skyscraper complex Torres del Poeta, the country's second-tallest structure, towers ominously opposite Plaza San Francisco's massive church, the urbane battling the spiritual. Flow like a migratory salmon as you navigate the jam-packed, pedestrian-filled streets.

Hang out at Plaza Murillo, where at least two Bolivian leaders have been hanged, including the plaza's namesake, Juan Murillo. Grab a bag of B$2 *pipoco* (popcorn) as hundreds of pigeons flock to their daily feeding. Groovy Calle Jaén has several museums, a couple of well-appointed cafes and bars to rest and refresh. You'll also be drawn to the large public markets where you can buy everything from passion fruit *(maracuyá)* to potatoes.

La Paz Loves a Parade

The devil wears out El Prado

Sauntering along El Prado, the sound of a brass band strikes your ears. Suddenly you notice a large gap in the traffic; children of all ages are adorned in festive costumes and marching in a somewhat coordinated fashion. Many days of the year, for a variety of reasons, *paceños* love a parade – and you will, too.

It could be the **Gran Entrada** at the end of July, when brightly costumed students from around Bolivia gather to celebrate the onset of the school year. You'll see *morenadas* and other traditional dances as celebrants twirl down El Prado. It's a lovely spectacle and makes for great photos.

The **Nuestra Senor de Gran Poder** (Our Most Powerful Lord) festival and parade happens in May or June, and gets a

HIGHLIGHTS
1 Iglesia de San Francisco
2 Mercado de las Brujas

SIGHTS
3 Calle Jaén
4 Museo Costumbrista Juan de Vargas
5 Museo de Instrumentos Musicales
● Museo de Metales Preciosos (see 4)
6 Museo Nacional de Arte
7 Peña Huari
8 Peña Jamuy
9 Plaza Murillo

SLEEPING
10 Gran Hotel Paris Hotel
● Altu Qala Design Hotel (see 20)

EATING
11 Ali Pacha
12 Ayluri
13 Cafe Mundo
14 Dumbo's
15 Jawitas Mi Chulumani
16 Mercado Camacho
17 Mercado Lanza
18 Popular Cocina Boliviana

DRINKING & NIGHTLIFE
19 English Pub
20 Hb Bronze Coffeebar
21 Lucky Llama
22 The English Lion's

ENTERTAINMENT
23 La Festividad de Nuestro Señor Jesús del Gran Poder
24 Teatro Municipal Alberto Saavedra Pérez

SHOPPING
25 Mercado Negro
26 Mercado Rodriguez
27 The Writer's Coffee

TOP EXPERIENCE

Mi Teleférico

Public transit just shouldn't be this much fun. But in La Paz, it is. Brought to the capital by former president Evo Morales, the Mi Teleférico system of aerial cable cars has accidentally become one of the city's great tourist attractions, offering panoramic views and a way around the steep city valleys without losing one's breath. Eleven lines connect from El Alto down to Zona Sur.

TOP TIPS

- Avoid rush hour, when it's harder to buy tickets and cars get crowded.
- Buy a 'credit card' *(tarjeta)* if you're staying a while or have a family-sized group.
- If connecting to another line buy a B$5 transfer ticket rather than a single B$3 fare.

PRACTICALITIES

- *miteleférico.bo*
- 6:30am-10:30pm Mon-Sat; 7am-9pm Sun and holidays
- B$3 single-line fare; B$5 for a two-line transfer ticket

Helping Hands

Color-coded maps make it fairly easy to get around and attendants are at every station to help scan tickets and answer any questions.

Local Flavor

The Yellow and Red lines connecting El Alto remain the most popular, by far. Sometimes you'll find yourself sharing a car with a *cholita* or businessperson on their way to work; other times it may be a gaggle of students on their way home from class (Bolivian students pay half fare). Mi Teleférico is a rather unique system and a wonderful way to explore La Paz – as the old airline commercials once said, the only way to fly.

Bird's-Eye Views

The steepest descents – and the most breathtaking – are on the Purple line from El Alto down to the Obelisk station, and combining Sopocachi's Yellow and Green lines for a hair-raising jaunt down to Irpavi and the Zona Sur. Observing the soccer games and traffic from this vantage point is startling. On the Sky-Blue line connecting the Green to downtown, you can check out the incredible layout of the Christmas Fair and its hundreds of multicolored shacks from above; similarly, you can view the Alasitas Fair in January. If you want to see some *cholets* without walking the streets of El Alto, quite a few are visible from the Blue line.

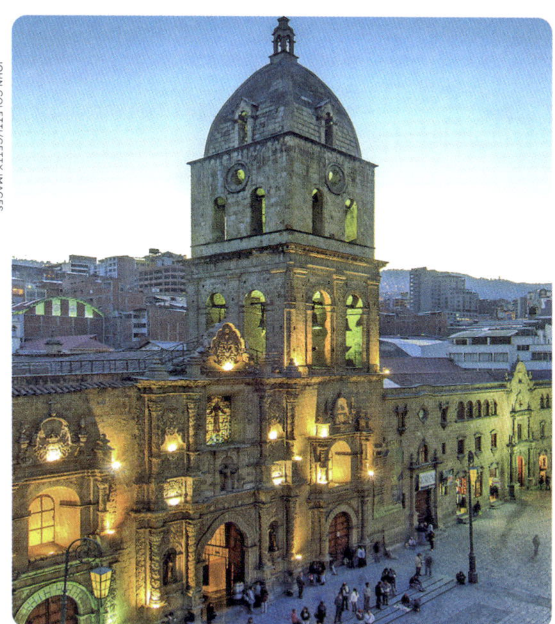

Iglesia de San Francisco

bit wilder than the uni kids. There is a copious amount of alcohol spilled on the Prado for this one, so step a bit carefully.

Other smaller parades on El Prado and other neighborhoods, celebrating minor saints or local anniversaries, happen occasionally throughout the year. Our recommendation: stop and enjoy!

Andino Baroque at the Basilica San Francisco

A holy stroll through La Paz's past

Before you even enter the doors of **Iglesia de San Francisco**, from the plaza of the same name, you're immediately struck by the city's, and nation's, heritage: three stone facings representing the Aymara, Inca, and Tiwanaku cultures. As you enter the main doorway, notice the first features of Baroco Andino (Andean baroque) – the facade is filled with carvings of birds, fruits, and pine cones. It's a mix of Spanish colonial and indigenous heritage that speaks to the country's chequered past.

Walking past the rather plain wooden benches and kneelers for Catholic congregants, you'll notice looking up another piece of the building's five-century history: a 'new' roof which replaced the original, which collapsed under the weight of heavy snows accumulating over the winters of 1608-1612.

Upstairs in the cloisters, in a walkway connecting the church to the adjacent and small museum, you'll note that the stained-glass windows are irregularly damaged – another remnant of local history. They are bullet holes from the violent eruption of the famed 1952 revolution. In fact, despite the holy designation, Plaza San Francisco is often the focus of civil unrest when the citizenry get their dander up – which in Bolivia, is quite often.

BOLIVIAN FUTBOL

Bolivian *futbol* (soccer) has never risen to the standard of its South American neighbors. No Bolivian club has advanced to the final of the Copa Libertadores, the annual South American championship. In the first World Cup, played in 1930, Bolivia played two matches and lost each 4-0. Interestingly, Bolivia coach Ulises Saucedo was allowed to referee some matches. In 1950, Bolivia was demolished 8-0 by eventual champion Uruguay and eliminated after one match. One bright spot came in 1963: Bolivia won the Copa America. Bolivia qualified for the 1994 World Cup, and they did manage their first point, and goal, in 64 years of World Cup play.

TRANSIT TANGLE

Initially built to connect El Alto with downtown La Paz 400m in altitude below, and previously accessible only by serpentine roads clogged with minibuses and other traffic, Mi Teleférico became a reality in 2014, with the Red, Yellow and Green lines representing the nation's flag.

COFFEE CULTURE

One business that seems not to have suffered Bolivia's recent economic downturn is the cafe and coffee business – there are more places to drink coffee than ever before for *paceños* and visitors. Being a cultivator of the bean, rather than an importer, has placed the country in an advantageous position, and the taste for local coffee is growing.

Roaster Café (p80) in San Miguel of the Zona Sur was a pioneer in roasting national coffee from Caranavi – officially dubbed 'the coffee capital of Bolivia' – and brewing it through Chemex presses. This coffee house grows, harvests, roasts and brews its own coffee – field to cup – working with Finca Kantutani and Geisha, Catuaí and Typica varietals. It also offers monthly barista classes.

After passing through a museum populated with religious paintings, you can unwind in a peaceful garden filled with fruit trees (like pear) and flowers, before taking a gander from a rooftop walkway of the urban maelstrom surrounding the tranquility of the church. Imagine yourself as President Hernán Siles Zuazo returning from exile in 1982, and give the people a little wave.

Coffee Tasting at HB Bronze

Tropical valleys produce rich beans

Walk through the doors on Plaza Tomas Frias into a new world. If you've never felt pampered by drinking coffee, a rather elite opportunity *(facebook.com/hbbronzecoffeebar; coffee tasting B$350)* is on offer at **HB (Hierro Brothers) Bronze** cafe.

The menu is a cool primer in itself, with carefully written explanations – did you always wonder what a *ristretto* was, but were afraid to ask? – along with an illustration of the cup in which it is served. No judgement here, just a welcoming to the cafe culture.

Finally your barista comes out and offers a trio of coffees, from the various family *fincas* (farms) in La Paz's rich valleys. You may get a 'Bourbon' varietal, a 'Geisha,' or others, each filtered through a different mechanism: a Japanese Hario V60, for example. As with wines, you'll notice different textures, colors, and flavors.

More good coffee spots are scattered across the city. Around **Plaza Avaroa** (p77) in Sopocachi there are boutique, all in one coffee shops like **Café Yanaloma** (p79) serving up fresh stuff from a remote La Paz Department village of Apolo. **Mugen Coffee Project** (p79) roasts on-site and serves its coffee in Japanese porcelain, a tribute to the proprietor's heritage. **Biofilia** (p79) is focused on conscious food but also offers French press and Chemex-filtered catuaí Rojo variety beans from Maximo Fuentes in Villa Tunari, Cochabamba.

Bolivia's Food Revolution

Regional pride in Downtown restaurants

In a country rife with possibility and ripe with ingredients, it still took an adventurous handful of culinary entrepreneurs to lift the lid on Bolivian cooking. The results have been nothing short of miraculous: the past 10 to 15 years have seen a revolution in the kitchen that's brought Bolivian ingredients and recipes to the foreground.

DRINKING IN DOWNTOWN LA PAZ: OUR CAFE PICKS

HB Bronze: The high-water mark, as it were, of new Bolivian coffee purveyors. Tastings of coffee – and fine wine – make you feel pampered. *8:30am-10pm*

The Writer's Coffee: A coffee shop inside a bookshop that has wonderful chocolate concoctions from the Amazon. More please. *9am-7:30pm*

Cafe Mundo: Spot that's been making visitors comfortable for years. 'Meet the world' over an acai bowl or a hearty stack of American pancakes. *7am-10pm*

Typica Centro: A multigenerational hangout stuffed with funky chairs, old stereos, and staffed by friendly, youthful servers. Win-win. *7:30am-11pm*

MARK GREEN/SHUTTERSTOCK

Plant-based dish at Ali Pacha

Interestingly, this revolution was kickstarted in 2013 by Danish 'gastronomic entrepreneur' Claus Meyer and his compatriot, executive chef Kamilla Seidler. Meyer's Zona Sur spot, **Gustu** (p82), is still one of the leading Bolivian restaurants in La Paz, and Seidler's successor, Marsia Taha, has been picking up prestigious awards for her pioneering work in showcasing heretofore unsung Bolivian ingredients.

The revolution quickly spread, and today some of the country's finest Bolivian cuisine is concentrated in La Paz's Downtown neighborhood.

Sebastián Quiroga trained at Gustu before launching all vegan **Ali Pacha** in the Casco Viejo. Just blocks from Plaza Murillo, he serves up incredible 11-course menus using only Bolivian ingredients.

There's also **Popular Cocina Boliviana**, in the heart of the Witches' Market, serving up affordable three-course meals with morsels from La Paz's fecund markets. So popular is 'Popular' that the line forms hours before it opens for a limited lunch-only seating.

The regional pride is often reflected in the choice of Aymara names, like Downtown's new and innovative restaurant **Ayluri**, headed by Mariana Calderon-Goldstein, who has been serving up small-plate menus to acclaim just off Av 16 de Julio.

Other expressions of Bolivian gastronomic pride include the use of purely local ingredients, and the revival of recipes generations old in the kitchens of youthful enthusiast chefs who are rescuing traditions one plate at a time.

Some of the Bolivian cuisine highlights in the wider city include **Manq'a** (p77) in Sopocachi, which goes the extra step in actually teaching the next generation of Bolivian chefs how to creatively prepare indigenous foods. And, in Zona Sur, **Phayawi's** (p82) menu is made up of dishes from all over the country.

CHEF STROLL THROUGH LA PAZ

Mariana Calderon-Goldstein, proprietor and chef of Ayluri Restaurant *@ayluri.restaurante*

Start in early morning with quinoa with apple, a hot drink and empanadas. You could do worse than **Jawitas Mi Chulumani** (p68) serving up their traditional empanada with a piping hot *api* (purple corn drink). At mid-morning it is the *salteñas'* turn.

Noon is synonymous with the *marraqueta* (the city's signature bread) paired with *llajwa* (tangy salsa) and classic soups like *maní* and *chairo* (made with herbs and freeze-dried potatoes). Mercado Lanza is a lunch hotspot, as is de Doña Paulina in Miraflores – try the *sándwiches de chola* (pork sandwiches) . Don't miss an afternoon *api* with cake.

At dinner, *anticucho* (skewered beef hearts) is a classic street food. The best are found on Sopocachi's Calle Aspiazu, Calle 15 and Ballivan in Calacota.

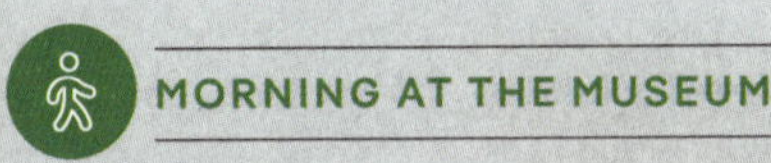

MORNING AT THE MUSEUMS

Discover La Paz's artistic and historic past with this short stroll beginning at Plaza Murillo.

START	END	LENGTH
Museo Nacional de Arte	Galeria Mamani Mamani	3 hrs; 2km

Start at the 1 **Museo Nacional de Arte**, featuring a permanent collection of Bolivian artwork and rotating themed exhibitions. Then, perambulate the cobblestone passageway one-and-a-half blocks to the 2 **Museo Nacional de Etnografía y Folklore** and its outstanding collection of Bolivian traditional dress, including a stunning and vibrantly displayed mask collection.

Clamber up a block and left two blocks to Calle Jaén, make a right one more block to the entryway of the 3 **Museo Costumbrista Juan de Vargas**, where you buy your four-in-one ticket for all the Calle Jaén attractions. In quick succession you'll pass through the 4 **Museo de Metales Preciosos** (some fine pre-Columbian goldwork on display), 5 **Museo de Litoral Pacifico** (which delves into Bolivia's obsession with its territorial loss to Chile), and the colonial home of 6 **Casa Murillo**. Last, but not least on your list is the 7 **Museo de Instrumentos Musicales**, showcasing a collection of more than 7,500 instruments from more than 200 world countries and territories.

You'll end up with a fine shopping opportunity at the 8 **Galeria Mamani Mamani** (a bit more like a storefront disguised as a gallery).

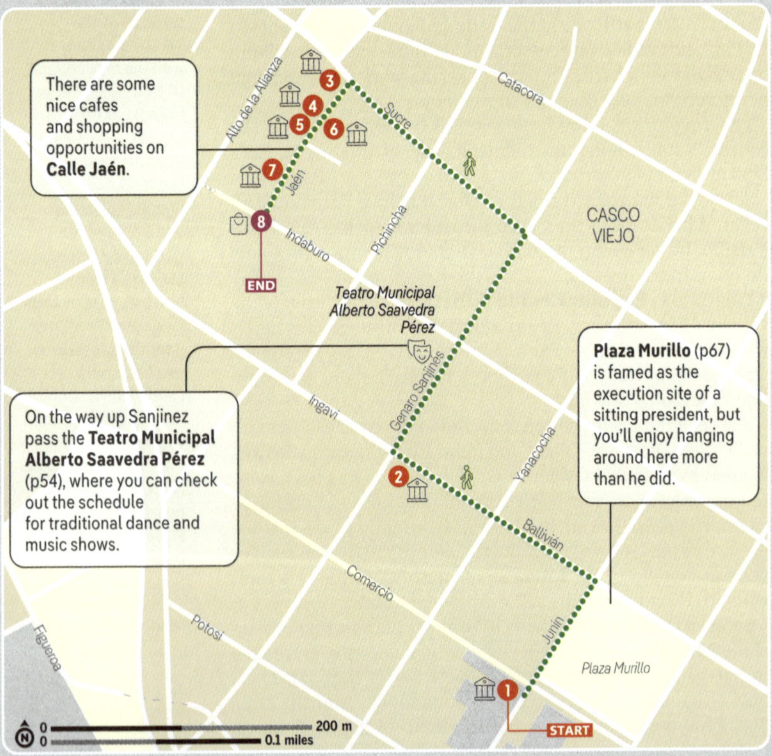

KAROL MORAES/SHUTTERSTOCK

Feria de las Alasitas

Las Alasitas: the Little Man Rules

The little man with big dreams

While Christmas is certainly a festive time in La Paz, it may be true that *paceños* look forward to a date one month later with even more anticipation. January 24 begins the Festival of Las Alasitas (the little things), where people buy things in miniature with the hopes that the full-size object will manifest itself in the coming year.

More than 6000 vendors and dozens of *curanderos* (native healers) offer their services at the massive Campo Ferial Bicentenario, just below El Prado.

Ekeko (the chubby, munificent god of abundance) and the **Feria de las Alasitas** is where Catholicism meets Aymara culture head on. A day before the Feria, there is a procession in honor of the Virgen de La Paz, for which many people get dressed up as Ekeko and distribute Bolivianos or miniature dollars to the crowd.

The fair can extend up to 30 days, and is truly regional in influence – more Aymara than national in spirit.

Like many things in the Altiplano, Ekeko and the fair can be traced back to the Tiwanaku civilization, where the god Tunupu, of fire and water, was celebrated.

The tradition is now honored bi-nationally: in Puno, Peru it was declared a Cultural Heritage of the Nation of Peru, and

continues on p66

EKEKO ABOUT TOWN

Ekeko is a figure derived from Tiwanakan culture – the smiling, colorful, and generous god of abundance and principal figure of Las Alasitas. A chubby, mustachioed fellow, Ekeko comes with various adornments: he can be festooned in colorful ribbons, affixed with coins and paper money with a cigarette dangling jauntily from his mouth, a fancy fedora or woolen *chulla* hat atop his head, and with *charangos* (mandolin-like instrument) or *zampoñas* (pan pipes) attached as musical accompaniment.

You can see a roomful of 160 Ekekos in all their colorful manifestations – of metal, clay, wood, and leather – in the **Museo Costumbrista Juan de Vargas** on Calle Jaén, in the Casco Historico district.

EATING IN LA PAZ: BEST COMFORT FOODS

Horno Camba: (Sopocachi) Mouthwatering *zonsos* (yucca and cheese pastry). Other treats include *keperi*, a hearty meat-and-yucca plateful. *8am-6pm* $

Salteneria El Hornito Cafeteria: A favorite of local workers. They get the braided top of the *salteña just* crispy enough. *8:30am-9pm* $

Jawitas Mi Chulumani: The pride of the nearby valleys, bite-sized cheese-filled empanadas served up with fresh *api*. *7am-9pm Mon-Sat, from 2pm Sun* $

La Soperia: The Bolivian tradition of lovely and warming soups continues here in Sopocachi. *11am-6pm Wed-Thu, 11am-11pm Fri, 12-11pm Sat, 12-4.30pm Sun, 11am-4pm Mon-Tue* $

LAURA FACCHINI/SHUTTERSTOCK

Mercado de las Brujas

TOP EXPERIENCE

La Paz's Magical Markets

It would be hard to overestimate the importance of La Paz's many markets in the public consciousness or in the general health of the country. They are the lifeblood of the city, providing fresh food and other products in an urban space that still relies greatly on the surrounding country. Most of all, they are colorful and lively, picturesque and vibrant.

DON'T MISS

- Saturdays at any market
- The Flower Market
- 'Macho Camacho' sandwich at Mercado Camacho
- *Mocochinchi* juice at Mercado Rodriguez
- Musical instruments at the Witches' Market
- Fresh juice at Mercado Lanza
- Electronics at Mercado Negro

Mercado Rodriguez

On the **corner of Zoile Flores and Belen** streets, just a few blocks uphill from the Obelisk and the Mi Teleférico Morado station, is one of Bolivia's most picturesque markets. The action starts at 4am daily, when many of La Paz's chefs arrive to take their pick of the very freshest produce. You'll find the market lively all week, but Saturdays and Sundays are ideal days for a wander as the surrounding streets are closed. Get a glass of cold *mocochinchi* (dried

PRACTICALITIES

- Most markets are open from dawn until evening
- Cash is king; only bolivianos, please

peach boiled with cinnamon and sugar). Sample the spicy red fruits of the *ulupicas*, a wild pepper measuring 30,000 SHU (Scoville Heat Units)! Delight in the sight of *pasankallas* (Aymara for 'toasted corn'), giant piles of multicolored toasted corn snacks smothered in sugar, being gobbled by the handful by the young and young at heart.

Mercado Camacho

Five joyous stories of food. A fave of tourists and locals alike looking for quick bite to eat, including the noteworthy 'Macho Camacho' sandwich named for the boxer of the same name: a heart attack waiting to happen with chorizo, fried egg and sliced hot dog atop a fresh *marraqueta* roll. You'll get a coffee to wash it down. There are other healthier choices, including fresh fruit juices, so don't fret.

Mercado Lanza

Mercado Lanza is a nice reward after a walk up from Plaza San Francisco. Get yourself a glass of *api* and some tasty accompaniments like a *salteña* (meat and vegetable pasty). You can also get a full meal. More structured than other markets, if you're staying in La Paz a while, it's a good place to stock up on groceries.

Mercado Negro

Dare we say that the **'black market'** is aptly named, with plenty of goods of unknown origin, like (pirated?) CDs and DVDs, along with a raft of electronics. Perhaps you need a charger? A Blu-ray of *Titanic*? You'll find them here – but please, no photos! Also a site for buying brand-name jeans and other fashion accessories, which (ahem) may not be genuine.

Mercado de las Brujas

An obligatory stop in La Paz, the **Mercado de las Brujas** (Witches' Market) is conveniently located perpendicular to the popular **Calle Sagarnaga**. You'll want to stroll here, admiring the carvings, handmade belts, sweaters, ponchos and indigenous amulets like the famed llama fetuses. La Paz residents and visitors who have met a certain someone may buy a love potion here to win them over. If you don't want to spend, there are stalls of tchotchkes like dolls, ashtrays, Tiwanaku statuettes, and postcards that are charming but not heavy on the wallet. At the far end are the musical instrument shops, where you can get a nice *charango*, guitar or other well-made music maker.

MODELS IN SUSTAINABILITY

Not many crops peek up through the cobblestones of La Paz. For produce, the city relies on the verdant valleys and surprisingly productive Altiplano for a range of food. One moment you might be buying oranges from Las Yungas, and the next, coffee beans from northern La Paz. By inquiring of vendors where the produce is from, you learn about the country's edible geography, and aid in its sustainability.

TOP TIPS

- Markets are liveliest on the weekend. Come earlier in the morning if you like things a bit less crowded.
- A bit of haggling is acceptable, but appreciate that many vendors will have comparatively low income and don't be cheap.
- Markets are picturesque, but always ask before snapping any photos.
- Come hungry! The markets are a great place to try local foods and dine side-by-side with *paceños*.
- For the sake of Pachamama (Mother Earth), bring your own bag and water bottle.

PEÑAS: CULTURAL BASTIONS

If you've somehow arrived in the city and there's no parade on, don't fret – much of the representative dance and music of Bolivia lives on in the *peñas*, or folk clubs, of La Paz. The word has its origin in Spain, where flamenco musicians and dancers gathered at *peñas flamencas*, but came to represent the 'new music' of the progressive 1960s and 1970s in Chile and South America. In La Paz, a trio of stalwart locales are conveniently found on Calle Jaén (Marka Tambo) and Calle Sagarnaga (**Peña Huari** and **Peña Jamuy**), where for two hours you'll enjoy colorfully clad dancers and top-notch acoustic musicians knocking out *morenadas* (folk dances) and other traditional numbers.

continued from p63

in 2017 UNESCO named the Bolivian tradition a Cultural Patrimony of Humanity. Large praise for such a small fellow.

El Super Clasico: La Paz's Soccer Showdown

Twice annually, city rivals clash

Twice a year in Miraflores, a 21st-century battle is enjoined that would rock the ancients: the *'super clasico'* held twice a year in **Estadio Hernando Siles** *(bolivar.com.bo; tickets B$40-270)* between traditional local rival teams Bolivar and the Strongest.

In the plaza, everything is for sale, including yellow and blue balloons to support either side: Bolivar wear sky-blue uniforms, and *'los tigres'* of the Strongest wear yellow-and-black stripes, naturally. The brave of stomach take their chances with the pork sandwiches; the more timid settle for popcorn and soda.

Hawkers selling valid tickets (or not) shout out their wares: *'Curva prefencia! Curva azur!'* Canny fans line up two or three days before and buy genuine tickets at the stadium windows; usually not necessary for league games, but this is El Super Clasico. Of the 231 encounters up to 2024, Bolivar won 93 and the Strongest 61, with 77 ties. Technically, the stadium holds 41,000 fans, but they pack in closer to 50,000, nose to nose on the concrete bleachers, for this game.

Black-vested police patrol at least as vigorously as the ice-cream vendors, while Polaroid photographers wander the crowd trying to make a buck selling instants. As the crowd settles in, the usual smoke bombs come from each end of the stadium along with an acrid sulfur odor and yellow smoke, naturally, from the Strongest side.

The Bolivian league will never be mistaken for the English Premier League or Spain's La Liga – there just isn't enough money behind it, and few foreign players ply their trade here – but there is a general enthusiasm that's hard to bottle. And this showdown is a guaranteed sellout as it generally happens just twice a year.

Buy tickets in advance. Arrive one or two hours early, partly for the atmosphere, partly to get your gear – plenty of scarves, kits, and face-painting on sale – and to find a seat, if you've chosen the concrete bleacher ducats. The afternoon temps vary wildly, so dress in layers, and bring a B$2 Styrofoam seat cushion to make the cement seats survivable. You will see that these also make for excellent projectiles – they soar like frisbees into the lower decks whenever a referee's decision is questioned (often).

Viva la Revolucion Nacional

Revolutionary history through spectacular murals

Coups and revolutions have been so commonplace in Bolivia's history that visiting the **Museo de la Revolucion Nacional**, anchoring the northern end of Plaza Villoroel, you might wonder, 'which revolution?' The answer, the popular revolt of armed miners in April 1952, not only resulted in the nationalization of Bolivian mining interests and massive land reform but set the stage for the country's modern political conflict.

AIZAR RALDES/AFP VIA GETTY IMAGES

Bolivar football club, Estadio Hernando Siles

Photos with accompanying text in Spanish and busts of historical figures tell the story, relatively dryly. Besides the brutalist style concrete building itself, the not-to-be missed highlight is a series of massive, vibrant murals by Miguel Alandia Pantoja Almaraz, similar in style to Mexican painter Diego Rivera's own (an admirer and friend of Almaraz), that heroically depict peasants, laborers and revolutionary leaders fighting injustice throughout Bolivia's history.

A Snapshot of La Paz Life in its Plazas

Snacks and people watching

Perambulating La Paz's many plazas immediately immerses you in the life of the city, its hubs of commerce, festivities, and social interaction. Set aside an hour or two to grab a snack or drink, people watch and soak the city in.

Recently renovated **Plaza San Francisco** is the city's largest open space, and one of its most historic. In the shadow of a 400-year-old **church** (p59), this plaza is a site of transit and public protests, among other things. Stroll down from Sagarnaga and enjoy a drink or snack from one of the many informal vendors.

Across the Prado, hike up to **Plaza Murillo** and grab a bag of popcorn, the favored snack. Gaze at the colonial buildings surrounding the square, and ponder whether you want to give any of that popcorn to the hundreds of pigeons who flock here. There are ample benches to sit on, as well as steps if you miss out.

At the south end of the Prado sit **Plaza de Estudiante** and **Plaza Bicentenario**, the boundary between downtown and Sopocachi. A statue of Bolivia's first president, Sucre, is often surrounded by fresh-faced army recruits. At the roundabout, here's another chance to get a street-food favorite, *anticuchos*. You may see a group of students dancing, in preparation for one of La Paz's many parades.

BEST PLACES TO WATCH FOOTIE

Dead Stroke (Sopocachi): Classic two-level billiards hall with a few screens for big sporting events.

The English Pub: Where Old Blighty expats feel at home drinking with the staff.

The English Lion's: In the heart of the Sagarnaga action, come for the beer and the footie, but not the food.

Invictos (Sopocachi): Good pub food and reliable coverage of local and international footie.

The Lucky Llama: The 'world's highest Irish bar' – need we say more? And classic Irish breakfast with a pint!

El Alto

GRITTY HIGH-ALTITUDE AYMARA STRONGHOLD

GETTING AROUND

El Alto's bustling **16 de Julio** (p75) market is the reason most folks come up here (Thursday and Sunday only) and its miles of stalls are made for walking. Of course, the Red, Purple, or Yellow lines of the *teleférico (single/ transfer B$3/5)* will take you up here and the Silver and Blue lines take you around. Taxis and *trufis* (minibuses) work their way up the crowded thoroughfares from downtown, but the streets are often jammed, so budget your time.

TOP TIP

Take the *teleférico* up and enjoy the views while avoiding the traffic. While walking, especially in the crowded market, do mind your personal effects – pickpocketing is known to happen here – and don't be so obvious about selfies and other tourist trappings. Nighttime is riskier.

A satellite city set 400m above downtown, El Alto is a rough-edged working-class district, unforgiving in temperament and climate. Recently, it's become a bit of a showcase for what La Paz can be, showing off its salty demeanor with popular demonstrations of wrestling, and the oh-so-bold architecture of the '*cholets*.'

El Alto has some of the city's most spectacular views, from terrestrial miradors and from two of the *teleférico*'s most stomach-churning descents. It's also home to Latin America's tallest statue of revolutionary Che Guevara.

If you've forgotten anything at all, you can likely purchase its equivalent at the miles-long 16 de Julio open air market – active on Thursdays and Sundays, the same days you can catch *cholita* wrestling. Do mind your p's and q's as you navigate this hustler's paradise occupying more than 400 blocks. You may just want to settle on one of the walking tours of El Alto, where there's greater safety in numbers.

Cholets: Nouveau Riche Mansions

Ostentation in El Alto

If you were walking along unawares in El Alto, the sight would stop you in your tracks: a building in the shape of the RMS *Titanic*; another with a to-scale replica of the *Statue of Liberty* jutting out from the top; yet another with characters from *The Avengers* seemingly leaping into the street. These are the *cholets*, the result of competition between prosperous El Alto merchants to create the most fantastical, whimsical buildings yet.

The name *cholet* is a portmanteau of *cholo*, formerly an insulting word for Aymara men, and the French *chalet*. The trend began in the early 2000s, when a businessman with a building on the Cochabamba–La Paz road built the first. The competition was on, and they began to spring up all over El Alto. No fools, these businessmen rent the buildings for weddings and other social events, and some double as hotels.

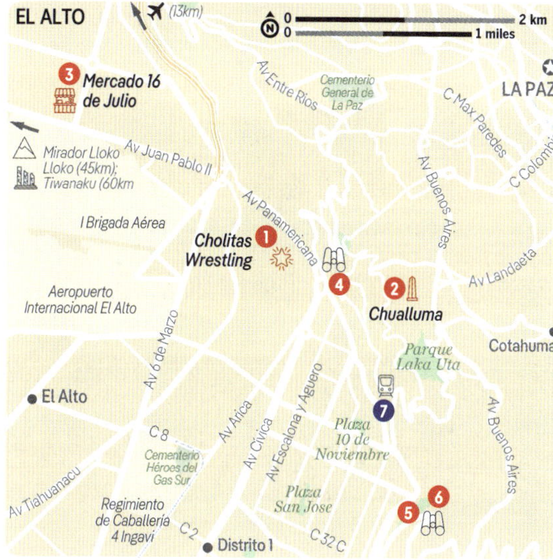

HIGHLIGHTS
1 Cholitas Wrestling
2 Chualluma
3 Mercado 16 de Julio

SIGHTS
4 La Tea/Faro Murillo
5 Mirador Virgen Blanca
6 Tupac Katari Mirador

TRANSPORT
7 El Mirador Teleférico Station

You can take a tour of El Alto with **Red Cap Walking Tours** that includes the *cholets*, or you can see many from the comfort of the *teleférico*'s Blue line.

Cholita Wrestling

Aymara women show their strength

One enters the arena, armed with a colorful ticket etched with a drawing of the main attraction: the **fighting cholitas**, staunch Aymara women of the Altiplano, punching back at centuries of racism and machismo by showing their mettle in the square circle. Dressed in traditional flowing skirts *(polleras)*, their braided pigtails dangle from beneath bowler hats; slippered feet allow for stealth.

Entering the ring, *cholita* pride is evident in more than their dress: traditional *sayas* (folk dances) play over the intercom as the combatants enter the arena; some dance the centuries-old *morenada*, an underclass mockery of their oppressors. *'Que pasión!,'* enthuses the ring announcer – 'what passion!'

Dubbed with names like Benita la Intocable ('the Untouchable'), Juanita la Cariñosa ('the Affectionate'), Nelly la Pankarita (the only masked participant, named for the ever-resilient cactus flower), these young women train twice a week and battle in three different locales. The more experienced and notorious out-earn their male counterparts.

There's no best evening to attend, but on Thursdays you can ride the *teleférico* Blue line conveniently nearby (and also catch market day at the famed **16 de Julio** (p73) market, the country's largest). The matches *(reservas.cholitas.*

continues on p73

QUEENS OF THE MOUNTAIN

You thought the wrestling *cholitas* were tough? In 2015, a group of *cholitas* formed their own mountaineering club, the Cholitas escaladores (Climbing Cholitas). Their first target was nearby Huayna Potosí.

Kitted out in traditional skirts and lugging up to 25kg of equipment, the group continued undaunted, scaling three more peaks in the next two years: Acotango (6050m), Parinacota (6350m) and Pomarapi (6650m). At last in 2017 they were ready for the heavily symbolic Illimani, at 6400m their most ambitious climb yet. They made it, of course.

A film documenting the climbing cholitas by Jaime Murciego and Pablo Iraburu entitled *Cholitas* was released in 2020.

DAMIAN RYSZAWY/SHUTTERSTOCK

TOP EXPERIENCE

Tiwanaku

Coming out of La Paz 72km toward sacred Lake Titicaca, and turning down a dirt road, not much is visible but a typical, modern Altiplano village. Hidden behind are the ruins of Tiwanaku, a civilization which dominated the region in the first millennium CE and came to a halt rather suddenly around 1000 CE, in unknown circumstances. Its temples, stone carvings and pottery shards tell tales still unfolding, with much conjecture remaining.

DON'T MISS

- Akapana Pyramid
- Temple of the Sun
- Mirador Lloko Lloko
- Pumapunku
- The Sunken Temple
- Museo Litico
- Museo Ceramico
- Stone Megaphones

A Typical Visit

A typical tour will depart La Paz around 8 or 9am, arrive at the site two hours later, and tour the two museums first before breaking for a traditional Altiplano lunch. In the afternoon, you'll visit a couple of the temples before heading back to the city for a late afternoon arrival. One of the more experienced companies for this itinerary is **Buhos Tours** *(buhostours.com)*.

What Was It?

Tiwanaku is thought to have been an ancient ceremonial center, with an elite population protected by a moat, or perhaps a bustling city of as many as 40,000 with complex terraced crops, fish ponds, and aqueducts connecting to

Titicaca. Its close-fitting stonework is a marvel of masonry; the extensive pottery collection spans four distinct eras; and evidence of architectural and astronomical wisdom abounds. How its massive stones were moved into place and carved is still a puzzle.

It's surmised that the stone for the various temples, courtyards and other structures was quarried far away and moved long distances to the site. The idea that these stones, some weighing tons, were also carved with mathematical precision has led some outside of the main body of anthropology to conjecture that extraterrestrial intervention was involved – these same theorists have noted similarities in the 'Andean cross' patterns between Tiwanaku's stones and those of other sacred sites across the globe.

Whatever it took to move these stones, modern efforts showed how hard it is: in 1966 the Bolivian army tried to shift one of the ancient monolithic stones with ropes and manpower, and failed to move it more than a few inches. The sandstone and andesite blocks of **Puma Punku** were cut so precisely that they interlock without any mortar, and were moved from quarries at least 10km from Tiwanaku. English anthropologist Ephraim Squier called Tiwanaku 'South America's Stonehenge.' Mysterious indeed.

Climb the Akapana

The **Akapana** is a terraced platform, and its top level was a sunken court, covered with blue-green gravel brought all the way from the Quimsahata Range, south of Titicaca. As you stand at the top, imagine that there was once a cleverly engineered drainage system which ran through Tiwanaku all the way to Lake Titicaca.

Gates of the Sun and Moon

President Evo Morales tried to imbue his initial election in 2005 with the Aymara spirit of his ancestors by holding his presidential swearing in ceremonies at the **Gateway of the Sun** in Tiwanaku. The site's largest gate, it was carved from a single massive stone 3.82m by 2.85m.

Ringing in the New

Although the equinoxes of March 21 and September 21 draw many visitors to Tiwanaku, June 21, South America's winter solstice and the Aymara New Year, is the most important date on the local calendar. Up to 5000 people come from all corners of the globe to watch the rising sun's beams illuminate the eastern temple. Locals don colorful ceremonial dress and visitors are invited to join the party: offerings are made and traditional food is prepared; there's also revelry fitting the occasion, with much *singani* (brandy) drinking, coca chewing, and spirited dancing.

Special buses leave La Paz around 4am to arrive in time for sunrise on these dates. Dress warmly because the pre-dawn hours are bitterly cold.

MUSEO LITICO: STEERING BY STARLIGHT

The **Museo Litico**, an indoor facility, houses the famed 7.3m Bennett monolith – a massive piece carved from a single sandstone slab. There's also the Puerta de las Estrellas, a complex drawing illustrating that the Tiwanakans could calculate astral patterns. Not only were they architects and metallurgists, but also astronomers.

TOP TIPS

- The weather comes up fast and heavy on the Altiplano. Be prepared with layers, sun protection and rain gear.
- If visiting between May and December, take the once-monthly night tour of the site, when the stones are illuminated with atmospheric light.
- If not on a guided tour, pay the extra fee for a guide. The history is long and complex here and a guide can sort it out for you in a more logical fashion.
- Plan to spend quality time here. There's a lot to see, and not to rush through.
- Have lunch in the village and support the local community.

ARTURO AND THE ANCIENTS

Arthur 'Arturo' Posnansky was an Austrian who never fit into the European rubric of his time; he visited Easter Island, captained steamers in the Amazon, fought for Bolivia against Brazil, and eventually was awarded citizenship. His landmark 1945 publication *Tihuanacu, the Cradle of American Man*, contains some far-flung ideas on the site that have since been disproved, but some theories still hold their weight, and his basic research remains valuable.

Lloka Lloka Mirador

Fifteen kilometers from the main Tiwanaku site is where many pilgrims gather on the June **solstice**, trekking from Tiwanaku to make offerings to Pachamama (Mother Earth) and eat a collective meal. It's the highest point on the Altiplano, save the surrounding Andean Cordillera of which it offers spectacular views. Some tours will stop here and it's highly recommended to do so if you can.

Monoliths on the Move

Giant monoliths built in honor of the Tiwanakans' mythical giant ancestors and named after personages in the (recent) history of Tiwanaku dominate the landscape and the visitor's imagination: the Bennett monolith, uncovered by American archaeologist Wendell Bennett in the 1930s, is the largest at 7.3m high. It moved around a bit: first to El Prado in La Paz, then to a plaza next to the city's main **football stadium** (p66) and now finally back 'home' in Tiwanaku.

The Ponce monolith, still impressive at 3m tall, is named for Bolivian archaeologist Carlos Ponce Sanginés, a key researcher from the 1970s to 1990s, who uncovered it in 1957.

The Bennett monolith resides in the **Museo Litico** (p71), which houses many stone sculptures including the Chacapuma. The Ponce monolith was placed in the center of the **Kalasasaya**, the 'place of standing stones,' which is also home to the 3m-high Fraile monolith, or Monolito Fraile, named for the early Spanish priests who came to the region.

Akapana Pyramid (p71)

MARK GREEN/SHUTTERSTOCK

continued from p69

wrestling@gmail.com; tickets B$100) are held in a *cholet* (p68), one of the Wonderland mansions constructed in El Alto by competing local entrepreneurs. On Tuesdays, the event at the Casa de Cholita includes a lecture/tour on the women's cultural context. On Sundays at a cement coliseum, the Bolivian crowd is more visible, and vocal. You'll want to grab a front row seat and a beer – both will provide some personal interaction with the wrestlers, and you may be invited to dance as the wrestlers approach the ring. If you want to go on a Sunday, it's best to book through a tour company, as the area is difficult to find.

The women theatrically fling off hats and *mantas* (shawls) and leap to the top rope like Spartacus of old; sleeves are rolled up to flex their biceps, among other crowd-winning gestures.

As they join battle, the *cholitas* draw on a surprising agility to employ all kinds of tricks against their rivals: aerial assaults, stinging slaps, and, cruelest of all, pulling one's opponent down to the apron by her pigtails.

Their ranks are replete with villains and heroines, corruption and redemption, all while flying around the ring fully costumed. All play their role, including the evil referee, obviously in cahoots with one of the glam gladiators. The audience clamor for justice not to be found. The only concessions to bodily harm are kneepads.

As the women tumble from the ring to battle at eye-level with the audience, alternative weaponry is employed: beer cans are battered against enemy skulls, suds soaking combatants and audience alike. A plastic gas-can jug is employed as a noggin-knocker. When the ladies approach the local Bolivian crowd – far more enthusiastic than the foreigners – the fans spray *cerveza* and epithets on the perceived enemy. Some find these staged battles belittling; others feel they empower the *cholitas*.

In the end, wounded warriors limp off into the Altiplano sunset as heroines pose for fan photos.

BEST VIEWS IN LA PAZ

Mirador Laikakota: (Downtown) Take the tram or bust a lung walking, the views and children's museum are worth your while.

Mirador Killi Killi: (Miraflores) You can almost peer inside the football stadium from up here, and Illimani dominates the picture.

Hotel Madero Cielo Bar: (Downtown) A different view of El Prado, from above: humans scurry like ants below.

Torre Verde: (Zona Sur) Bolivia's tallest building and highest bar are an unbeatable combo.

Devil's Point: (Zona Sur) Worth the 45-minute trek through creepy formations at the Valle de la Luna.

America's Biggest Rummage Sale

(Almost) anything you want, for a price

Imagine the world's biggest rummage sale spread out over 5km. Then imagine thousands of people jammed into it. That's what you'll get on Thursdays and Sundays at El Alto's main event (after the **cholitas wrestling** (p69), of course!). Welcome to **Mercado 16 de Julio**, Bolivia's largest open-air market, and one of the largest on the continent.

The thousands of stalls with colored canvas coverings make for an impressive site from the *teleférico* as you ride up (disembark at 16 de Julio station, naturally). You wanted car parts, or a whole car? Bike helmets? How about a whole bike? If you look hard enough, you can find nearly anything here.

BEST VIEWS FROM EL ALTO

La Tea/Faro Murillo: Fifty meters from the Purple line of the *teleférico*, watched over by a gentle *cholita*.

Mirador Virgen Blanca: The impressive presence of the virgin's statue is part of a larger park.

Mirador Lloko Lloko: A sacred site at the highest point on the Altiplano, overlooking the holy mountain of the same name.

Mirador Tupac Katari: Site of high importance to the indigenous community; tread lightly here.

El Mirador Teleférico Station: There's a reason it's called 'the lookout' station – take a moment to appreciate as you depart.

'Almost anything' includes rich platefuls of food: you can get *churrasco,* (steak) *charqui*, (dried meat jerky) or *chicharron* (pork rinds) and wash it down with a bottle of Fanta or Coke. Want to fill up on *picarons* (doughnuts) fried up in a big tin *caldo*? Step right up.

Caution: some parts of the market are open to vehicular traffic, and pickpockets have been known to hover, but it's generally safe, with a police presence.

Signs for public bathroom say 'Baño Publico' and the experience generally costs B$1.

Murals of Chualluma: a Splash of El Alto Color

El Alto's rainbow-painted barrio

When La Paz authorities decided to renovate and rebuild the neglected El Alto neighborhood of **Chualluma** in 2018, they indirectly created another phenomenon: a genuine tourist attraction built on local talent.

Riding up to El Alto from the Obelisk on the *teleférico*'s Purple (Morada) line, take the city in; this stretch of the cable car is one of the highest. Before you arrive, you will already see the brilliant colors of Chualluma's murals against the orange-red brick façades and corrugated metal roofs that define much of La Paz. Aymara cosmology, geometric patterns, indigenous faces – it's like turning a television monitor from black and white to color.

The *barrio* is a rainbow of hues since the municipality consulted with La Paz-born artist Knorke Leaf *(instagram.com/knorke_leaf)* – and, crucially the local population – on how to both bolster and beautify the neighborhood. Incredibly, a project that covers 10 blocks and encompasses 144 homes took only 140 days to complete.

A low-key option is to remain on the *teleférico* and see the murals: as you ride up and over the neighborhood, you'll see one wall emblazoned with the Aymara words Chu'wa Uma, meaning 'crystalline slopes.' Another wall depicts four *cholitas* in ponchos and traditional bowler hats.

At the last stop of the Purple line, simply stay on as the *teleférico* circles back around.

To get up and close with the murals, departing at the **Faro Murillo** station, you'll walk about 15 minutes to reach the neighborhood. The climb is steep and through narrow streets, but fortunately the landscape doesn't allow for automobiles.

The murals, created by El Alto residents, reflect their lives and dreams: one features a woman in traditional *pollera* skirt sprouting condor wings; yet another shows a child playing among the Andean constellations. Take a breath and take in the art, and reddish hills in the distance. Feel the energy of a barrio reborn.

As one local woman said to a reporter, 'now when we wake up in the morning, we don't see brick and dirt. We see colors.'

Sopocachi

THE CITY'S SOULFUL, BOHEMIAN LIGHT

If New York had Greenwich Village and Paris, Montmartre, La Paz will always have Sopocachi. Just far enough from the bustle of El Prado to allow for some breathing (and walking) space, the steep streets of this bohemian enclave teem with cultural opportunities, night and day. There are probably more cafes here than anywhere else in La Paz, clustered around the people-watching pedestrian byway Plaza Avaroa. Dotted with embassies, bars, heaps of vegetarian eateries, and a smattering of galleries, this eminently walkable district could serve as the focal point of your stay, for it also hosts a handful of boutique hotels and quality hostels. Plaza España, in addition to its expansive urban views, is also convenient to the Sopocachi *teleférico* station. Playing pool with a cigarette dangling daringly from your lips, sipping on a *chuflay* (Bolivian brandy and lemon soda), browsing the galleries of local and international renown, you may discover your inner artiste here – and find it rather difficult to leave.

GETTING AROUND

The neighborhood's streets are often steep, but very walkable. Any *trufi (B$2)* from downtown labeled Plaza España will get you here; so will a taxi, but at a higher price. The *teleférico's* Sopocachi station is a convenient connection between El Alto all the way to Irpavi (you'll have to switch to the Green line en route and buy a B$5 two-line ticket).

TOP TIP

This is a strolling neighborhood, so enjoy the plazas of Avaroa, España, and the views from the Monticulo. Traffic gets jammed up here as in most of La Paz; walking is often the best, and most relaxing, option.

Las Flaviadas: Classical Blast

Classical tunes and a fireplace

Through a hinged gate on Avenida Ecuador, and up a cobblestone path bordered by purple and yellow *boca de sapo* flowers from the Mediterranean, up another challenging staircase, is the home of a century-old La Paz musical tradition: *las Flaviadas*. The sessions are named for Don Flavio

EATING VEGGIE IN SOPOCACHI & AROUND: OUR PICKS

Armonía: Long time all-inclusive health spot in Sopocachi housing the Altramuz cafe and health food store. Wonderful juices. *noon-10pm* $$

Go Green: Substituting normally meat-based dishes like burgers and tacos with veggie varieties is the genius here. *noon-10pm Mon-Sat, to 4pm Sun* $

Valhalla: A small stand that pops up out of Plaza Avaroa, with a surprising selection of coffees, chocolates, and honey from Los Yungas and the Amazon. *9am-5pm* $

Sweet Fit: Grab some walking fuel and ascend the steps of this corner shop to get nuts, fresh empanadas, and other boosters. *8am-8pm Mon-Sat, to 5pm Sun* $

SOPOCACHI

HIGHLIGHTS
1 Mi Teleférico

SIGHTS
2 Espacio Fundación Patino
3 Fundación Solón
4 La Casa Museo Inés Córdova y Gil Imaná
5 Las Flaviadas
6 Museo Fernando Montes
7 Plaza Avaroa
8 Plaza Isabel la Católica
9 Salar Galeria

SLEEPING
10 Anami Hotel Boutique
11 Casa Fusión
12 El Museo Boutique Hotel
● Greenhouse (see 19)

EATING
13 Armonía
14 Biofilia
15 Cafe Yanaloma
16 Go Green
17 Horno Camba
18 La Rufina
19 La Soperia
20 Manq'a
21 Mi Chola
22 Mugen
23 Sabor Gaucho
24 Sultana Cafe-Arte
25 Sweet Fit
26 Valhalla Industrias

DRINKING & NIGHTLIFE
27 Dead Stroke
28 Invictos
29 Reineke Fuchs
30 Roaster Café

Machicado Viscarra, a Bolivian industrialist and patron of the arts who started the (initially, by invitation only) tradition in 1922 with a pile of LPs from his student days in Boston, USA.

The **weekly event** *(flaviadas.org; entry free, donations welcome)* grew so popular that it was opened to the public in 1938. Notable figures like Catalan cellist Pau Casals wrote to Sr Viscarra; renowned conductor Leonard Bernstein of the New York Philharmonic even paid a visit to the Avenida Ecuador home in 1954. In recent decades Flavio's youngest son, Eduardo Machicado Saravia, has kept the tradition alive, with a brief respite during the darkest days of COVID-19. Once again the doors are open to the public on Saturday evening; a paper program is handed out as Eduardo announces each composition in turn, with a brief biography of the composer and information about the track and specific recording.

A warm fire crackles along with the old LPs (sometimes CDs) as the attendees are transported back in time under the watchful eye of stained glass reproductions of Bach, Mozart and Wagner; a moody Beethoven remains vigilant at the top of the staircase.

Note that the living room is large, but likely only accommodates about 20 persons comfortably. Arrive early to ensure you have a seat and don't interrupt the program, which begins punctually.

SOLON'S QUIXOTES: POLITICS & ART

Walter Romero Solón remains one of Bolivia's most important artists, and it is fitting that the exterior of his workshop, now **Museo/Casa Solón** (p78), is adorned with one of his many renditions of Don Quixote de La Mancha.

Solón used the character of Don Quixote, patron of the noble lost cause, to express himself politically, whether through *Quixote and the Dogs*, authored when Solón's own son was 'disappeared' by the military government in 1971, or *Quixote and the Angels*, another sideways condemnation of the same right-wing regime. Coincidentally, the Casa Solón is just a few hundred meters from the statue of Miguel Cervantes (Quixote's creator) in Plaza España.

Views & Brews in Sopocachi's Plazas

Shopping, coffee and a viewpoint

Between your forays to the cultural hubs, cafes and excellent restaurants of Sopocachi, reserve a little time to explore the neighborhood's pivotal plazas.

Walking up to **Plaza Avoroa**, the heart of Sopocachi, dotted with palm trees, you'll see tons of families, children playing on various rides, dogs gamboling on grassy knolls. Shop the vendors' stalls or enjoy a coffee at one of the nearby cafes. Salute Eduardo Avaroa, the plaza's namesake and hero of the War of the Pacific.

Tranquility is the watchword as you walk up to **Plaza España**, centered around a statue of esteemed Iberian author Miguel de Cervantes of Don Quixote fame. Pine trees are flanked by placards bearing pithy local poetry; scale the Monticulo's steep steps to earn a stupendous view of the Andes through a tiled portico.

EATING IN LA PAZ: BEST BOLIVIAN FOOD

Manq'a: Socially conscious training ground for new chefs, with local food and opportunities for disadvantaged youth. *noon-9pm Mon-Sat, to 3pm Sun* $$

Ayluri: (Downtown/El Prado) New kid on the block serving up small-plate magic, from a veteran chef in the Bolivian new cuisine movement. *noon-3pm* $$

Mi Chola: Chef Franco's creative 11-course rotating menu, featuring local ingredients, satisfies and surprises diners. *noon-3pm, 7pm-11pm Mon-Sat* $$$

La Rufina (p82): Both the Sopocachi and Zona Sur locations are known for their fab presentation of seemingly standard Bolivian fare. *noon-10pm Tue-Sat, to 9pm Mon* $$$

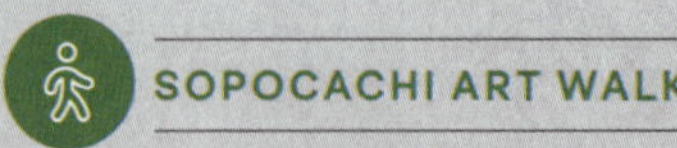

SOPOCACHI ART WALK

This walk, through the heart of the barrios and up Avenida Ecuador, brings you to artists old and new, dead and living, including galleries, embassies, cafes and even the former homes of the artists themselves.

START	END	LENGTH
La Casa Museo Inés Córdova y Gil Imaná	Museo Casa Solón	3km; 3 hrs

Begin on Avenida 20 de Octubre at **1 La Casa Museo Inés Córdova**. The Potosina artist (1928–2010) attended the fine arts academy of La Paz and made this gallery her home. Proceed to Calle Fernando Guachalla and the museum in the home of **2 Fernando Montes** (1930–2007). Piped in jazz brings you in tune with the master of Altiplano imagery, in a museum set in the home and studio he cherished. Pop into **3 Alianza Francesa's** multilevel site, attached to the French Embassy, and a wonderful cafe that hosts regular art shows.

Head up to **4 Espacio Fundación Patino**, which contains a performing arts theater, a cafe and galleries with regular exhibits. Take Avenida Ecuador to **5 Galeria Salar**, the former studio of the late contemporary artist Gastón Ugalde (1944–2023). Salar now opens its doors to many modern artists through partnerships with galleries in Miami and Bogotá. Finish your tour at the foundation dedicated to Bolivia's Uyuni-born, outspoken and prolific artist **6 Walter Solón** (1923–1999).

After a morning or afternoon full of art, you might want to stop at **7 Sultana** (p79), right down the street from Salar and Solón, for a bite, a coffee, or a drink – it too has fabulous rotating art shows on its ample wall space.

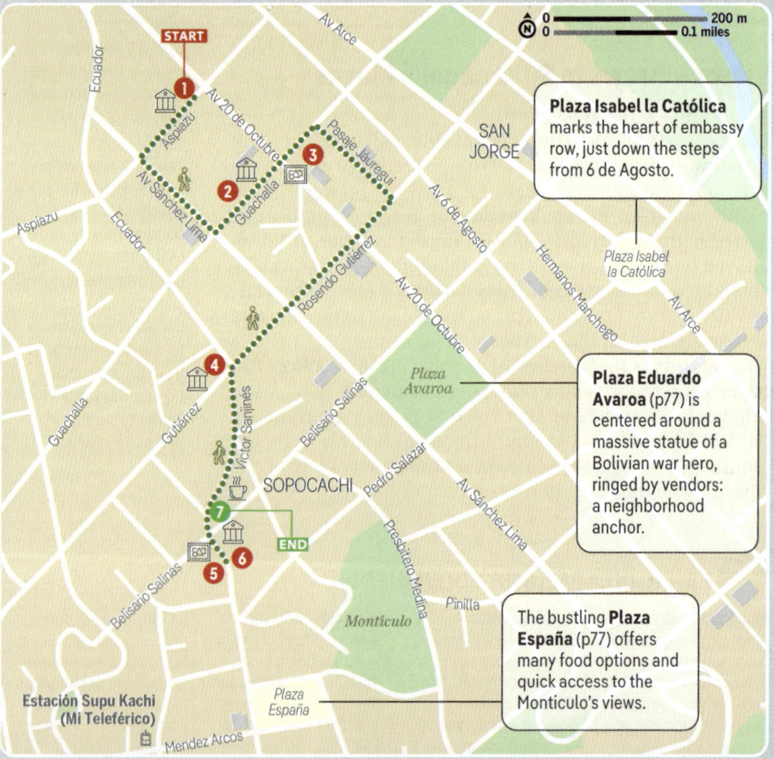

Plaza Isabel la Católica marks the heart of embassy row, just down the steps from 6 de Agosto.

Plaza Eduardo Avaroa (p77) is centered around a massive statue of a Bolivian war hero, ringed by vendors: a neighborhood anchor.

The bustling **Plaza España** (p77) offers many food options and quick access to the Monticulo's views.

Parapente: Flying High in La Paz's Valleys

A true bird's-eye view

Parapente, according to the Cambridge dictionary, is the 'sport of jumping off a cliff or hill with a sheet-like parachute'.

Who doesn't want to jump off a cliff with only a 'sheet-like parachute?'

In La Paz, once you've conquered your fear of heights via the *teleférico*, you may consider graduating to *parapente*. There is one licensed group of fliers based in Sopocachi, **AndesXtremo** *(andesxtremo.com; B$1200-130 single, group discounts)*, and they have a spotless history of getting people to the ground safely.

Better still, you can begin the adventure – and get your heart racing – with a bit of mountain biking in the inter-Andean valleys. This is a sort of high-adrenaline preparation for the great leap of faith later – a few hours on full-suspension bikes, bumping along the hills just south of the city proper. There's a proper bike park in **Valle de la Luna** (p81), where you'll get a primer on using the bike and avoiding disaster, after which you'll partake in two descents. The leaders will select routes for you based on your experience level, so don't fret.

Once you've dismounted your bicycle you'll head off to one of three takeoff points, depending on weather and winds: Llakhasa, Yanari, or Chanka. Then it's time to strap into your seat and run headlong down the hill until you're airborne. (Easier said than done: this author did not elevate until his third attempt!). The most important factor here is to run as fast and as normally as you can – no gazelle-like bounding, please. Running in tandem off the side of a hill takes some getting used to.

Once your feet are dangling gravity-free, there's little to do but enjoy the 20–30-minute flight over the valley (the licensed pilot is in complete control of the glider the entire trip, though he may let you steer for a moment if you wish). If you're lucky you'll see eagles and other birds actually below you – a completely amazing perspective. In the winter when the group goes a bit further afield for takeoffs, you may even see condors.

You'll also want to look cool and confident for the camera attached to your apparatus. Landing is bit tricky – you'll have to anticipate the ground and try to run a bit here, too. Then unstrap yourself, and you'll have a lifetime memory, all captured on video.

WHY I LOVE SOPOCACHI

Brian Kluepfel, Lonely Planet writer

I lived in Sopocachi from 1999 to 2000, and though businesses may have come and gone, the cool character of this boho barrio remains. Its appreciation for Bolivia's great artists, past and present, is evident in the galleries – art that tells a cultural and political history. The food choices are eclectic, and I could tour Plaza Avaroa's cafes all day, only to dip into the bars when darkness falls.

The international character: from the uber-German **Reineke Fuchs** *bierhaus (reinekefuchs.com)* to Argentina's finest beef at **Sabor Gaucho**

It's challenging, aerobically, to climb its winding pathways, but so worth it when you reach Plaza España and the Monticulo!

DRINKING IN SOPOCACHI: CAFES

Biofilia: Cool vibe with probiotic drinks, lots of Amazonian cacao including brownies, cheesecakes with seasonal fruits *8:30am-9:30pm Mon-Sat* $

Yanaloma: Straight outta North La Paz Department like a caffeinated express, Apoyo village brings the caffeinated energy. *7:30am-4pm Mon-Fri* $

Sultana Cafe-Arte: Coffee, artful drinks listed in a chapter-book-replica menu. Charming all the way around. *3pm-10:30pm Mon-Sat* $$

Mugen: A tribute to Japanese-Bolivian culture with functional wood decor, meticulously maintained plants and great coffee. *8:30am-9pm* $

Zona Sur

SUBURBAN EDGE WITH A REFINED TOUCH

GETTING AROUND

Zona Sur is like its American suburban counterparts: there's heavy traffic and you often need a car. The streets aren't great for walking, and minibuses and taxis fill the space that cars do not. (Some areas do have sidewalks, so it is possible to walk around, paying careful attention when crossing the busy intersections.) The saving grace is the *teleférico*, which services Calacoto and Irpavi from Sopocachi and Downtown.

You'll hear the *voceros* (callers) for the afternoon *trufis* calling out exotic sounding locales: Calacoto! Irpavi! Obrajes! Cota Cota! Chasquipampa! But what are they all about?

Zona Sur is a city within (or without) the city – a bit distant from downtown, and with more oxygen and warmth, as well as Bolivia's tallest building, the imposing Torre Verde (Green Tower). Somewhat a replica of suburbs throughout the world, but with enough outstanding restaurants and hotels to draw you in.

This is the neighborhood where you'll find fashionable diplomats and businessmen chatting over cafes, and kids in the latest American or European fashions devouring hand-churned ice cream.

Just outside the zone, easily reachable by taxi, *trufi* or tour company, are Valle de la Luna and Siete Lagunas, justifiably popular natural areas that are great for walking, communing with nature, birding, or just acclimatizing to the altitude.

TOP TIP

Take the *teleférico* down from Sopocachi or the Prado; you'll beat the traffic from the town center, at the same price as a *trufi*, and with better views. Some of the establishments here require a reservation for dinner so don't just drop in and expect to be served.

Climb the Green Tower

Speakeasy in the sky

Given the chance, who wouldn't want to go to the top of Bolivia's tallest building? The Calacoto subdivision is home to the architect Gustavo Dellien's imposing, impressive **Torre Verde** (Green Tower). At 46 storys (163.4m, or 536ft), it is Bolivia's tallest building. Its viewing platform with a 360-degree perspective of the urban surroundings is a must-see.

From the distance, it shines like *The Wizard of Oz*'s Emerald City. It is truly green, too: the Spanish glass windows regulate the amount of sunlight entering the building, thus controlling its temperature as well. Tests were done up to 70m underground

DRINKING IN ZONA SUR: BEST CAFES

Roaster: Started the national growing, roasting and drinking revolution and still a strong favorite in San Miguel. *7:30am-11pm* $

Typica Calacoto: A unique chain with other locations in Oruro and Sucre. Try the 'big rooster' – a mega espresso that's sure to wake you up. *7:30am-10pm* $

Cafe Épico: The classic bicycles and movie star posters belie the modern coffee techniques (just watch) that produce a flavorful cup. Pancakes to kombucha. *8am-10pm* $

Otoño Café y Vinos: Combining a coffee and wine bar is a stroke of genius from these purveyors of caffeine and alcohol. *8am-11pm Mon-Sat, 9am-8:30pm Sun* $

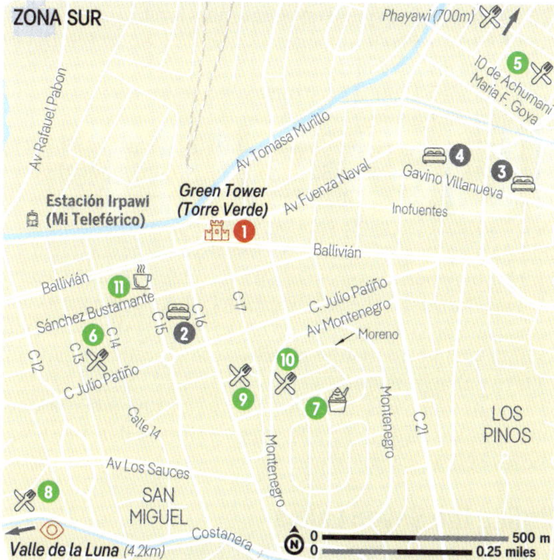

HIGHLIGHTS
1 Green Tower (Torre Verde)

SLEEPING
2 Atix Hotel
3 Met Hotel
4 Mitru Sur

EATING
5 Ancestral
6 Cafe Épico
7 Gigibonta
8 Gustu
9 La Rufina Sur
10 Roaster Cafe

DRINKING & NIGHTLIFE
11 Typica Calacoto

to ensure its stability against the seismic shocks that have been known to rock this sector of South America.

There's a restaurant and a bar on the 38th floor, and some cafes and other attractions including restaurants with spectacular views.

Hiking the Lunar Landscape

Scaling mountains of the moon

One of the more popular trips to the outskirts of La Paz is the **Valle de la Luna**, or Moon Valley *(entry B$15)*. Popular lore has it that Neil Armstrong, the first man to walk on the moon, named the region while visiting here after his famous Apollo 11 mission in 1969 (he and other NASA personnel had also visited in 1966 to prepare for what they thought would be a similar terrain). Regardless of its truthfulness, it's a great story.

You don't have to go to the moon to get to Moon Valley. You can hook up with a tour group, grab a Mallasa-bound *trufi* 231 from Calle Mexico, or if you're really into the overall travel experience, take the *teleférico* to Irpavi and jump on a Mallasa micro at nearby Plaza Humbolt. *Trufi* drivers will let you off at the park entrance if you tell them that's where you're headed. The valley is open from 9am to 4pm all week and until 5pm on weekends.

RED-TAILED COMET

In 2024, La Paz made the red-tailed comet its official bird.

This hummingbird is particularly loyal to habitats with flowering cactus; thus it is a common presence in the cacti-heavy natural areas just outside of the Zona Sur. Its color scheme, a gold-green body with a shimmering red tail, matches the tricolors of the national flag.

It appears on murals throughout the city and is emblazoned on students' backpacks. It is hoped that publicizing the beautiful *colibrí* (hummingbird) and its habitat will help drum up support for the reforestation of natural areas around the city.

EATING IN LA PAZ: BEST ICE CREAM

Helados Splendid: A seven-decade decadent tradition in San Miguel, and now, in Zona Sur. *8:30am-5:30pm Tue-Sun* $

Dumbo's: If you're feeling a bit hot and bothered on El Prado (Downtown), make a pit stop at this local haunt, right next to the cinema. A family favorite. *7am-11pm* $

Frigo: If you've survived, or are steeling yourself for a football match in Miraflores, there's no better sustenance than their ice cream sandwiches. *9am-6pm* $

Gigibonta: The city's best gelato, served with love and social consciousness from the owners, who employ recovering substance users. *10:30am-7:30pm Sun-Thu, to 8pm Fri & Sat* $

LA PAZ: OUTDOOR EXTREMES

Miguel Alem Morales, bicycle/paragliding tour guide Andes Extremo

I love La Paz for its proximity to the mountains and varied ecosystems, and being able to go up or down thousands of meters in an hour of travel, which allows many options for the practice of adventure sports. The entire valley of La Paz is an ancient riverbed, presenting crazy clay formations on its slopes, such as the **Valle de La Luna** and **Valle de las Ánimas**, where you can enjoy beautiful hikes, both to train and acclimatize via its demanding altitude gains, or just for the pleasure of enjoying our unique landscape with very little walking: and both options are practically within the city limits!

Two basic routes depend on your fitness level: a short 15 minute walk to a lookout; a longer 45 minute loop to the Devil's Point is worth the effort.

You'll understand Armstrong's sense of wonder seeing the spires and depressions caused by eons of erosion – it is otherworldly. Local legends come alive in the formations: The Cholita's Hat, The Turtle Shell and The Kind Grandfather are among the images you may conjure from the muddy spires.

The 32 species of cactus add a prickly sense of differentness, while various species of *lagartos* (lizards) and the odd *vizcacha* (a rabbit-like rodent) pop out of various subterranean hideouts.

Among the cacti is the infamous San Pedro, known for its hallucinogenic properties, and one of the reasons the park shuts down at night – too many hippies were literally tripping off trails to unhappy endings.

There are some ups and downs, as well as hanging bridges and stairs, but also guardrails, so generally you'll be fine if you proceed at a reasonable pace.

Birding the Seven Lakes

Indigenous hospitality and hawk-watching

Just 11km from downtown La Paz are the Seven Lakes (Siete Lagunas), a series of lakes and neighboring indigenous community that is growing in attraction for nature lovers and hikers. A half-day or day trip here *(turismoelalto.com/tours/ecoturismo/birdwatching/half-day/siete-lagunas)* often encompasses a meal with the community, and in addition to seeing some of the great outdoors bordering the city, you'll be supporting the Siete Lagunas town.

In reality, only three of the seven lakes are used frequently for birding, but all have well-made trails as well as blinds from which to spot the birds without interrupting them. You'll get a nice variety of up to 30 species of waterfowl and some other migratory species, including the barn swallow. Coots, ibis, ducks, herons and gulls populate the lakes in good numbers.

The local Ornithology Club of La Paz *(facebook.com/COLP.Bolivia)* is a good contact point for tips on visiting the lakes, and what potential birds are around. A typical birder might find the following on a half day trip, divided between a morning viewing aquatic species and the afternoon looking for raptors.

Among the waterbirds you may encounter are the lesser and greater yellowlegs, giant coot, and yellow-billed teal. There may be aplomado falcons and mountain caracaras up above in afternoons.

EATING IN ZONA SUR: BOLIVIAN RESTAURANTS

Phayawi: Specialty plates and decor from around the country, served in Zona Sur. *noon-3:30pm, to 9pm Thu-Sat* $$

Gustu: Eleven-course meals served with love at the restaurant that kicked off a revolution in Bolivian cuisine. *12:30-10pm* $$

La Rufina Sur: Like its twin eatery in Sopocachi, this is Bolivian 'fast food but artesanal,' with treats like *ispi*, a tiny fried fish. *12:30-3pm & 7-10pm Mon-Fri, noon-4pm Sat-Sun* $$$

Ancestral: Wood-fired goodness dominates this Achumani favorite. *7-10pm Wed-Fri, noon-3:30pm Sat-Sun* $$$

Places We Love to Stay

$ **Budget** **$$** **Midrange** **$$$** **Top End**

Downtown/ El Prado

MAP p57

Madero Hotel and Suites $$ A relative newcomer, this fine business-style hotel sits just above the Plaza de Estudiante and El Prado and has a bar with a fabulous view.

Gran Hotel Paris $$ The grand old lady of Plaza Murillo has revived its century-old glory, strangely managed by the local police! Get a room with a balcony if you can.

Altu Qala Design Hotel $$$ Five-star winner featuring indigenous-themed decor from repurposed colonial homes, a first-rate coffee shop/ restaurant, and stunning bar views.

Hotel Europa $$$ Conveniently a few steps from the Prado and still a nice modern option after a quarter-century in business. Tiwanaku museum is just down the block, as are cafes and restaurants.

Sopocachi

MAP p76

Anami Boutique Hotel $$ Wonderful old house hidden behind a wall, filled with historic bric-a-brac, an immense shade tree and garden, and a French creperie on site.

El Museo Boutique Hotel $$ Nice option on edge of Sopocachi, also an old house up a narrow alleyway. Close to the city center, yet peaceful; colonial feel with modern amenities.

Casa Fusion $$ Being one block from the *teleférico* is just one of the niceties of this boutique option, as well as solicitous staff, local art, delicious breakfasts, and coca tea.

Greenhouse $ Perfect place for solo backpackers with spacious shared kitchen and large library. Next to a great soup joint for lunch or dinner.

Zona Sur

MAP p81

Mitru Sur $$ Irpavi's top choice, with a rooftop pool and first-rate business amenities, too. Close to nearby churches and Mamani Mamani Gallery.

Hotel Atix $$$ A first-rate boutique Zona Sur option with matching quality restaurant and high-altitude bar, super city views. Ticks all the boxes.

Met Hotel $$$ Views of the Andes, a spa, a pool...shall we go on? Contemporary Bolivian artwork enhances the vibe.

Gran Hotel Paris

For places to stay in Lake Titicaca, see p108

MIROSLAW SKORKA/SHUTTERSTOCK

Above: Basílica de Nuestra Señora de Copacabana (p90); Right: Chincana Ruins (p100), Isla de

Researched by
Joe Sills

Lake Titicaca

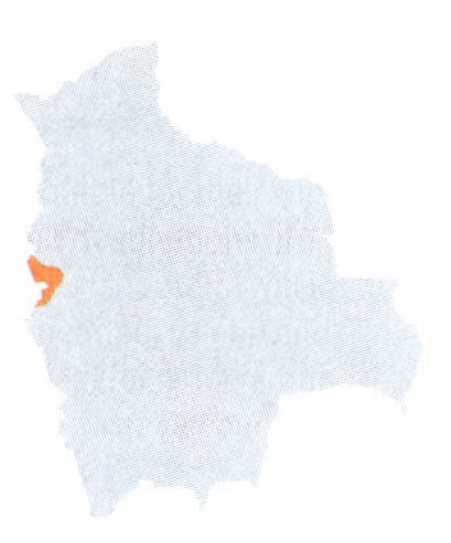

ANCIENT HEART OF ANDEAN CULTURE

Uncover the origins of the Inca and captivating, lesser-known legends cradled by this freshwater diamond on the roof of the Andes.

A halo of ancient terraces etches along the valleys and hills surrounding Lake Titicaca, a remnant of a civilization that once rivaled ancient Egypt and Rome. Centuries before the Inca, the Tiwanaku civilization called Lake Titicaca home, and many of the terraces they carved into the landscape still bloom with carefully tended crops like potatoes, maize and beans.

This is the heartland of the Aymara people, an Andean culture permeating the shores of Lake Titicaca in Bolivia and Peru. Thought to be descendants of the Tiwanaku, the Aymara endured the Inca, remained unconquered by the Spanish and now welcome the trickle of tourists who make their way into their homeland each year.

At 3812m, Lake Titicaca is the highest major navigable waterway in the world. Though boat traffic is scarce, a smattering of motorboats and hydrofoils ferry travelers through this hauntingly beautiful landscape of farms, casitas and legends.

On Isla del Sol, travelers can hike across a Mediterranean microclimate to the mythical birthplace of the Inca. In Copacabana, the sounds of silver trumpets mingle with lively markets brimming with bags of sweet *pansakalla* – a popped maize.

In contrast to its Peruvian neighbor, the Bolivian side of Lake Titicaca is a place that still feels entirely local. Tourists are welcomed, but not pandered to. Along its shores, the gateway to a deeper understanding of Andean culture opens wide.

THE MAIN AREAS

COPACABANA
Urban center with markets, pilgrimage sites and port. p90

ISLA DEL SOL
Incan origin legend and pre-Incan societies. p96

HUATAJATA
Shoreline settlement with Andean history museums. p102

Find Your Way

Base camp in urban Copacabana, backpack through hostels on Isla del Sol, sleep off-grid on Isla de la Luna or road trip around towering, mortuary chullpas and the monolithic ruins of Tiwanaku. Here's how to get around.

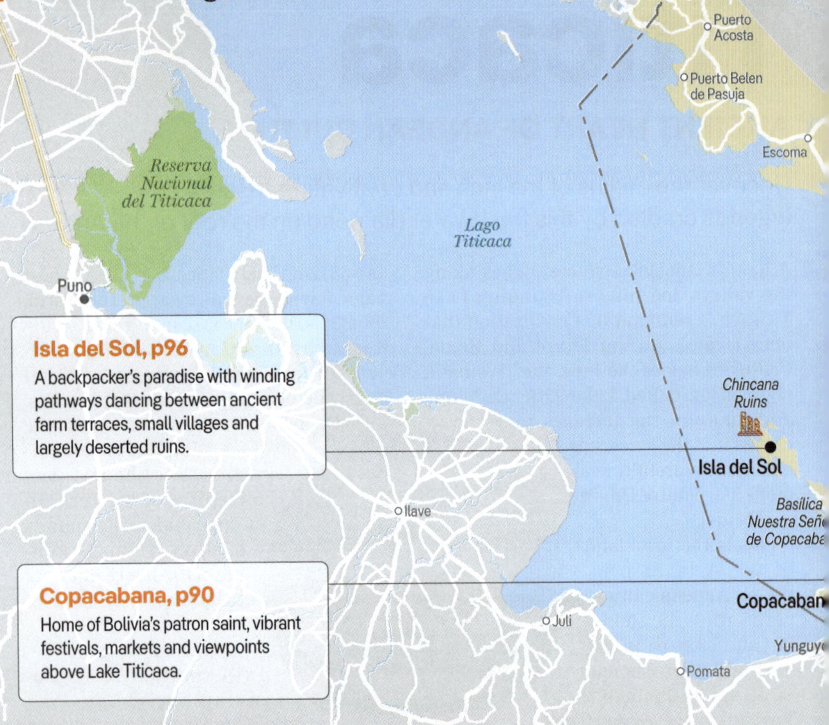

Isla del Sol, p96

A backpacker's paradise with winding pathways dancing between ancient farm terraces, small villages and largely deserted ruins.

Copacabana, p90

Home of Bolivia's patron saint, vibrant festivals, markets and viewpoints above Lake Titicaca.

FERRY

Ferries from Copacabana are the most popular way to get around the lake. **Asociación Union Marinos Titicaca**, located on the northern end of the Copacabana waterfront, offers daily ferries from Copacabana harbor to Isla del Sol. Tickets cost about US$8.

BUS

Bolivia Hop offers bus tours of Lake Titicaca for about B$275. Buses depart from **Plaza Sucre** in Copacabana and also connect to La Paz and Puno, Peru.

PRIVATE DRIVER

The best way to travel around Lake Titicaca by land is to book a private vehicle from La Paz or Copacabana, with prices ranging from B$275 to B$700 per day, depending on the luxury level. Many drivers coordinate with boat captains.

Huatajata, p102

Small port city on the lake's south-eastern shoreline where travelers can immerse in authentic Andean history and the kitschy legacy of Bolivian tourism.

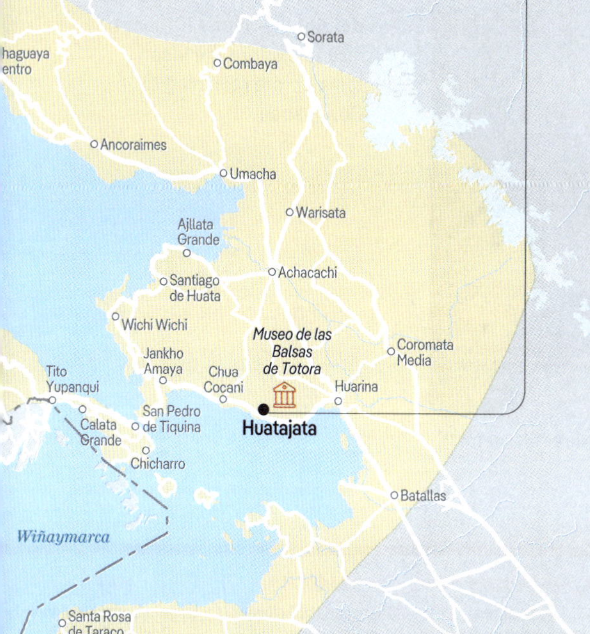

Plan Your Time

While several of the highlights on Lake Titicaca can be experienced in a long day, the best move is to devote several to this spectacular, underrated region.

JULIAN PETERS PHOTOGRAPHY/SHUTTERSTOCK

Inca ruins, Isla de la Luna (p97)

Just One Day

- Start your day in Copacabana, visiting **Basílica de Nuestra Señora de Copacabana** (p90) before strolling to the city's port.

- Take a boat to Isla del Sol. Climb **Escalera del Inca** (p96) at Yumani Village to view a sacred spring before descending the stairs and taking the boat to the **Templo del Sol** (p97) for a 10-minute hike to explore the Incan ruins before returning to Copacabana.

Seasonal Highlights

Rain showers and thunderstorms dot shoreline settlements during the wet season, while islands within the lake remain perfect for day hikes and exploration year-round thanks to Lake Titicaca's unique microclimate.

FEBRUARY

Experience Copacabana's major festival, the **Fiesta de la Virgen de la Candelaria** (p90), when the streets come alive with brass bands and pop-up bars.

MARCH

Thousands of Bolivians make a pilgrimage to Copacabana for **Semana Santa**, many walking for days to seek blessings.

MAY

Copacabana celebrates **Alasitas Festival** on May 24. Purchase miniatures of chalets, cars and symbols of property and join the party.

Over a Long Weekend

- Start the day at the **Basílica de Nuestra Señora de Copacabana** (p90) in Copacabana before hiking to **Cerro El Calvario** (p94) for a bird's-eye view.

- Take an afternoon ferry to **Isla del Sol** (96) with a gameplan to spend two nights. Enjoy a day of hiking the **Inca Trail** (p96) through terraces to visit the **Chincana Ruins** (p100).

- Stop by **Isla de la Luna** (p97) and **Iñak Uyu** (p98) ruins on the ferry ride back.

Around Titicaca in Five Days

- Spend a night in **Copacabana** (p90) enjoying nightlife and fresh lake trout before heading out for two nights on **Isla del Sol** (p96).

- Enjoy hiking the Inca Trail to the **Chincana Ruins** (p100), **Titikala** (p101) and **Templo del Sol** (p96).

- Explore **Isla de la Luna** (p97) before overnighting in Huajata beside the **Andean Roots Eco-Village** (p103) at Huatajata.

- Learn about Bolivia's reed boat builders before venturing on to **Tiwanaku** (p70) archaeological site.

JUNE

Peak winter around Lake Titicaca brings chances of on and off snow and rain, though temperatures remain above freezing. Aymara people celebrate the **Andean New Year** on Isla del Sol with sunrise ceremonies on June 21.

AUGUST

Overnight lows hovering just over freezing with mild afternoons make for pleasant traveling and hiking weather. Bolivia celebrates its **Independence Day** on August 6 with fireworks and parades in communities across the region.

SEPTEMBER

Cars, buses, and trucks are blessed with flowers, beer and holy water in Copacabana. Cloudy conditions general prevail over shoreline communities, while Isla del Sol receives sun. Temperatures begin to warm as winter fades.

NOVEMBER

Bolivia celebrates **Todos Santos** (All Saint's Day) November 1 and 2 and communities on Isla del Sol pay homage to the dead by bringing the skulls of lost loved ones and community leaders to gatherings in village cemeteries.

Copacabana

TRAVELER'S BLESSING | FOOD & HANDICRAFTS | ISLAND FERRIES

GETTING AROUND

The streets of Copacabana are hilly but not mountainous. Travelers can comfortably see the town's main attractions on foot, though bike rentals are available at **Aventura MTB**. A hike to **Cerro El Calvario** can be achieved from the city center on foot, and the port lies just a few minutes downhill from **Plaza 2 de Febrero**.

For travelers entering from Peru, the port of Copacabana serves as a first taste of Bolivian culture. There's a stark contrast between the relatively hectic Peruvian side of Lake Titicaca and the more scenic, natural-feeling Bolivian side. The city's population of around 6000 pales in comparison to the 1.2 million residents of Puno, Peru; yet the streets of Copacabana feel lively, especially around Plaza 2 de Febrero, the city's main square.

In Copacabana, tourists are largely left to their own devices. Though markets are free to browse, vendors are typically laid-back and low pressure.

In February, the square turns into a stage for brass bands blaring celebratory sonatas for la Virgen de la Candelaria, Copacabana's patron saint. Year-round, Catholic pilgrims converge on Basilica de Nuestra Señora de Copacabana – a 17th-century cathedral constructed over a Tiwanaku monolith – whose statue of the Virgin Mary is said to grant blessings to travelers.

Gain the Blessing of the Dark Virgin

A pilgrim's blessing can't hurt

The **Basílica de Nuestra Señora de Copacabana** (Basilica of Our Lady of Copacabana) rises like a whitewashed fortress against the deep blue of Lake Titicaca, a beacon for pilgrims and curious travelers. It's here that wanderers of all backgrounds convene to gain the blessing of the **Virgen de Copacabana**, the Dark Virgin. Carved in maguey wood by a descendant of the third Incan emperor, **Huayna Capac**, the legend of this deity rippled across the Andean landscape long before Bolivia and Peru were separated as nations.

It's said that the Virgen de Copacabana rescued fishermen from stormy waters on the nearby lake, descending as a vision of the Virgin Mary guiding them to safety.

TOP TIP

Copacabana makes a convenient pit-stop on the way to Isla del Sol, but the city itself is worth at least one night. Consider extending your stay, and make note of ferry times. Lake Titicaca is vast, and ferries to Isla del Sol take at least an hour.

Continues on p94

COPACABANA

Piedra Sagrada (10km)

0 — 2 km
0 — 1 miles

Cerro Pukhara
YAMPUPATA
Ferry to Copacabana
SAMPAYA
SICUANI
TITICACHI
Cerro Huara Huara
SANTA ANA
Isla Jiskha Huata
Río Jinchaca
HINCHACA
Cerro Jankho Khaua
Cerro Pucara
CHANI
KUSIJATA
Cerro Calvario
COPACABANA
See Enlargement

Enlargement

Cerro Calvario
Avaroa
3 de Mayo
Ballivián
Junín
San Antonio
Pérez
Oruro
Jáuregui
Michel Pérez
Baptista
Plaza 2 de Febrero
La Paz
Costañera
6 de Agosto
Plaza Sucre
Av Busch
Pando
José Ballivián
Copacabana Beach
Lake Titicaca
Basílica de Nuestra Señora de Copacabana
Murillo
Potosí
Paredes
Av 16 de Julio
Av Tejada
Beach

0 — 400 m
0 — 0.2 miles

HIGHLIGHTS
1 Basílica de Nuestra Señora de Copacabana
2 Cerro Calvario

SIGHTS
3 Baño del Inca
4 Horca del Inca
5 Playas Blancas de Yampupata
6 Plaza 2 de Febrero
7 Sampaya
8 Sicuani
9 Titicachi
10 Yampupata

ACTIVITIES, COURSES & TOURS
11 Gruta de Lourdes

SLEEPING
12 Hostal Flores del Lago
13 Hostal Piedra Andina
14 Hostal Sonia
15 Hotel La Cúpula
16 Hotel Lago Azul
17 Hotel Rosario del Lago
18 Las Olas
19 Suma Samawi

EATING
20 Flotanta Qhana Pacha
Islas Flotantes Pacha Gira (see 5)

TRANSPORT

WALKING TOUR

Sampaya to Yampupata

Incan pilgrims made the journey to Isla del Sol by following the same route on the Yamputata Peninsula that you can today. From its farthest point, they boarded reed boats bound for Isla del Sol and the Titikala – the sacred stone said to be the spot where their empire began.

1 Iglesia San Roque de Sampaya

Begin your journey in the village of **Sampaya**, a 45-minute taxi ride from downtown Copacabana. Stock up on last minute supplies at one of Sampaya's *tiendas* (stores), soak in a bird's-eye view of the Yampupata Peninsula and prepare for a stunning, downhill trek to the modern pilgrimage site.

The Hike: The journey to the Gruta de la Virgen de Lourdes covers about 6km and takes just over an hour. There is no entrance fee for the shrine, but people may ask for tips at the entrance.

2 Gruta de la Virgen de Lourdes

Wooden crosses flank the entrance of a shoreline cave shrine that draws modern, Catholic pilgrims. Here, a 1905 effigy of the Virgen de Lourdes serves as a prayer site for devout followers. This is a Bolivian version of a similar figure in Lourdes, France that served as a prayer site for Pope John Paul II and Pope Benedict XVI.

The Hike: Retrace your steps for 15 minutes before the trail begins to level out on the way to Titicachi. Keep the shoreline on your left until you see soccer fields at the edge of town.

Gruta de la Virgen de Lourdes

DAVID VILAPLANA/ALAMY

3 Titicachi

From a photographer's perspective, the small community of Titicachi gives Sampaya a run for its money. Titicachi overlooks a spectacularly photogenic bay whose shores form a crescent around the lake's lapping waters. A lone tienda serving soft drinks and snacks can help you stave off hunger before pushing onward to Sicuani.

The Hike: Continue along the road for about 40 minutes, enjoying views of tranquil potato fields before reaching the outskirts of **Sicuani** and a living legend of Lake Titicaca.

4 Sicuani

A faded sign, a small totora-reed boat and a series of benches mark the boundary of Hilario Paye Quispe's domain. Since the late 1990s, Hilario has been entertaining travelers by sharing a collection of postcards from around the globe and an optional paddle in a traditional reed boat. Hilario is something of a local legend, having been featured in *The New York Times* and countless Lonely Planet guidebooks.

The Hike: From Sicuani, the road climbs slightly, winding through a dense scrubland and a series of agricultural terraces leading to the finish line at Yampupata.

5 Yampupata

A fistful of boat docks cling to life along **Playas Blancas de Yampupata.** Twin restaurants on man-made islands of reed flank this beach. Spend the afternoon walking along the beach, swimming in the lake and bouncing between plastic patio chairs. Sample fresh fish and hard-earned beverages at **Flotanta Qhana Pacha** and **Islas Flotantes Pacha Gira.**

Make a call back to your housing in Copacabana to arrange a taxi back to town or a private boat transfer to Isla del Sol.

COUSTEAU CONNECTION

French oceanographer Jacques Cousteau left a legacy at Lake Titicaca that's still whispered about today. In 1973, Cousteau and company undertook a mission to search for ruins beneath the lake. While unsuccessful in that quest, the team did film and document a rare species of giant amphibian: the Titicaca water frog.

One of the largest amphibians in the world, these giant frogs grow up to 20cm in length and feature a unique adaptation to high altitude. The frogs feature a thin, wrinkled skin that helps them absorb additional oxygen directly from the water.

Due to habitat destruction, mining pollution, invasive species and over-harvesting, the Lake Titicaca water frog is now considered a critically endangered species.

Continued from p90

More than 400 years later, she still watches over those willing to journey to the altar below her feet for a blessing.

The air in Copacabana, Bolivia, is tinged with the scent of burning incense and the sound of passing seagulls as you step through the grand Moorish-style arches of this 16th-century masterpiece. Inside, light filters through stained-glass windows, casting kaleidoscopic patterns across gold-draped altars and centuries-old stone. Perched above the pews, a finely carved wooden statue laminated in gold leaf watches over her domain. The Virgen de Copacabana - Bolivia's patron saint - sits cloaked in intricate robes, her presence commanding curiosity and admiration. Legend says her altar is built over a buried, pre-Incan monolith that drew travelers here long before Catholicism arrived. Today, this modern monument protects travelers who journey here from across Bolivia.

Outside, a tradition that continues in the streets where - at times - priests bless cars, drenching them in beer, flower petals and holy water in an only-in-Bolivia ritual of faith and festivity.

Walk through **Plaza 2 Febrero**, where vendors sell miniature cars, houses, and dollar bills—symbols of Andean prosperity rituals—and soak in the sounds of blaring brass and drumbeats celebrating the festival of the hour. Stop by a market stall to grab your fill of pasankalla, a toasted corn invented in these streets that comes by the bulging bagful, while browsing lanes of pop-up shops lining a path from the basilica to the lakeshore.

Climb to Cerro El Calvario

Bridging the present and the past

The hike to **Cerro El Calvario** is a short but steep pilgrimage that rewards hikers with the best panoramic views of Lake Titicaca outside of **Isla del Sol.** Rising 200m above the city

FABIO LAMANNA/SHUTTERSTOCK

Summit of Cerro El Calvario

below, the summit was a significant location for ancient cultures living around the lake. While only about 1km from the Copacabana town center, high altitude at the trailhead and a relatively steep climb can make this a strenuous journey, especially for travelers who have not had time to acclimatize to Bolivia's lordly position above sea level yet (Copacabana sits at 3810m).

The trail begins near the cathedral (p90), winding past 14 stone crosses, each marking a **Station of the Cross**. Reminiscent of similar crosses on the legendary Camino de Santiago Compostela in Spain, these shrines are central to local religious rituals, especially during Semana Santa, when pilgrims climb the hill to reflect and seek blessings. These crosses are meant to depict the walk Jesus of Nazareth took on his final journey to the top of the hill of Calvary, where he was crucified by Roman soldiers.

The path itself is rocky and takes 30 to 45 minutes to reach the summit, depending on your pace and altitude adjustment.

At the top, prayer shrines and Andean spiritual altars stand against a backdrop of Titicaca's shimmering waters. Ribbons fly in the Bolivian breeze and candles burn around the clock near the summit. Protected from the wind by miniature caverns built into the rocks, their flames mark sites of prayer and worship used by believers from across the globe.

In pre-Columbian times, Cerro El Calvario is said to have been a notable place of worship to Pachamama, the embodiment of mother earth. Today, as in ancient times, pilgrims often leave offerings on this summit. Enterprising vendors will sell you offerings at stalls along the way – each selling tokens of prosperity in this life while perching atop the relics of the ancient world.

THE MANY RUINS OF COPACABANA

Local lore suggests the Basilica of Our Lady of Copacabana is built on a sacred, pre-Incan site left by the **Chiripa** culture, but it's indisputable that numerous remnants from previous inhabitants pepper the city. Most of these sites bear names harkening back to the Inca; names conjured by Spanish priests. **Horca del Inca**, translated as 'Incan Gallows,' is likely an observatory left by the Chiripa. **Baño del Inca**, 'the Incan Baths,' half a mile outside of town, may have been used by the Inca, but had likely been a leisure source used for centuries by Chiripa, Huari and Tiwanaku peoples.

Isla del Sol

TEMPLES | TRAILS | TUBERS

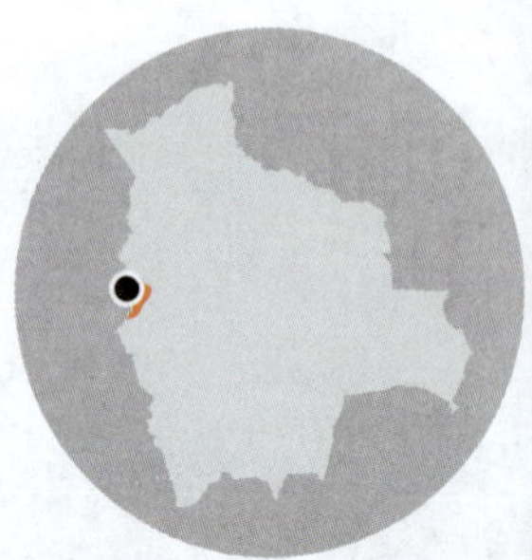

The largest island in Lake Titicaca, Isla del Sol is a destination well worth traveling the long road to Bolivia to reach. If the archaeological ruins at Tiwanaku represent the heart of the ancient Titicaca region, Isla del Sol symbolizes its soul. Here, on a verdant island towering above the deep, blue water below, footpaths of dirt and stone pave the way to Andean legends.

GETTING AROUND

Ferries from Copacabana deposit travelers on the southern shore of the island, near Yumani. Walking is the only way to get around the island, though some residents linger around docks offering llamas for hire to transport luggage.

Hike the Inca Trail

Day hike through history

The Inca Trail is Isla del Sol's most popular attraction and the top reason to spend several nights on the island. This winding, 18km loop trail takes between two and three hours to transect the island's backbone from **Yumani** to the **Chincana Ruins** (p100; *entry B$10*), the best-known ancient remnants on the island.

On the way, the Inca Trail passes through potato terraces, forests and llama pastures. Signature pit-stops include the Titikala (p92), said to be the very birthplace of the Incan Empire; **Templo del Sol**, an Incan temple whose origins date to Tiwanaku; and the **Escalera del Inca** stairway leading to **Fuente del Inca**, a spring misinterpreted as the Fountain of Youth by the Spanish.

Each stop offers a new perspective on the antiquity of humanity and the fleeting nature of life, though few information signs and research papers exist to tell the tales of these far-flung monuments to a bygone age.

Plan to spend the night either in **Challampa**, about an hour from Chincana, or back in Yumani. If you're pressed for time, try snagging a ride from a local fisherman. They can be found at ports such as Challpampa and Playa Japapi and will sometimes ferry you from one side of the island to the other for about B$100.

No guide is needed for this hike, but a sturdy pair of hiking boots is recommended. Start by mid-morning and follow the

TOP TIP

It's tempting to make this destination a day trip. Resist the urge and plan at least two nights to allow for a proper exploration of the island's trail system and ruins. It is possible to hike from the southern end of Isla del Sol to the north comfortably in a day.

HIGHLIGHTS
1 Chincana Ruins
2 Templo del Sol

SIGHTS
3 Challapampa
4 Escalera del Inca
Fuente del Inca (see 4)
5 Piedra Sagrada
6 Yumani

EATING
7 Restaurant Uñtasiwi

trail clockwise from Yumani. Amble back past beaches and the Templo del Sol as daylight begins to fade.

From 2017–2022, the Inca Trail north of Yumani was closed to tourists due to a localized conflict that culminated in a newly built hostel near the Chincana ruins being blown up with dynamite. For a time, this resulted in blockades along the trail restricting tourists from venturing towards the communities of Challa and Challampapa. Relations between the towns have improved and an agreement with tourism authorities in Copacabana has reopened the island in full. However, it's still advised to enjoy this hike with company. The mysterious disappearance of a lone Korean hiker in 2018 set off international alarm bells. While conflict has dissipated and crime is not prevalent on the island, tourists have been heckled for fictional 'tolls' on the route. Paying them is a matter of your discretion.

Proceed with your wits and enjoy this spectacular stroll through the open pages of history.

Sail to Isla de la Luna

A twin island next door

Resting just a few minutes by ferry from Isla del Sol, diminutive **Isla de la Luna** is a worthy day trip destination that only takes about an hour to investigate. Hop on a ferry at Yumani for the short trip over to this neighboring island, where the magnificent ruins of **Iñak Uyu** await. Vastly different in character from both the Chincana ruins on Isla del Sol, the rooms, passages and courtyard of Iñak

ENJOYING THE SIMPLE LIFE

Raul Piaggio,
Isla del Sol guide
(7-323-0678)

Like most people, when I first came here I thought it was amazing – maybe the most beautiful place in Lake Titicaca. Most people only do a day trip because they don't really know what to expect and what they are going to find here.

I think many tourists are looking for a specific reason to be in a place; they want the largest tree or the oldest temple. A lot of people consider it a waste of time to be in a place just to walk and enjoy a place. I don't agree.

When people say they want to see Lake Titicaca, I normally say they should skip Peru and go to the Bolivian side.

AN ELDER'S VIEW

Every day, **Señor Isaac** waits by the docks near Templo del Sol with an oxygen tank and a llama, ready to help ferry travelers and bags to their lodgings.

I've only had to use the oxygen tank once, but I have been a boat captain, a gardener and a security guard. I grew up on the island, and I've seen almost eight decades go by. In that time, tourism has changed a lot. About 25 years ago, our first hotels started to open up. Before, people just came here for the day to see the ruins. Now, they usually spend the night, because so many families are running hostels. I want people to know that tourists are welcome here. We want people to visit our home.

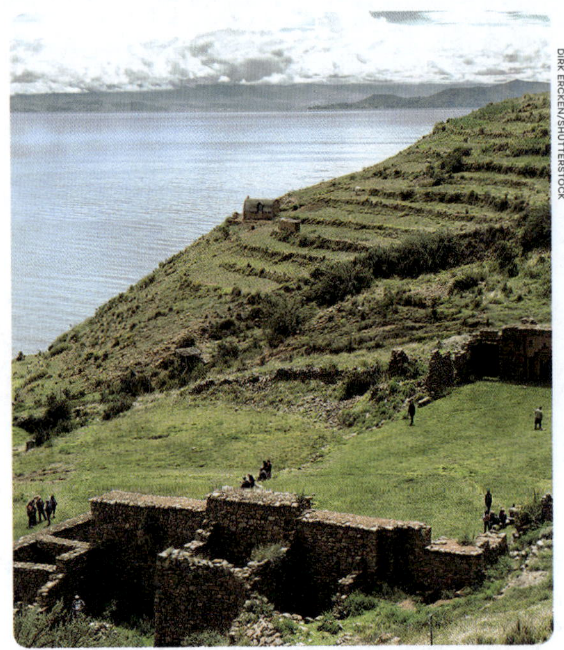

DIRK ERCKEN/SHUTTERSTOCK

Templo de las Vírgenes

Uyu are carved into a terraced hillside. Sections of plastered facade remain, giving these ruins an appearance that feels like more like a relic of the American desert southwest than a close relative of Machu Picchu.

This courtyard is home to the legend of the **Templo de las Vírgenes** (Temple of the Sun Virgins). Archaeologists believe that this complex was an Incan nunnery, a dedicated home for noble women who were selected to live a celibate life in order to perform sacred duties for the state. Makeshift shrines around the site still pay homage to their spiritual might centuries after their bodies departed this place.

Travelers are free to explore the ruins at their leisure, offering a rare chance to harness your inner Indiana Jones.

A short trail leads from the dock to the ruins. Nearby, a public bathroom, handicraft stands and dockside cafes offer services for travelers waiting for the ferry back to Isla del Sol. Several families on Isla de la Luna also run rustic hostels. Most are located about 400m from the ruins of Iñak Uyu and accessed via a well-marked hiking trail beginning at the dock below the ruins.

If off-the-grid is your thing, overnighting on Isla de la Luna might be for you. Hostels here generally cost about B$240 per night and include a home-cooked dinner. Bear in mind, electricity is generally powered by generator and – when available – hot water usually depends on solar power. Accommodationss are rustic, yet tranquil. Local hosts have a reputation for hospitality.

Soak in Sunset over Yumani

Cliffside feasts and stunning sunsets

Don't skip this slow travel experience if you're overnighting on Isla del Sol.

A cluster of cliffside restaurants huddle atop Yumani, perched high on the southern edge of Isla del Sol. Each one serves near-identical menus – variations on simple, hearty fare like wood-fired pizza, spaghetti with meat sauce, and Bolivia's beloved *pique macho*, a chaotic pile of beef, sausage, fries, onions, peppers, and boiled egg. While the food here is entirely serviceable, no one's come to this perch on Lake Titicaca in search of a Michelin star. This mission is something much simpler: slide into a plastic chair, pop the cap off a bottle of cold Huari, and watch one of the most jaw-dropping sunsets in South America unfold right in front of you.

From the western fringe of Yumani, clouds drift lazily above the lake, blurring the line between earth and sky as they blend with the snow-capped peaks of Peru in the distance. The evening sun sets the whole scene ablaze – clouds pulsing with orange, magenta and lavender. The glassy surface of Lake Titicaca shimmers beneath the display, catching every color like a giant mirror reflecting the sky. It feels ancient here. There are no cars, no blaring horns, no buzz of modernity. Instead, the soundtrack is made of braying donkeys, barking dogs, soft footfalls on dusty trails and the distant laughter of children. Twilight settles slowly over the terraces of Yumani, just as it has for thousands of years.

At **Restaurant Uñtasiwi**, the bartender cracks open another Huari with a smile, happy to swap your last few crumpled US dollars for Bolivianos at a (presumably) fair rate. As night deepens, the lights of the restaurants flicker on, warm and inviting. This is a place for the slow life, far removed from group chats and email threads. Your hostel and its sporadic wi-fi signal are just a short walk away, down a dirt path lined with mud-brick homes, small gardens, and the occasional sheep grazing quietly in the dark.

HYDROFOILS ON LAKE TITICACA

As your ferry plods along the surface of Lake Titicaca, you may notice an unusual fleet of red and white vessels blazing by. These are hydrofoils, boats that ride above the waves. They are the property of **Crillon Tours**, a private tour company that has served as Bolivia's de-facto marketing department since the 1950s.

The legacy of Crillon Tours is complex. Founded in 1959, the company rose from an outfitter supplying rustic journeys to Tiwanaku into an almost inescapable force of tourism. In 1966, they brought hydrofoils to Lake Titicaca. They eventually opened museums, built lodges and trained many of Bolivia's tour guides. This transformed Bolivian tourism, but has also created a disparity between luxury travel and public services that still exists today.

MATYAS REHAK/SHUTTERSTOCK

TOP EXPERIENCE

Chincana Ruins

A stone labyrinth on the north end of Isla del Sol has puzzled archaeologists for decades. Around it, terraced hillsides cascade towards the water, their crops bearing testament to the forgotten people who worked this land eons ago. Yet, it is the ruins that lure adventurous travelers here, offering a reason to spend another night on Isla del Sol.

DON'T MISS

- Palacio del Inca
- Titikala
- Playa de las Gemelas
- Mesa Ceremonica
- Templo del Sol
- Fuente del Inca

Walking into the Labyrinth

An intriguing archaeological site lies hidden among the rocky outcroppings and ancient terraces ringing Isla del Sol, welcoming travelers whose curiosity has pushed them this far. The **Chincana Ruins**, estimated to be nearly 700 years old, snake across the island's side like a maze of myths and mysteries. Though less imposing than Machu Picchu and far younger than neighboring Tiwanaku, the stones of this labyrinth are a worthwhile destination for archaeology buffs.

PRACTICALITIES

Bring B$10 for entry. Sometimes this fee is collected dockside or included in tour rates.

When the Spanish arrived here in 1621, the site's original name was already forgotten. By then, residents had taken to calling the ruins Chincana, 'the place where one gets lost.' Here, rectangular rooms meander through doorways, niches and stairs, forming an actual maze.

Like their original name, however, the original purpose of these ruins has been lost.

Theories of a Purpose

Thanks to their remote location and relative lack of fame, the ruins at Chincana draw few crowds. In the silence, they can even take on a life of their own. Stepping beneath the remnants of Chincana's stone archways, the silence can be almost disorienting. There are no cars, no distant hums of modern life. Only the rhythmic lapping of the Lake Titicaca far below and the chirping of the island's songbirds interrupt your thoughts here.

These stones seem to have stories, but few signposts linger to tell their tales.

In truth, much of what is known about the Chincana ruins is theory. 'El Laberinto' sprawls across a high plateau with commanding views of the lake. It's believed that these walls were built by the Inca in the 15th century, during the reign of the great Pachacuti. And it's possible that the site served as a palace or ceremonial center. Some believe this was an Incan retreat for priests, a sacred sanctuary dedicated to Inti, the sun god. And then there are those who whisper of hidden chambers and secret tunnels still buried beneath layers of earth and stone.

A Combination of Cultures

The site's original use could also predate the Inca. When the Inca arrived at Isla del Sol, the **Aymara** were already living here. And centuries before Pachacuti's empire stretched across the Andes, the **Tiwanaku** civilization flourished around the lake as well. Prior to Tiwanaku, the **Chiripa** culture also worked in agriculture and stone here. It is believed that all of these cultures also viewed Isla del Sol as an important site, a place for rituals and astronomical observations. And it's known that many of the agricultural terraces ubiquitous on this island were first constructed millennia ago.

At Chincana, the legends of each of these cultures converge. Incan stonework interweaves with Aymara oral traditions that tie ancient civilizations together like the corners of this maze. A short walk from the ruins leads to **Titikala**, a massive sacred rock believed to be imbued with energy from the sun itself. Pilgrims once traveled here from across the Incan empire to pay homage at this place. Like the ruins, the rock stands silent, weathered by time but still drawing travelers to its perch above the lake.

KNOW BEFORE YOU GO

Even in a location this remote, handicraft vendors may sometimes set up shop around the ruins or along the Inca Trail leading towards Titikala.

Most of Isla del Sol's eco-lodges, hostels and hotels are located on the southern end of the island at Yumani, but a few do operate in **Challapampa**, about an hour's walk away from the ruins.

TOP TIPS

- Be prepared for UV rays. Isla del Sol has a Mediterranean microclimate that means full sun for much of the day.
- It is possible but not advisable to hike the Inca Trail (p96) and visit the Chincana Ruins in a day trip from Copacabana.
- **Unión Marinos Titicaca** operates a ferry twice per day.
- Public ferries arrive and depart from **Yumani** and run from early morning until late afternoon.
- Though not located inside of the Chincana complex, Templo del Sol (p97) on the island's southern end offers another glimpse into Bolivia's monumental ancient architecture.

Huatajata

BOAT BUILDERS | ECO-VILLAGE | ISLAND-HOPPING

GETTING AROUND

Huatajata is a compact, walkable community. Buses from La Paz run hourly and reach the town in about two hours for about B$500. Private transfers from La Paz range from B$500 to B$1000 depending on group size.

Scattered boat docks, lakeside restaurants and a handful of hotels and hostels make the small town of Huatajata, the best of a limited number of base camps for exploring numerous smaller islands on Lake Titicaca. Huatajata offers a chance to learn more about the maritime tradition of indigenous people living around Lake Titicaca.

The town's main attraction, the Andean Roots Eco-Village, sits beside the Inca Utama Hotel & Cultural Resort. Visiting this signature attraction requires an overnight stay at the hotel that also includes access to an on-site observatory. Andean Roots Eco-Village also employs a Kallawaya (medicine man) that demonstrates traditional healing practices and educates visitors on natural medicines used in the region.

The fleet of hydrofoil boats lingering off the coast of Huatajata should be your clue that most of the infrastructure and attractions in this town are products of early Bolivian tourism efforts from Crillon Tours, one of the country's most expensive but most well-connected guide services.

TOP TIP

Bite the bullet and book a room at **Inca Utama Hotel & Cultural Resort**. Understand this experience may feel kitschy. This place is the product of another era in tourism; however, the on-site museum is of high quality, and you'll need to spend two nights here to fully experience the nearby islands.

Reed-Boat Builders of Lake Titicaca

Titicaca artisanry is still alive

A peculiar site rises from the shoreline of **Huatajata**: square sails and a mast. From them, the waving flags of dozens of nations billow under a constant breeze. Beneath them, a pair of alpacas pluck grass from a lawn. This is the workshop of **Fermin Limachi**, a Bolivian national treasure.

Limachi is a legend in the world of boatbuilding, an artisan that has crafted and sailed boats made of reeds from Lake Titicaca around the world – literally. Limachi has the receipts in his workshop to prove it. Pages of newspaper clippings and magazine articles are testament to his life's story. On his workshop wall, there's **Abora IV**, a 14m reed boat that Limachi constructed in Bulgaria and that sailed to Egypt from the Black Sea. Beside it, **Ra II**, one of the most famous vessels of legendary Norwegian explorer Thor

Heyerdahl, built by Fermin's father and sailed from South America to Africa.

When Fermin isn't contributing to a greater understanding of ancient seafaring, he's hosting travelers at his workshop inside Huatajata's **Museo de las Balsas de Totora**. The immersive museum invites visitors to witness the captivating art of crafting organic vessels that once helped ancient sailors navigate not only Lake Titicaca, but the globe. The museum's extensive collection (complete with a replica of Ra II) documents the intricate process of constructing these unique boats, from the meticulous harvesting of totora reeds to their final assembly.

Meet with Médicos Kallawaya

Insight into traditional medicine

The Aymara people are not the only descendants of Tiwanaku still living around Lake Titicaca. A culture of traditional healers also calls this region home – the **Kallawaya**. These neuropathic healers travel by foot (and bicycle) to communities across the Andean and Amazonian regions of Bolivia practicing an ancient form of medicine. Using a pharmacopoeia of more than 900 native plants and a series of rituals passed down through a secretive language, the Kallawaya once served as the healers of Incan royalty.

Today's Kallawaya healers still play an important role in communities throughout Bolivia, and travelers have an opportunity to explore a museum based on their craft at the **Andean Roots Eco-Village** inside **Inca Utama Hotel & Cultural Resort**. The museum includes a robust gallery of plants gathered from the Andes and the Amazon that are used in Kallawaya medicine. Often, the hotel will arrange for an on-staff Kallawaya healer to greet visitors inside the museum, a practice they have maintained for decades.

CHULLPAS

Built by the Lupaca, Aymara and Inca civilizations, *chullpas* date back to the 12th century or earlier. Archaeologists believe they housed the mummified remains of priests and other elite figures. Inside, people have been found buried in fetal positions with ceramics, textiles, and food for the journey into the afterlife.

The best-known *chullpas* in Bolivia are near **Parque Nacional Sajama**, but lesser-known sites like **Isla Kalahuta** and **Cutimbo** hold their own secrets. Recent studies suggest some were reused by different cultures over centuries, blending Aymara and Inca traditions. Facing the rising sun, these towers are thought to have been spiritual beacons. Today, they serve as reminders of cultures that saw death as a doorway, not an end.

THOR HEYERDAHL'S REED BOATS

Norwegian explorer Thor Heyerdahl forged a deep connection with the indigenous reed boat builders of Lake Titicaca during his quest to understand ancient maritime travel. In the 1970s, Heyerdahl sought out Aymara artisans, including the Limachi family. He enlisted their expertise in building Ra II (p102), a vessel modeled after ancient Egyptian papyrus boats, to test theories of transoceanic contact between early civilizations.

The Aymara craftsmen constructed the boat using traditional techniques. Ra II successfully sailed from Morocco to Barbados in 1970, proving that such vessels could endure long oceanic voyages. Heyerdahl's collaboration with the Aymara revived global interest in their ancient skills and reinforced theories of pre-Columbian contact across the Atlantic.

The encounter can feel both humbling and somewhat manufactured. This is an arrangement made for tourists, though the museum has an air of reverence. The Kallawaya performs real rituals with real ingredients. Visitors are taught how to treat the healer with respect – before being given the opportunity for them to read the future via flaming alcohol and coca leaves.

Like most activities in Huatajata, a visit with the Kallawaya is reserved for overnight guests of the resort, a tradition that dates back to a time when Bolivian tourism was dominated by its operating company, Crillon Tours.

Visit Funerary Towers on Isla Kalahuta

Superstition surrounds these ancient tombs

If you're the type who loves ancient mysteries and windswept landscapes, **Isla Kalahuta** delivers in spades. Sitting quietly off the southern coast of Lake Titicaca, protected by a maze of shallow channels, this small, often-overlooked island is home to some of the lake's most intriguing pre-Inca burial towers, called *chullpas*. While the Andean Roots Eco-Village showcases miniature replicas of these towers, Kalahuta Island is home to the real deal.

Recent archaeological digs have revealed **Lupaca** and **Tiwanaku** tombs, with remains suggesting high-status burials dating back at least eight centuries. The island's oral history tells of horrible fates for those who disturb the tombs, and it's said that the souls of those who spend the night on the west side of the island – alongside the tombs – depart to be with the dead. Residents take these legends seriously. They refuse to live beyond the confines of the island's only settlement, **Quegaya**.

It's easy to spend a half day traveling to the island and investigating its ruins. As with most sites around Lake Titicaca, this is a place to savor the slow lapping of time along the lakeshore. Plan to pack a lunch and picnic.

Public ferries don't run to Isla Kalahuta. The best way to get here is to hire a private tour from Huatajata. Crillon Tours facilitates these for about B$1000. Be sure to take a few hundred Bolivianos to tip your captain and crew.

Investigate Tiwanaku Pottery on Isla Pariti

Handcrafted by the ancients

Tiny, unassuming and yet one of Lake Titicaca's most important archaeological sites, Isla Pariti is a must for history buffs and anyone intrigued by the lake's ancient civilizations. Located in the Wiñaymarka section of Titicaca about 9km from Huatajata, this island shot to fame in 2004, when archaeologists uncovered a stunning cache of Tiwanaku-era ceramics, including finely crafted zoomorphic vessels depicting pumas, frogs and llamas. This discovery led to an

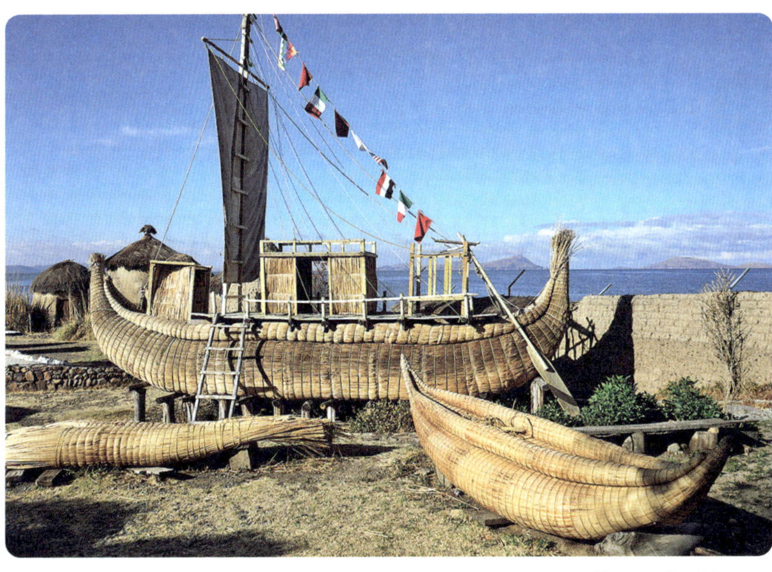

ANDY SUTHERLAND/SHUTTERSTOCK

Reed boat, Lake Titicaca

increased understanding of the ways in which pottery was used by the Tiwanaku people and spawned new theories about how widespread its use in ceremonies became.

Researchers believe Isla Pariti was once a ritual and trading hub, where pilgrims from Tiwanaku communities across their sprawling civilization journey to offer elaborate pottery to the gods. According to archaeologists, most of the pots and vessels found on the island were broken into pieces and buried nearly a thousand years ago in a ritual thought to release their spiritual energy as an offering.

Once shattered, they were deposited into a pit alongside the bones of sacrificed llamas, potentially as an offering to the lake. After their find, archaeologists from Bolivia and Finland pieced many of the vessels back together, recreating the faces of both animals and people that once called the island home.

Much of the collection has made its way to Museo Nacional de Arqueología in La Paz; however, many artifacts remain on the island. For travelers, a visit to the island offers a rare opportunity to see ancient objects actually used by people in daily life in the location they were used at. **Museo Arqueológico Isla Pariti** houses many of the relics discovered here, including artifacts from Tiwanaku and the even older Chiripa culture. Isla Pariti takes a few hours to explore, making a great day trip from Huatajata. To get there, hire a private boat at Huatajata or Puerto Pérez.

POTTERY POWER

Crafted between 500 and 1000 CE, Tiwanaku pottery was used in ceremonies across the Andean world. Archaeologists have found thousands of deliberately broken ceramics at ritual sites like **Isla Pariti** and **Puma Punku**, a practice known as ritual termination.

In Tiwanaku belief, objects had spiritual energy. Breaking them released their essence, offering it to deities, ancestors or Pachamama (Mother Earth). This ritual destruction created a connection between the physical and divine realms. The fragments provide clues to Tiwanaku's vast influence, from Lake Titicaca to the distant valleys of northern Chile and Argentina.

HELP ME PICK:

A Lake Titicaca Tour

Day trip destination or week-long pit-stop on your way around Bolivia? Lake Titicaca can easily play the role of both. For travelers basing out of La Paz, the temptation of a two-day tour makes for an easy photo-op beside these tranquil waters. But if you're the kind of traveler that seeks a deeper understanding of place, Lake Titicaca offers an almost limitless amount of extraordinary sites that can redefine your perception of humanity and time.

If You Like...

Self-Guided Tours

If you've arrived at Lake Titicaca without much of a game plan, consider yourself in good company. In contrast to other areas of the altiplano, the Lake Titicaca region is compact enough to explore on your own. **Bolivia Hop** buses allow you to jump on and off at leisure (thus the name), and the area's reliance on boat travel generally makes transfer between communities a user-friendly experience.

All of the area's major attractions can be navigated on foot, be that the markets of Copacabana, the Inca Trail on Isla del Sol or the museums in Huatajata. This is a friendly area for self-guided travelers, as long as you squirrel away a few contacts for cab drivers, hostels and boat pilots on WhatsApp. Contact an Isla del Sol hostel or start at Copacabana's **Asociación Unión Marines** and network from there.

MATYAS REHAK/SHUTTERSTOCK

To Splurge

Luxury is a subjective term in Bolivia. If you're accustomed to five-star resorts in Europe, you'll be shocked by how far the term 'luxury' is stretched here. The silver lining? Top-flight services in Bolivia remain relatively affordable by upmarket standards, and tour operators (mostly out of La Paz) can take the logistics out of traveling here.

Research outfitters such as **Dream Makers Bolivia** or **Crillon Tours** for higher end experiences that provide guided tours of area highlights like religious sites, ruins and hiking trails. Guides and guide company also come in handy when making the tedious border crossing from Puno, Peru, which involves an unusual amount of printed paperwork and forms.

Outdoor Adventure

It's possible to see some of Lake Titicaca in one or two days, but if you prefer to make memories etched in dusty boot prints, this region is worth spending four or five days in. The **Sampaya to Yampupata** hike is a perfect introduction to modern, rural Bolivian while the **Inca Trail** (pictured) on Isla del Sol offers rare opportunities to visit archaeological sites that remain largely overlooked by mass tourism.

For peak baggers, the snow-capped range flanking the lake's eastern shore beyond **Omasuyos** offers treks deep in the heart of Andes. These adventures; however, are best undertaken with an experienced local guide capable of navigating the area's complex social structure revolving around their community leaders, the **Ponchos Rojos.** Try experienced trekking outfitters such as **Pukina Travel** or **Epic Travel** in La Paz.

JENS_BEE/SHUTTERSTOCK

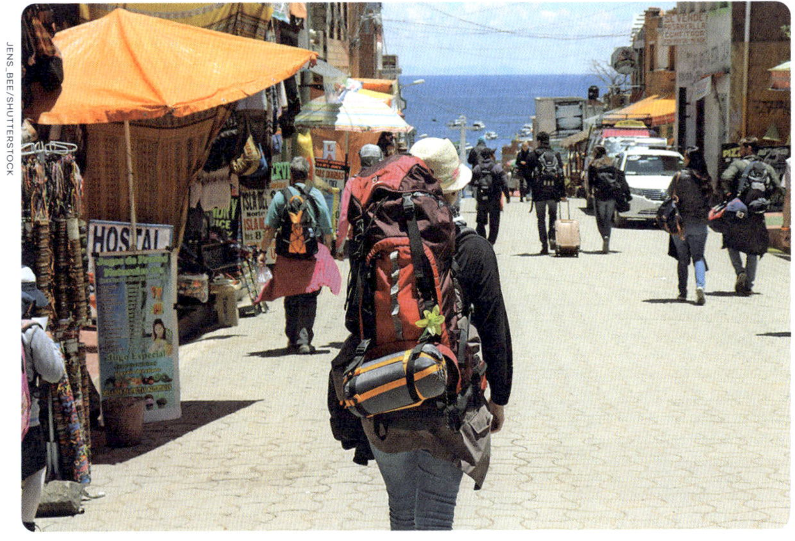

HOW TO

Acclimatize
Lake Titicaca sits at 3812m (12,507ft). Most people's blood will oxygenate less efficiently here. Take it easy for the first day or two before hiking.

Pack ahead
Bring plenty of sunscreen and UV-protective hats or shirts. The sun is harsh at high altitude and sunburns can develop quickly.

Budget
Bring cash. In urban areas, Bolivianos are preferred. In rural areas like this, U.S. dollars can still get you out of a bind.

Be respectful
Traditional clothing is common here. Treat locals respectfully and ask before taking their photo. Unlike neighboring Peru, most won't ask for compensation for photos.

Complete the Story

Even for experienced students of ancient history, Lake Titicaca can feel an introduction to an alternate timeline. To visit this place is to gain a deeper understanding of the breadth and depth of the pre-Columbian and pre-Incan worlds. The Chiripa culture flourished here not long after Trojans and Greeks clashed in modern day Turkey. Tiwanaku was reaching its height while Charlemagne held court over the Holy Roman Empire. And the Aymara began to establish themselves around Lake Titicaca while Genghis Khan pushed his armies towards modern Beijing.

Much more than a site of incredible natural beauty, Lake Titicaca is a deeply significant cradle of human civilization. But the story uncovered here cannot be fully appreciated on its shores alone. A richer context awaits travelers who venture to the UNESCO World Heritage site at Tiwanaku, the Pre-Columbian Precious Metals Museum in La Paz, the Rio Lauca Burial Towers in Oruro and Incan sites like Saqsaywaman and Machu Picchu in Peru.

At these sites, a more complete picture of Lake Titicaca's influence on world history unfurls. The ancient people living in the places we consider unspoiled, natural terrain today carved the landscape by hand. They mastered masonry, metallurgy and agriculture in ways that rivaled more famous peer civilizations around the globe. And they left a tantalizing trail of breadcrumbs for curious travelers to follow in their wake.

Places We Love to Stay

$ Budget $$ Midrange $$$ Top End

Copacabana

MAP p91

Hostal Sonia $ The budget-friendly sibling of upscale Hotel Lago Azul features comfortable but basic rooms. Some include lake views, all provide access to a roof terrace.

Suma Samawi $ A beachside camp that happens to also have private rooms. A rustic option that's more for the vibes and location than a luxury experience.

Hostal La Cúpula $ A quaint, bohemian hostel with spacious lawns, roaming alpacas and sweeping views of Copacabana. Cash only but all of the amenities of home at a great rate.

Hostal Las Olas $$ This eye-catching, artistic marvel overlooking Copacabana's harbor is the passion project of German architect Martin Stratker. Guests stay in adobe rooms whose spiraled domes command unbeatable views of the water.

Hostal Flores del Lago $$ Self-heated adobe rooms and apartments located on the outskirts of town. Great for quiet nights or group travel.

Hostal Piedra Andina $$ Positioned on a hill overlooking Copacabana and Lake Titicaca. Walled gardens and a roof terrace offer plenty of outdoor communal space, while rooms usually have views of the lake.

Hotel Rosario del Lago $$$ An expansive hacienda whose gates open towards Copacabana's harbor. Rooms styled with Andean artwork, lake views from the shower and a highly regarded in-house restaurant.

Hotel Lago Azul $$$ An upscale, beachside retreat just steps from Playa de Copacabana. Spacious rooms with hot water, on-site breakfast overlooking the lake and easy access to ferries to Isla del Sol.

Isla del Sol

MAP p97

Inka Pacha $ Budget option popular with backpackers. Located in Yumani and affiliated with Hostelling International.

Inti Kala Hostel $ Located in Yumani. This hostel features recently remodeled rooms with solar-heated showers and Andean artwork.

Hostal Jallalla $$ Excellent views of the Peruvian Andes from the western side of Yumani. Comfortable rooms with views that are ideal for sundowners.

Hostal Puerta del Sol $$ A step up from the basic with rooms that overlook commanding views of the water and feature solar heating. Outdoor terrace is a bonus.

Ecolodge La Estancia $$$ Private, adobe cottages with thatched roofs that sit atop pre-Incan farm terraces on the path from Yumani to Templo del Sol. As many amenities as can be found on the island and a concierge for ferries and hikes.

La Posada del Inca Eco Lodge $$$ The first hotel on Isla del Sol is also its grandest. This *posada* (hotel) was once a hacienda for a powerful politician, prior to the 1952 Bolivian Revolution.

Isla del Luna

MAP p97

Hostal Qhanapacha $ This charming, basic hostel sits atop a hill overlooking Temple de la Luna. The property has no electricity or hot water, but does offer food and water alongside the chance to spend the night on Isla de la Luna.

Luna del Titikaka Lodge $ Basic shared rooms with multiple beds and dramatic lakeside views. The owners specialize in arranging boat transportation to their island.

Hostel Mirador de Luna $ A simple homestay whose owners, Isabel and Max, take special care to teach travelers about Aymara tradition and culture.

Huatajata

MAP p103

ALAXPACHA Hostal $ Clean but basic rooms in a large, concrete and brick tower across the highway from the Andean Roots Eco-Village. Most offer lake views.

Inca Utama Hotel (p103) **$$$** One of Bolivia's original tourist resorts. The on-site museum is legitimately well curated and spending the night opens up a visit to an observatory used by NASA astronomers for social nights.

JAM TRAVE_S/SHUTTERSTOCK

Hostal La Cúpula

Researched by
Ryan Ver Berkmoes

The Cordilleras & Yungas

INCA TRAILS, UPHILL CLIMBS, DOWNHILL THRILLS

A land of soaring peaks and plunging valleys, where ancient trails trodden by Incas and llama caravans snake across sheer mountainsides and today's adventures await.

Caught between the Andes and the Amazon, this rugged region has just about everything you could ask for from your Bolivian adventure – except cities. However, La Paz is near at hand, only three hours by car from some of the region's greatest highlights.

For the vertically inspired, there are plenty of glacier-capped 6000m peaks and adrenaline-charged mountain bike descents, such as the vaunted World's Most Dangerous Road. Nature lovers can seek out the cloud forests and lush climes of the Yungas. Coroico is the region's main town for travelers and it rewards with good food and drink, mellow places to stay and plenty of nearby activities. Sorata has a spectacular location right on the edge of high-altitude beauty and is at the center of trekking routes. You can even trek or bike to a boat that will take you deep into the Amazon.

Throughout the Yungas you can hike to waterfalls, laze away in villages such as Chulumani and hike on perfectly laid stone highways originally built by the Incas. On long-distance treks like the El Choro, you can start high in the clouds and end in the tropics.

In the Cordillera Real, the 6000m charmer, Huayna Potosí, leads the array of peaks begging to be climbed. It's a high-altitude wonderland. In the far north, you can explore the ruins of a lost culture at seldom-visited Iskanwaya.

JOSEMAR FRANCO/SHUTTERSTOCK

THE MAIN AREAS

CORDILLERA REAL
One snow-capped peak after another. **p116**

COROICO
Balmy climes and mellow vibes. **p125**

SORATA
Hub of spectacular hiking. **p138**

For places to stay in The Cordilleras & Yungas, see p143

WWW.MARIOMARTIJA.ES/SHUTTERSTOCK

Left: Cordillera Real (p116); Above: World's Most Dangerous Road (p128)

Find Your Way

Long and narrow like the ridge of the Andes running down its western flank, dividing the high plains from the Amazon to the east, the Cordilleras and Yungas shift from high-altitude arid to subtropical lush.

Sorata, p138

Peer out over the sheer drops to the valleys below and up high to the glacier-clad peaks above.

4WD & CAR

Roads in the region are only good and car-friendly along the main routes: La Paz to Coroico and La Paz to Sorata. After that, paving rapidly disappears and it's the domain for tough 4WD vehicles.

Coroico, p125

Hang out on the square catching the mellow vibe and warm climes of this gateway to adventure.

Cordillera Real, p116

A jagged row of peaks that offer sublime climbing and trekking for all tastes at lofty altitudes.

BUS

There's bus service throughout the day to Coroico and Sorata. Minibuses and *trufis* provide service. The vagaries of the weather mean that schedules are unreliable during the rainy season when washouts and closures are common.

EVGENY SUBBOTSKY/SHUTTERSTOCK

El Choro Trek (p134)

Plan Your Time

Decide what you want to do: Trekking? Climbing? Cycling? Ruins? Some of several? Then figure in the weather and logistics to see what's possible. Independent travel is not easy.

With Limited Time

- The most popular way into the region is coasting downhill via the 'Death Road.' Yes, the cycling trips on the **World's Most Dangerous Road** (p128) are popular: you cruise from misty high altitudes down to sub-tropical languor near **Coroico** (p125). Or go high in the **Cordillera Real** (p116) by climbing the world's most attainable 6000m summit, **Huayna Potosí** (p118), only three hours from La Paz.

With More Time

- Sail down the Death Road, explore the Coroico region and scale Huayna Potosí. But then try one of Bolivia's great long-distance hikes, the **El Choro Trek** (p134), which follows an Inca highway. Head north to the **Sorata** (p138), where ancient trails lace mountains in all directions and you can explore the mysterious ruins at **Iskanwaya** (p142). Also, consider a riverboat trip to the **Amazon** (p137).

Seasonal Highlights

MARCH–MAY
Bolivia's fall sees the downpours of the rainy season ending in April and the dry months beginning, which are best for trekking and climbing.

JUNE–AUGUST
Head off in the dry months of winter along Inca trails on multi-day hikes that span the Cordillera Real and the Yungas. Book ahead with agencies.

SEPTEMBER–NOVEMBER
The peak winter season continues into the spring. Climbing conditions are great and roads are dry everywhere. Watch for rain in November.

DECEMBER–FEBRUARY
Summer brings downpours that can turn trails and roads into rivers of mud or wash entire roads away. But the bounty of the Yungas fills markets.

HELP ME PICK:

Treks & Climbs

For long-distance hauls and shorter day trips along ancient Inca paving, down cloud-encased valleys and through regions of untamed wilderness, trekking options abound in the Cordilleras and Yungas. Trails lead from high Andes glaciers to the edge of the Amazon, taking you through diverse ecosystems. Strap on your crampons and ice axe for an ascent of the summits of the Cordilleras Real. Famed peaks ideal for novices and little-known summits ideal for experts await.

Where to Trek for...

A Classic Hike

The popular **El Choro Trek** (p134) takes you from the easily reached La Cumbre at a lofty 4725m and over three days and 57km takes you down to the sub-tropical Yungas. Along the way you'll spend a lot of time following ancient Inca paths, with stones so close-fitting, it's like they were laid yesterday. You'll manage several river crossings on swinging suspension bridges and camp in places where mountain people will prepare local meals.

Following the Incas on the Takesi trek

Multiple peoples – including the Incas – have used this at times challenging route that takes a relatively low pass over the Cordillera Real to reach the Yungas and eventually the Amazon. But it was those superlative engineers the Incas who left behind segments of highway that are among the best engineered of their many legacy highways in South America. This **three-day trek** (p136) mixes climbs with downhill stretches and raw nature with historical vestiges.

A Gorgeous Day Hike

Sorata, three hours north of La Paz, is a hub for hiking and trekking. A great day hike starts above town at the summit at **Cumbre Ch´Uch´U** (p140), which has been a hub for trails – and now roads – since time immemorial. On a winding trail down to town, you pass through cloud-misted landscapes with primordial views of treeless peaks and sheer drops. Everything gets more lush as you go down.

Where to Climb for...

An Easy Summit

'I bagged a 6000m peak.' That's a major bragging right for climbers and at 6088m, Bolivia's qualifies for the boast. Even better, **Huayna Potosí** (p118) is considered one of the easiest peaks of that height to climb in the world. In addition, it's only three hours from La Paz, where you can find excellent mountaineering agencies that can guide nearly any fit person to the summit in three days.

A Challenging Climb

Easily seen from all over La Paz, soaring, iconic **Illimani** (p123) is another of the Cordilleras Real peaks within reach. Attaining the 6438m summit is a very technical climb that is a test for skilled climbers. The ascent covers 10km and requires four days. Complicating factors include multiple crevasses, vast ice fields, frequently dangerous wind conditions and precarious walks along sheer cliffs. Reach the summit and you're on top of the world.

Illimani (p123)

FROM LEFT: TUNDE GASPAR/SHUTTERSTOCK, ALEKSANDAR TODOROVIC/SHUTTERSTOCK

La Cumbre pass (p129)

HOW TO

Choose a guide
There are many questions to ask and qualifications to check about the people you'll be entrusting with your adventure's success. See p122.

Calculate gosts
Prices for trekking and mountaineering vary widely. Guiding services charge different prices depending on their experience and what's included in the trip. See p117.

Select gear
The right gear is critical to your adventure's success. Deciding what to bring and not to bring and where you'll source it is important. See p124.

Check the weather
The drop-down menu of *mountain-forecast.com* lists most of the main peaks in Bolivia: *mountain-forecast.com/subranges/bolivian-andes/locations*

Guides & Agencies

La Paz

America Tours *(america-ecotours.com)* Long-running trekking agency with deep experience organizing all manner of adventures across the region. Excellent for custom trips; works with many of the best guides.

Bolivian Journeys *(bolivianjourneys.org)* Mountaineering agency with experience on all the peaks of the Cordillera Real. Assists newbies and skilled technical climbers. Plans trips to rarely climbed peaks.

Climbing South America *(facebook.com/climbingsouthamerica)* Specializes in getting people with limited or no experience to the top of Huayna Potosí.

Deep Rainforest *(deep-rainforest.com)* Specializes in trips from the Yungas to Rurrenabaque in the Amazon. Besides traditional boat journeys, offers rafting trips and options for various departure points. Also organizes jungle treks in Madidi National Park.

Gravity Bolivia *(gravitybolivia.com)* Legendary cycling company that runs lauded trips on the World's Most Dangerous Road (WMDR). Does long biking treks from the Cordillera Real to the Amazon, including from Sorata. Excellent for custom trips.

Terra Bolivia *(voyage-bolivie.com)* Trekking agency with broad knowledge of out-of-the-way places across the region. Good for custom treks on seldom-trodden trails. Specializes in immersive experiences.

Xtreme Down Hill *(xtremedeathroad.com)* Good WMDR tour leader with rides aimed at younger riders.

Coroico

Coroico Star *(facebook.com/coroicostar)* Does treks, rafting and cycling tours plus custom adventures.

Sorata

Felix Chino (p139) Top point of contact for guides and drivers, plus he arranges logistics in the region.

Cordillera Real

SOARING PEAKS | ACCESSIBLE CLIMBS | HUGE ADVENTURE

GETTING AROUND

Access throughout the region is entirely overland and the predominantly unpaved roads can get mucky and washed out in the rainy season. Public transportation to many trekking and mountaineering base camps is infrequent, so chartered private transportation from La Paz is often the mode of choice, or you'll simply rely on your outfitter or tour organizer.

Public buses to Paso Zongo leave from near Plaza Ballivian in El Alto in La Paz when full. Buy tickets on board.

TOP TIP

If you're newly arrived in Bolivia, spend at least a couple of days in La Paz adjusting to the altitude at 3600m before heading higher. If you're unfamiliar with high altitudes, there's no way to predict if you'll suffer from altitude sickness. As they say, your body will tell you.

Looking from the west, you see a stunning, jagged white line across the horizon. Bolivia's Cordillera Real has more than 600 peaks over 5000m, most of which are easily reached and some are just a few hours' drive from La Paz. They're also still free of the bureaucracy attached to climbing and trekking in the Himalayas and elsewhere. Many peaks will entice the experienced climber, and whether you choose a well-known climb or one of the lesser known, climbing in the Bolivian Andes is an accessible adventure. And plenty of treks, bikes and hikes don't involve climbing at all.

The best season for climbing in the Cordillera Real is April to September. Most of the climbs are technical and require climbing experience, a reputable climbing guide and proper technical equipment. Still, many are drawn here simply because Huayna Potosí is one of the world's most easily accessed 6000m peaks.

Summit the Condoriri Massif

Thirteen peaks of the condors

Condoriri (Kunturiri) Massif is actually a cluster of 13 peaks ranging from 5100m to 5648m. The highest of these, Cabeza del Cóndor (Head of the Condor) has twin winglike ridges flowing from either side of the summit. Known as Las Alas (the Wings), these ridges cause the peak to resemble a condor lifting its wings. According to local legend, the massif is the last refuge of the biggest and most ferocious condors in the Andes, which kidnap children and educate them to become 'man-condors', then return them to the human population to bring terror and death.

Cabeza del Cóndor is a challenging 14km climb following an exposed ridge and should be attempted only by experienced climbers. It usually takes two to three days. You'll need a 4WD to access the start of the walk at the dam at Laguna Tuni (or Riconada, about an hour closer). A driver and a guide is a good

idea. You can also trek the 24km from Milluni to the Laguna Tuni dam on the road to Paso Zongo. Take everything you'll need with you, as there's nowhere to buy provisions once you begin the trek. It isn't possible to drive beyond the dam because a gate bars the road. If you need to hire pack animals, you'll have to do so before you reach the dam. Again, this is where a guide is essential.

At Laguna Tuni, take the rough road to circle south around the lake and continue up a drainage channel trending north. Once you're in this valley, you'll have a view of the Cabeza del Cóndor and Las Alas.

From the end of the road, follow the obvious paths up along the right side of the valley until you reach a large lake, Chiar Khota. Follow the right shore of the lake to arrive at the base camp, which is an easy three hours from Laguna Tuni. There are toilet facilities here. The community offers paid campsites and basic huts.

Leave base camp at about 3am and follow the path up the east-trending valley through boulders, passing some lakes on your left. Keep heading up the main trail, on the right-hand side of the valley, until you reach the glacier. You should reach this point in about 1½ hours from base camp.

Here you should rope up and put on crampons. Head left across the glacier before rising to the col (lowest point of the ridge), taking care to avoid the crevasses. Climb to the right up the rock-topped summit Tarija (5240m), which affords impressive views of Pequeño Alpamayo, before dropping 100m down a scree and rock slope to rejoin a glacier on the other side. From there, follow the main ridge to the summit. The ridge has some exposure.

HIGHLIGHTS
1 Ancohuma
2 Condoriri Massif
3 Huayna Potosí
4 Illimani

SIGHTS
5 Paso Zongo

SLEEPING
6 Refugio Casa Blanca
Refugio Huayna Potosí (see 5)
Refugio Vista Panorámica (see 5)

DETERMINING COSTS

Some guiding services include just about everything you could imagine in their trip fees, others, precious little. It's hard to know what specific things to ask about. The service should be able to answer any questions about what is covered.

Foremost is what equipment is supplied for the trip. Most services can rent you gear if you need it, but the price varies greatly. Others include anything you need in the package price.

The quality of tents and mountain huts *(refugios)* greatly affects the cost of the trip, as does food. Nail down the specifics. Porter or animal handler fees can also add up if you require many or if they are with you for the entire trip.

KARL BERNAL/SHUTTERSTOCK

TOP EXPERIENCE

Climbing Huayna Potosí

Imposing beauty and ease of access and ascent are just two reasons why **Huayna Potosí** is Bolivia's most popular major peak. What really draws climbers from around the world is that it's 88m over the magic 6000m figure, a critical bragging right in mountaineering circles. (That it's 26ft under the magic 20,000ft figure is swept under the glacier, as it were.)

DON'T MISS

- The summit
- Minimalist High Andes beauty
- Views across Bolivia and Peru
- More stars than you've ever seen
- Learning how to use an ice axe
- Tackling 45-degree inclines

Planning

Though some people attempt to climb Huayna Potosí in one day, it's not recommended. Unless you're skilled and fully acclimated to the altitude, three days is considered optimal for high-altitude newbies to ensure you properly acclimatize and learn necessary skills before you make for the summit. It's the option chosen by about 80% of La Paz tour company clients, about 95% of whom make the top.

Even experienced climbers should take two days as trying to cover the entire 11km route (one-way) to and from the usual start point at Paso Zongo in one go is foolhardy.

WEATHER

Check the weather conditions on Huayna Potosí: ***mountain-forecast.com/peaks/Huayna-Potosi/forecasts/6094***

MATYAS REHAK/SHUTTERSTOCK

Refugio Huayna Potosí (p121)

AVERAGE DAYTIME TEMPERATURES ON HUAYNA POTOSÍ

At **Paso Zongo**, where almost all climbs begin: 0°C

At the **High Camp**, last stop before the summit: -2°C

At the **Summit**: -8°C

Temps are for noon during the peak season. In recent years conditions have been trending warmer, but can vary in either direction. Winds are another big variable.

La Paz agencies run trips up the mountain all year but the months with the best weather are from April to September. The difficulty of the climb is officially rated as 'moderate,' which contributes to its popularity. Experienced guides like to say that any reasonably fit person not suffering from altitude sickness can climb Huayna Potosí.

Although you won't see scenes like those horror shots of Everest with long queues of brightly clad climbers waiting their turn for a minute at the summit, in peak season Huayna Potosí will see up to 40 people a day at the tip.

The Climb – Day One

There are a number of routes to the top of Huayna Potosí; the following describes the North Peak route, which is most popular with visitors and tour companies. It's appealing because it can be climbed by beginners with a competent guide and technical equipment.

Experienced climbers skip everything that happens on this day and begin their climb with the activities on day two.

For everyone else, the day begins and ends at one of the guesthouses at **Base Camp** at **Paso Zongo** (4700m). Climbers spend the morning learning about their gear and how to put it on and use it. Then there is a short hike to a glacier at 4900m where people learn how to use their ice axes, a skill that will be essential the next day.

Day Two

Climbers leave Paso Zongo in the morning for a hike that will only take two to three hours, but which is an important opportunity for people to get used to their gear and conditions on the trail.

TOP TIPS

- It bears repeating: spend enough time in La Paz to make certain you don't have altitude sickness before starting your climb. Symptoms usually appear within 24 hours and clear up within three days.

- If you hire a car to take you to Paso Zongo, don't assume the driver will know the way. Minibuses from La Paz (El Alto) to the villages around Zongo pass by the guesthouses and namesake lake at Paso Zongo. The journey only takes an hour.

- Make certain your phone or camera can handle the cold temps at the summit.

- Don't forget your sunglasses, it's all very white.

UNEXPECTED CHALLENGES

Plenty can go wrong, even on a climb with 'moderate' difficulty, so even in favorable conditions you'll need to guard against overconfidence. Veteran guides identified two common problems encountered by new climbers. Firstly, all climbs are physically demanding, and as the air thins, this gets compounded. Even barely perceptible altitude sickness prevents people from sleeping so climbers are trying to tackle new problems with brains scrambled from lack of sleep. Another challenge is clear snow: it may be so hard it's great for walking, but when you go to grab purchase with an ice axe, it bounces off and bonks you in the head.

You first cross the dam on Laguna Zongo and follow the aqueduct until you reach the third path on your left, signed 'Glacier Huayna Potosí.' This path leads to a glacial stream, then through and across rocks to reach a moraine ridge. Near the end of the moraine, there's a slight descent followed by a climb up steep scree gullies. At the top, you bear left and follow the cairns to reach the **High Camp** (5150m) at **Campo Rocas Glacier** (5130m). There are sleeping huts and dry places for tents. Almost all tours stop here, and people are usually surprised by how tired they are after just a few hours of hiking.

Day Three

Headlamps are lit for the 2am start. This is the big day that will culminate in the summit. Most climbers forget to look up in the first hours for a spectacular star show – if it's clear.

The first glacier is crevassed, especially after July, so everyone ropes up while crossing it. Next comes a steady ascent of the initial slopes and then a long, gradual traverse to the right, before turning left and climbing steeply to a flat area between 5500m and 5700m known as **Campo Argentino**. It takes two to three hours to reach this point, which is a logical place for a break as hints of dawn appear.

Some experienced climbers stop at Campo Argentino on their first day instead of Campo Rocas Glacier as that makes the final ascent that much easier. They camp just to the right of the path as the area beyond is heavily crevassed, especially later in the season.

Continue on the path/trench out of Campo Argentino, and head uphill to the right until you join a ridge. The steepest climbs are found all through here and the ice axe is essential for dealing with the 45-degree inclines.

Cross a flat stretch to reach the steep and exposed **Polish Ridge** (named in honor of the Polish climber who died while soloing in 1994). Navigate a series of rolling glacial hills and crevasses to arrive below the summit face. Either climb straight up the face to the summit or cross along the base of it to join the ridge that rises to the left. This ridge provides thrilling views down the 1000m-high west face. Either route will bring you to the **Summit** (6088m) in four to six hours from Campo Argentino.

The descent to Campo Argentino from the summit takes two to three hours; from there, it's only another one or two hours back to Paso Zongo.

Other Activities

While most people come to Huayna Potosí to climb, you can also stay at the Paso Zongo guesthouses and head out for high-altitude hikes or cycling rides (bring your own bike). Circling Laguna Zongo is just the start; trails go in all directions.

CARLOSLIMA/SHUTTERSTOCK

Summit of Huayna Potosí

Paso Zongo Guesthouses

A cluster of hostel-style mountain guesthouses cluster around Paso Zongo and the namesake lake. Reachable by road when bad weather doesn't close the pass, this is the traditional starting point for Huayna Potosí climbs. Here at 4700m, you're well above the treeline and the stark landscape is an austere yet entrancing introduction to the High Andes.

Beds at the guesthouses are often reserved by mountaineering groups out of La Paz. That, and the lack of easy means of contact, mean that you're gambling in a big way if you turn up just hoping to score some beds. Still, if you're not planning an entire expedition up Huayna Potosí and can return to La Paz if there's no room at the inn or you're content to camp and just use the bathroom and cooking facilities, then you might try your luck. Not driving? The guesthouses are right by the La Paz–Zongo road and buses will let you off outside.

All the following charge around B$200 per night, including hearty meals.

Run by a lovely couple, **Refugio Vista Panorámica** offers 12 beds and guiding services. You can even learn to herd llamas.

Refugio Huayna Potosí *(huayna-potosi.com)* is run by a La Paz tour company, and makes a fine place to acclimatize – there's sublime walking and plenty of advice and good cheer on hand. It has room for 20. No walk-ins.

Refugio Casa Blanca is a simple but hospitable mountain hut with camping. People praise the gracious owners, who also offer guiding services.

GEAR FOR THE CLIMB

Tour companies typically supply the following gear:

- **Headlamp** For early morning hikes or if you fall into a crevasse.
- **Balaclava** For full facial coverage.
- **Heavy-duty gloves**
- **Harness & ropes**
- **Windproof jacket**
- **Heavy pants**
- **Gaiters** An extra layer to keep pants dry in deeper snow.
- **Double boots** with crampons Crampons are sharp triangular spikes for snow and ice.
- **Ice axe** Used for the 45-degree inclines.

HOW TO PICK A GUIDE

Always get the basics from any potential trekking and mountaineering guide. Key details: Years of experience, professional credentials and deep knowledge of the mountain you intend to climb.

While several organizations claim to train guides in mountaineering skills, the most effective is the Asociación de Guías de Montaña (AGMTB; Bolivian Mountain Guides Association; *agmtb.org*). This organization has met the strict requirements for guide training and certification established by the International Federation of Mountain Guides Associations (IFMGA).

Also, hire at least two guides for a group, that way if someone goes down with altitude sickness, one guide can take them to a lower altitude while the rest press on. Note that English-language skills among guides can vary widely.

For recommended guiding agencies, see p115.

ROBERT DELLER/SHUTTERSTOCK

Trek to Ancohuma

Difficult and rewarding hike, with glaciers

Ancohuma (Janq'u Uma) is the highest peak in the Sorata Massif, towering on the remote northern edge of the Cordillera Real. It was not climbed until 1919 and remains a very challenging climb that should only be attempted by very experienced mountaineers with a guide. It's a 15km climb to the summit and will usually take five days there and back.

One real attribute is that it is less crowded than other more famous Bolivian peaks. But note: its proximity to Lake Titicaca means that you can encounter rain and snow at any time of the year. Still, as one guide told us, the whole range is paradise for real climbers.

The peak is accessed via Sorata, where you'll travel by vehicle up to La Mina. From here it's just one hour by foot up to the trailhead at Laguna Chillata (4200m). Your guide can organize any needed pack animals, which requires local knowledge as mining has taken a toll on mountaineering services.

Ancohuma is most often climbed from the more easily accessed western route, using Laguna Glacial as a base camp. Hike from Laguna Chillata (p141) to the base camp at Laguna Glacial. From here the route climbs the obvious moraine and then ascends the huge glacier, over fields of extremely dangerous crevasses. Most climbers make a high camp at 5400m or 5800m. The route then climbs to the bergschrund (crevasse) and across a relatively level ice plateau to the summit pyramid. This is most easily climbed via the north ridge; the first part is quite steep and icy but then gets easier toward the summit.

Illimani

It's essential to hire guides (probably before you leave La Paz, although you can check with our source in Sorata, p138) as Ancohuma offers some of the most difficult – but rewarding! – climbing in Bolivia.

Climb Illimani

Superb mountain climb within sight of La Paz

Illimani, the 6438m giant that beckons you from La Paz, is the second highest peak. Its technical difficulty is hard, which is compounded by the combination of altitude and ice conditions that make it a very serious four-day climb for people with great experience.

A notorious side note: on January 1, 1985, Eastern Air Lines Flight 980 crashed into Illimani killing all 29 aboard. Little of the debris has ever been recovered, although regular expeditions try to find remains revealed by the receding glacier.

The easiest way to reach Puente Roto, the first camp, is via the climb's start and end point at **Pinaya**, a bracing three-hour trip by 4WD from La Paz. As always, professional guides secured in La Paz are essential and will organize all the details for the 10km trek to the summit.

The normal route to **Pico Sur**, the highest of Illimani's five summits, is straightforward but heavily crevassed. At Pinaya you set out with porters and mules to carry your gear to the first camp at **Puente Roto** (a two- to three-hour walk) or to the high camp at **Nido de Cóndores** (5400m), a rock platform beside the glacier, that is a four-to-six-hour slog up a rock ridge from Puente Roto.

TRANSPORT

Bus travel between larger cities in Bolivia is usually scheduled and there is a range of services on offer, with some deluxe services rivalling the luxury of business-class on an airline. That's not the case in less-traveled routes like those of the Cordilleras and Yungas, where transport services are often ad hoc. Buses will not follow any formal schedule but will instead leave when they fill up. Note, too, that rainy season can render roads impassable for days or even weeks on end. Fortunately, residents are very helpful in trying to convey useful information despite language barriers.

THE RIGHT GEAR

Most guides and guiding services use good equipment. It's one area that is immediately apparent to prospective clients and makes an early and important impression. Note, however, that technical climbing gear is built with a fair degree of extra strength and even old and well-used equipment can be generally safe even if it doesn't look new out of the box.

Make sure you also pay attention to tents, which can be critically important on high-altitude and difficult climbs, especially those that experience a lot of wind. Check them over carefully. Guides should carry a radio, a cell phone or both. There's no reason to be out of touch should help be needed. And you should confirm you're happy with the food being provisioned.

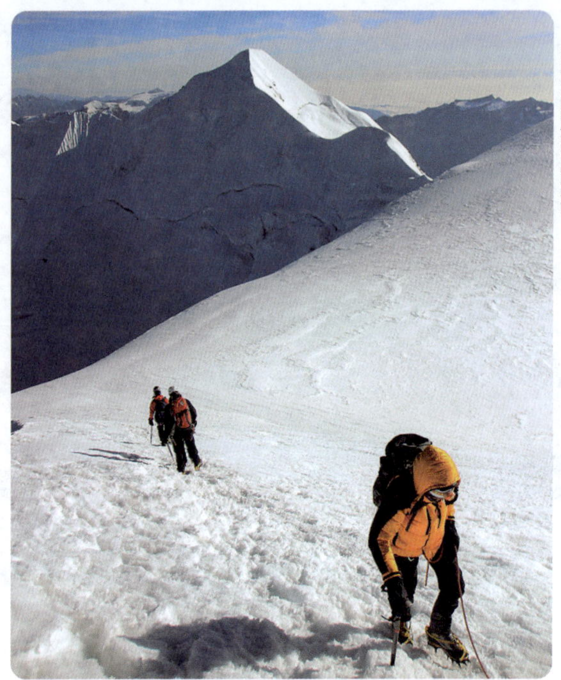

ROBERT DELLER/SHUTTERSTOCK

Summit appraoch to Illimani (p123)

From Nido de Cóndores you set off at about 2am and follow a steep and snowy path that crosses a series of crevasses. Caution is especially needed on this exposed section, where several climbers have perished. Knowledge of self-rescue techniques from a crevasse is essential.

Continuing, you aim for the large break in the skyline to the left of the summit, avoiding two major crevasses and crossing one steep section that is iced over from July onwards. Ascending the final three vertical meters involves walking 400m along the summit ridge at over 6400m elevation while looking down upon Lilliputian La Paz.

The six to 10 hours for the climb from Nido de Cóndores to the summit and three to four hours back down makes for a long arduous day and is the most challenging aspect of ascending Illimani.

If possible, continue down from Nido de Cóndores to Puente Roto on the same day. The 1000m descent is not appealing after a long day, but your body will recover more quickly at the lower altitude.

On the fourth day, you can walk from Puente Roto back out to Pinaya in about two hours.

Coroico

SWEEPING VIEWS | MELLOW SQUARE | TRAVELER'S REST

With warm weather, spectacular views, good resort-style hotels for all budgets and an infectious laid-back air, Coroico is easily the most visited tourist town in the Yungas. It's perched eyrie-like on the shoulder of Cerro Uchumachi and commands a far-ranging view across forested canyons, cloud-wreathed mountain peaks, patchwork agricultural lands, citrus orchards, coffee plantations and dozens of small settlements.

Coroico is derived from the Quechua word *cory-guayco*, meaning 'golden hill.' The town's biggest attraction is its slow pace, which allows plenty of time for swimming, sunbathing and hammock-swinging. When ambition permits, enjoy good walks in the lush surrounds.

Wandering the streets, you'll be rewarded with fine views in all directions. A strip of benches on the north edge of town just beyond the welcoming main square form a selfie viewpoint backed by endless Yungas vistas. At night you can enjoy the best restaurant in the region and the best bar, too.

Kick Back on the Main Square

Coroico's engaging heart

Coroico's **Plaza Principal de Coroico** is a leafy central square that's studded with minor pleasures and is the focus of town life. Start on the west side where you'll find a large statue of an Andean cock-of-the-rock (aka *tunki*), the locally beloved red bird that's a symbol of the region. It's perched atop a rainbow, not as a sign of sexual enlightenment but rather as a nod to the large local indigenous Aymara population and the national flag adopted in 2009. The gourd-like thing hanging from the tree behind is the nest of an *uchi*, another common local bird with a striking black body and bright yellow tail feathers. You'll see these unique nests throughout the Yungas.

On the east side of the square in the shadow of the **Catedral San Pedro y San Pablo de Coroico**, a sober **memorial** honors native son Manuel Victorio García Lanza who was born

GETTING AROUND

Frequent buses serve La Paz, taking about three hours. Other services are more sporadic. During the rainy season, the road for Chulumani may not be open and you may have to go via La Paz. You can get to the Amazon and points east via Caranavi, but buses are infrequent. The **main bus terminal** is outside of town and you may need a taxi to reach the center, especially in the rainy season. Go here for tickets and to find out when buses may depart.
Taxis for La Paz and the region leave from close to the main square.

TOP TIP

The center of Coroico is pleasant and it's worth staying as close as possible to enjoy wandering the streets, the main square and sampling the nightlife.

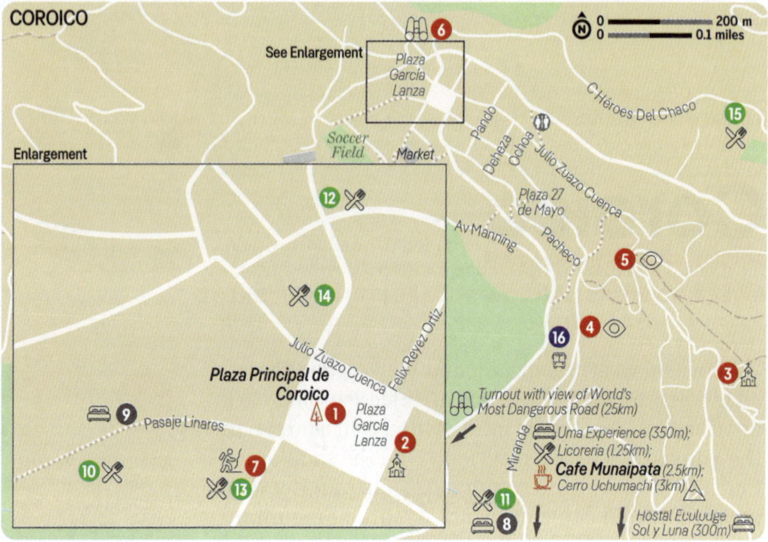

COROICO

HIGHLIGHTS
1 Plaza Principal de Coroico

SIGHTS
2 Catedral San Pedro y San Pablo de Coroico
3 El Calvario
4 El Chawi
5 Hotel Esmeralda
6 Selfie Viewpoint

ACTIVITIES
7 Coroico Star

SLEEPING
8 Hostal El Cafetal
9 Hostal Kurmi

EATING
10 Carla's Garden Pub
11 El Cafetal
12 Pub Don Vito
13 Ristorante & Pizzeria Toto
14 Tea House
15 Villa Bonita

TRANSPORT
16 Main Bus Terminal

LOVE BUT A SIP AWAY

To find love and make your stay in Coroico permanent, all it takes is a short 500m walk southeast of the main square and a little thirst. **El Chawi** is a spring and fountain by the side of the road that comes with a legend that says all those who partake of these cool, clear waters direct from the earth will not only find true love in Coroico but will then settle down and never leave. Drink at your own risk!

in Coroico in 1777. Lanza was killed in 1809 after helping to lead one of many unsuccessful rebellions against the Spanish. His head was left on display in the square.

On the square's south side, a string of Italian cafes aimed at tourists offer up indifferent fare hawked by touts (our 'spaghetti Carbonara' was more like scrambled eggs over noodles). A better bet for an afternoon treat are the many **ice cream shops** (*heladerías*) on the north side and throughout town.

Hike to an Airy Chapel

From spiritual to secular awe

For a lovely and possibly inspirational walk, head uphill toward **Hotel Esmeralda** and on up to El Calvario, an easy 20-minute hike. At **El Calvario** the Stations of the Cross lead to a grassy knoll and a surprisingly large, mustard-yellow chapel.

From here the trail continues 3km to **Cerro Uchumachi**, which towers above the town and affords terrific valley views. It's at an elevation of 2533m (Coroico is at 1525m); the round-trip hike from the chapel should take about five hours.

Taste (& Smell) the Coffee

And maybe a rice ball

Getting a great cup of coffee in Bolivia can be a struggle, what with the plethora of weak, watery brews. But after sampling the products at **Cafe Munaipata** *(cmunaipata.wixsite.com/munaipata-caf--de-al; tours B$40-300)*, you'll know that at least in Coroico, they've got the necessary ingredients for a good cup. This slick operation is the tourist-friendly front for a **local coffee plantation**. Set in lush gardens 4km south of town (it's a decent, mostly level walk, but the road is ghastly so cars can't travel much faster than people on foot), you can stop in for a coffee or for a tasting of a house brew. Tours of the plantation and roastery last from one to five hours.

On your drive (or walk) out, watch for the unadorned and functional **Licoreria**, a brick stall selling beer, booze and phone cards. If the sign for 'Rellenos de Arroz' is hanging out front, you are in for a superb treat. A popular street food, the **fried rice balls** made by the ladies here may be the best you'll have in Bolivia. Only B$6, this meal in your hand comes with various fillings (eggs, potatoes, chicken etc), has a perfectly golden thin and crispy shell and is served with a dreamy peanut sauce.

Your Local Ticket to Adventure

Cycling, rafting, hiking and more

You don't have to organize your descent on the Death Road from La Paz; **Coroico Star** (*facebook.com/coroicostar*) is a great local adventure sports outfitter that rents bikes, organizes cycling trips on the WMDR and other local trails and leads canyoning trips. They also run river rafting trips (p133) and have developed a popular 9km trek that takes in three remote waterfalls *(B$100)*.

Best Restaurant in the Yungas

Oh, the pizza! Oh, the pesto!

Modest from the outside (and inside), **Ristorante & Pizzeria Toto** *(WhatsApp 7-151-2707)* serves superb Italian that's the product of a talented French family of chefs. It only has five tables, the decor verges on stark and the open kitchen is more utilitarian than atmospheric. Yet the dishes that pour forth are all the beauty you need. Thin-crust pizzas come cracker crisp from the cauldron of the oven. Homemade tagliatelle, gnocchi and ravioli come with delicious sauces, including a sublime pesto (which you can also get on the pizza). Finish with their creamy homemade ice cream. Try calling as you may be able to book; this mid-priced pizzeria is open from 6pm to 10pm from Thursday to Sunday.

RIDING THE DEATH ROAD TO HEAVEN

Every October Coroico sees the streets fill with especially fit people in the days before a mid-month Saturday. That's when the grueling annual 'El Ascenso al Cielo por el Camino de la Muerte' (The Ascension to Heaven by the Road of Death; *facebook.com/yolosalacumbre*) is held. Dozens of cyclists set off from nearby Yolosa (p132) and zip up the gravel road for more than 3600m to the summit at La Cumbre.

It's a nearly unthinkable feat, especially for those who struggled just to coast down the World's Most Dangerous Road (p128) on one of the daily tours. The average incline is 7%. The average time for winners is well under four hours, or an average speed of 16km/hr over the 63km. Phew!

EATING & DRINKING IN COROICO: OUR PICKS

Carla's Garden Pub: Down stairs on the pedestrian walkway west of the plaza, serves German classics plus pasta; has a beer hall vibe in an open-air setting. *noon-10pm* $$

El Cafetal: Secluded spot with unbeatable views; an easy 1km walk south of town. Frenchified dishes, vegetarian treats and daily specials. *8am-8pm Wed-Mon* $$

Tea House: Engaging owner welcomes travelers to this upstairs spot. Excellent coffee. Serves breakfast and lunch in the dry season, plus organic snacks. *7am-8pm* $

Pub Don Vito: Welcoming upstairs pub has microbrews on tap from La Paz's female-centric Cerveza Warmi. Menu includes six burgers, nachos and fries. *6pm-midnight* $

Don't miss the Warmi Beer Cacao Porter!

ALEKSANDAR TODOROVIC/SHUTTERSTOCK

La Cumbre pass

TOP EXPERIENCE

World's Most Dangerous Road

It's one of the world's great rides: the wild 3600m descent down the aptly named World's Most Dangerous Road, complete with perilous cliffs, spectacular views and enough thrills and chills to provide the full quota for an entire trip. Best of all, tour companies from La Paz have devised programs that make this remarkable 63km journey possible for nearly anyone.

DON'T MISS

- Views from WMDR
- Long stretches of downhill coasting
- Challenging gravel riding
- Waterfalls
- Entrance to WMDR
- Yolosa
- La Cumbre

History of the Road

Before a modern replacement highway opened in 2007, the road between La Cumbre (the eponymously named summit above La Paz) and Coroico enjoyed the moniker 'the World's Most Dangerous Road' (WMDR, aka Death Rd or mundanely, the Yungas Rd), which was first coined in an NGO report outlining the extreme challenges of transport in the Bolivian Andes. The nickname was – and is – well deserved: from its opening in the 1930s to 2007, dozens of vehicles per year disappeared over the edge into the great abyss and hundreds were killed. Local drivers and tourists alike feared the road and

FOR LUNATICS ONLY

Every October exceptionally fit cyclists race up the Death Road (p127); the winners take less than four hours.

MARK PITT IMAGES/SHUTTERSTOCK

Cyclists prepare to descend

truckers who plied it had prayers and superstitions built up around ensuring their safety. And its fearsome reputation hasn't dimmed as over three dozen cyclists have died on the road in recent years.

The WMDR is still in use by vehicles today, although traffic is a fraction of what it once was. From morning until midday, about 100 or more bicycles whizz down it as part of heavily marketed adventure tours out of La Paz. They are accompanied by support vehicles (most with a stretcher strapped to the side...). Or you may see the odd tourist bus with bug-eyed passengers within.

Starting the Ride

All the Death Road bike tours follow a similar course. You make the long trek uphill through the seemingly endless reaches of La Paz, passing innumerable bus repair shops and sidewalk mattress factories that use piles of *pajá* (a type of straw grown high in nearby mountains).

Cyclists mount up at **La Cumbre**, which is its own scenic destination at 4725m, well above the tree line. Herds of llamas roam around the shore of a large lake and people from La Paz make the journey to burn ritual fires (you'll see kindling vendors on the drive out of the city) as part of offerings to Pachamama (Mother Earth). Look for old trails switchbacking far up into the mountains. These were used as recently as the 1930s by people from La Paz harvesting ice from glaciers that have since vanished due to climate change.

The first portion of the ride is along the shoulder of the waterfall-lined modern highway. It's a breezy downhill run, which if the clouds cooperate offers sweeping views of the vast chasms cleaving the mountains. You can spot an original segment of the WMDR below as well as small gold mines. After 24km,

THE DAY'S TIMETABLE

On a Death Road bike tour, you ride almost entirely downhill for a total of 64km. Hotel pickups in La Paz are around 7am and you start your ride after 8am at La Cumbre. Stops and breaks punctuate the route. Most riders are on bikes for four to five hours and reach the finish point in Yolosa around 2pm. Tours get back to La Paz around 8pm.

TOP TIPS

- The tour operator should provide ample water, helmets and all protective gear plus layers of clothing to handle rain and temperatures that can be cold at the start and tropical at the finish. If they don't, choose another operator.
- Bring sunscreen, bug spray, a swimsuit and a small towel for the mist you'll likely encounter en route – even if it doesn't rain.
- If you're traveling by car, there are myriad viewpoints to savor the scenery. For a sweeping view of the WMDR, look for the turnout marked by a series of boulders 2.5km uphill from the Las Orquideas Eco Parque Restaurante.

FOOD FOR THE ROAD

Tours usually include a breakfast served either in the van on the drive up from La Paz or at La Cumbre. Then there's a snack break at some point along the way, which typically includes fresh fruit. Finally, a buffet lunch is the norm at journey's end at whichever venue the tour company has chosen for the final stop.

the highway begins an extended uphill climb. The tours stop and bikes are loaded onto support vans for an 8km jaunt to where the actual WMDR adventure starts.

The Serious Part

A cluster of snack stands marks where the fun really begins. A gravel turnoff from the modern highway leads onto the access road that plunges down and joins the WMDR. Here, you've descended just far enough that you're in the cloud forest and the sides of the road are thick with ferns.

A sign plastered with tourist stickers proclaims 'Bienvenidos al Camino de la Muerte' (Welcome to Death Road). On many days, mist shrouds the road's entrance, making it all the more foreboding. The descent is initially steep and soon you are on the legendary WMDR. It's rough, it's gravel, it's narrow (a little over 3m wide) and it has precipitous cliffs, up to 1000m drops and few safety barriers along its 31km length.

The weather rapidly changes as you descend, quickly becoming temperate and humid. Banana trees and other subtropical stalwarts appear. You'll spot the small plots growing coca. A major challenge for cyclists is keeping their eyes glued to the road (vitally important, given the blind curves and rough conditions), what with the spectacular scenery that only gets better around each of the innumerable bends.

Most tour companies have support vans trailing their groups, so if your butt tires of the deep potholes or your spirit tires of the challenge, you can surrender to a seat within and ride the rest of the way down.

Start point of descent on WMDR

MARK PITT IMAGES/SHUTTERSTOCK

As the heat builds, roadside waterfalls provide refreshing relief. At some there's no need to dismount; rather, you can coast right through the cooling torrent.

Ride's End at Yolosa

When you hit 1100m elevation, you'll reach the small riverside village of Yolosa (p132), a tidy place with minimarkets. Most tours end here and many tour companies have arrangements with nearby guesthouses for a buffet lunch and the use of a pool. You can always opt not to return to La Paz and instead head up the hill to Coroico (p125) and continue your trip from there.

Tragedies

Crosses (aka 'caution signs') lining the WMDR testify to the frequency of past vehicular tragedies. The most notorious of these occurred in 1983 when a *camión* (flatbed truck) plunged over the precipice, killing the driver and 100 passengers.

Because the old road was the commercial link to the east and the Amazon, it was crowded with trucks day and night, which added to its danger. Many unique practices emerged to make the journeys survivable. At the entrance point off the new highway near the 'Bienvenidos al Camino de la Muerte' sign, look for an old and battered sign in Spanish and English that says 'Welcome Death Road Keep Your Left.' Because heavily laden trucks struggling slowly uphill did less damage to the road by driving close to the mountain rather than the cliffside edge – which was (and still is) prone to collapse, the WMDR is a left-side-only route. New and tired drivers often forgot this vital rule. Collisions on blind curves were common.

And because collapses were common, parts of the road were regularly reduced to barely the width of a single truck. When two trucks met on these narrow stretches, the rule was that the truck going downhill had to back up until the truck edging uphill could pass. To avoid this dangerous situation, local men and boys served as flaggers (called *barritas*) signaling when the narrow stretch was clear. Their pay was tips from thankful drivers.

Still, as one veteran trucker told us, trucks unable to pass led to a disaster he witnessed in the old days. A Coca-Cola truck was heading downhill at night and met another truck on an unpassable portion. It began backing up, but the driver's assistant was inexperienced and let the truck get too close to the edge of the road, which collapsed, plunging the truck and driver to their doom.

'I saw many bodies on the Death Road,' the trucker said, 'but our bosses said "Schedule! Schedule!" so we could not stop."

CHOOSING A TOUR COMPANY

It's easy to spot cycling groups in their jackets with matching colors. Each tour company has its own scheme and the differences don't stop there. Prices range from B$350 to B$900. You get what you pay for: higher-end companies have top-quality, well-maintained bikes with excellent brakes (essential) and sophisticated suspension (very essential on the rugged WMDR).

Be sure the operator has guides at the front and back of groups so that slower riders won't be left to their peril and faster riders won't unwittingly get in trouble.

Two recommended La Paz operators for those exploring WMDR are **Gravity Bolivia** (p115; *gravitybolivia.com)* and **Xtreme Down Hill** (p115; *xtremedownhill.com)*.

Beyond Coroico

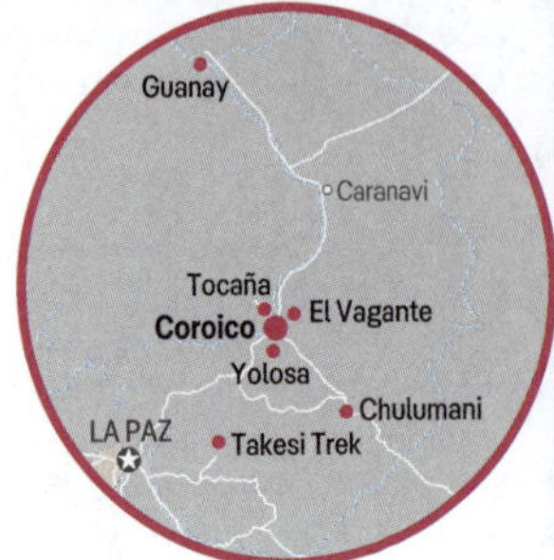

Yungas means 'warm lands' in Aymara, the Indigenous language spoken by over 1.7 million people, and you'll find myriad outdoor pursuits here.

Places

GETTING AROUND

If you are scared of heights or don't have much faith in Bolivian bus drivers, ask for an aisle seat. Roads are narrow; drops are steep; and some of the routes, such as to Chulumani, are hairy.

Traveling between towns in the region can require backtracking to La Paz or taking a somewhat costly taxi ride across a valley. This is especially true in the rainy season (Nov-Apr) when roads become perilous and access is impossible.

Buses from Coroico leave sporadically, when full. Buy tickets and make inquiries at the main bus station. Elsewhere, ask locally.

Coroico sits on a perch overlooking the vast Yungas, the transition zone between the dry highlands and humid lowlands, where the Andes fall away into the Amazon Basin. Above the steaming, forested depths rise the near-vertical slopes of the Cordillera Real and the Cordillera Quimsa Cruz, which halt altiplano-bound clouds, causing them to deposit bounteous rainfall. Vegetation is abundant, and tropical fruit, coca, cacao and more grow abundantly.

Coroico, the main town, and Chulumani are the only population centers. Most people here claim Aymara descent but there's also a noticeable Afro-Bolivian population. Coroico makes a good base to explore this vast region with water adventures, hidden villages, hikes and treks and journeys further into the Amazon.

Yolosa

TIME FROM COROICO: **10 MINS** 

Death Road's end

Although you may call it an oasis of bliss after you've been jiggled like a colorized can of paint on the region's roads, the village of **Yolosa** is located about 7km down from Coroico. It boasts a serene riverside setting – good for picnics procured from a string of minimarkets with winsome owners that line the *smooth* main road. If you need to cool off, several guesthouses offer day passes for their swimming pools.

High noon locally begins around 1pm when cyclists begin rolling in from their World's Most Dangerous Road (WMDR) bike tours, which end here. Many still wear looks of terror.

Compelling home for wildlife

On the banks of the Río Coroico, **Senda Verde Wildlife Sanctuary** *(sendaverde.org; tours from adult/child B$150/75, reserve ahead)*, gives shelter to scores of indigenous wild species that have been rescued from lives as pets, as sideshow attractions in shop windows or from illegal traffickers. Monkeys, toucans, caimans, Andean bears, ocelots and margays are among the residents.

In a switch from other animal displays, visitors mostly walk through chain-link cages while the residents roam free all around (watch out for the diabolical birds above). The excellent 75-minute tours are ecologically minded and offer serious insight into the animals. You'll learn the often-depressing stories of how many of the residents came to live out their lives in this oasis.

Note that the riverside location is buggy, so bring repellant. The on-site restaurant is excellent with organic snacks, great locally grown coffee and a lunch buffet (Gravity Bolivia's WMDR bike tours finish here, p131). If you're smitten, you can volunteer or stay at their ecolodge (p143).

Zip over the jungle

At **Zipline Bolivia** (Zzip the Flying Fox; *facebook.com/ziplinebolivia; from B$250*) three zipline sections take you flying at speeds of up to 85km/h through the forest canopy near Yolosa. The 1500m zipline can be combined with trips down the WMDR. There's an office right in Yolosa.

White-water rafting

The **Río Coroico** is the country's most popular commercially rafted river and is convenient to La Paz, Coroico and Yolosa. The river features over 30 rapids, great surfing holes, dramatic drops and challenging technical maneuvers. It alternates between calm pools and 50m to 900m rapids.

The white water normally ranges from Class II to IV, but may approach Class V during the rainy season (when it's too dangerous to raft).

Access is from the highway between Yolosa and Caranavi; the best put-ins are 20 minutes north of Yolosa and near the confluence with the Río Santa Bárbara, 50 minutes north of Yolosa.

Another popular rafting river, the **Río Huarinilla** flows from Huayna Potosí and Tiquimani down into the Yungas to meet the Río Coroico near Yolosa. Although it's normally Class II and III, high water can swell it to Class IV to V.

Coroico Star (p127) and La Paz agencies organize trips down these rivers.

El Vagante

TIME FROM COROICO: 2¼ HRS

A hike and wild swimming

A good day out will take you to El Vagante, an area of lovely natural stone swimming holes in the **Río Santa Bárbara**.

Follow the road from Coroico toward Arapata for about two hours. Turn left at a fork in the road and head steeply downhill past Comunidad Miraflores; at the second fork, bear right. After two hours along this 7km route, which features a stretch with some pre-Columbian terraces, you'll reach a cement bridge. Turn right before the bridge and follow the river downstream for 20 minutes to a series of swimming holes and waterfalls (follow your ears). The return is all uphill, so you might want to arrange a pickup.

continues on p136

COCA IN THE YUNGAS

Traditionally, coca is used in Bolivia for leaf chewing, drinking in *mate* (herbal tea) and during religious ceremonies.. Its mild alkaloids help with altitude sickness and fatigue. It's also, of course, used to produce cocaine.

Under former president Evo Morales, production of coca for non-illicit purposes was promoted under a policy of 'coca yes, cocaine no.' Today you'll see small, family-run coca farms in the valleys around Coroico. The plants are easily spotted: bushy, with oval leaves (which you'll likely see in hotel tea services) and reddish berries.

Observers note that the coca leaves sold through the legitimate wholesale markets in La Paz are only a portion of the overall estimated harvest.

MARK PITT IMAGES/SHUTTERSTOCK

TOP EXPERIENCE

Incas & Grandeur: The El Choro Trek

Traversing the Cordillera Real and Parque Nacional Cotopata, the El Choro trek is one of Bolivia's premier hikes. It begins at La Cumbre (4725m) and climbs to 4859m before descending 3250m into the humid Yungas. Among the hallmarks are spectacular scenery and a rapid change in climate, vegetation and wildlife as you leave the altiplano and plunge into the subtropical forest.

DON'T MISS

- Views in the Upper Half
- Apacheta Chucura
- Abra Chucura
- Choro
- Puente Colgante suspension bridge
- Casa Sandillani
- Río Jucumarini

Day 1

El Choro's trekking route begins at La Cumbre's **Statue of Christ**, where there is a park registration office. Traditionally this is also the place for ritual *challas*, which asks for blessings from the gods and good luck with the journey. In former times it was an Aymara sanctuary. From here, follow the well-defined track to your left for 1km, then turn off onto the smaller track that turns right and passes between two **small ponds** (one often dry). Follow the track up the hill until it curves to the left and begins to descend.

PRACTICALITIES

● **Start** La Cumbre ● **End** Chairo ● **Duration** 3-4 days
● **Distance** 57km ● **Difficulty** Medium

Now follow the light track leading up the gravelly hill to your right and toward an obvious notch in the barren hill before you. This is **Abra Chucura** (4859m), and from here the trail runs downhill all the way to its end at Chairo. At the high point is a pile of stones called **Apacheta Chucura**. For centuries travelers have marked their passing by tossing a stone atop it (preferably one that has been carried from a lower elevation) as an offering to the mountain *apus* (sacred places). An hour below Abra Chucura lies the remains of a ***tambo*** (wayside inn) dating from Inca times.

One hour below the *tambo* is the hamlet of **Estancia Samaña Pampa**, where there's a store that sells water, a grassy campsite, a shelter and another registration hut.

A short way further on is the village of **Chucura** (Achura; 3600m), which has basic supplies. An hour's walk from here leads to some **campsites** along the river.

Day 2

Continue on the beautifully paved **Inca road** to **Cha'llapampa** (2825m), a lovely village with a roofed campsite and simple shelters approximately seven hours from the trail's start point. There are toilets, and water is available from a convenient stream below a bridge close to town.

After two hours following beautiful but slippery stretches of pre-Columbian paving, you'll reach a **rustic suspension bridge** across huge boulders and the Río Chucura at **Choro** (2200m). The track continues descending steadily along the true left (west) side of the river, passing through dense vegetation to **campsites** (charging B$180 or less per night) and a minimarket.

Day 3

From the ridge above Choro, the trail alternately plunges and climbs from sunny hillsides to vegetation-choked valleys, crossing streams and waterfalls. You may have to ford the **Río Jucumarini**, which can be intimidating in the wet season, although logs are often set across the waters allowing for a precarious balancing act. Further along, the trail crosses the deep gorge of the **Río Coscapa** via the substantial **Puente Colgante suspension bridge**.

The trail continues through the almost-not-there hamlet of **San Francisco** and nicely organized **Buena Vista** (with **campsites**), which are separated by the stiff ascent and descent of the **Subida del Diablo**. Some five to six hours from Choro is the remarkable **Casa Sandillani** (2050m), a home surrounded by beautiful gardens with **campsites**.

From Casa Sandillani it's an easy 2½ hours downhill to **Chairo**, where camping is possible in a small, flat, grassed area with no facilities, near the bridge above town.

TRANSPORT & LODGING

It's easy to reach La Cumbre from La Paz on the many buses heading towards Coroico and the east.

From Chairo, you can walk the appealing 12km to Yolosa and then get a ride to Coroico. This could be your trek's fourth day.

There's camping all along the route, or you can try the growing number of guesthouses on the latter half of the trek

TOP TIPS

- Prepare for a range of climates. It can be cold, even snowy, on the first day, but it soon gets much warmer.
- For the lower trail, light cotton trousers offer protection from sharp vegetation and biting insects.
- The Inca paving can be slippery; make sure you've got shoes with traction and consider using trekking poles (which also help your knees on the long downhill sections).
- For the best chance of clear views of the stunning scenery, start early before the Yungas mist rises.
- Conditions are best during the May to October dry season.
- La Paz agencies (p115) can arrange treks.

continued from p133

Tocaña

TIME FROM COROICO: **30 MINS**

Visit an Afro-Bolivian village

Hillside **Tocaña** is one of the hidden Afro-Bolivian villages in the Yungas. Although you can see Coroico across the Rio Coroico valley, it exists in another world. The long, rough road of switchbacks up from Hwy 3 passes banana and coca farms and arrives at the impressive **Museo del Centro Cultural de Tocaña** *(facebook.com/tocanatuoportunidad; by donation)*, a cultural, historical and craft center that's also a vibrant community hub. It's an excellent place to start a visit; listen to examples of Afro-Bolivian Saya music (a haunting hybrid of African, Aymara and Spanish styles). Beautiful murals outside honor notable community members.

A bit further uphill, the **Plaza Principal** has sweeping views and inspirational slogans. A side note: the museum and Tocaña's clinic were both built with money from the United States Agency for International Development (USAID), when that organization represented the bipartisan commitment of the United States to fund humanistic causes worldwide.

Takesi Trek

TIME FROM COROICO TO VENTILLA: **3½ HRS**

Hike along the Inca Trail

Also known as the **Inca Trail**, the **Takesi trek** is one of the most popular and impressive walks in the Andes. The route was used by the early Aymara, the Inca and the Spanish as a major route to the humid Yungas over a relatively low pass in the Cordillera Real.

The 48km route includes a significant segment of expertly engineered pre-contact paving; it's more like a highway than a walking track. The walk itself is demanding and takes at least three days, but plan on longer because of unreliable transportation to and from the trailheads at **Ventilla** and **Yanacachi** (you'll likely need taxis). On the first day you'll make a tough ascent to 4650m. Don't try it in the rainy season when the mud and cold will defeat you. Scenery includes soaring peaks, glacial lakes, plunging valleys and, after the village of **Takesi**, lush tropical Yungas beauty.

Plan on camping along the way. La Paz agencies (p115) can supply guides, transportation and arrange logistics like mules as you'll have to carry water and food.

Chulumani

TIME FROM COROICO: **3 HRS** 

A peaceful perch (until the party)

Perched on a hillside, this large village has a lively main square, a heaving weekend market, vibrant Afro-Bolivian culture and tropical attitude (and altitude: 1700m). With far fewer international visitors than Coroico, it's much more tranquil – except during the 10 days after August 24, when **Chulumani** stages the raucous **Fiesta de San Bartolomé**, a riot of drinking, dancing, bands, parades and, yes, more drinking. The region is a paradise if you're into birds and butterflies

THE HIDDEN MINORITY: AFRO-BOLIVIANS

The hill villages of the Yungas such as Tocaña are home to a high proportion of the country's Afro-Bolivian population. (The ceremonial king lives just north in the village of Mururata.)

An estimated 23,000 Bolivians are descended from enslaved Africans brought to Bolivia by the Spanish in the 17th century to work in the Potosí silver mines. Huge numbers died in the horrible conditions and the survivors were transferred to domestic labor and farm work.

Slavery in Bolivia didn't end until 1851, but the labor practices it spawned persisted for another century. Afro-Bolivians were forced to move to isolated villages in the Yungas, where many adopted aspects of the indigenous Aymara. Discrimination has always been rampant and Afro-Bolivians weren't recognized as an official group until 2010.

Traditional Yungas breakfast

LORENA SAMPONI/SHUTTERSTOCK

– there are clouds of the latter, and several endemic species of the former.

The current 'world's most dangerous road'

Since the original WMDR (p128) was superseded by the new road for vehicles, the perilous route from La Paz to Chulumani (approximately four hours), which extends on to Irupana, has claimed the title. White knuckles aside, it's an exceptionally beautiful route (if not closed in the rainy season), though it's hard to appreciate when your bus is reversing around a blind, muddy bend in search of a section wide enough to let oncoming traffic past. Expect plenty of thrills on the ride, whether by car or bus.

Guanay

TIME FROM COROICO: **6 HRS**

Take a beguiling river journey

The only reason to visit isolated **Guanay** is to hop a boat to Rurrenabaque. The down-to-earth miners and *barranquilleros* (panners) give this unadorned frontier town of 12,000 a bit of a tropical Wild West feel. Buses from La Paz take about 10 hours.

River travel was once the only lifeline connecting remote Amazonian communities to the rest of Bolivia. Today, roads have replaced many of the river routes and mining operations have taken over most of the rest. The wonderful exception is the journey between Guanay and Rurrenabaque.

Tour operators (p115) run riverboats that typically take about four days, starting on the Río Kaka. **Mayaya** is the last town before you enter a vast uninhabited area. Once past the mines, the myriad natural wonders of Parque Nacional Madidi (p301) and **La Reserva de Biósfera Pilón Lajas** predominate. You'll camp on beaches, spot wildlife, fish for dinner and visit remote communities before disembarking at the Amazonian Rurrenabaque (p298).

HEARTY YUNGAS BREAKFASTS

You'll see signs everywhere in its namesake region and also in La Paz for the *Desayuno en los Yungas* (Yungas breakfast), a classic meal beloved for its rib-sticking, hearty fare. Workers who go without lunch value a day's worth of fuel.

Costing no more than B$20, the centerpiece is a big chunk of fried meat, usually beef, with a fried egg on top. A piece of white bread or a bun is on the side to mop up the juice. A generous dollop of salsa picante adds spice.

Rounding out the plate is a fried banana or plantain and a big scoop of white rice. Deluxe versions include orange juice or lemonade and perhaps coffee.

Sorata

GRAND VIEWS | GREAT HIKES | DRAMATIC SKIES

GETTING AROUND

Sorata is a long way from other Yungas towns, and there's no road connecting it directly with Coroico, so you must go through La Paz.

Buses and *trufis* (minibuses) leave for Sorata from La Paz (3½ hours) throughout the day. The entire route is in good condition and paved. It's about three hours from La Paz with a car and driver.

The town is the jumping-off point for services to the more remote northern reaches of the region. Many of these roads are in dire shape and the vehicles are 4WD.

Head to the main bus stop to get an idea when transport might depart. Look for local taxis around the central Plaza General Enrique Peñaranda.

Like a gold nugget buried in the surrounding peaks, Sorata (2670m; *360.sorata.bo*) is a real find. While it doesn't have the reliable Death Road feed of its rival Coroico, this semi-tropical village, sitting high above verdant valleys, offers excellent treks, kick-ass downhill mountain biking, and an intoxicating atavistic air. Many are enthralled watching the ever-shifting clouds reveal snow-covered peaks. (Sorata comes from the Aymara word *shuru-ahta,* which means glowing peak.)

In colonial days Sorata provided a link to goldfields and rubber plantations and a gateway to the Amazon Basin. These days, mining is the main source of employment in the region. But it's worth your effort to hire a guide and explore this under-appreciated mountain idyll and its intoxicating surrounds.

Sorata suffered during the massive social unrest in 2003, which ultimately brought Evo Morales to power.

Stroll the Main Square

Views, posies, palms and more!

Sorata's manicured central square, **Plaza General Enrique Peñaranda**, is the focus of local life, with the town's best view of the *nevados* (snow-capped mountain peaks) and towering date palms. Grab a bench and watch the clouds rise like theater curtains to reveal the nearby peaks looming large.

Cheap and cheerful eateries line the perimeter while the **Iglesia Santa María Magadalena** has a forecourt filled with flowers. On the northeast corner, **Casa Günther** is a historic mansion that's an exclamation point of the square. It was built in 1895 for the Richters, a quinine-trading family, and was later taken over by the rubber-trading Günthers. Look for bullet holes in the doors.

An Extravaganza of Mountains & Valleys

Can you overload on awesome?

The main road into Sorata from La Paz passes through dry plains and then lifts over the mountains to present a spectacle of dramatic valleys. Some 20 minutes before you reach town, you'll notice a Jesus statue on a knob of rock. It's the sentinel for **Mirador Ulluntija**, a viewpoint with a 360-degree panorama of the Andes. If it's clear, your journey just got longer. There are snack stands by the road; the broad lookout is a 10-minute scramble up the hill.

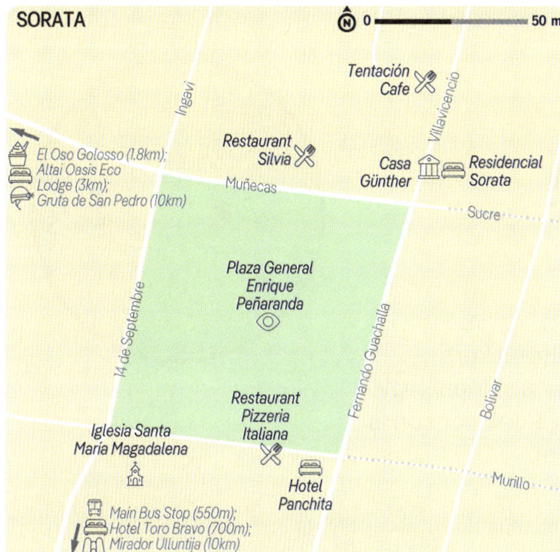

Thrilling Walk to a Fascinating Cave

Wonderful views near and far

The excuse for a great walk, **Gruta de San Pedro** (San Pedro Cave), known in the Aymara language as *Chussek Uta* (House of Owls), is 510m deep. Its highlight is a subterranean lagoon you cross in pedal boats. Guides show you around and offer crowd-thrilling details about the three species of nectar- and insect-eating bats who lurk in the pitch-black surroundings.

Underground joy aside, the real pleasure of this outing is the 10km walk from Sorata to get here. It's reasonably level and will take about 2½ hours. The first kilometer is twisty, dusty and scruffy, and will have you questioning your decision, but then the vistas open up to the majesty of the mountains and valleys and you'll be entranced. Brilliant greens and reds of the soaring, sheer mountainsides alternate with black and silver striations on bare rock. The sound of rushing water in rivers far below echoes up.

At the cave site, vendors include an outlet for the locally beloved ice-cream maker **El Oso Golosso** (p139). There's a big pool you can pay to use (the walk gets hot) and even some simple rooms to rent. Consider making arrangements to get picked up and driven back to Sorata.

TOP TIP

Felix Chino *(WhatsApp +591 7-194-8128; felixsorata@gmail.com; facebook.com/trekkingsorata)* is an excellent source for local guides and drivers, most of whom have responded to the dearth of tourists by going to work in the mines.

BOUNTY OF THE SORATA REGION

The balmy climate is ideal for growing fruits and vegetables, which vary by altitude. **Chuñu** are small potatoes grown in the high plains that are left to freeze-dry under snow all winter. In spring they are hard and black and have more bite than fresh spuds. *Chuñu* are used in soups and stews or mashed as a side dish. Fried up, they are a treat and served around the main square with salsa picante. **Tunta** is the deluxe version of *chuñu*. Once dry, the potatoes are placed in mountain streams which wash all the color away; the resulting white flesh has a delicate flavor.

Sorata is also renowned for white sweet corn, fava beans, big tomatoes and luscious peaches.

EATING & DRINKING IN SORATA: OUR PICKS

Tentación Cafe: Fab coffee drinks just off the main square. Creations include fruity delights, milkshakes, Irish coffee; plus cakes and sandwiches. *9am-7pm* $

Restaurant Silvia: Busy, place on the main square; big menu of local faves. Daily soup and stew specials are musts. Big breakfasts. Counter sells *chuñu*. *7am-9pm* $

El Oso Golosso: Name means Greedy Bear, and you'll be one after you taste this ice cream that's flavored with fresh fruit. Widely sold in town. *10am-6:30pm* $

Try the karicari (wild blackberry)!

Restaurant Pizzeria Italiana: Main square veteran serves up reliable thin-crust pizza and good pasta. Heaping plates of meaty Bolivian fare. *noon-9pm* $

Beyond Sorata

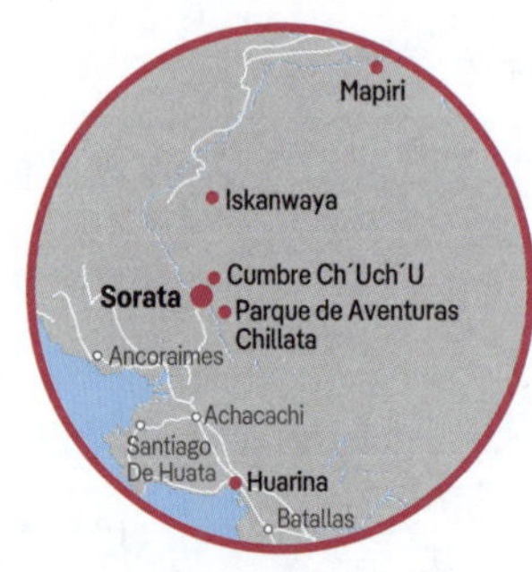

Sorata is a great base for hikers pursuing some of Bolivia's finest high-mountain landscapes. Peak season is from April to November.

Places

GETTING AROUND

Sorata is effectively the end of the line for independent transport. To reach trailheads and sites in the mountains around town, you can arrange for a driver through your guesthouse or Felix Chino (p139). He can also help with longer journeys and treks in the region. Or you can go with one of the La Paz agencies with experience in the area such as America Tours (p115). Regardless, 4WD is the order of the day.

The mountains about Sorata are a wonderland of soaring beauty above the tree line, where ancient Inca trails once trodden by llama caravans link glaciers, lakes, peaceful valleys and more.

However, the explosion in gold mining, especially illegal mining, has not been good for tourism in the region. To the north, outsiders are often viewed with suspicion and even hostility and once popular treks like El Camino del Oro are no longer recommended both because of the environmental destruction and safety concerns. The same is the case for much of the Cordillera Apolobamba region.

There are exceptions, such as the remarkable and all-but-unvisited pre-contact city of Iskanwaya. And there are long-distance treks and mountains to climb with the right guides.

Cumbre Ch´Uch´U

TIME FROM SORATA: **90 MINS** 

Hiking, trekking and biking paradise

The historic summit, Cumbre Ch´Uch´U (4700m), was once the hub of a network of trails throughout the Andes. For centuries, and until as recently as 1982, llama trains would bring salt from Uyuni to trade for corn and potatoes.

Today the summit is a hub for roads and can be easily reached on a fascinating 4WD drive up from Sorata. For a great introduction to hiking in the area, get a local guide (p122) and follow the ancient trading trails (which are in danger of falling into disrepair as the guides who maintained them have had to seek work in the mines) for five hours (25km) back to town. There are myriad more possibilities.

Or get a mountain bike. The beer bottles you see at the summit are not litter but offerings to Pachamama for safe passage down. Each October, the **Jach´a Avalanche** *(gravitybolivia.com)* sends scores of riders from around the world careening down the mountain to Sorata. The record time is an astonishing 32 minutes.

Parque de Aventuras Chillata

TIME FROM SORATA: **40 MINS**

Explore a mysterious burial site

In the green mountains at 3600m, the municipal **Parque de Aventuras Chillata** is undeveloped but for a gravel road and hut. Good. On a broad, grassy plain (good for camping) near the entrance sign, is one of Sorata's unheralded mysteries: a vast area of what's thought to be an **Inca cemetery** *(Cementerio Inca)*, although the **burial tombs** could date from before. Undocumented, over 100 lichen-covered stone mounds sprawl over the landscape. Wander amongst them and try for your own answers.

Hike to a beautiful lake and beyond

Laguna Chillata (4200m) is a popular hike from Sorata or within the park. It's reached by ancient trails that lace the region and allow for hikes that last for hours of days, taking in high-altitude vistas and linking glacier-clad peaks.

About 13km (two hours) from the Inca burial tombs, it's a serene spot with great views of the surrounding sierra and Lake Titicaca. Guides can show you various options for getting here from Sorata as well as further highlights, such as the much further Laguna Glacial at 5100m.

Huarina

TIME FROM SORATA: **1¾ HRS**

A tasty stop

You can see the source of your lunch, Lake Titicaca, out the back door of your restaurant in Huarina, a town of roadhouses about midway between La Paz and Sorata. It's an excellent place to break the journey as a string of restaurants serve up delicious meals of freshly caught lake fish. You'll have your choice, but the most prized is locally known as *cakachi*. Get it fried with potatoes or in a soup.

Mapiri

TIME FROM SORATA: **3 DAYS**

By foot or bike to the Amazon

This is not a DIY adventure. But for wilderness thrills taking in some of Bolivia's most arresting and remote mountain and sub-tropical regions, it's possible to **trek** on foot or with a mountain bike from Sorata to the riverside mining town of Mapiri. The town itself is charmless, but from here you'll get a boat onwards to Rurrenabaque (298).

It's a remarkable journey you have to arrange through an agency (p115) as you'll need logistical help and guides. Gravity Bolivia (p131) leads mountain bike trips on this incredible route.

HIGHLIGHTS IN THE MOUNTAINS

When exploring the mountains above Sorata, watch for the following:

From January to April, you'll see children selling bags of a leafy, green herb known as *tucus tucu* in Aymara. Much loved in the region, it makes a strong mint-like tea and is used in a cheesy corn chowder.

Watch for the medium-sized black and white mountain caracara, known locally as the *suerte maria* – these birds of prey are thought to bring luck, such as 'I won't fall off a cliff.'

On the road to Cumbre Ch´Uch´U, watch for a rare food outlet, **Pension Doña Antonia**, which is beloved for its delicious takeaway lunch specials of spicy, roast llama, potatoes, *chuñu*, cheese, an egg and corn.

TOP EXPERIENCE

Lost Ruins at Iskanwaya

Isolated and mysterious, the major but near-forgotten ruins of Iskanwaya, on the western slopes of the Cordillera Real, are little visited. Of the few who visit, none can suppress their awe when first encountering this dramatic site in a cactus-filled canyon, perched 250m above the Río Llica. A center of the Mollo culture, it predates the Inca's Machu Picchu.

GITANA TROPICAL/SHUTTERSTOCK

Iskanwaya

TOP TIPS

- Without a vehicle, the ruins are a 1500m descent from the main road above (with a corresponding climb back up).
- During peak wet season (Dec-Mar), roads to Aucapata and Iskanwaya may be impassable.
- Bring food as local sources are limited.

PRACTICALITIES

Self-navigating to Aucapata and Iskanwaya is difficult as apps like Google Maps show no roads in the region at all. Go with a guide.

A Magnificent Site

Given the complexities of visiting the 13-hectare site, the chance to explore Iskanwaya in solitude is a rare treat. Thought to date from between 1145 and 1425, the ruins are attributed to the Mollo culture, which predated the Incas.

The large citadel was built on two platforms and flanked by agricultural terraces and complex networks of irrigation canals. It contains more than 100 buildings (most with running water), plus delicate walls, narrow streets, small plazas, storerooms, burial sites and niches.

Aucapata

The tiny settlement of Aucapata – a charming mountain town at 2640m with a serene plaza – is far off the beaten track. Reaching the ruins from town requires a walk of several hours, as the route is roughly over 7km-long with myriad switchbacks. Most local drivers now work in the mines.

How to Visit

For now, the best way to visit Iskanwaya is to start from Sorata on a day trip. In dry season (May to October), the scenic drive will take four hours one-way. You can either set this up in Sorata (p138), or through a La Paz agency (p115). In the past, there were a couple of guesthouses in Aucapata, but they are hard to contact.

Places We Love to Stay

$ Budget $$ Midrange $$$ Top End

Coroico
MAP p126

Hostal Kurmi $ Ideally located just off the main square; family-run guesthouse across several floors. Large rooms have views and terraces; nice gardens.

Hostal El Cafetal $ South of town, this French-owned hotel has tremendous views, a nice pool on large grounds and a noted cafe.

Hostal Ecolodge Sol y Luna $ On a jungle-covered hill; appealingly rustic cabañas (cabins), basic rooms and camping spots. Yoga, pools and a hot tub.

Villa Bonita $$ Charming and colorful cabins on the east side of town; has a popular cafe and offers yoga and massage. Great views along the road.

Uma Experience $$$ Boutique resort with sweeping views and an infinity pool. Large, forested grounds and modern cottages that open to nature. Healthful cuisine.

Around Coroico

El Eden Yolosita-Tocaña $ Newish riverside campground and motel with a bit of style and a large pool. Good food and simple, tidy rooms. On the road to Tocaña.

Senda Verde Eco Lodge $$ This delightful spot in the animal refuge has cabins and a treehouse. Bed down to the sounds of the thousands of four-legged and feathered residents. Good restaurant.

Chulumani
p136

Hostal Dion $ Best of the central options. Homey setting has sparkling, simple rooms, a courtyard garden and a location convenient for partaking in town life.

Country House $$ Gorgeous home 10 minutes west of the plaza offers a fabulous welcome. Delicious meals and oodles of hiking and tourism advice. Artful rooms and gardens.

El Choro Trek
p134

Villa Teresa Casa de Campo $ In Chairo at the end of the El Choro Trek, has a sprawling riverfront setting with basic rooms and a large pool.

Urpuma Ecotourism Lodge $$ Restful country retreat near Sandillani on the trail. Three comfortable cottages built using local methods with materials from the surrounding forests. Serves meals.

Sorata
MAP p139

Hotel Toro Bravo $ Just south of town, outlandish statues dominate the entrance; inside is a serene garden and pool. The owner is active in promoting the community.

Hotel Panchita $ Built around a sunny courtyard right on the main square, has small rooms (avoid dark ones). Good central location close to restaurants, cheery staff. *(7-120-5651)*

Residencial Sorata $ Within the Casa Günther, the colonial-style mansion oozes atmosphere. Rooms are variable, newer ones are better, ask to see a few. Big garden. *(7-322-4200)*

Altai Oasis Eco Lodge $$ Lush garden spilling down to the river and a tasty cafe (amazing house-grown mushrooms). Grassy campsites, comfortable rooms and rustic *cabañas* (cabins). Book ahead.

For places to stay in Southern Altiplano, see p178

MAPIMARF/SHUTTERSTOCK

Left: Salar de Uyuni (p155); Right: Reserva Nacional de Fauna Andina Eduardo Avaroa (p16

Researched by
Joe Sills

Southern Altiplano

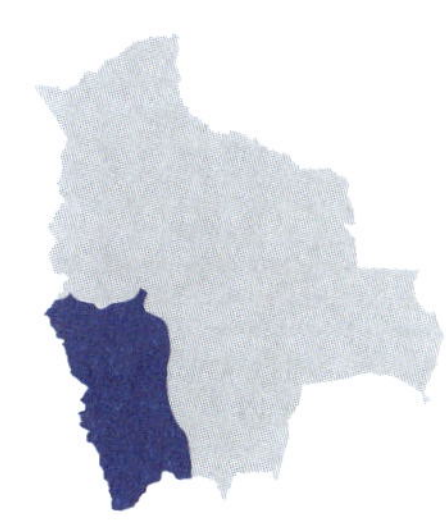

OTHERWORLDLY ADVENTURES AT EXTREME ALTITUDE

Windswept plains, dreamlike natural features and an ancient human history atop one of the highest inhabited areas on the planet.

The Southern Altiplano – a vast highland plateau stretching across western Bolivia – is one of the most mind boggling landscapes on Earth. Sitting at an average altitude of 3600–4000m above sea level, this rugged terrain is home to otherworldly geology, vibrant indigenous cultures, and scattered populations of quizzical Andean wildlife. The Altiplano harbors Bolivia's tallest peaks and a deep legacy of lore dating back millennia. This is a home of ancient gods, desert tombs and the modern-day descendants of people whose civilizations thrived here long before the Inca and Spanish arrived.

Near the center of the Altiplano lies Salar de Uyuni – the world's largest salt flat and the lifeblood of Bolivian tourism. Mercurial salt hotels ring this transfixing wasteland that transforms into a natural mirror during the rainy season and a wanderer's dream when clouds run dry. Here, travelers are compelled to ponder their own existence in what feels like an endless world trapped between Earth and sky.

In the Altiplano's southwestern corner, Reserva Nacional de Fauna Andina Eduardo Avaroa harbors geothermal geysers and one of the world's largest strongholds for flamingos. Nestled against the borders of Chile and Argentina, its heights hold the keys to the still-beating heart of the Andes. And a bookend of 'Wild West' history lies in Tupiza, a desert outpost where famed outlaw legends met their end.

THE MAIN AREAS

PARQUE NACIONAL SAJAMA
Hiking, hot springs and geyser fields. **p150**

SALAR DE UYUNI
The largest salt flat on Earth. **p155**

RESERVA NACIONAL DE FAUNA ANDINA EDUARDO AVAROA
Volcanic lagoons and flamingos. **p164**

TUPIZA
Bolivia's 'Wild West' adventure hub. **p171**

Find Your Way

Parque Nacional Sajama, p150

Bolivia's first national park rests below its tallest peak. Hike through dwarf trees in its Queñua forests, plod through geyser fields and soak in natural hot springs.

Salar de Uyuni, p155

The world's largest salt flat is a blank canvas for photographers and an ethereal landscape for adventure seekers searching for their own slice of solitude.

Tupiza, p171

The famed final refuge for Wild West outlaw Butch Cassidy is an adventure hub for rock climbing, hiking and horseback riding perched on the border of Argentina.

Reserva Nacional de Fauna Andina Eduardo Avaroa, p164

A wildlife wonderland, this magnet for birders is home to tens of thousands of flamingos as well as pumas, Andean foxes and geothermal marvels.

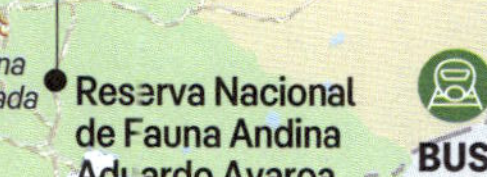

PLANE

A handful of daily flights operate between Uyuni's Joya Andina Airport (UYU) and La Paz. **Boliviana de Aviación** is the most reliable carrier, though occasional EcoJet flights may pop up.

BUS & TRAIN

Buses are the most affordable way to get around the Altiplano, though they generally only move from city to city. **Bolivia Hop** offers travelers the opportunity to jump on and off with more freedom. Meanwhile, plodding trains still run between **Oruro** and **Uyuni** four days per week.

OFF-ROAD VEHICLE

Motorcycles and 4WDs are the most common methods of transport across the Altiplano. It is possible to rent your own vehicle in a major city and drive yourself, though an experienced driver is highly recommended (and often required) on the salt flats.

Plan Your Days

Experiencing everything the Southern Altiplano has to offer requires a deep dive. Expect to spend long days on bumpy roads and plan off days for recovery time in civilization.

HUGO TURNER/SHUTTERSTOCK

Parinacota Volcano

If You Only Do One Thing

- If you only have a few days earmarked for the Altiplano, plan your trip to coincide with a new moon to maximize the night skies and head directly to Uyuni from La Paz.

- You'll need to arrange for a salt flats tour via an operator like **Hidalgo Tours**, **Andes Salt Expeditions** or **Quechua Connection** to make the most of your time on the salt flats. Book a salt hotel like **Hotel Palacio de Sal** (p178) or **Hotel Luna Salada**.

- Explore the **Uyuni Train Cemetery** (p155).

- Hike to the top of **Incahuasi Island**. Watch sunset over the salt flats and stargaze beneath the Milky Way.

Seasonal Highlights

Dry months open up vast swatches of salt flats to cruise across and high peaks to summit. Wetter weather makes for dazzling mirror effects on the salt flats but tougher travel.

JANUARY

Rainy season brings the famous mirror effect to the Salar de Uyuni. Some roads may be impassable, but the landscape is at its most surreal.

FEBRUARY

Rainy season may still be at its peak during the early weeks of February, but the last echoes of the month bring drier weather and Carnaval celebrations throughout communities.

MARCH

The rains begin to subside, leaving a thin layer of water over Salar de Uyuni and opening up more favorable driving and trail conditions elsewhere on the Altiplano.

A Week on the Altiplano

- Cross over from San Pedro de Atacama, Chile to begin a weeklong journey through Bolivia in **Reserva Nacional de Fauna Andina Eduardo Avaroa** (p164) with the stunning combination of the arsenic lake of **Laguna Verde** (p167) and flamingo haven of **Laguna Colorada** (p168).

- Make a stopover at a high altitude hostel before spending three nights in **Uyuni** to photograph the salt flats, visit cacti-covered islands and stargaze before breaking north towards **Parque Nacional Sajama** (p150) for two nights in the village of **Tomarapi** (p178) for hiking, hot springs and geyser fields.

- Coast into La Paz on the final day.

More Than a Week

- A few extra days on the Altiplano go a long way. Savor a slower pace that opens up time for camping, horseback riding, summiting volcanic peaks or more thoughtful photography in this otherworldly landscape.

- Camp beside geyser fields and visit the **Rio Lauca Burial Towers** in Sajama National Park.

- Spend two nights in a remote cabin above **Tomarapi**. Climb to the top of **Parinacota Volcano**. Pay respects to the **Coqueza Mummies** resting in the caves above Salar de Uyuni.

- Climb over cacti islands, visit the site of Butch Cassidy's legendary last stand in **San Vicente** and ride horses through **Valles de los Machos** in Tupiza.

JUNE

The dry season offers crisp air, intense blue skies, and frigid nights – perfect for trekking Andean peaks, stargazing on salares, and high-altitude driving tours through landscapes that resemble few others on Earth.

AUGUST

Bolivia celebrates its independence day with parades, music and dancing across the country on August 6th. Plan to join celebrations in the streets after long days of adventure in wilderness areas around Uyuni, Tupiza and Oruro.

SEPTEMBER

Warmer temperatures make exploration more comfortable. Flamingos gather in larger numbers for mating season on the lagoons, where they perform ritual dances with each other and march in unison in shallow, thermal lagoons.

DECEMBER

Rain starts returning, creating dynamic landscapes during a transition period with a mix of dry salt flats and the season's first mirror reflections. Tourism traffic begins to increase as photographers fly in for the mirror effect.

Parque Nacional Sajama

VOLCANIC PEAKS | GEOTHERMAL SIGHTSEEING | AYMARA COMMUNITIES

GETTING AROUND

The region is remote, roads are made of dirt or sand and supplies are only available in villages. The only reliable form of transportation around the park is a 4WD. Rent your own at **Forza Rent a Car** or **Fox Rent A Car** in La Paz. This is an area visitors can experience on their own, but a dedicated GPS device and experience driving off road are recommended. Roads are comprised of gravel or loose sand and have sizable ditches and holes to cross. Be prepared to dig your vehicle out of the sand if you go it alone.

The snow-covered peak of **Volcán Sajama** lords over the Southern Altiplano south of La Paz. Dominating an arid, windswept landscape peppered with ancient *chullpas* – the mud-brick, funerary towers of the ancient Aymara people – **Parque Nacional Sajama** ushers you into Bolivia's high plains southwest of La Paz. Since 1939, Bolivia's highest peak has been a sentinel for a surrounding national park stretching more than 1000 sq km around the Oruro department near the Chilean border.

Here, you can marvel at a 6542m (21,463ft) stratovolcano while bathing in geothermal hot springs at its feet. You can stroll through ancient forests of dwarf trees and watch seemingly endless herds of alpaca, llama and vicuñas saunter over the plains while Andean thunderstorms roll over the remnants of rural bell towers.

Whether exploring thermal springs, hiking beneath the Andean peaks volcano, or discovering centuries-old Aymara culture, visitors to Parque Nacional Sajama are immersed in one of Bolivia's most awe-inspiring and rugged natural landscapes.

Hike the Lagunas de Altura Trail

Day hike above geysers and clouds

A soft, burbling field of primordial geysers flanks the Rio Junthama along a dirt road several miles past **Sajama Village**. Their rising steam marks the way towards a spectacular, high altitude day hike that climbs more than 360m above the valley floor towards a trio of lakes on the Bolivian border with Chile – the **Lagunas de Altura**. Resting nearly 5000m in the sky, **Laguna Castro Macho**, **Laguna**

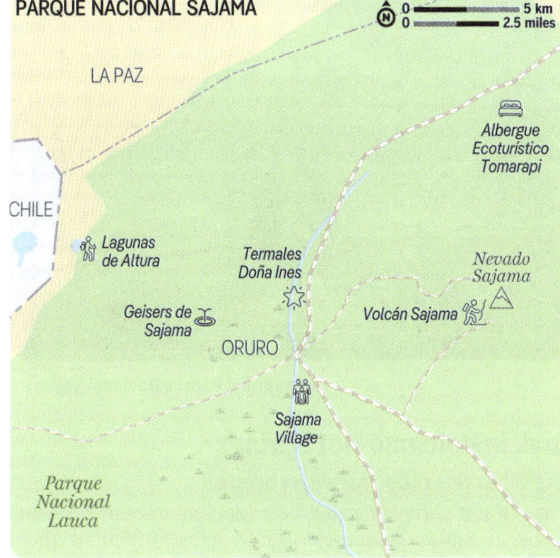

Cata Cuevas and **Laguna Casiri-Hembra** offer travelers a chance to hike above the clouds. Their shores ripple with cobalt waters and snow-capped peaks, and it's unlikely you'll pass many other hikers on the trail.

Park at the geyser field to extend the hike or continue along the dirt road for about 1.5km until you see a parking area that marks the trail head. From there, the trail travels alongside and over the increasingly narrow Rio Junthama before climbing through a series of switchbacks above the tree line.

Travelers can spend a half day trekking to Laguna Castro Macho and back or opt for a longer, full-day hike to visit all three lakes. Though the distances are relatively short (Laguna Castro Macho is less than 4km from the trailhead), the high elevation makes for a challenging hike over trails made of volcanic rock. The reward is strolling through a section of the park that remains uncrowded even during peak season while zig-zagging over an international border.

Hikers take note: During rainy season, weather conditions can shift in an instant at this elevation, changing from bluebird skies and sunshine to pelting hail storms at higher elevations and downpours of rain closer to the valley floor. Keep a rain jacket and hat handy, and have a plan for lighting.

Adventurous travelers can even camp at the **Geisers de Sajama** geothermal area. A series of stone fire rings about 100m west of the geysers themselves denote designated, dispersed camping sites open to visitors with their own gear. Bring your own tent, a campfire meal and warm sleeping bags to enjoy the night.

TOP TIP

Parque Nacional Sajama receives fewer than 5000 international visitors each year. Don't expect gift shops and infrastructure at this national park. Fewer than 10 rangers patrol the park so be sure to have a map and a grasp on where you are going.

A RANGER'S VIEW

Javier Huarachi is one of a handful of full-time rangers residing within Parque Nacional Sajama. The rangers rotate shifts between park regions.

Our job is to protect the park's forests from logging, ensure visitor safety and help people interact with the local communities. The people here live pastoral lives. They mostly raise alpacas. They also sell warm clothes made from their wool and tend to the lands. The park provides a way of preserving that lifestyle. Most visitors stay at hostels in Sajama Village or at **Tomarapi Eco Lodge** (p178), but camping is also allowed. You can bring a tent or rent one in La Paz to camp at **Termales Hot Springs** and **Geisers de Sajama**.

HIKING ON THE ALTIPLANO

Juan Carlos Cardenas, owner of Pukina Travel in La Paz, has been guiding day hikes and multiday treks through the Andes for more than two decades. *pukinatravel.com.*

Spend two or three days at high altitude in La Paz before your hike to acclimatize. Drink plenty of water and wear sunscreen. UV rays are harsher at elevation and hydration helps your blood oxygenate more efficiently. Nights in Parque Nacional Sajama can reach -15°C. Bring warm layers like a down jacket, warm hat and gloves. Bring snacks and supplies and make sure to have 4WD transportation. It's the only way to access the best trails. Plan a multiday visit if fauna like condors and flamingos are on your wishlist.

JAMI TARRIS/GETTY IMAGES

Hot spring, Parque Nacional Sajama

Soak in Volcanic Hot Springs

Barebones relaxation for weary hikers

A trio of hot springs located between Tomarapi and Sajama Village at **Aguas Termales**. Run by Aymara families, these springs provide an opportunity to rinse off and relax beneath the snow-covered peak of Bolivia's tallest mountain. At **Termales Doña Ines** *(entry B$15)*, a bare-bones, back-to-nature experience awaits.

Dams of loose stone in the middle of soggy llama pastures form natural baths camouflaged in the landscape. These springs are a far cry from five-star wellness retreats. And that's all the better.

For a modest entry fee of B$15, you can park beneath Volcán Sajama and saunter over to a natural spa of warm geothermal water lined with evergreen algae. Though some smaller, scattered springs can be found at geothermal features around the park, the waters of Aguas Termales are a safer bet that feature a smattering of amenities for travelers.

Water temperature is typically warm, but not scalding. And the pools range from hot tub temperatures to barely warm bathwater, depending on the area you choose to rest in.

On-site changing areas provide a semi-private place to trade trail clothes for bathing suits. In contrast to natural hot springs in a Japanese *onsen,* for instance, bathing suits are preferred here. Owing to its heavy Spanish colonial influence, Bolivia remains a generally modest country when it comes to public bathing.

The mineral-rich waters beneath Volcán Sajama are heated by its volcanic activity. It's no surprise that they are believed to have therapeutic properties like soothing sore muscles and promoting mental health. In these springs, steaming waters contrast with the crisp, cool air of the Altiplano. And as you soak, you may spot wandering herds of llamas, alpacas and vicuñas strolling by. The occasional flyover from flamingos, or even an Andean condor, might occur for the supremely fortunate. This natural setting – free from large crowds, wristbands, towel rentals or massage services – enhances the experience, making these springs feel like a secret oasis in the towering Andean wilderness.

Beyond Parque Nacional Sajama

The Altiplano's largest city is home to its best-known Carnaval celebration, making it a can't-miss in February and March.

Oruro rises from the Altiplano's horizon like an urban oasis, a city of dust, devotion, and dancing. For much of the year, this overgrown mining town feels tranquil. But for a few electrifying days in late February and early March, Oruro transforms.

Here, Carnaval is at its best. Carnaval de Oruro is no ordinary festival. It's a kaleidoscope of sound and motion, where ancient Andean traditions collide with Catholic saints in a parade of fire-breathing devils and thundering brass bands on streets that pulse with the rhythm of Bolivia's soul. At its heart is the **Diablada**, the Dance of the Devils – a spectacle of swirling capes, golden masks, and a battle between light and darkness.

Oruro

TIME FROM PARQUE NACIONAL SAJAMA: **4 HRS** 

Delight in the Diablada

Every February, this high-altitude mining town explodes into a riot of color, sound, and myth during **Carnaval de Oruro**, considered by many to be Bolivia's most elaborate Carnaval festival. The streets of Oruro become a stage and its people performers. Thousands of dancers and musicians flood the city, parading in a tide of brass and rhythm, weaving their way toward the Sanctuary of the Virgen del Socavón beneath the blare of trumpets, trombones and bass drums.

The **Diablada** –the Dance of the Devils – is the center of it all. Beneath golden masks and colorful Andean headdresses, costumed dancers twist through the streets, locked in a battle between good and evil. Archangels with billowing wings lead the charge, while devils with glowing red eyes fight back in a hypnotic swirl of motion. This performance symbolizes a spiritual war, a centuries-old fusion of Andean folklore and Catholic tradition that served to keep indigenous stories alive after Spanish occupation.

For the best views, stake out a spot along the **Avenida Cívica**, where the largest crowds gather, or head to the **Plaza 10 de Febrero**, where the city's colonial bones shake under the weight of a thousand marching feet. **Carnaval Saturday and Sunday** are peak chaos, though the dates very slightly by year.

GETTING AROUND

Oruro is a relatively small city that can be explored easily on foot, especially if you're focusing on the central areas where most of the attractions are located. Bike rentals, taxi services and minibuses are also available. All of these services can be found at local vendors surrounding **Mercado Simon Bolivar**. Irregular trains to Uyuni depart from Oruro Station on Tuesday, Wednesday, Friday and Sunday. **Trans Atlas** runs six daily buses to La Paz.

CARNAVAL LIKE AN EXPERT

Valeria Arias, local photographer, guide and Dream Makers Bolivia founder shares her tips for making the most of Carnaval in Oruro, Bolivia's top destination for the festival. *DreamBolivia.com*

If you're traveling from La Paz or Cochabamba, book in advance. Buy bus tickets ahead of time. Buses fill up quickly and hotels will be booked. The best viewing spots are from **Plaza 10 de Febroro** at the heart of the parade. **Avenida Civica** is great for seeing dancers up close. **Calle Bolivar** is a good balance between the view and your own personal space. Most of all, respect the tradition. Carnaval is a religious festivity honoring the **Virgen del Socavón**. Some groups perform for faith rather than entertainment, so be respectful, especially during the Saturday pilgrimage.

CURIOSO.PHOTOGRAPHY/SHUTTERSTOCK

Carnaval de Oruro (p153)

By Monday, the dust settles, and Oruro exhales, breathing back into form as laid-back, high-altitude hub of commerce.

Climb to the Virgen del Socavón statue

Perched on a hill overlooking the city, the Sanctuary of the **Virgen del Socavón** is one of Oruro's most important and revered sites. This Catholic church, dedicated to the Virgin of the Mine, stands at the crossroads of Oruro's religious and mining history, reflecting the deep devotion of the city's people. Its significance is intertwined with the Carnaval de Oruro, where thousands of dancers and pilgrims make their way to the sanctuary as part of the festival's sacred procession.

Visiting the sanctuary is a powerful experience. The church itself is a striking blend of colonial and indigenous architectural styles, adorned with intricate altars, gold leaf, and murals that tell the story of Oruro's spiritual journey. The altar at the heart of the church houses a revered statue of the Virgin, believed by locals to protect miners and bring them good fortune. Many of Oruro's miners visit the sanctuary before embarking on dangerous work, seeking the Virgin's blessing.

The journey up to the sanctuary is as rewarding as the destination. You can climb the steps leading to the hilltop, which offer panoramic views of the city below and the surrounding Altiplano. The towering Monumento a la Virgen del Socavón, a massive statue of the Virgin, overlooks the city and adds to the site's spiritual and scenic allure.

EATING IN ORURO: OUR PICKS

La Casona: High-quality pizza, *salteñas* (meat and vegetable pasties) and a basic bar in a cozy space around the corner from Plaza 10 de Febrero. *9am-8:45pm Mon-Sun* $

Ay Jalisco Oruro: Ay Jalisco serves up nachos, tacos and ramen Mexicana close to Museo Nacional Antropológico Eduardo López Rivas. *5pm-9:30pm Wed-Sun* $

Restaurante El Criollito: Traditional Bolivian dishes dominate a menu of classics like *pique macho* (layered meat, potatoes and vegetables) and peanut soup. *9am-5pm Mon-Sun* $$

1221 Steakhouse: Carne experts specializing in burgers and chorizo steak in an upscale atmosphere. *6pm-9:45pm Mon-Wed, 12-3:30pm & 6-10pm Sat, 12-4pm Sun* $$$

Salar de Uyuni

LIMITLESS HORIZONS | WORLD-CLASS PHOTOGRAPHY | NATURAL WONDER

The salt flats of Uyuni are an unimaginable, bewildering sight. Spanning more than 10,500 sq km, this vast landscape of mineral-plated topsoil dazzles beneath both sun and moonlight – and it's still growing at a rate of 50km per year. In a time when many of Earth's natural wonders are disappearing, **Salar de Uyuni** is expanding.

There is a feeling here of being trapped between heaven and Earth. To travel through the salt flats is to be frozen in a static embrace, to be floating inside of a mirror reflecting mountains and machinery. It is here that the world-famous Dakar Rally reinvented itself into a South American tradition. And it's here that travelers flock for the most trip-defining photographs in Bolivia.

From December to March, the wet season coats the salt flats with a shallow layer of water, forming a mirror now famous around the world as Bolivia's main tourist attraction.

Visit the Uyuni Train Cemetery

A haunting monument of industrialization

A graveyard of iron and steam lies on the outskirts of Uyuni, where the last of the city's streets begin to give way to the nothingness of the salt flats beyond. This is **Cementerio de Trenes**, the Uyuni Train Cemetery, a place where the skeletons of industry sleep in the dust, their hulking frames scorched by sun and scarred by wind. These are the rust-bitten remains of Bolivia's rail empire, once the steel veins pumping tin and silver from the mines of Potosí to the edges of the Pacific coast.

Now, the engines lie still. Some sleep under layers of graffiti. Others corrode into the sand like ill-forged monuments to forgotten gods. Numbering in the dozens, these trains haven't moved in over 70 years, but their presence still carries weight. You can feel it in the silence between your footsteps on the gravel here. You can hear it in the clang of boots

GETTING AROUND

4WD is the only way to go on the salt flats. Most rental companies in Bolivia explicitly ban travel on the salt flats due to wear and tear on their fleet. For this reason – and the lack of navigational markers on the *salar* – local vehicles are owned and controlled by tour companies. You'll need to hire a guide or rent a vehicle insured for the salt flats in La Paz or Sucre. For the latter, mention you are planning to go to Uyuni. You'll be charged a premium.

TOP TIP

Stay an extra day or two. Salar de Uyuni feels tailor-made for photography, and while it's tempting to stop in for a photograph and carry on, this place rewards slow travel with a more immersive experience that allows for more photo-ops, more self reflection and relaxing recovery days in an otherwise harsh region.

SIGHTS
1 Cementerio de Trenes
2 Coqueza Mummies
3 Isla del Pescado
4 Kachi Lodge Hotel Ruins
5 Playa Blanca Salt Hotel
6 Tunupa Volcano

ACTIVITIES, COURSES & TOURS
7 Esmeralda Tours
8 Red Planet
9 Salty Desert Aventours

SLEEPING
10 Hostal La Magia de Uyuni
Hotel Boutique Andina (see 1)
11 Hotel Kachi de Uyuni
12 Hotel Palacio de Sal
13 Jardines de Uyuni
14 Piedra Blanca Hostel

EATING
15 Memos Cafe Bistro
Minuteman Revolutionary Pizza (see 1)
16 Restaurant 16 de Julio
17 The Hot Spot

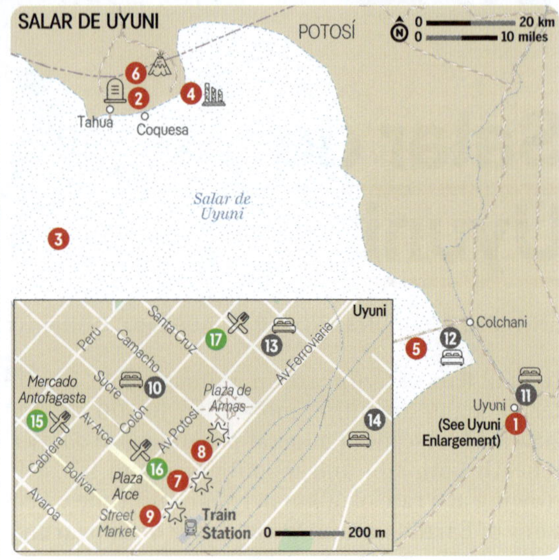

SIMÓN PATIÑO'S LOST EMPIRE

As WWI stoked the world's hunger for tin, Bolivian mining mogul Simón Patiño built railways to funnel the country's mineral wealth to the coast. Patiño's fortune soared, earning him a reputation as the 'Andean Rockefeller.' His miners' toil fuelled his European palaces. When Bolivia's 1952 revolution seized the mines, Patiño had already vanished into exile, dying in Buenos Aires in 1947. His legacy? A rusting iron and steel graveyard. Today, railways that once cut across the salt flats now corrode, slowly withering into the landscape they once steamed across.

against metal, as travelers clamber aboard – sans conductor – for a motionless ride.

Once, these iron horses hauled minerals that helped fuel the global economy and powered European wars. Today, they power a different kind of commerce. At the gate, vendors peddle salt-crusted souvenirs and llama keychains. Local artists weld pop culture icons from scrap metal – Transformers like Optimus Prime and giraffes welded from brake pads. The place feels like a post-apocalyptic art park mashed up with a museum exhibit no one bothered to curate.

And yet, it's beautiful. Stark. Wild. Perfect? The Uyuni Train Cemetery feels like a place where the past hasn't quite faded into obscurity. It's taken root in the earth.

Come at dawn or just before dusk and plan to spend at least an hour here. That's when the shadows stretch long, and the golden light dances across the iron. Bring a tripod. Bring a friend. Climb high and look out across the nothingness. Enjoy dancing with the ghosts of industry through this haunting portal to another time.

Catch Sunset on the Salar

A natural optical illusion

At sunset, the greyscale world of the *salar* transforms into a kaleidoscope of purple, red and silver hues bounding towards the horizon line. In the rainy season, soil and sky melt into one as a shallow coat of rainwater transforms the salt flats into a giant mirror. It's a striking visual at any time of day, but the mirror effect is most spectacular at sunset.

In the late afternoon, silhouettes of 4WD vehicles dot the horizon like a convoy of ghost ships, floating in a reflection so perfect it's difficult to tell where Earth ends and the sky begins. Beside them, the shadows of travelers wearing

ESTEBAN ALEJANDRO/SHUTTERSTOCK

Uyuni Train Cemetery (p155)

plastic rain boots wade into the shallows. They run, laugh, clasp hands and strike poses crafted by Uyuni's resourceful off-road guides.

Since the early 2010s, when new roads and a small regional airport cracked the region open to the world, these guides have turned photo ops into performance art. They carry props like plastic dinosaurs and chairs, transforming the featureless terrain into a canvas for optical illusions. Groups climb atop trucks, line up in folding chairs, and stage scenes that appear to bend the laws of light and scale.

Even in the dry season, when the mirror effect retreats and water is more scarce, the drivers usually know where to find it. Pockets of water still cling to the *salar*'s sunbaked surface, and with the right angle, they'll fool your senses just the same.

Uyuni's guides are more than prop crews; however. The thin sheets of water coating the *salar* move, and there is no guaranteed location to find them. Instead, finding the effect is a coordinated game of hide-and-seek played out between nature, guides and intermittent cellular service every day.

PHOTO TIPS FOR THE SALT FLATS

Carlos Cojinto, a professor of photography and visual arts at Sucre's University of San Francisco Xavier, shares his tips for getting the best photos on the *salar*. @caed_05

Wear bright colors. Primary and secondary colors are great against the dominant, white backdrop of the salt flats. Shadows are harsh during the day. Plan your trip around exploiting golden hours to look for dramatic silhouettes around sunset.

Trust the drivers! Most of them are very experienced in handling all kinds of cellphones and cameras, and they've seen every clever picture you could ever imagine on the *salar*. They can help you with composition. To that end, embrace the fun and let your inner kid out. How often can you be in a place like these salt flats? Have fun!

EATING IN UYUNI: OUR PICKS

Minuteman Revolutionary Pizza: A staple for high-quality pizza and affordable beer. Some say it's the best pizza in South America. *5-9:30pm Wed-Sun* $

Restaurante 16 de Julio: *Pique Macho* and pastas with balconies overlooking Uyuni's main drag. Great for a casual night on the town. *9am-10pm Mon-Sun* $$

The Hot Spot: Bolivian fusion including stuffed peppers, root vegetables and mussels. Michelin-level menu. Refined drinks selection. *5-9:30pm Tue-Sat* $$

Memos Coffee Bistro: Expertly crafted espresso drinks in a quant setting with light sandwiches, healthy bowls and snacks. *8am-1pm* Wed-Sat $$$

KICKSTARTED BY NEIL ARMSTRONG

Famed astronaut Neil Armstrong, best known as the first person to walk on the moon, was also among the first tourists to visit Salar de Uyuni.

During the Apollo missions, Armstrong recalled seeing what appeared to be a massive mirror reflecting from South America. This was the Salar de Uyuni full of water during the rainy season, a scene so striking that Armstrong made it a personal mission to visit the giant mirror when he returned to Earth. After concluding his media obligations following the moon landings, Armstrong followed up on his mission. In the early 1970s, he brought a moonstone gift to Bolivian astronomers on a visit to the salt flats, kickstarting a wave of tourism that has yet to subside.

The cottage industry revolving around photography here depends on finding a mirror. That mirror could be just a few kilometers from the *salar*'s most popular entrance at Colchani – or it could be an hour out into the featureless void.

Stargazing on the Salar

Stand beneath the Milky Way

After watching the vibrant colors of the sunset reflect off the salt crust, stay on the flats to experience the night sky. Salar de Uyuni takes on another personality as the sun settles on the Altiplano. At more than 3600m, the atmosphere is thin. The air is crisp. And on evenings with little moonlight, the Milky Way wraps its arms around the salt flats from one horizon to the next. Up here, when night falls, the white salt crystals coating the *salar* glint with faint echoes of starlight. At times, the crunch of salt beneath your shoes feels like stepping through the stars.

Many tour operators in Uyuni offer evening stargazing experiences that start with the sunset over the salt flats and merge into an astronomical adventure. Most tours include a guide with telescopes, helping travelers identify constellations like Orion and the Southern Cross, planets like Venus, Mars and Saturn, as well as our own galaxy overhead.

Even for experienced stargazers, the ultra-dark skies here offer a rare treat. Very little meaningful light pollution exists for hundreds of kilometers. The high altitude of Bolivia makes for less atmospheric distortion, the visual effect that causes stars to twinkle. There are fewer dust particles, moisture molecules and air currents between your eyes and the stars. The skies are literally clearer up here.

While anytime after dark is a good time, the very best views come between midnight and 4am. Some agencies like **Red Planet Expeditions** *(redplanet-expedition.com)*, **Esmeralda Tours** *(esmereldatoursuyuni.com)* and **Salty Desert Aventours** *(saltydesert-uyuni.com)* also organize overnight 4WD journeys that allow you to sleep directly on the salt flats – under the stars – to take advantage of peak viewing time. Most include dinner around a campfire, tents, sleeping bags and stargazing equipment. Bring plenty of warm clothing to make the most of your time in the brisk night air. The best months for overnight stargazing trips are during the peak of dry season from May to October.

Climb the Cactus Islands

Day hike above the *salar*

Towering islands of petrified coral and enormous cacti interrupt the flat, blank desolation of the salt flats. If the salty soil itself serves as a blank canvas for creatives, the islands are a lab for scientists.

They're a bizarre spectacle that often double as the only landmarks in sight. Though they number in the dozens and most are undeveloped, each island offers an opportunity for

Isla Incahuasi

exploration and a break from the sheer flatness of journeys across the flats.

On most of these islands, travelers can hike to a bird's eye view of the Salar de Uyuni on trails made of petrified coral. And these remnants of the area's prehistoric past tell a story. Look carefully, and you'll see layers of ancient sea life interwoven with pumice from deep below the surface of the Earth. Millions of years ago, that pumice bellowed from the belly of Tunupa volcano and skyrocketed through the atmosphere before crashing into the sea.

These eruption cycles repeated themselves over a geologic timespan that stretches for millennia. Scientists estimate that the volcano's last eruption took place around 1.4 million years ago. By those standards, the *salar* is still sporting a fresh coat of paint—its sunbaked crust remained a lake until about 40,000 years ago.

The largest islands, **Isla Incahuasi** and **Isla del Pescado** house waves of tourists during the dry season. Facilities have been built to accommodate those throngs on Isla Incahuasi, but travelers seeking a more isolated slice of the *salar* are free to venture onto its less developed, mostly unnamed siblings at their own choosing.

On the islands, hikers can spend anywhere from a few minutes up to several hours basking in the prickly shadows of trichocereus cacti, an endemic species that can reach 900 years in age, only found on the Altiplano. Evidence from major eruptions of Tunupa volcano lies on these trails, where hikers can spot volcanic rock coating remnants of an ancient seabed. You'll need a guide to tackle these trails; local tour companies know how to find each island and when weather conditions permit access for each.

A TALE OF FIRE AND SALT

Curious travelers can spot the ruins of a modern, domed village beneath a cacti-coated island near the town of Jirira. Here, the burned husks of geodesic domes sit atop wooden platforms that resemble a floating dock on a barren sea. These are the ruins of **Kachi Lodge Hotel**, a luxury tourist retreat owned by a joint Bolivian and Swiss group that was burned down in 2021 for violating a law that restricts any permanent structures on the salt flats.

At one time, the lodge was a prominent feature on major media roundups of the world's most beautiful places to glamp. And while search listings for the hotel still appear online, the platforms once housing domes going for nearly US$2000 per night are all that remain.

THE FAMED DAKAR RALLY

The **Dakar Rally** has a storied history on the Salar de Uyuni, marking one of the most iconic and challenging stages of the race. The overland rally – which originally began in Paris and ended in Dakar, Senegal – made its way to Bolivia for the first time in 2014, bringing competitors to the world's largest salt flat. Since 2020, the event has been held in Saudi Arabia.

The Uyuni stage became legendary for its sheer beauty, spectacular aerial photography and the technical difficulty that the disorienting terrain presented. For many drivers, racing across the salt flats became one of the most memorable and surreal parts of the Dakar Rally. Since then, Uyuni has become a recurring stop and a destination for racing fans.

R. AUGUST/SHUTTERSTOCK

Playa Blanca Salt Hotel

Visit the First Salt Hotel

Pit-stop at a curious construct

Though best known for its vast, otherworldly emptiness, the Salar de Uyuni is not utterly without its landmarks. In fact, in a landscape defined by the absence of features, the few that do exist tend to feel larger than life. Chief among them is the **Playa Blanca Salt Hotel** – a surreal structure built entirely from salt blocks pulled straight from the *salar* itself.

Constructed in the early 1990s, Playa Blanca is said to be the first salt hotel ever built on the flats. It was a bold idea: a lodge made from the very terrain it stood on, offering weary travelers the rare chance to sleep in the middle of the world's largest salt desert. But as tourism increased, so did the hotel's logistical problems. With no plumbing and no sanitation infrastructure, waste from the hotel began to threaten the fragile ecosystem of the *salar*. By the early 2000s, the Bolivian government stepped in, shuttering the operation and leaving the structure to slowly decay in the sun.

For a time, it sat in silence – just another curiosity being slowly reclaimed by salt and wind. Then came the Dakar Rally.

In 2014, the abandoned hotel was repurposed as a relay station for communications gear during the internationally renowned off-road race. Radio towers sprouted nearby. Satellite dishes blinked into the sky. And with that, Playa Blanca got a second wind.

Today, the hotel is no longer a place to sleep – but it is a place to gather, and a standard stopover on most salt flats tours. Inside, you'll find a small salt museum, a bar serving cold beers and soft drinks, and an ever-changing monument built from flags left by travelers from around the world. It's part watering hole, part time capsule, part art installation. Salt sculptures like flamingos and a monument to the rally dot the exterior. And in a place where nothing seems to stick, Playa Blanca endures. The building is crumbling, salty to the core, and, like all hotels, it's full of stories.

Hiking to the Caves of Mummies

Cultural history of the salt flats

In the desolate mountains that fringe the Salar de Uyuni, the area's surreal beauty takes a darker, more haunting turn. Hidden among the red rock canyons and wind-scoured plateaus lie ancient cave mummies, left behind by the Uru-Chipaya people more than a thousand years ago. Preserved by the dry, high-altitude air of the Altiplano, these naturally mummified remains offer an eerie, unfiltered window into pre-Columbian life – bones folded in fetal position, sunken faces wrapped in woven shrouds, staring out from hollowed stone chambers.

These aren't sterile museum exhibits tucked behind glass. The mummies linger here in the open. They are considered revered members of the wider Andean community. And, like most things in Bolivia, they haven't been fully cordoned off from the curious. Local tour companies have leaned into the mystery, crafting full-day expeditions that lead travelers through remote desert terrain to reach the caves.

Most tours depart from Uyuni and cost around B$500. Operators like **Red Planet Expeditions** *(redplanet-expedition.com)* fold the mummy caves into broader adventures across the high desert – often including visits to *chullpas*, the ancient stone burial towers that rise like weathered sentinels across the Altiplano.

Expect a full day of high-altitude driving, bouncing through valleys dusted in salt, past surreal rock formations twisted by wind and time. Eventually, you'll reach the **Coqueza Mummies** *(entry B$30)*, near the isolated village of San Juan, perched in the shadow of Tunupa volcano.

There's no velvet rope here. Just you, your guide, and the kind of silence that makes time feel like it is in from all sides. As you step into the caves, past lichen-stained stones and dust-covered, brittle offerings, you're standing face-to-face with the actual people who called Bolivia home long before it was ever a concept of a nation.

If you go, remember that these mummies are human remains. Most lie in minimally managed sites that depend on visitors to be respectful. It goes without saying, but no flash photos and (really) no touching. Fewer than a dozen visitors per day visit these remains.

THE LEGEND OF TUNUPA

The lore surrounding **Tunupa volcano** (5321m) adds even more mystique to the *salar*. According to Aymara and Quechua mythology, Tunupa was a powerful goddess, often depicted as a beautiful young woman. Long ago, she conceived a child while warring gods battled over her affection. To end the war, Tunupa exiled herself to a land with no mountains or gods. Eventually, her location was discovered, and a vengeful warrior came to destroy her unborn child. Tunupa wept endlessly, her tears mixing with her breast milk as she mourned. Her sorrow was so immense that her tears and milk flooded the valley, drying into a vast white desert below her peak. Tunupa herself was turned into the massive volcano now standing guard over the salt flats.

Beyond Salar de Uyuni

The second largest salt flat in Bolivia offers an even more remote experience than its larger neighbor.

Places

GETTING AROUND

Entrances near the towns of Sabaya and Tauca offer DIY access to Salar de Coipasa. The best way to access the area is by hiring a custom 4WD tour from Uyuni or Oruro.

With a map of the Salar de Uyuni in your hands, the giant, white question mark to the north is hard to miss. What is that? Yes, there is another stunning salt flat within arm's reach of Salar de Uyuni—**Salar de Coipasa**, the most remote of the remote.

A playground for adventure bikers crossing the Altiplano on two wheels, or wildlife tours passing through from Sajama, Salar de Coipasa offers allure to travelers who want to get completely off the beaten path. At its closest point, Salar de Coipasa sits just 20km from Salar de Uyuni; but to get there, you'll have to improvise a custom route from Uyuni or Tupiza.

Salar de Coipasa

TIME FROM SALAR DE UYUNI: **2-3 HRS (DRY SEASON ONLY)**

Spot wildlife at Lake Coipasa

While most travelers head to Eduardo Avaroa National Reserve for their share of Bolivian wildlife, Salar de Coipasa offers an alternative experience closer to cities like La Paz and Oruro. Though the salt flat is remote - six hours from Oruro and just over two hours from Salar de Uyuni - it cuts the travel time for bird-watching nearly in half if you're more interested in seeing wildlife and less concerned with the geologic features further south.

Accesible only during dry season, Salar de Coipasa remains largely untouched by tourism, and its location close (as the bird flies) to the now defunct Lake Poopó means migrating Andean flamingos have been descending on **Lake Coipasa** in greater numbers since 2015. In addition to flamingos, you're likely to see vicuñas, silvery grebes, and Puna ibises around the lake. There's also a remote chance of spotting an elusive Andean fox.

Bear in mind that Salar de Coipasa is more prone to flooding than Salar de Uyuni, and its crust is often more saturated with liquid. For this reason, access may be impossible during the rainy season.

Overnight on Coipasa Island

Chipaya Village is not the only community thriving inside the *salar*. In the center of the salt flats huddled beneath a volcanic island, the small town of Coipasa harbors a single hotel, a cave most often used by campers and a handful of cafes. Aside from camping, the town of **Coipasa** is the only practical outpost for overnighting in Salar de Coipasa. Fortunately, this rustic town seemingly perched on the edge of infinity is well-known for friendly residents ready to welcome travelers in this bizarre land.

See salt mines on the salt flats

Salar de Coipasa doubles as a salt extraction location for common table salt. While passing through, sporadic commercial saltworks can be seen on the shoreline, but for a closer look at the intricacies of salt mining, consider paying a visit to the market in **Colchani** on the way back to Uyuni. Many families in Colchani have harvested salt from the *salares* by hand for generations, and homegrown salt refineries are located behind numerous storefronts.

More compact than commercial factories, these family-run businesses feature salt drying locations, small furnaces, blending and bagging stations. Travelers have the opportunity to purchase salt from the area to transport home to the dinner table.

Chipaya Village

TIME FROM SALAR DE UYUNI:
6 HRS VIA HIGHWAY; 3 HRS OFF-ROAD

Visit a living ancient culture

Chipaya Village, nestled in the mountains about 6km from the shores of Salar de Coipasa, offers a glimpse into human life as it was thousands of years ago. Home to one of three oldest living cultures in the world – the **Uru-Chipaya** – this remote community has lived in the harsh Altiplano for more than 4500 years.

Walking through the village, you'll see locals dressed in traditional woven garments, speaking Chipaya, a language older than both Aymara and Quechua. Circular adobe homes here are topped with conical thatched roofs, designed to withstand both strong winds and flooding. Meanwhile, cultivated salt-marsh fields provided quinoa, potatoes and *cañawa* (an Andean grain) for the community.

Travelers who arrive with respect and curiosity are generally welcomed and well received. A journey to this village can take a full day from Uyuni, but pairs well with an overnight at Salar de Coipasa. Prepare to spend two or three hours strolling the streets, and be prepared to converse in Spanish.

THE STORY OF LAKE POOPÓ

Another memorable water feature populates maps of the Southern Altiplano – **Lake Poopó**. Once Bolivia's second largest lake, Poopó has all but disappeared. Once a critical stopover for more than 200 species of wildlife, the waterway has struggled to amount to much more than wasteland with a few marshy areas since 2015. Migrant flamingos have been forced westward towards Salar de Coipasa and Parque Nacional Sajama.

Government sources blame the lake's decline on climate change, but the mining industry may have also had a hand. River diversions between Lake Titicaca and Lake Poopó have siphoned much of the lake's inflow. People living in shoreline fishing communities are departing, leaving behind a graveyard for fishing boats slowly sinking into the soil.

Reserva Nacional de Fauna Andina Eduardo Avaroa

GEOTHERMAL MARVELS | FLAMINGO COLONIES | MARTIAN LANDSCAPES

TOP TIP

It's dangerous to go alone. Take a dedicated GPS. Even with a local eSIM, cellular coverage in this remote region is scarce. Do not rely on smartphone apps to help you navigate. It's best to lean on an experienced driver or a dedicated GPS device with satellite connectivity here.

Few landscapes on Earth compare to the otherworldly kaleidoscope of multicolored deserts, lagoons and volcanic peaks tucked into Bolivia's southwestern border with Argentina and Chile. At **Reserva Nacional de Fauna Andina Eduardo Avaroa,** travelers are pitted into a race against time down dusty roads of volcanic sand. Located a full four hours from Uyuni with scarce accommodations within, a visit to Bolivia's most frequented national reserve requires a dedicated effort and an off-road vehicle.

The reward for that effort is access to a landscape that often feels like a portal to another planet. Shallow lagoons of sulfur, borax and arsenic

GETTING AROUND

Travelers venturing here have two choices: hire a driver or go it alone in a rental vehicle. Either way, a 4WD is essential. There is no other way.

The reserve is accessible via a bouncing, four-hour drive from Uyuni or an even rockier, one-hour route over the passes of the Atacama Desert from San Pedro de Atacama, Chile.

The vast majority of travelers rely on private guide services to navigate the reserve, though its roads are also popular with adventure bikers.

Extremely experienced off-road drivers may attempt the journey; though GPS is absolutely essential and apps like iOverlander *(ioverlander.com)* also help.

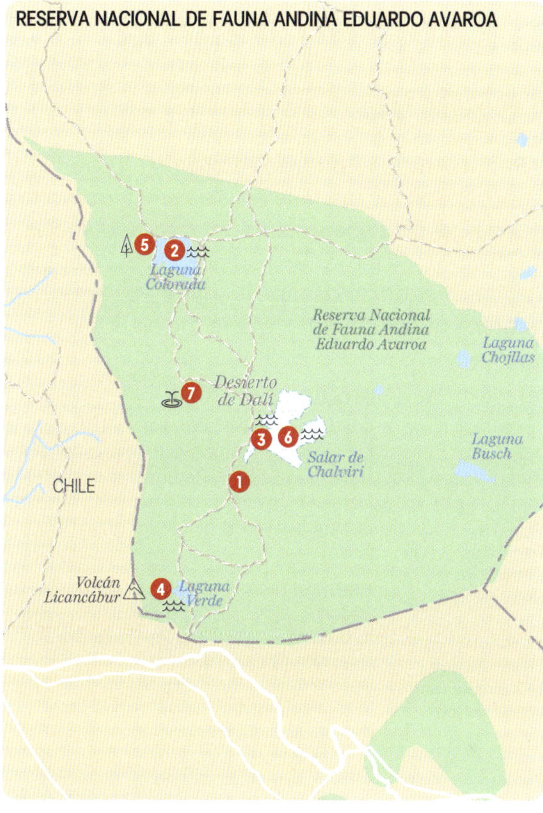

SIGHTS

1. Desierto de Dalí
2. Laguna Colorada
3. Laguna Salada
4. Laguna Verde
5. Reserva Nacional de Fauna Andina Eduardo Avaroa
6. Salar de Chalviri
7. Sol de Mañana

send hues of gold, ruby and emerald rippling across valleys filled with the fluttering, pink wings of flamingos. Volcanic fumaroles spout steam and primordial goo into the atmosphere; and vehicles bound down trails used by the world famous Dakar Rally – on roads that careen over the desert well above 15,000ft.

SPRING INTO ACTION

Interested in checking out other nearby geothermal sites? Visit Parque Nacional Sajama's selection of hot springs (p152).

ROAD TRIP

Driving the Eduardo Avaroa National Reserve

Reserva Nacional de Fauna Andina Eduardo Avaroa is an untamed, high-altitude fever dream of geologic marvels where flamingos wade through blood-red lagoons, geysers spew sulfuric steam, and ancient rock formations haunt windswept valleys. Tucked deep in the Andes near the Chilean border, this rugged landscape is shaped by time, tectonics, and the raw forces of nature. Here, where the air is thin, a mind-bending road trip awaits.

1 Aguas Termales

Hot springs cut through the high-altitude chill beside **Laguna Salada**. This rare way station within the park borders welcomes travelers with the opportunity to take a warm plunge beside flocks of flamingos and wandering maize birds. A trio of hostels located within walking distance provide hot meals and bare-bones lodging for around B$80 per night.

The Drive: Continue south for 20 minutes to a barren valley known as **Desierto Salvador Dalí**. Roadside parking provides an opportunity to soak in the surreal scenery.

2 Dalí Desert

Resting 15,583ft high, the Dalí Desert is named after Catalan artist Salvador Dalí. Here, haunting, isolated rock formations formed by wind erosion pepper a perplexing landscape capped by sulfuric volcanic peaks.

The Drive: The wide highway in the Dalí Desert leads directly to Laguna Verde. Continue south for about an hour until you see the **Volcán Licancábur** piercing the horizon. Follow the highway towards the Chilean border crossing. Bear east at Laguna Blanco and climb the hill to its neighbor, Lagunda Verde.

GALYNA ANDRUSHKO/SHUTTERSTOCK

Geyser, Sol de Mañana

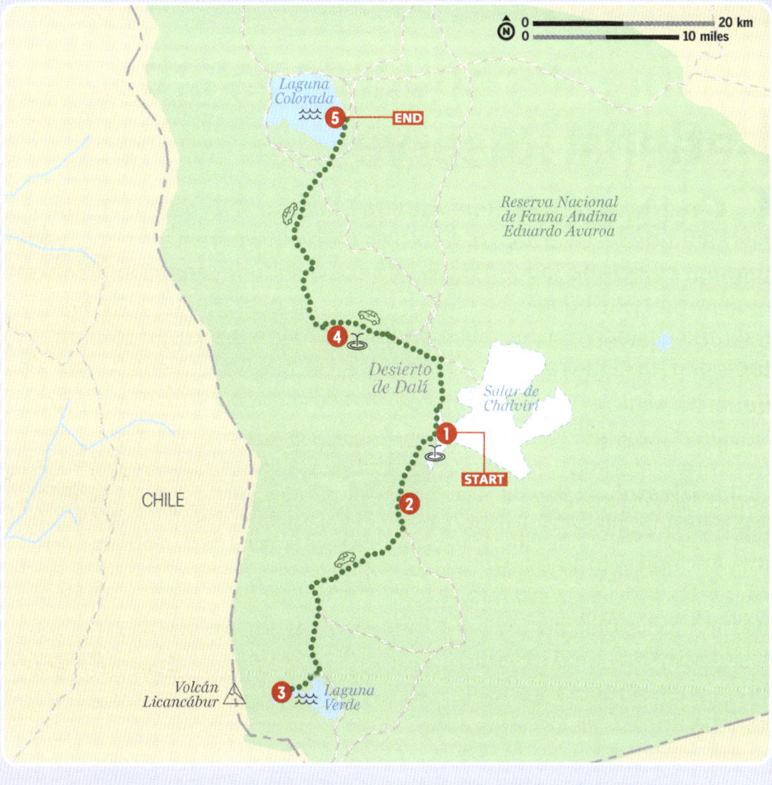

3 Laguna Verde

At the foot of a volcano on the Chilean border, this lagoon filled with arsenic creates an emerald illusion. It's best to visit Laguna Verde no later than mid-morning, when arsenic-laced breezes are calm.

The Drive: Retrace your steps towards Aguas Termales, passing **Salar de Chalviri**. Bear west on Camino Hito Cajon Villa Mar for about 15 minutes before continuing onto Camino Hito Cajon – Laguna Colorada. This black sand road climbs to 16,040ft before cresting to reveal a geothermal research facility and the entrance to the Sol de Mañana Geothermal Fields.

4 Sol de Mañana Geothermal Fields

At **Sol de Mañana**, visitors get a (smelly) front row seat to the slow growth of the Andes. Fumaroles, hot springs, geysers and mud pools fill a primordial landscape where travelers can get precariously close to pools of slippery, pungent soil. Use caution in this area. Steam vents can be dangerous.

The Drive: Pass through the last of the Sol de Mañana fields and climb through a winding, rocky terrain for about an hour before descending above **Laguna Colorada** (p168).

5 Laguna Colorada

As the road from Sol de Mañana descends, borax islands appear like icebergs amidst the rippling, ruby surface of Laguna Colorada. This mystifying lagoon of shallow, geothermal water has become a world famous hub of flamingos thanks to the ecosystem forming around the snow-colored mineral. Make for the observation tower located on a peninsula in the center of the lagoon to find parking areas, a coffee shop, a toilet (B$15) and shoreline access to thousands of flamingos year round.

TOP EXPERIENCE

Laguna Colorada

Laguna Colorada is considered by most to be the crown jewel of Reserva Nacional de Fauna Andina Eduardo Avaroa. The bustling flamingo colonies here are the primary reason some 40,000 travelers each year venture deep into this Andean wilderness on rugged backroads, and this destination is unlikely to disappoint any time of year. Bring your binoculars and join the flock.

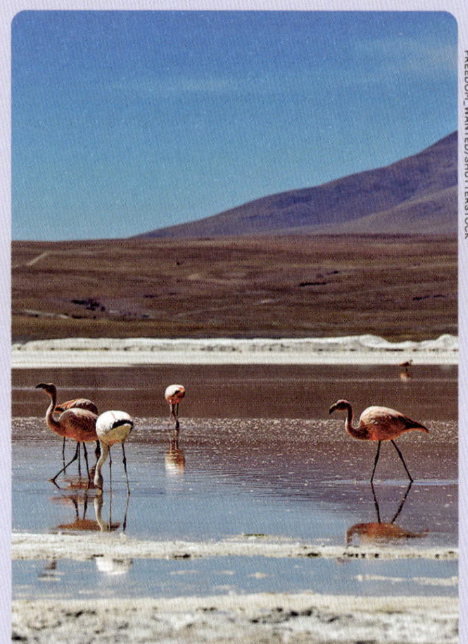

FREEDOM_WANTED/SHUTTERSTOCK

Laguna Colorada

TOP TIPS

- Flamingos dance together during mating season from September to December.
- During hatching season, from December to March, flamboyance (groups of flamingos) numbers are reduced as parents fly far and wide to find food for chicks.
- Bring small change for the bathroom in the observation tower.

Wildlife Tips

Avoid distressing wildlife. This is a strict no drone zone. Never wade into the lagoons.

Flamboyances of Flamingos

Up to 60,000 flamingos from three different species mingle in the warm, geothermal waters here. From viewpoints on shore, flamingos can be found plying the lagoon's waters for microscopic algae and shrimp, using their scoop-like beaks to filter tiny creatures into an easy meal. These mercurial birds play an underrated role in the history of evolution. They are one of just three bird species (the others being penguins and doves) that produce milk for their young. Both male and female flamingos possess this trait, which scientists believe may be an evolutionary holdover from 30 million years ago.

While the largest, brightest flamingos here may draw your eye first, pay special attention the smaller, paler James' flamingos. This species was thought to be extinct until the 1950s, when the colony here was discovered.

Flamingo populations are healthy in the area, but scientists say climate change will impact Laguna Colorada. Increased rainfall in the Andes produced by rising temperatures can alter the pH balance of the salty lagoon, shifting its color from red to teal. Stronger storms can even flood flamingo nests and destroy colonies.

Beyond
Reserva Nacional de Fauna Andina Eduardo Avaroa

A secluded desert highway leads to Bolivia's best bird-watching.

Past a military checkpoint on a northbound route out of Eduardo Avaroa National Reserve, one of Bolivia's best-kept secrets delivers a final treat for wildlife fans venturing to the southwest corner of the country, the **Route of the Andean Jewels**. Barely more than a Jeep trail, this ribbon of crushed rock and rubble careens through shallow ravines used by Dakar Rally racers before depositing daring road trippers on the shores of a remote group of lagoons beloved by Andean fauna.

Though colorful and breathtaking in their own right, these lagoons lay outside of the reserve's boundaries. They are smaller and flamingos gathered here are more condensed, enabling photographers a closer look at Bolivia's most famous avian attractions.

The Andean Jewels

TIME FROM EDUARDO AVAROA NATIONAL RESERVE: **5HRS**

Road trip around flamingo lagoons

A less-frequented group of flamingo lagoons lay on the northern outskirts of Eduardo Avaroa Fauna National Reserve near the Chilean border. Together, **Laguna Honda**, **Laguna Charcota**, **Laguna Hedionda** and **Laguna Cañapa** are known as the Andean Jewels. According to flamingo researchers operating in the area, these lagoons offer even better viewing opportunities than their renowned sibling to the south, Laguna Colorada.

Wildlife in the Andean Jewels are more accustomed to humans coming closer for photo-ops. Though a respectful distance is still required, the location of these lagoons outside the reserve itself makes access easier. In fact, researchers say Laguna Hedionda is the best place in Bolivia to view flamingos.

GETTING AROUND

The Route of the Andean Jewels is even more remote than Laguna Colorada. The easiest way to find this road of volcanic dirt and desert rock from outside the national reserve is to begin in **San Cristobal** and follow Highway 701 to **Los Flamencos Eco Hotel** (p178). Interior park roads leading past **Laguna Pastos Grandes** towards **Tapaquilcha** will also take you there.

WHY I LOVE THE ANDEAN JEWELS

Joe Sills, Lonely Planet writer

For weeks, dreams of flocking flamingos dancing over blood red waters at Laguna Colorada filled my head. Laguna Colorada – I was sure – would be a travel highlight I would never forget.

Thanks to a sudden hailstorm and a close lightning strike, that sentiment proved true. But while there are more flamingos at Laguna Colorada and the water itself is undeniably more photogenic, the birds in these lagoons made for better wildlife photography and fonder memories.

These flamingos are more adjusted to human visitors. They are not easily spooked by photographers roaming the banks, particularly at Laguna Hedionda, 'the stinky lagoon.' What's more, the roadside was also brimming with viscachas – a kind of hybrid between a jack rabbit and a chinchilla.

CHRISSY VASQUEZ/SHUTTERSTOCK

Laguna Hedionda (p169)

This sulphuric lagoon is colloquially known as 'the stinky lagoon,' and contains as many as 7000 flamingos condensed into an area only 13% of the size of Laguna Colorada.

During winter months, the lagoons can freeze over. Flamingos will gather together for warmth near Laguna Hedionda's hot, geothermal springs. Often, their bodies freeze into place with one leg punching through the ice. This unique survival adaptation helps the birds retain warmth from the lake during the area's coldest months. These flamingos can remain "frozen" in ice until it thaws, producing feeding opportunities for predators like Andean foxes and pumas.

The area's crafty predators are notoriously difficult to spot. Foxes are omnipresent but wary of humans. It's likely that an Andean fox may be watching you from a secluded hideout during your visit. Pumas are less common, but encounters between humans and the apex predator of the Andes have occurred.

Throughout the Andean Jewels, your chances of encountering most of the area's wildlife increases. More condensed than Laguna Colorada and less visited than most of the already sparsely-populated reserve nearby, this grouping of lagoons offers a glimpse into wild Bolivia without straying far from the vehicle.

Most visitors spend a few hours in the area; but **Los Flamencos Eco Hotel** (p178) provides a rare chance to spend the night beside Laguna Hedionda.

Tupiza

'WILD WEST' | OUTDOOR ADVENTURES | STUNNING LANDSCAPES

Cradled by cacti-peppered peaks peering up from valleys of sandstone spires, Tupiza feels like a world removed from the salt flats of Uyuni. This small but bustling town is home to horse stables, backpacker hostels and a land of legends tethering the history of South America to its northern neighbors.

Brimming with tuk-tuks and horse tack, Tupiza feels like Bolivia's farthest frontier – an outpost where fiery canyons split a desert landscape ripe for rock climbing, mountain biking, hiking and horseback riding. Today, Tupiza is a gateway to natural areas of towering rock cathedrals and cactus-studded ridgelines, a town that beckons travelers slowly making their way through the Altiplano to stay an extra day or two.

Most travelers stumble into Tupiza on their way to or from Uyuni, expecting a dusty layover before the salt flats steal the show. But those who linger soon find themselves under its spell. This is cowboy country, the kind of place where you can stretch your legs and immerse in the landscape on horseback or pack a box lunch for a picnic beneath bedrock.

The town itself is laid-back. In Tupiza, a handful of streets shaded by palm trees are flanked by market stalls selling fresh fruit, empanadas and gelato. The smell of grilled meat drifts from roadside barbecues and coffee shops packed with high school students and backpackers.

GETTING AROUND

Though Tupiza is small enough to navigate on foot, tuk-tuks are ubiquitous in this region and found on nearly every street corner. Originally an import from Argentina, they now line the streets of Tupiza and seem to appear out of thin air in the dusty canyon trails outside of town. Both tourists and residents constantly make use of these diminutive, puttering taxis. In fact, it's nearly impossible to take a photo in Tupiza without one in it.

TOP TIP

The compact, scenic streets of Tupiza make for a perfect break between long days of battering down rutted dirt roads. Take advantage and slow your pace.

Horseback Riding in Bolivia's 'Wild West'

Colorful canyons, cacti and caballeros

Tupiza delivers dramatic red canyons, towering cactus fields, and rugged landscapes best explored on horseback. Whether you're a seasoned rider or a novice, several local outfitters provide guided tours to immerse you in this breathtaking terrain.

SIGHTS
1 Plaza de la Independencia

ACTIVITIES, COURSES & TOURS
see 3 La Torre Tours
2 Valle Hermoso Tours

SLEEPING
3 Hotel La Torre
4 Hotel Mitru
5 Hotel Mitru Anexo

EATING
6 Alamo
7 Restaurant La Torre
8 Restaurant Pizzeria Pastipizza
9 Salteñas Especiales Marianita

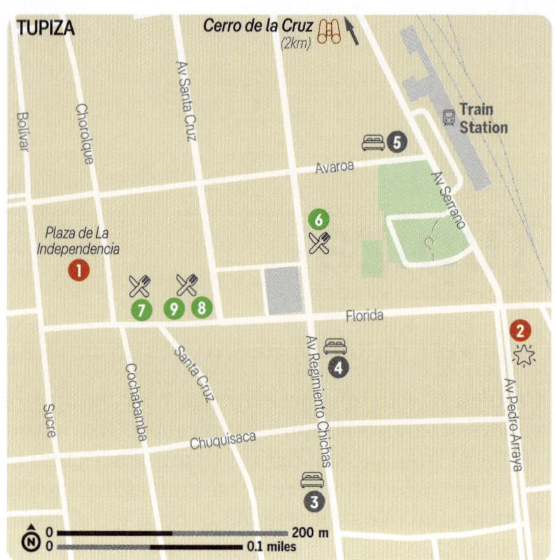

THE DRIVER'S SEAT

Agencies de Viajes owner **Ramiro Ancasi** has been manning the wheel for travelers across Bolivia for three decades. He gives his best advice for drivers that are new to the country. *(+5 917-129-1880)*

Be patient. Things do not happen quickly here. Roads close in the rural areas. Traffic in the cities can be heavy. The most important thing is to find a reliable car. Bolivia only imports used vehicles, so the reliability of a vehicle is more dependent on maintenance than age. Our highways have improved a lot, but dirt roads are common. Those roads are not marked well so you need to use GPS, a map or a driver to know where you're going.

Operators like **La Torre Tours** (*latorretours-tupiza.com*) and **Valle Hermoso Tours** (*vallehermosotours.com*) offer horseback adventures ranging from three-hour excursions to multiday treks. Shorter rides typically take you through mudrock and sandstone canyons to geologic wonders like Quebrada de Palmira, Puerta del Diablo, and Valle de los Machos, showcasing stunning rock formations and multicolored mineral deposits. For a more extensive experience, their seven-hour ride includes additional attractions such as **Cañón del Duende** and **Toroyoj**, where you'll traverse riverbeds and marvel at towering monoliths like La Torre. Prices start at B$200 per person for a three-hour tour, which includes horse and equipment, a Spanish-speaking guide, and guaranteed departures with a minimum of two participants.

For those seeking a combination of activities, some outfitters also offer a full-day 'Triathlon' tour. The day includes a 4WD tour, hiking, and horseback riding, allowing you to explore the wide range of canyons, peaks and springs around Tupiza comprehensively. This option is ideal for travelers looking to maximize their exposure to the region's natural beauty in a single day.

Hike to Cerro de La Cruz

The best view of Tupiza

For travelers looking to get a bird's-eye view of Tupiza's rugged beauty, a hike to **Cerro de la Cruz** is a must. This hilltop lookout offers a stunning panorama of the town, framed by dramatic red rock formations, rolling hills, and the distant peaks of the Bolivian Andes. It's an accessible, rewarding walk that's perfect for sunrise or sunset.

ALINA ZAMOGILNYKH/SHUTTERSTOCK

Cerro de La Cruz

The trail to **Cerro de la Cruz** starts just outside the town center, making it an easy trek for independent travelers. From **Plaza de la Independencia**, head south toward the Cementerio General, where a dirt path winds its way uphill. The route is well-trodden but can be steep and dusty, so sturdy shoes are recommended.

The hike takes about 30 to 45 minutes at a steady pace, with plenty of opportunities to pause and take in the changing views. Along the way, you'll pass scattered cacti and dry, rocky terrain that feels straight out of a Wild West movie. At the top, a simple white cross marks the summit, offering a peaceful resting spot with 360-degree views of the town below.

For the most breathtaking scenery, aim for sunset or sunrise, when the red rocks glow in the golden light. The trail is safe to hike alone during the day, but if going in the early morning or evening, consider bringing a flashlight.

Be sure to pack water, a hat, and sunscreen, as the sun in Tupiza can be intense. Whether you're a seasoned trekker or just looking for an easy adventure, Cerro de la Cruz delivers a rewarding escape with unbeatable views.

A TALE OF TUK-TUKS

You may be surprised to see a signature public transportation vehicle most associated with Southeast Asia in the middle of the Bolivian desert. Throughout Tupiza and the surrounding canyons, tiny tuk-tuks putter along dusty roadways that seem better suited for horseshoes. They serve as taxis, delivery trucks and makeshift school buses.

You'll find eager drivers waiting on nearly every corner of Tupiza. Just flag one down for a ride. You can even ask some tuk-tuk drivers for a sightseeing tour.

Nowhere else in Bolivia will you find this concentration of tuk-tuks. The reason? Argentina. The two regions share a common history and culture (Tupiza is just 30km from the border). And, as it turns out, transportation methods.

EATING IN TUPIZA: OUR PICKS

Restaurant La Torre: Excellent coffee shop and student hangout. A rare chance to find iced latte in rural Bolivia, plus tacos and other snacks. *3pm-10pm Mon-Sun* $

Salteñas Especiales Marianita: Fresh chicken and beef *salteñas* are prolific in Bolivia and these are some of the best. A perfect mid-morning snack. *8am-5pm Mon-Fri* $

Restaurant Pizzeria Pastipizza: Handmade pizzas with crispy dough. A favorite for celebrations; not far from Independence Square. *9am-10pm Mon-Fri, to 11pm Sat* $$

The Alamo: Incredibly kitschy international restaurant reminiscent of a Route 66 diner. Surprisingly good food and lively, fun vibes. *6pm-10pm Mon-Sat* $$

Beyond Tupiza

Legend has it that Butch Cassidy's final showdown took place here.

GETTING AROUND

The roads from Tupiza to San Vicente are rough, and you'll need your own 4WD vehicle if you want to make the journey on your own; otherwise join a tour group. Tuk-tuks won't carry you to San Vicente.

The region around Tupiza is forever linked to the legend of Butch Cassidy and the Sundance Kid, the infamous American outlaws who roamed South America in the early 1900s. After years of robbing banks and payrolls across Argentina and Bolivia, the duo found themselves cornered near the town of San Vicente, about 100km from Tupiza. Bolivian soldiers allegedly ambushed them in a final shootout, ending their storied run.

San Vicente serves as the gateway to retracing the outlaws' final days. The rugged, red rock canyons and winding trails around the town echo the Wild West landscapes they once rode through. Whether or not Butch Cassidy truly met his end here remains debated, but the legend lingers on nearly every dusty road in the region and especially in San Vicente, which now has a cottage industry built on the outlaw's name.

San Vicente

TIME FROM TUPIZA: **1 HR**

Chasing the ghost of Butch Cassidy

For history buffs, outlaw chasers, and anyone with a taste for the Old West, the remote route from Tupiza to **San Vicente** is a backcountry pilgrimage into the final, murky chapter of one of the Wild West's most enduring legends. Spend a half day visiting the town where Butch Cassidy and the Sundance Kid are said to have met their fate in 1908 – cut down in a shootout with Bolivian soldiers after robbing a mule train loaded with payroll.

Start your journey early in Tupiza where fresh *salteñas* and coffee can be found at the cafes near Independence Square. From here, hire a 4WD or join a guided tour. The drive over winding dirt roads takes about an hour, passing through scenery that has changed little in the century since the outlaws traveled this highway themselves. Squint, and it feels like their horses could still be riding just over the next ridge.

TIMOTHY THEIS/SHUTTERSTOCK

San Vicente Cemetery

When you reach San Vicente, head first to the **San Vicente Cemetery**, where Butch and Sundance are rumored to be buried in unmarked graves. There's no sophisticated monument, or elaborate fanfare. Faded hand-painted billboards and a humble blue street sign linger over the as-yet unverified graves. Some say the bodies were never positively identified. Others claim Butch survived and disappeared into anonymity. Most likely, though, they're beneath your feet.

Next, visit the **Museo Butch Cassidy & Sundance Kid** *(B$10)*, a humble but fascinating spot with period photographs, handwritten reports and oral histories from Bolivian soldiers who witnessed the ambush. The museum offers context and contradictions in equal measure.

Afterward, take a walk through the village – or, for the adventurous, follow a trail that traces the bandits' final flight, snaking through the same arid valleys and sandstone outcrops they once rode.

By late afternoon, begin the journey back to Tupiza, watching the long shadows fall across the land where legends make their final ride into the sunset.

BUTCH IN BOLIVIA

Butch Cassidy, the infamous American outlaw, fled to Bolivia in the early 1900s to escape increasing pressure from domestic police and Pinkerton detectives. After years of robbing banks and trains across the American West, Cassidy and his partner, the Sundance Kid, left the United States in 1901, settling in Argentina before moving to Bolivia around 1906. There the duo sought a new life, possibly hoping to live quietly, but soon resumed their outlaw ways, robbing payroll transports and mining company funds. Their final stand came in 1908 near the village of San Vicente, after robbing a local silver mine's payroll. Bolivian authorities tracked them down, and after a shootout, both were reportedly killed in a small adobe house.

Which Wilderness to Visit

The Southern Altiplano is roughly the size of California, a massive destination with an immense diversity of landscapes and cultures. While Uyuni makes the short list of most itineraries, the Altiplano's other wilderness areas require time and dedication to reach. Here are the pros and cons of each.

Where to go if You Love...

Photography

Look no further than **Salar de Uyuni** for filling up that social media feed. While photographers of all kinds can flourish on this alabaster dreamscape, the site is particularly well-suited for travelers seeking influencer-style portraits. During the wet season, the *salar*'s natural mirror effect produces a backdrop that's nearly impossible to replicate anywhere else on the planet. Local guides have mastered the art of portraiture here, and almost all of them come equipped with photo props ranging from chairs to miniature dinosaurs. In the dry season, the *salar*'s remote areas become more accessible, providing a surreal stage for stargazing photos under the Milky Way.

Wildlife

It's possible to see wildlife almost everywhere on the Altiplano. Alpacas, llamas and their cousins the wild vicuñas populate roadside pastures. The occasional flock of rhea (Andean ostriches) can also be spotted from the road; but the very pinnacle of wildlife watching here is **Reserva Nacional de Fauna Andina Eduardo Avaroa**. If you're a wildlife photographer toting a telephoto lens, consider spending several nights inside of the park. Don't expect luxury accommodations, however. Rustic hostels are the name of the game here. Thankfully, a few are located near the hot springs of Aguas Termales and provide an opportunity to soak your bones while flamingos saunter through shallow lagoons nearby.

Hiking

Sajama National Park is the unquestionable queen of day hiking on the Altiplano. The sprawling national park surrounding Bolivia's tallest peak offers excellent day hikes on the **Lagunas de Altura Trail** and also provides opportunities for treks to lesser-visited sites like **Sajama Base Camp** and **Wisalla Mountain**. Base camp in Sajama Village or Tomarapi for several nights to maximize your trail time in the Andes.

Adventure Sports

While each of the Altiplano's hubs offers a healthy dose of adventure, the highest concentration of adventure sports activities is in **Tupiza**. Horseback riding and hiking are the area's signature activities, but this striking desert landscape also serves as a gateway to more adrenaline-pumping sports. Rock climbing, rappelling, canyoneering and off-roading are all popular pastimes in the wilderness areas surrounding town. And local outfitters are well-equipped to get your blood pumping.

LOUIELEA/SHUTTERSTOCK

Laguna Colorada, Reserva Nacional de Fauna Andina Eduardo Avaroa (p168)

HOW TO

Before you go
Decide whether to visit during wet or dry season. Dry season offers more hiking and camping opportunities, while wet season brings the mirror effect to the *salares*.

When to go
The Southern Altiplano is a year-round destination. The best combination of wet and dry seasons tends to be in early December or early March.

Book ahead
Wet season means peak travel time for international travelers, especially in Uyuni. If you plan to visit between December and March, book well in advance.

Budget
Carry cash in local currency. While some rural vendors will accept US dollars, bolivianos are the preferred currency. As a rule, ATMs are only available in cities.

Finding Drivers & Guides

For experienced travelers, recommendations to hire guides and drivers in Bolivia may feel superfluous. Outside of La Paz, the roads here are sparsely populated and rarely suffer from traffic jams. This belies the logistical challenges of traveling in Bolivia.

Fuel shortages are frequent throughout the country. It can take several hours to wait through long lines at gas stations. Roads often lack proper signage and are more frequently than not still built out of a combination of sand, dirt, gravel and tarmac. Frequent toll checkpoints manned by corrupt police have also been known to shake down travelers for a few extra bolivianos.

During times of political unrest – which are common in Bolivia – travelers are likely to encounter roadblocks. While not likely to be dangerous, these blockades can force detours on even more rustic roads with even fewer signposts.

It is not lightly that we recommend hiring a guide and driver to navigate the Southern Altiplano. Fortunately, favorable conversion rates and an abundance of outfitters make this process relatively painless.

Places We Love to Stay

$** Budget **$$** Midrange **$$$ Top End

Sajama National Park

MAP p151

Hostal Oasis $ This modest but well-run hostel near the entrance of Sajama Village can provide transportation, private rooms and meal services to travelers on a lean budget.

Hostal Sajama $ Adobe, thatch-roofed huts near the town square of Sajama Village. Great for climbers: owner Eliseo is a climbing guide and arranges treks to the surrounding volcanos.

Albergue Ecoturistico Tomarapi $$ Community-owned lodge located beside a historic church and snow-capped peaks. Comfortable, (heated!) rooms and cultural tours hosted by local families.

Salar de Uyuni

MAP p156

Hotel Kachi De Uyuni $ Well-run, modestly priced 'salt hotel' in Uyuni. Unrelated to the glamp ruins on the *salar*. A great way to experience a salt-hotel-like experience without the price tag.

Piedra Blanca Hostel $ Warmly decorated rooms in a modern, concrete building with a bright central courtyard near Uyuni's town center. Group and private rooms available.

Hostal La Magia de Uyuni $$ One of the first hotels in Uyuni. Hacienda-style property featuring antique furniture, reliable utilities, and breakfast included in price.

Jardines de Uyuni $$ An upscale, Spanish-style hotel located on Uyuni's main drag. It's a favorite among veteran drivers and guides making their way to Uyuni from La Paz.

Palacio de Sal $$$ Built on the eastern shore of Salar de Uyuni in Colchani, Palacio de Sal is as its name suggests – a palace made of salt. Remote location means once you're in the palace, you're in the palace.

Crillon Tours Airstream $$$ A high-end, once-in-a-lifetime option for travelers without budget concerns. This camp spends wet season beneath Volcan Tunupa and dry season in the middle of the salt flats. Bolivia's peak salt flats experience.

Hotel Boutique Andina $$$ Upscale option with heated pool and rooftop restaurant overlooking the Uyuni Train Cemetery. Rooms are stylish and comfortable. Feels like a Colchani salt hotel dropped into Uyuni.

Eduardo Avaroa National Reserve

MAP p165

Hostal Efames $ The best of a trio of hostels o-perating inside the reserve at Aguas Termales Chalviri. This is the best of the limited options in the park. Location by the hot springs is unbeatable, but this is an extremely rustic experience.

Los Flamencos Eco Hotel $$ As close to flamingos as you can stay, this eco-lodge is on the shore of Laguna Hedionda. Rooms are well-appointed with views of the Andes and lagoons. Features a shared viewing area inside of a geodesic dome.

Hotel Tayka del Desierto $$ A stay here feels like walking onto a set from *Star Wars*. This lodge began life as an NGO project designed to provide villagers with an opportunity to make income outside of smuggling rings operating on the Chilean border.

Tupiza

MAP p172

Hotel La Torre $ Tidy boutique hotel in a colonial-era home. Clean bathrooms, and shared roof terrace and kitchen areas where you might meet other travelers.

Hotel Mitru Anexo $$ A slightly trimmed down extension of one of the nicest hotels in town, the adjacent Hotel Mitru. Guests have access to the main hotel's pool and reliable hot water.

Hotel Mitru $$ A charming desert oasis just a short walk from the center of Tupiza. The courtyard houses a scenic, palm-lined swimming pool set beneath murals of the desert. Rooms are modestly appointed but comfortable.

JOE SILLS/LONELY PLANET

Hotel Tayka del Desierto

Researched by
Michael Grosberg

Central Highlands

HISTORIC CITIES AND ALPINE SCENERY

The Central Highlands encompasses traditional rural villages and vibrant, architecturally significant cities, both set amidst beautiful mountainous countryside.

Judging by the ruins of the Incan settlements found here, this lofty, rugged territory, sandwiched between Bolivia's Altiplano to the west and its tropical lowlands to the east, has long been recognized and valued for its fertility and temperate climate. But it was the discovery of Cerro Rico's vast silver reserves that jump-started the Spanish empire in the Americas. The wealth that was spawned, and the needs of servicing Potosí's mining industry, whatever the cost to indigenous labor, led to the region's development.

Gorgeous Sucre, which originated as a graceful living quarters and administrative center, later became the birthplace of Bolivia's independence in 1825. Its architecture and laid-back appeal, surviving centuries, draw travelers also looking to get out to trekking trails of the uniquely contoured and multicolored Cordillera de los Frailes. Once-glorious Potosí's treasure trove of ornately designed religious buildings and pastel-colored homes sit under the shadow of Cerro Rico, whose still-operating mines can be visited.

Lower-altitude Cochabamba, possibly Bolivia's most pleasant city, has an ideal climate and culinary scene worth tasting. Throughout, there are lovely, little-known colonial towns; it's well worth eschewing the city-to-city mode of travel to explore them. A more distant past is evoked by the Inca ruins in the Cochabamba Valley, but Parque Nacional Torotoro has the last laugh on the age front: it's bristling with dinosaur footprints and fossils, some of which date back 300 million years.

DEVIN BEAULIEU/SHUTTERSTOCK

THE MAIN AREAS

COCHABAMBA
Great food and nearby outdoor adventures. **p186**

SUCRE
Architectural elegance, history and lively street life. **p202**

POTOSÍ
Empire's beginnings revealed at elevated mining town. **p216**

For places to stay in the Central Highlands, see p231

AGUSTIN JOYA SOTO/SHUTTERSTOCK

Left: Fiesta de la Virgen de Guadalupe, Sucre (p205); Right: Cristo de la Concordia (p186)

Find Your Way

Geographically the heart of the country, the Central Highlands is a vast, pastoral and mountainous region dotted with remote villages and three major population centers, the latter well served by intercity buses.

Cochabamba, p186
This big city surrounded by mountains and blessed with a Mediterranean climate is considered Bolivia's culinary capital.

TRUFI

Whether a minivan, *micro* or *trufi* (shared car/minibus), these collective vehicles servicing fixed routes are often the most comfortable and efficient means of getting around. Most especially for the Sucre to Potosí and Cochabamba to Torotoro routes.

BUS

Getting between towns can be slow and sometimes uncomfortable – if venturing beyond the Potosí–Sucre paved highway, the route between Cochabamba and Sucre is particularly slow. Coming from La Paz, most travelers choose to reach Potosí and Sucre from the south via Oruro.

PLANE

There are frequent flights to Cochabamba and Sucre from La Paz and Santa Cruz; Cochabamba has connections to various regions. It's a quick and cheap flight between Cochabamba and Sucre. There's no functioning airport in Potosí

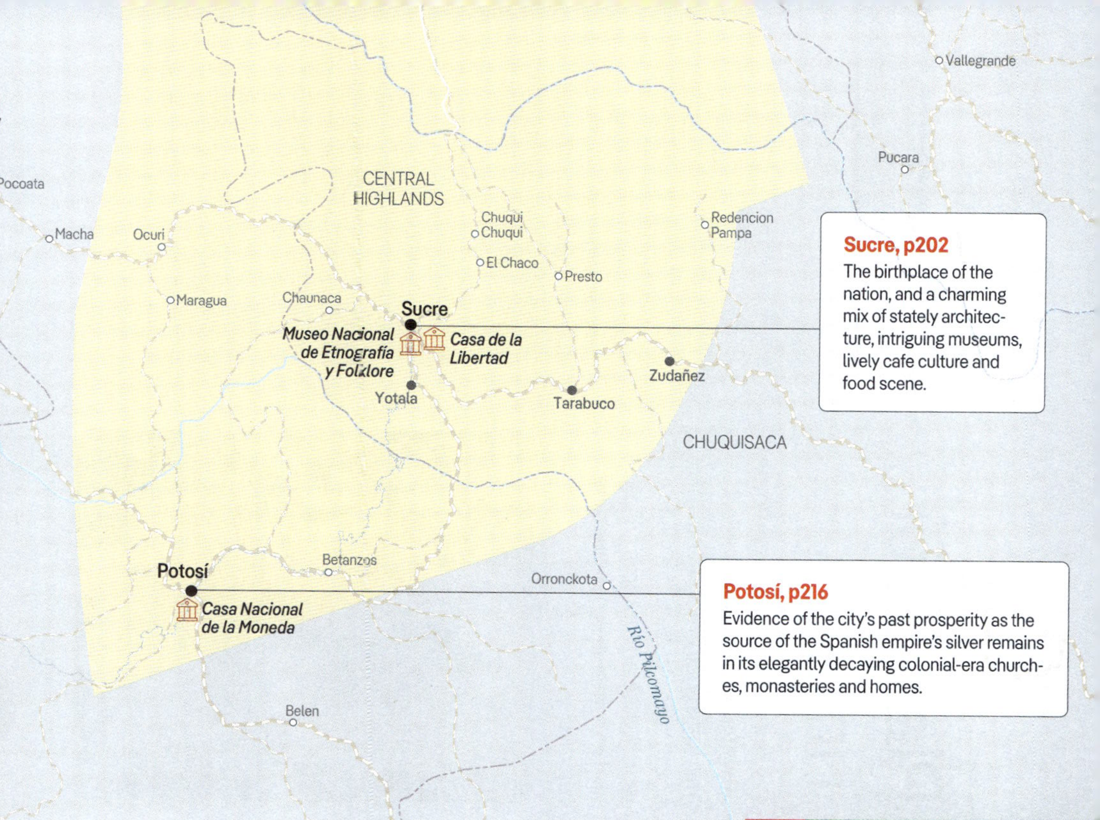

Sucre, p202

The birthplace of the nation, and a charming mix of stately architecture, intriguing museums, lively cafe culture and food scene.

Potosí, p216

Evidence of the city's past prosperity as the source of the Spanish empire's silver remains in its elegantly decaying colonial-era churches, monasteries and homes.

Plan Your Time

Cochabamba, Sucre and Potosí are aligned in a geographical and logistically helpful north–south axis. All deserve visits with worthwhile adventures, villages and mountains in surrounding regions.

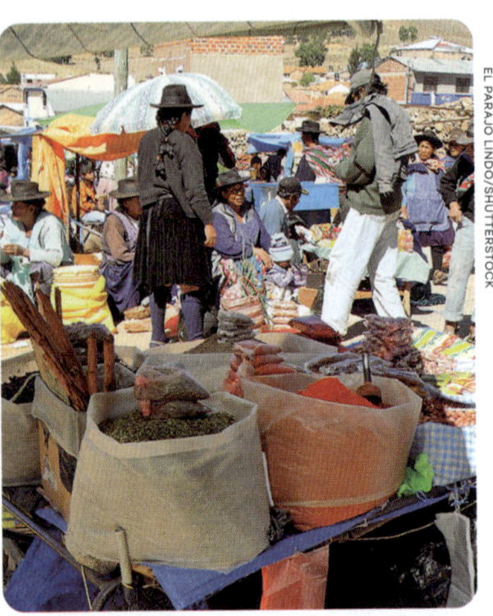

EL PARAJO LINDO/SHUTTERSTOCK

Sunday market of Tarabuco (p211)

If You Only Do One Thing

- Beeline it to the architectural jewel-box city of **Sucre** (p202) and plan to stay for several days; try to arrange your visit to include a Sunday in order to get out to the major market at **Tarabuco** (p211).

- Make reservations at one or two of Sucre's outstanding **tasting menu restaurants** (p207), and otherwise enjoy the city's excellent cafe scene, particularly those with breathtaking views.

- There's no shortage of fascinating **museums** (p209) to choose from, whether on Bolivia's independence history, indigenous textiles, mineral wealth or palaeontology. Accommodations are highlights as well, since many, regardless of budget, are housed in restored colonial-era buildings.

Seasonal Highlights

The region's climate is mostly mild with ideal temperatures for daytime hiking. Evenings can get frosty, especially at highest elevations. Religious and cultural festivals fill the calendar.

FEBRUARY

Bring your earplugs for dynamite, a loud brass band and dancing with cross-carrying miners around Cerro Rico in Potosí on **Dia de los Compadres** (p228).

MARCH

Tarabuco's indigenous festival **Pujllay** (p205) bursts into life on the third Sunday in March with a Quechua mass, folk dancing, music and traditionally clad *campesinos* (subsistence farmers) from surrounding communities.

MAY

For the brave and curious, in the northern part of Potosí department, several towns host ***tinku* 'festivals'** (p228), essentially semi-choregraphed brawls that last for two to three days. An associated traditional dance is performed elsewhere, like Potosí.

A Week-Long Trip

- Head to **Sucre** and follow our one-day itinerary, experiencing the best of the city, from its fine dining to its museums.

- As soon as you arrive, book a two-day hiking trip into the **Cordillera de los Frailes** (p213), a stunningly beautiful region dotted with small traditional villages.

- Grab a ride to the high-altitude city of **Potosí** (p216). After catching your breath, take your time wandering its cobblestone streets, appreciating the finely preserved architecture, and take a guided tour of the **Casa Nacional de la Moneda** (p216), one of Bolivia's best museums.

- Consider the physically fraught but memorable underground mining tours of **Cerro Rico** (p218).

Two Weeks to Travel

- Begin in **Cochabamba** (p186), where you can plan a few days around dining out, whether sampling the city's signature *salteñas* (meat and vegetable pasties), or lively *churrasquerias* (BBQ restaurant).

- Wander the massive market, take a convent tour and get views on the entire valley from the **Cristo de la Concordia** (p186).

- Take two full days visiting the spectacular geology and caverns at **Torotoro National Park** (p194); back in the city, choose a day out climbing **Pico Tunari** (p193), visit the ruins at **Incallajta** (p198) or relax at **Laguna Corani** (p201).

- Next, fly or bus it to **Sucre**, possibly the country's loveliest city with museums galore, before getting a ride to **Potosí** to learn about its silver mines, both past and present.

JULY

Middle of the long, dry period that's ideal for climbing **Pico Tunari** (p193) and hiking the **Cordillera de los Frailes** (p213). No matter the daytime temperatures, at altitude things can still get chilly at night.

AUGUST

Catch merrymaking at the **Fiesta de la Virgen de Urkupiña** (p205) in Quillacollo, just outside Cochabamba and **Día de la Patria** (Independence Day) in Sucre, with parades, traditional dancing and live music.

NOVEMBER

Make your way to Aiquile for the **Festival del Charango** (p228) when the country's premier *charango* (stringed instrument like the Spanish mandolin) musicians compete for the top accolade – the 'Golden Charango.'

DECEMBER

Pack a raincoat and umbrella (really through February) for the occasional downpour, and sometimes river flooding. Nevertheless, sunny days aren't uncommon and city streets are festooned with lights and decorations for Christmas.

Cochabamba

FINE FOOD | MARKET SHOPPING | HISTORIC BUILDINGS

GETTING AROUND

Taxi hire app Yango Lite works well, does airport pickups and is often cheaper than taxis hailed off the street. Cash only. Convenient *micros* and *trufis* (shared cars/minivans) display their destinations and run to all corners of the city *(B$3)*.

Walking the city center during the daytime, as well as the leafy, upscale neighborhoods of La Recoleta and Queru Queru, is safe and recommended.

Cochabamba's light-rail system has two functioning lines: the 15km long Green running east to Quillacollo and south to Sipe Sipe; the 7km long Red line runs south. Tickets available at all stations.

A place of contradictions, Cochabamba, Bolivia's second largest city, is definitively urban with a Mediterranean climate and well-off, fashionable neighborhoods. It's also the heart of the country's Quechua-speaking, most agriculturally significant region. Widely considered one of Bolivia's most livable cities, with a foot firmly planted facing forward, Cochabamba's also a stronghold for left-leaning political activism and protest. The city lies in a fertile green bowl, 25km long by 10km wide, amidst a landscape of fields and low hills. But just to the northwest rises Cerro Tunari (5050m), the highest peak in central Bolivia. The roomy, ever-developing new-town avenues have a wide choice of restaurants and a lively bar scene driven by students and young professionals. It's also the base for outdoor adventures further afield, including a do-not-miss trip to Parque Nacional Torotoro. You might find yourself staying longer than planned.

Sublime Valley Views

City sights from a mountaintop

It's all about perspective. Flying into Cochabamba, the **Cristo de la Concordia**, the immense Christ statue that's become the city's iconic landmark, seems almost diminutive. And Cerro de San Pedro (2800m), the mountaintop just to the east of the city center on which it stands, is dwarfed by a surrounding broad range with several peaks over 5000m. Up close, however, it's easy to appreciate the massive size of the 2000-ton statue. It's in fact the second largest of its kind in the world, 44cm higher than the famous Cristo Redentor in Rio de Janeiro, which stands 33m high, or 1m for each year of Christ's life. Cochabambinos justify the one-upmanship by claiming that Christ actually lived *'33 años y un poquito'* (33 years and a bit). Truly breathtaking 360-degree panoramic views are worth the trip. The city, hemmed in by mountains, sprawls below. Other than scenery, there's not much else going on up top: a couple of

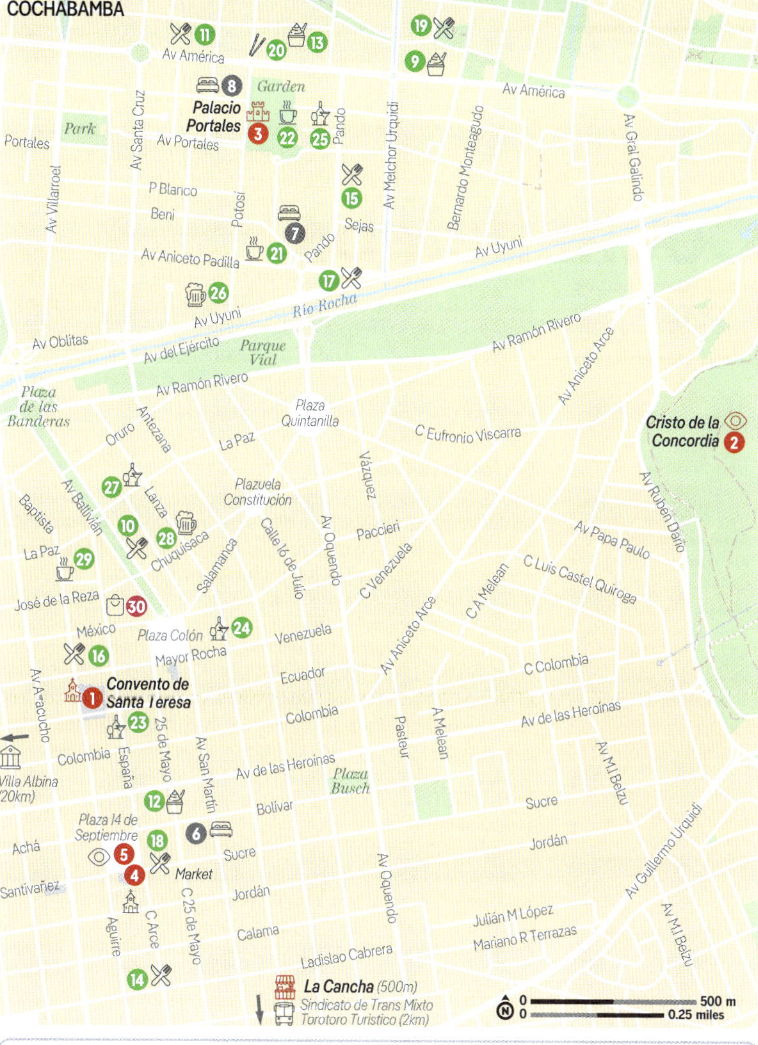

HIGHLIGHTS
1 Convento de Santa Teresa
2 Cristo de la Concordia
3 Palacio Portales

SIGHTS
4 Catedral Metropolitana
5 Plaza 14 de Septiembre

SLEEPING
6 Cesar's Plaza
7 Gran Hotel Cochabamba
8 Hotel Aranjuez
Hotel Boutique La Casa de Margarita (see 19)
Running Chaski Hostal (see 16)

EATING
9 Amalfi Helados Acai
Casa de Campo (see 17)
10 Chipotle
11 Clementina
12 Cristal
13 Donal
Dumbo (see 12)
14 Empanadas Otah
15 Globo's
16 La Cantonata
17 La Estancia
18 Mikuy Cafe Cultural
19 Pizzeria La Casa de Margarita
20 Sansei Oscar Kotoriy Restaurante
Wist'upiku (see 10)

DRINKING & NIGHTLIFE
Espresso Café Bar (see 4)
21 Hoy Hay Café
22 Huayllani La Hacienda del Té
23 Incantatio Café Temático
24 La Tirana
25 Mandarina Lounge
26 Muela del Diablo
27 Novecento
28 Suassuna by Fragmentos
29 Typica Café

SHOPPING
30 Asarti
Sombreros Boston (see 4)

TOP TIP

The flight between La Paz and Cochabamba's Jorge Wilstermann International Airport must be one of the world's most incredible (sit on the left coming from La Paz, the right from Cochabamba), with fabulous views of the dramatic Cordillera Quimsa Cruz and a (disconcertingly) close-up view of the peak of Illimani.

WATER WARS

The eyes of the world turned to Cochabamba in 2000, when its citizens took to the barricades to protest water rate increases. The World Bank had forced the Bolivian government to sell off its water company to US giant Bechtel to provide financing for a tunnel that would bring water from the other side of the mountains. The rate hikes brought hundreds of thousands of citizens out in protest, sparking national uprisings and eventually driving Bechtel out. Dubbed 'the Water War,' it helped usher Evo Morales and his party Movement Towards Socialism (MAS) to power.

souvenir stalls, quick eats and families and couples, especially on weekends, enjoying themselves.

The very steep, shade-free footpath from the base of the mountain (1250 steps), near the eastern end of Av de las Heroínas, is only worth considering if you're in the mood and shape for an intense cardio workout at high altitude. Locals warn of the threat of robberies, so it's safest to avoid going solo, though plenty of locals jog up for exercise. The *teleférico (round-trip B$15)*, when not shut down for maintenance, is the way to go (irregular hours when open). The station is at the edge of a public park near the corner of Heroínas and Ruben Dario. Taxis charge B$40 for the round trip to the top, including a half-hour wait; the best option if you're visiting in the early evening to get a glimpse of the city being transformed into a sea of sparkling lights.

Street Marketing

Get lost in La Cancha

Looking for herbal diabetes medicine, several gallons of vodka or a car-sized dresser? What about a llama fetus? The paradigmatic Bolivian market, and one of the largest in South America, Cochabamba's **La Cancha** sprawls across a vast acreage of maze-like streets, as well as an equally large network of indoor stalls, all to the east of the city's old bus terminal. Wednesday and Sunday are busiest and absolutely overwhelming in their combined crush of humanity and vehicles; best avoided if you prefer even a little elbow room. There's nary space to walk, and the streets themselves turn into one massive traffic jam. Safety isn't a concern, but watch out for pickpockets as you would in any dense urban area. If accessing the market by taxi, best to be dropped off a good ways to the north around Av Calama or Ladislao Cabrera.

Stalls selling similar types of goods or services are grouped together. For example, more than a dozen barbershops line Av Barrientos. The largest and most accessible area is Mercado Cancha Calatayud, which spreads across a wide area along Av Aroma and south toward the former railway station. It's your best opportunity to see local dress, which differs strikingly from that of the Altiplano. The Mercado de Ferias spills out around the old railway station. *Artesanías* (stores selling locally handcrafted items) are concentrated along the alleys near the junction of Tarata and Arce, at the southern end of the market area (you can also scour the stalls behind the main post office for inexpensive souvenirs). Food of course is abundant, from pyramidal piles of strawberries, sacks of quinoa and every butchered cut of meat.

EATING IN COCHABAMBA: QUICK EATS

Wist'upiku: Chain serving *pasteles* (fried dough with a variety of stuffings), empanadas and *wist'upiku* (an empanada variant). *7:30am-6:30pm Mon-Sat* $

Mikuy Cafe Cultural: The light-filled atrium at this restored colonial-era building has sandwiches, crepes, pastries and good cappuccinos. *8am-9pm* $

Empanadas Otah: Hole-in-the-wall spot where you can quickly tackle large, juicy empanadas washed down with a juice. *8am-4pm Tue-Sat* $

Amalfi Helados Acai: Deliciously refreshing, whether as a dessert or meal; acai served by weight, with all the toppings. *9am-8pm* $

GRAYSONSTOCK/SHUTTERSTOCK

Silpancho

The sidewalks of several avenues running north to south between La Cancha and downtown, nearly all the way to Av Heroínas, are chock-a-block with street vendors selling a similar variety of goods. Foot traffic can be slow going, especially midday, as there's not much room for pedestrians.

Fo more sedate shopping, try **Asarti** *(asarti.com)* for expensive, export-quality alpaca clothing; cheaper alpaca- and llama-wool *chompas* (sweaters) can be found in the markets. And check out **Sombreros Boston** for handmade straw hats. The city's largest and most modern mall with relatively upscale shops, Hupermall, as well as upscale clothing boutiques, are in la Recoleta to the north of downtown.

Sample Cochabamba's Duelling Desserts

A sweet-tooth tour

In the center of town, on Av de las Heroínas, between España and 25 de Mayo, are a jumbo-sized **Dumbo**, **Cristal** and **Donal**, crowding one another in a kaleidoscopic jumble of lights, signs, and displays of gelato flavors, cakes and other elaborately crafted desserts. All serve a range of foods throughout the day, from pancakes to mediocre burgers, but families flock here in the evenings for gut-busting servings of dessert.

Competing for *cochabambinos'* bolivianos is **Globo's**, with three locations across the city – the multistory outlet on Av Pando in La Recoleta, perhaps the most festive of the lot

CULINARY SMORGASBORD

Cochobamba has a dazzling array of local specialties, commonly on restaurant menus, including the gut-busting *pico a lo mancho* (meats and sausages, onions, spicy peppers and tomatoes on thick french fries); *silpancho* (schnitzel-style meat, rice and potatoes); *lomo borracho* (beef with egg in a beer soup); and *picante de pollo* (chicken in spicy sauce).

There's tasty street food and snacks all over Cochabamba; the *papas rellenas* (potatoes filled with meat or cheese) at the corner of Achá and Av Villazón are particularly delicious. Great *salteñas* (meat and vegetable pasties) and empanadas are ubiquitous, and locals swear by the sizzling *anticuchos* (beef-heart skewers). Argentine-style *churrasquerías* (restaurant serving barbecued meat) can also be found on a pedestrian plaza called Blvd La Recoleta.

DRINKING IN COCHABAMBA: CAFES

Typica Café: Locations downtown and in Recoleta; oases of bohemian bric-a-brac with garden seating, coffee varieties and quick bites menu. *7:30am-10pm*

Hoy Hay Café: Full-bodied espresso drinks, along with pastries in plant-filled, sophisticated space. *8am-9pm Mon-Sat*

Huayllani La Hacienda del Té: Idyllic setting in rear terrace of Palacio Portales, with cakes, pies and other small food plates. *8:30am-12:30pm & 3:30-8pm Mon-Sat*

Espresso Café Bar: Old-school spot with regulars, mostly men chatting with old buddies or perusing the papers while sipping large cups of espresso. *8am-6:45pm Mon-Sat*

CONVENT HIERARCHY

The first daughters of *cochabambino* families were strongly pressured to enter the convent. An elderly nun had to pass on before a new young nun was allowed in. Those who paid a considerable dowry (equivalent to more than US$150,000 in modern money) earned a *velo negro* (black veil) and a place on the council responsible for all decisions. They were blessed with a private stone room with a single window, and spent most of their day in prayer, religious study and activities such as sewing tapestries. Less-wealthy, second-class nuns wore a white veil and attended to the *velo negros*. The poorest, who couldn't afford any dowry, were *sin velos* (without veils), who attended to menial tasks.

– which mixes kid-friendly playground elements with a nightclub feel. Nearby, a two-story all-glass outlet of **Donal** in Queru Queru has a retro futuristic style that's enhanced at night by a ceiling of sparkling lights.

Religious Isolation

Imagine convent life

Contact with the outside world was forbidden. Even family visits were no-touch. That it was a heavily sought-after life speaks to the limited opportunities for women. Stepping inside the noble, timeworn **Convento de Santa Teresa** *(facebook.com/conventomuseosantateresacbba; tours B$30, an additional B$25 for photography)* is like stepping into a Gabriel García Márquez novel. Forty-five-minute guided tours, in Spanish, of this gracefully restored complex allow you to imagine the completely cloistered existence of the nuns who spent most of their lives within its heavily fortified walls. The tours start each morning hourly from 9am to 11am, with afternoon tours starting at 2:30pm, 3:30pm and 4:30pm.

A strict Catholic order with a strong devotion to the Virgin Mary, the Carmelites are thought to have been founded in the 12th century on Mt Carmel. The order believes strongly in the power of contemplative prayer and shuns the excesses of society. After the original building, built in 1760, was destroyed in an earthquake, a new church was built in 1790 with an excess of ambition, but was too big to be domed. Much of the building has been painstakingly restored over the past decade, including renewing access to the walkway around the domed roof with spectacular city views.

The rules inside the convent were strict. Personal effects weren't permitted and communication with other nuns was allowed for only one hour a day – the rest was spent in total silence. Bedrooms weren't exactly an oasis of comfort. The tour takes you through a fully furnished (one bed) austere replica bedroom. Meals were eaten without speaking and contact with the outside world was almost completely prohibited. Once a month each nun was allowed a brief supervised visit from her

EATING IN COCHABAMBA: OUR PICKS

Muela del Diablo: The outdoor patio of this hip, sophisticated place has a worthy menu, with more than a dozen varieties of artisanal wood-fired pizza. *5:30-11:30pm Mon-Sat* $$

La Estancia: Thick steaks (it's worth upgrading to the Argentine meat), fish and chicken, sizzled on a blazing grill. *noon-3pm & 6-10pm Mon-Sat, 3:30-10pm Sun* $$

Casa de Campo: A Cochabamba classic, this cheerful, partly open-air restaurant is a traditional spot to meet and enjoy Bolivian dishes and grilled meats. *noon-11:30pm* $$

Pizzeria La Casa de Margarita: Set in a boutique hotel's charming garden and living room, with many varieties of pizza, lasagna and tasty desserts. *5-11pm* $$

Clementina: Intimate and sophisticated, with a dimly lit back patio. Creative salads, burgers, a dozen pasta dishes and good cocktails. *6-10pm Wed-Sat* $$

La Cantonata: Top spot downtown for fine-dining; old-school Italian, hefty menus and waistcoated waiters. *noon-2:30pm & 6-10pm Mon-Sat, noon-3pm Sun* $$

Sansei Oscar Kotoriy Restaurante: Seriously high-quality sushi, ramen and sashimi, including massive 'sushi boats' at affordable prices. *noon-10pm Mon-Sat* $$

Chipotle: Not to be confused with the American chain, rather an open-air Mexican eatery with authentically done burritos, tacos, etc. *11am-11pm* $$

family, but this took place behind bars and with a black curtain preventing them from seeing and touching each other. You can check out this window onto the world near the entrance. The only other contact with the city was through the sale of candles (you can see the workshop where these were handcrafted) and foodstuffs, which was performed via a revolving door that kept vendor and client apart. Such transactions were the sole source of income for the nuns, who were otherwise completely self-sufficient. Other tour highlights are a fully-stocked, built-in herbal medicinal cabinet and a chapel, spectacularly renovated, sparkling with gold leaf and other jewels.

There's still a Carmelite community here, but its half-dozen or so nuns are housed in more comfortable modern quarters next door and they live with fewer restrictions.

CONVENT LIFE

If you're curious about the convent life, be sure to visit Potosí's own **Convento de Santa Teresa** (p221) and **Convento de San Francisco** (p222).

The House(s) That Tin Built

Relax in Palacio Portales' gardens

Some observers claim Bolivia suffers from the 'resource curse' and that its economy won't spread wealth to the masses despite an abundance of natural minerals. There's no better symbol of wealth disparity than Cochabamba's most regal home, an opulent mansion called **Palacio Portales** *(patino .org/visita-nuestros-museos; tours B$25)*. It's an ostentatiously grand, mustard-yellow building nestled amidst Queru Queru, an upscale neighborhood with palm tree-lined avenues, large homes peaking out above high adobe walls and loads of contemporary-style cafes and restaurants. Built in 1927 by the tin baron Simón Patiño in a mixed bag of European-styles with Carrara marble, French wood, Italian tapestries and delicate silks, it's the perfectly manicured Versailles-inspired gardens that are truly a magnificent oasis (no entrance fee). Open from 9am to 7pm, they're a wonderful place to pass the time with a book or just soak in the sun.

House tours are worthwhile; however, they're primarily in Spanish (available 3pm to 6pm Tuesday to Friday and 10am to noon Saturday and Sunday). Worth noting: the games room is an imitation of Granada's Alhambra and the main hall takes its design inspiration from Vatican City.

The property also houses an arts and cultural complex with private recitals and shows; there's a small shop at the entrance serving delicious soft-serve ice cream made with dairy products from a related farm; and a highly recommended **cafe** (p189) in back.

Despite the pretty penny it cost Patiño, he never actually inhabited the Palacio Portales. To further explore his story, you can visit **Villa Albina** *(museovillaalbina.fundacionpatino. org, entry B$25)* in the village of Pairumani and tour the home the tin baron actually occupied. This enormous white mansion, with its long, palm-tree-lined entrance roadway, was named after Simón's wife, Albina. She was presumably as fussy as her husband when it came to the finer things in life, and the elegant French decor of the main house seems fit for royalty. As well as

THE TIN TYCOON'S TARNISHED LEGACY

At the time of his death in 1947, Simón Patiño controlled more than a third of the world's supply of tin and was one of the wealthiest people alive. Much like American gilded age barons John D Rockefeller and Andrew Carnegie, workers' conditions and rights weren't respected and strikes in Oruro and Potosí in 1942 were met with violence. Like the tycoons in the US, Patiño left behind important philanthropic work (the Patiño Foundation focuses on education, pediatric health and eco-minded agricultural practices), but his tarnished legacy also included labor abuses so severe they led to the creation of a powerful mine workers' union.

TOUR ADVICE

Because tourism in Cochabamba is relatively low key, it can be challenging for solo travelers looking to book excursions to outlying destinations; unless in a group, prices can be prohibitively high. It's best to try arranging in advance, otherwise you'll likely have to stick around for several days at least before there's a departure. During December and January, the wettest months, few trips are scheduled. Many companies, including some we recommend, only have Spanish-speaking guides; **El Mundo Verde Travel** is a noteworthy exception. Otherwise, some La Paz-based trekking and tour companies can help.

GETTING TO TOROTORO

The most common side trip from Cochabamba is to Torotoro, 134km (a three-hour *micro* ride) to the south. Torotoro *micros* with **Sindicato de Trans Mixto Torotoro Turistico** *(B$35)* depart daily, when full, from around 7am until late afternoon, but waits can vary; 1½ hours isn't unusual. Arrive around 7am or go with a group. The stop is in the southern part of the city and traffic can be bad in surrounding streets. The road to Torotoro is now entirely paved and continues to be improved.

the house, there's a formal garden, complete with topiary, and the family mausoleum, made from Carrara marble, in which the don and his wife were laid to rest.

The villa is only 18km from Cochabamba, but traffic can be awful. Best to take a taxi and try to avoid rush hours. Alternatively, from Quillacollo, take a Pairumani *trufi* from the Plaza Bolívar and get off at Villa Albina.

Plaza Break

Park yourself in central square

Grab a bench for some people watching on the attractively landscaped and well-kept **Plaza 14 de Septiembre** in the heart of the city's downtown. Or stroll along the attractively arcaded circumference with flocks of pigeons competing for space. The plaza's name refers to the date when independence leader Pedro Domingo Murillo was executed by the Spanish authorities in 1810. Murillo's spirit lives on when large crowds gather, not infrequently, in civic protest. The southern side of the plaza is dominated by Cochabamba's **cathedral** *(free entry)*, the valley's oldest religious building. When construction began in 1542, the plan was for a tiny stone-and-adobe structure. Many later additions and renovations have removed some character, but a fine eastern portal has been preserved. It's light and airy inside with statues of several saints, a gilded altarpiece and a grotto for the ever-popular *Inmaculada* (Virgin of the Immaculate Conception).

When the Sun Goes Down...

Party with cochabambinos

There's a flourishing bohemian-style bar scene popular with mostly university-aged students along and around España, between Mayor Rocha and Colombia in the city's downtown. **Incantatio Café Temático** has decent food and cheap drinks. In La Recoleta, a slightly older, stylishly dressed crowd heads out, with popular spots including cocktail lounges. Some of these have live music, such as **La Tirana** along Paseo del Blvd. The area around El Pasaje Portales has several nightclubs playing Latin and electronic music; **Mandarina Lounge** wouldn't look out of place in Miami Beach. The nightlife along El Prado (Av Ballivián) mostly involves drinking at street-front restaurants, some very large, and can get crowded and raucous, especially with *fútbol* (soccer) on the TV. **Novecento** and **Suassuna by Fragmentos**, both just to the east of El Prado, draw 20-somethings for sophisticated cocktails and varied live performances. Couples meet up at one of the city's many fine cafes and, not to be outdone, families head to the dessert palaces scattered throughout the city.

Beyond Cochabamba

Outdoor adventures await on snow-capped summits, in a national park of prehistoric terrain and in some of the country's best preserved Incan ruins.

Stretching from the climbable high peak of forested Cerro Tunari, to the north of the city to the lower-elevation Chapare, the region that produces the most coca (the ingredient processed into cocaine), spreading to the northeast, this is a region of contrasts. The highest profile draw, Torotoro National Park, is a showcase for geology, palaeontology, spelunking and a simply joyful landscape to explore on foot. To the southeast in the Cochabamba Valley is Valle Alto, the country's 'breadbasket'. Sleepy rural towns function as marketplaces for Quechua-speaking, traditionally dressed farmers who till the fields of maize and wheat. Remote Incan ruins, alpine lakes and villages frozen in amber sit in bucolic countryside of the Andean foothills.

Places

GETTING AROUND

Micros to Quillacollo, Pahirumani and Sipe Sipe leave from the intersection of Avs Ayacucho and Aroma near the bus terminal.

Trufis and *micros* to eastern Cochabamba Valley villages leave from a variety of spots south of the center, along Av República at the corners of Barrientos, Av 6 de Agosto and Mairana.

From Cochabamba, taxis (30 minutes) leave for Tarata when full and *micros* (B$6, 45 minutes) from the corner of Av Barrientos and Magdalena. Or you can use Yango Lite to get to there.

Pico Tunari

TIME FROM COCHABAMBA: 1½ HRS

Summit this high-altitude peak

Cloud covered, fog encrusted, snow packed, rainy or clear skies – regardless of the extent of the panoramic pay off at the summit of snow-dusted **Cerro Tunari** (5050m), you'll feel exhilarated. And bone-tired. It's the second highest peak in central Bolivia (Cerro Pirhuata is only 45m higher) and the second peak from the left on the Taquiña beer label. Its flanks are 25km northwest of Cochabamba along the road to Morochata and Independencia. The more common ascent along the north face, which can take a good four hours (or faster depending on your group's pace), ascends from Estancia Chaqueri or Tawa Cruz, 12km beyond Cruce Liriuni at 4200m. There are a few alpine lakes, sections of scrambling and jumps over burbling streams, and you should be aerobically fit (and acclimatized to altitude). Views along the way are spectacular and you can spot the Cochabamba mountain finch (endemic to the area), Andean condors, llamas and viscacha (rabbit-like rodents).

Most people go with a tour company or guide out of Cochabamba. Rates for one- or two-day trips with **Andes Xtremo** and **El Mundo Verde Travel** (p192) depend on the number

continues on p198

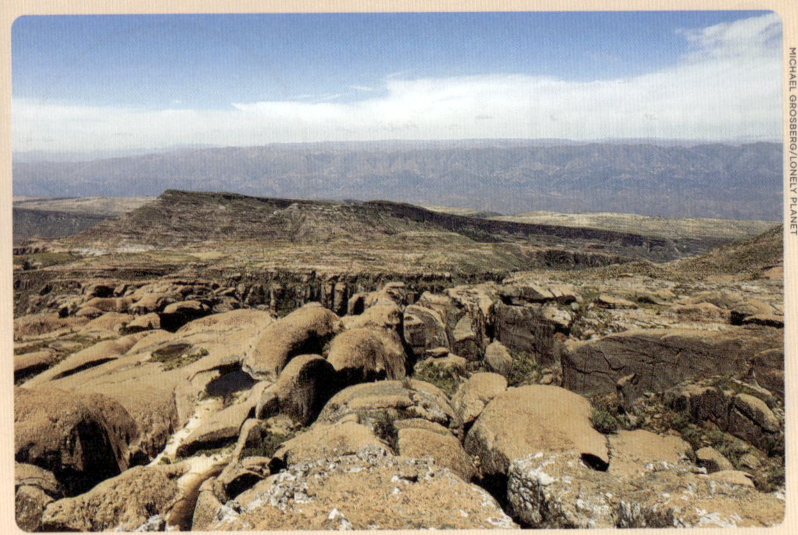

MICHAEL GROSBERG/LONELY PLANET

Torotoro National Park

TOP EXPERIENCE

Parque Nacional Torotoro

On the small size in terms of acreage for a Bolivian national park, Torotoro packs a memorable punch. Its geography showcases geology on an awe-inspiring scale. Beds of sedimentary mudstone, sandstone and limestone, bristling with marine fossils and – from drier periods – dinosaur footprints, have been twisted into otherworldly-looking terrain. Caverns, valleys and rocky escarpments can all be explored on foot.

DON'T MISS

- Dinosaur tracks at Torotoro village
- Ciudad de Itas
- Caverna de Umajalanta
- El Vergel waterfall
- Views over Cañon de Torotoro
- Dinosaur footprints in Carreras Pampa
- Red-fronted macaws

Dinosaur Tracks

If the Tyrannosaurus rex figure in the plaza, the dinosaur head sticking out of city hall or the pterodactyl-themed cafes weren't an obvious tell, Torotoro has become synonymous with palaeontology. The village, which sits in a wide section of a 20km-long valley at an elevation of 2600m, is flanked by enormous, inclined mudstone rock formations bearing bipedal and quadrupedal dinosaur tracks *(huellas)* from the Cretaceous period (spanning 145 million to

PRACTICALITIES

- sernap.gob.bo/torotoro
- B$120 to B$170 per person for a full day of guided excursions
- Guide office: 7-435-9152

NORADOA/SHUTTERSTOCK

El Vergel waterfall, Cañon de Torotoro

65 million years ago).

As obvious as impressions on freshly laid concrete, tracks of both herbivorous and carnivorous species are all over the place; interpretative work remains unfinished. The closest are at **Cerro Huayllas**, at the entrance to the village, on the other side of the river. They're behind a locked fence so you'll need an official guide to enter (most people visit as part of the hike to Cañon de Torotoro and El Vergel). Above the water but below the road are the area's largest tracks, made by an enormous quadruped dinosaur. Near here, just above the road, the angled plane of rock reveals a multitude of tracks, including a long set from a heavy quadrupedal dinosaur (possibly an armadillo-like ankylosaurus).

Along the route to Umajalanta cave, the flat area known as the Carreras Pampa site has several excellent footprint sets made by three-toed bipedal dinosaurs, both herbivores and carnivores.

Cañon de Torotoro & El Vergel

Three kilometers from Torotoro, the ground drops away into an immense and spectacularly beautiful canyon, more than 250m deep. From the mirador at the top you can gaze along it, watching vultures wheeling. From here, following the diminishing canyon to the left, you come to a flight of 800 stairs that lead down to a 10m-high waterfall, **El Vergel** (also called *Huacasenq'a*, meaning 'cow's nostrils' in Quechua), filled with incongruous mosses, vines and other tropical vegetation.

In addition to the mirador, there's a semicircle **viewpoint** pitched vertiginously out and over the canyon. The cliffsides are home to the critically endangered *paraba frente roja* (red-fronted macaw), which you have a good chance of seeing, or

FOOTPRINT FACTS

All the tracks in the Torotoro area were made in soft mud, which then solidified into mudstone. They were later lifted and tilted by tectonic forces. For that reason, many of the tracks appear to lead uphill. Many local guides, however, incorrectly believe that the footprints were made in lava as the dinosaurs fled a volcanic eruption.

TOP TIPS

- To join others and reduce costs, turn up at the guides' office around 7:30am to book morning and full-day trips. If you're only going in the afternoon, best to hang out there starting at around 1:30pm.
- Visiting any sights far from town (eg Cavernas Umajalanta, Turu Rumi or Ciudad de Itas), ask your guide in the morning to reserve lunch at Cabañas Umajalanta. It's cheap and filling.
- If using a vehicle to get to sights, bring as much water as possible for the entire day.
- Cash is available at the Banco Unión ATM at the central market.

RECOMMENDED ITINERARY

Most people combine Ciudad de Itas with one of the other two 'major' sights on one day (eg with El Vergel, it's B$670 for a group of five) and do the remaining one in the afternoon of their arrival or morning of departure. Doing Caverna de Umajalanta, Ciudad de Itas, Cañon de Torotoro and El Vergel in a day (B$855 for five) is tiring and overly ambitious. Our suggestion is Ciudad de Itas, Turi Rumi and Caverna de Umajalanta in one long day and Cañon de Torotoro and El Vergel the day after.

at least hearing. At the bottom, a crystal-clear river tumbles down through cascades and waterfalls, forming idyllic swimming pools. Be sure to pack a bathing suit if the weather's conducive or you don't mind a frigid plunge. Ask your guide to return via the longer alternative path, to avoid climbing the same 800 steps back to the top.

If walking and not going all the way to the falls, this is the least expensive of all the sights to visit.

Caverna de Umajalanta

The Río Umajalanta, which disappears beneath a layer of limestone approximately 22m thick, has formed the impressive **Caverna de Umajalanta**, of which 4.5km of passages have been explored. The entrance to this massive, gaping maw involves scrambling over truck-sized boulders and leap-frogging pools of water. Natural light fades at every step. By the time you switch on your headlamp, the descent takes on the feel of an Indiana Jones–type adventure. Parts involve crawling and wriggling through extremely narrow, tight spaces; several short, rope-assisted climbs; and even a waterpark-like slide or two down slick rock formations. It's a moderately physical trip – absolutely great fun, though possibly problematic for the claustrophobic. Expect to get both wet and very dirty (wear long pants and nonslip shoes you don't mind getting wet). Inside are interesting stalagmite and stalactite formations and waterfalls, as well as a resident population of vampire bats. You eventually descend to a small underground lake and river, which is populated by small, white, completely blind catfish. The ascent tends to be less strenuous than the descent, as it takes a more direct route.

Caverna de Umajalanta

MICHAEL GROSBERG/LONELY PLANET

A guide is mandatory as it's easy to get lost, and helmets with headlamps and gloves are provided. The walk from the parking area to the official entrance, and beyond to the cavern itself, is a completely exposed, mostly uphill slog of a couple of kilometers. On the way, keep an eye out for several sections of dinosaur footprints.

Ciudad de Itas

The long-ago refuge of isolated communities (a few spots of rock art are the most visible evidence), these weirdly shaped caverns are striking. However, they aren't the main reason to make the 21km, sometimes white-knuckle, drive to **Ciudad de Itas** from Torotoro. It's the breathtaking views you should come for, which, at nearly 4000m, provide an expansive perspective on the unique geology of the region. Visible cross sections of sloping mountains appear in isolation like massive spaceships that have been abandoned for millennia. Guides point out uniquely shaped rock formations, scurrying viscacha (a rodent that resembles a rabbit) and soaring Andean condors.

It's a mildly strenuous hike with a couple of tricky spots that involve climbing and scrambling over boulders.

Turu Rumi

There really should be more of a warning: Turu Rumi, an amalgamation of strangely sculpted rock formations, is not the best choice for the faint of heart or for those who suffer from vertigo. To reach the summit, you need to take a small leap or large step, depending on your height, across a narrow chasm. On the ascent and then again descent. On our trip, without the assistance of a tall, long-limbed fellow hiker, one or two others would have been too anxious to try. You'll see Andean condors floating on thermals and horizon-expanding views. El Mundo Verde Travel even offers rappelling.

Torotoro Town

This is a sleepy rural village, and therein lies its appeal. The biggest challenge when taking a leisurely stroll along its bumpy cobblestoned streets is the elevation gain from the Rio Rodeo at the northern edge of town. Accommodationss, though fairly interchangeable, are concentrated within several blocks of the main plaza. Most charge around B$80 per person. Outside the high season, booking in advance isn't necessary and you can check out a few in person before deciding. Several recommended spots are outside the center (moto-taxi drivers to take you there hang out around the plaza).

The centrally located local market has a few *comedores* serving simple dishes like fried chicken for B$15, and a handful of cafes and casual restaurants with irregular hours are within a block or two of the plaza; however, it's not uncommon for many dishes to be unavailable. **Café Cretácico** caters to gringos with a lovely back garden, board games, artisanal beers and a gluten-free raclette *(B$85)*.

KEEP IN MIND

It's compulsory to take a guide on any excursion outside the village; guides lead groups of no more than six. Entry tickets *(B$100 for four days)* are purchased at the park office next door to the office where you arrange guides. Hang on to your ticket at all times; it might be inspected by rangers. Guides are unlikely to speak English, but their knowledge of the surroundings greatly enhances your visit.

THE PATH TO INCALLAJTA

Remy van der Berg, owner of El Mundo Verde Travel *@elmundoverdetravel*

Of all of Bolivia's magnificent historical sites, Incallajta, for me, is most magical and its history a personal obsession. However, the journey itself is equally rewarding. The drive passes by farmers working their lands in a fashion not too dissimilar from Incan times. There's even an Incan-era bridge called *'incachaca'* that crosses a small river; vegetation can be so overgrown that the bridge is barely visible. You can stop to buy produce like strawberries, and even offer to pick some yourself. Nearby, there's an ancient Spanish church, evidence of the first Spanish in Cochabamba territory and an extremely old, utterly sleepy little village called Chimboata, a window on this very rural and isolated region of the country.

PULSAR IMAGENS/ALAMY

continued from p193

in the group. Trips involve an early-morning departure time and cold-weather gear.

However, budget-minded, experienced climbers can grab a *micro* or *camione* (flatbed trucks) toward Morochata. They leave on Monday, Thursday and Saturday at 7am from three blocks off the main plaza in Quillacollo and return to Cochabamba in the afternoon on Tuesday, Friday and Sunday.

A more challenging route begins from the beautiful forested Parque Pairumani near Quillacollo (the south-face route). It's a complicated, four- to five-hour ascent to the summit, with some sections requiring technical equipment. Experienced climbers can manage the round-trip in a long day, but the high-altitude ascent will be more pleasant if you allow two days and camp overnight. You'll need a guide to find your way.

Incallajta

TIME FROM COCHABAMBA: **3 HRS** 

Visit remote Incan ruins

A memento mori to civilizations past and the nearest thing Bolivia has to Peru's Machu Picchu is this remote, uncommonly visited site, 132km east of Cochabamba on a flat mountain spur (2950m) above the Río Machajmarka. **Incallajta** *(*meaning 'Land of the Inca'; *entry B$25)* was the easternmost outpost of the Inca empire; after Tiwanaku it's Bolivia's most significant archaeological site. Of the 50-plus structures scattered over 30 hectares, it's the immense stone fortification (5m tall in parts) sprawling across alluvial terraces above the river that jogs the imagination most easily. Because of the monumental scope of the ruins (from above,

Ruins of Incallajta

INCALLAJTA'S HISTORY

Incallajta was probably founded by Inca Emperor Tupac-Yupanqui, the commander who had previously marched into present-day Chile to demarcate the southern limits of the Inca empire. It's estimated that it was built in the 1460s as a measure of protection against attack by the Chiriguanos, who coveted its fertile agricultural lands. Some researchers believe it was also designed as a sort of ceremonial replica of Cuzco, the Inca capital. In 1525, the last year of Emperor Huayna Capac's rule, it was abandoned. This may have been due to a Chiriguano attack, but was more likely the result of increasing Spanish pressure and the unraveling of the empire, which fell seven years later.

it appears it was designed in the shape of an eagle) and their relatively isolated location, you need to take a cognitive leap to begin to grasp their importance. The illustrated map available at the park's entrance kiosk and on-site signage (in Spanish) are helpful, but a knowledgeable guide would be best (there's talk of having Spanish-speaking guides for hire at this entrance). Left to your own devices, at a leisurely pace, you could cover the territory in an hour.

Incallajta was made known to the world in 1913 by Swedish zoologist and ethnologist Erland Nordenskiöld, who spent a week at the ruins measuring and mapping them. However, they were largely ignored – except by ruthless treasure hunters – for the next 50 years, until the University of San Simón in Cochabamba launched its investigations.

Without your own transportationation or a guided tour, visiting Incallajta will prove inconvenient at best. There's no public transportationation and arranging a private taxi would be exorbitant. Still, for those determined few, if you can't arrange lodging in private homes or prefer the outdoors, you can camp at the site next to the ruins; be sure to take plenty of water, food and warm clothing, and have the proper gear.

Cochabamba agencies run day trips to Incallajta; easily most recommended is **El Mundo Verde Travel** (p192), which will do the trip for one or two *(US$260 for one, discounts for groups; includes food)*, and, of course, larger groups. Beware of tours that seem suspiciously cheap or that involve 'trekking.' That usually means getting a cab part way and walking a good distance to the site.

WALKING WITH DINOSAURS

The palaeontology-minded should head to Sucre's **Parque Cretácico** (p207) to get up close to an even larger concentration of exposed dinosaur footprints.

CHARANGO CAPITAL

The *charango*, the stringed instrument Bolivia is most known for, gained initial popularity in Potosí during the city's mining heydey. It has five courses of two strings and it's not usually picked, but rather played in a plucking manner, much like a banjo. Thanks to conservation efforts, it's no longer made from the shells of armadillos or tortoises.

Aiquile, known as Bolivia's *charango* capital, produces more than 400 a year, many exported to communities in Ecuador and Peru. The small Museo del Charango has some archaeological pieces and holds a collection of the instruments. The Feria del Charango is held here in late November. The town lies on the main route between Cochabamba and Sucre, but most intercity buses pass in the wee hours of the night.

MICHAEL GROSBERG/LONELY PLANET

Tarata

The most readily accessible ruins in the Cochabamba Valley at **Inca-Rakay** are decidedly less impressive, but there are spectacular views. This site of mostly crumbling stone walls was likely an Incan administrative outpost and storage facility for the largest corn deposits of South America.

The access town for the ruins is the quiet and friendly village of Sipe Sipe, 27km west of Cochabamba. If you're in Sipe Sipe on a Sunday between February and May, try to sample the local specialty, a sweet grape liquor known as *guarapo*. The best option for visiting is with El Mundo Verde Travel.

Tarata

TIME FROM COCHABAMBA: **45 MINS** 

Lovely village stroll

Picturesque and decaying, Tarata, 35km southeast of Cochabamba, is one of the region's loveliest towns. For those who appreciate a leisurely stroll with no destination in mind, it's worth a short visit. There's a gorgeous central plaza filled with palm trees and jacarandas. Heavily cobbled streets eventually peter out into dirt ones that turn rural. Midday and evenings, when it can feel eerily somnolent, many seem to be concealing rows of abandoned homes. Birds' nests grow unfettered on electrical wires and weeds the size of bushes grow on rooftops and out of adobe walls.

There are a few buildings of note to look out for: the enormous neoclassical **Iglesia de San Pedro**, constructed in 1788 and restored in the early 1980s, has several interior panels with mestizo-style details carved in cedar; the 1772 Franciscan **Convent of San José**, which contains lovely colonial furniture and an 8000-volume library, was founded as a missionary training school and contains the ashes of San Severino, Tarata's patron saint, whose feast day is celebrated on the last

Sunday in November; and the **Palacio Consistorial** (government palace) of President Melgarejo (built in 1872). None of these were open during our most recent visit.

The town's name is derived from the abundant tara trees, the fruit of which is used in curing leather. But Tarata is known as the birthplace of president General Mariano Melgarejo, who held office from 1866 to 1871 and whose remains lie in the town church. While citizens aren't proud of his achievements, they're proud of producing presidents (populist military leader General René Barrientos, who ruled from 1964 to 1969, was also born here).

It's also known for its particularly high-quality *chicha* (maize beer) made with organic corn grown in the area.

A couple of informal spots serving very basic set fare can be found near the taxi stands a block west of Plaza Principal. Your best bet for a good meal, however, is to stop at one of the fish restaurants serving up enormous plates of *trucha* (trout) or *pejerrey* (king fish), located 17km north on the return to Cochabamba, at the western end of **Laguna Angostura** (you can hire paddle boats and kayaks on weekends).

Laguna Corani

TIME FROM COCHABAMBA: 1¾ HRS

Mountain lake retreat

Far removed from Cochabamba's traffic-clogged streets, the pine forested area around this 9.5km-long reservoir has the look and feel of the Scottish highlands. Often enshrouded in fog, especially during wet winter months and despite its high altitude (3250m), there's a familiarity to the area's appeal, similar to mountain retreats the world over. Built in 1966 with the purely functional purpose of regulating waters for hydroelectric plants in the area, Corani doubles as a weekend spot for *cochabambinos* seeking a little fresh air and rural R&R. There's a handful of restaurants specializing in *trucha* and *pejerrey* dishes, but you need to overnight at one of the half-dozen lakeside lodgings to justify the journey. Nearly all offer kayaking, fishing, guided hikes and horseback rides, as well as motorized boat trips around the lake.

Villa Alpina *(facebook.com/villa.alpina.corani)*, perched on a heading on the lakes' northwestern slope, is a destination in its own right. A pioneering ecotourism project, every feature of its architecturally sophisticated A-frame cottages is designed to take advantage of and amplify the setting. And its style bonafides are only increased by its all-glass clifftop restaurant with breathtaking views and a kitchen run by top flight Cochabamba restaurant Muela del Diablo.

You'll need to rent a car or hire a taxi from Cochabamba to get up here; your lodging can arrange this for you as well. Once you've escaped Cochabamba's urban sprawl to the east and head north, you'll most likely get stuck behind slow-moving trucks chugging up mountainous switchbacks on their long journey to Santa Cruz. Best to be patient and appreciate the fine mountain scenery.

NO ORDINARY ALCOHOL

Chicha, a maize beer with a low alcohol content, traces its origins to pre-Hispanic religious ceremonies. Traditionally served out of large earthenware pots and drunk from *tutuma*, cups made from the crescentia (or calabash) tree, the ancient artisanal process of producing *chicha* is quite complicated and labor intensive (factory-made *chicha* is decidedly less palatable). Recipes, using different corn varieties, spices and fruit peels are passed down from generation to generation and techniques vary, though plastic and metal are never used. Especially renowned for its particular brew, **Punata**, an otherwise ordinary town 50km east of Cochabamba, has a small museum dedicated to *chica's* cultural importance and production.

Sucre

WHITEWASHED ARCHITECTURE | MUSEUM EXPLORATION | CULINARY SCENE

GETTING AROUND

The city center is easily and best navigated by foot. Traffic along the narrow one-way streets can get seriously backed up; it's sometimes advisable to walk several blocks out of the logjam before grabbing a taxi. The **bus terminal** is a 3km uphill walk from the center along Av Gutierrez and most easily accessed by *micros* A or 3 (B$2) from along Ravelo, or by taxi (*micros* are too crowded for lots of luggage).

A taxi between central Sucre and Sucre's Alcantarí International Airport 32km south should run around B$70. Buses leave from the intersection of Av República Federal and Atacama.

Known as 'the city of four names' (which actually constitutes a fifth, besides Chuquisaca, Charcas, La Plata, and of course Sucre), not to mention its moniker 'the White City of the Americas,' it's easily the country's most beautiful and cultured city. A survivor of centuries of historical ebbs and flows, it's nevertheless maintained its status as the symbolic heart of the nation. Founded on indigenous lands in the late 1530s by the Spanish, Sucre soon benefited from Potosí''s silver-mining wealth, with the non-laboring class choosing its salubrious climate over Potosí's chillier one. Later, it was here that independence was proclaimed, and while La Paz is the seat of government and treasury, Sucre is recognized in the constitution as the nation's capital. Surrounded by mountains with a glorious ensemble of whitewashed colonial-era buildings sheltering pretty patios, a vitality enhanced by a progressive university population and no shortage of museums, travelers tend to find themselves struggling to pick up and leave.

Altiplano Arts & Crafts

Museum with indigenous textiles

The intricacy, the level of detail, the hypnotizing patterns and complex symbolism. If you give yourself over, and allow time to focus on the textiles, framed, deservedly, like invaluable paintings, and the accompanying deeply explanatory texts (in Spanish, English, French and German), you could spend several hours at the superb **Museo de Arte Indígena** *(4-645-6651; admission B$25)*. It's a must for anyone interested in the indigenous groups of the Sucre area, with a particular focus on the woven artistry of the Jal'qa and Tarabuceño cultures. The Jal'qa's elaborately patterned Escher-like red-and-black garments called *axsus* (an apron-like skirt) are especially resonant. Search for their inventive

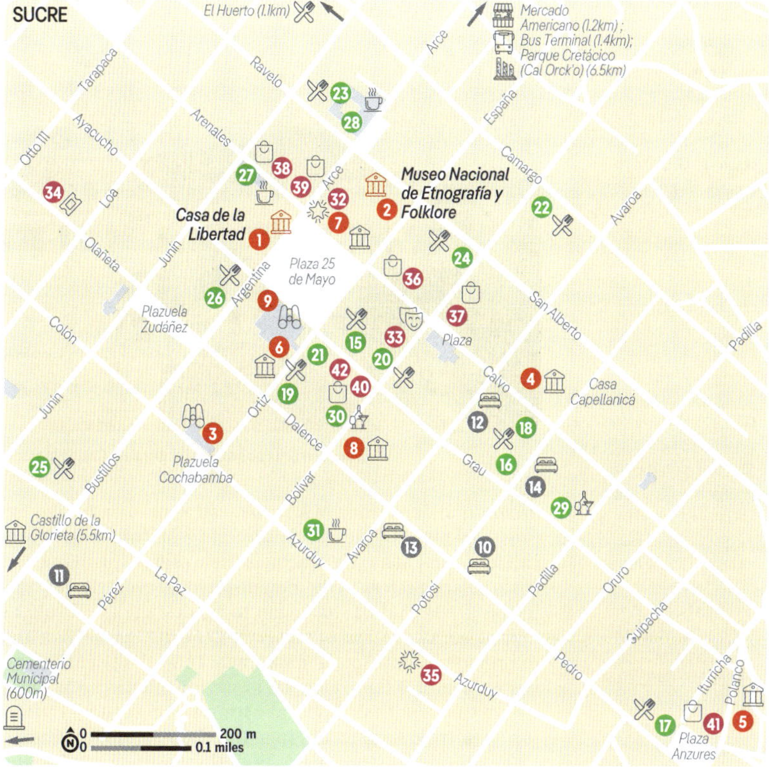

HIGHLIGHTS
1 Casa de la Libertad
2 Museo Nacional de Etnografía y Folklore

SIGHTS
3 Convento de San Felipe Neri
4 Museo Convento de Santa Clara
5 Museo de Arte Indígena
6 Museo de la Catedral
7 Museo del Tesoro
8 Museos Universitarios
9 Prefectura de Chuquisaca

SLEEPING
10 Casa Verde
11 Hostal CasArte Takumba
12 Kultur Berlin
La Posada (see 15)
13 Mi Pueblo Samary
14 ON Hotel Boutique

EATING
15 Augustina Tetería
16 Bienmesabe
17 Café Time & Coffee
18 Coffee Bike Roastery
19 El Solar
20 Florín
21 Joy Ride Café
La Posada (see 15)
22 Male Salteñería
23 Mercado Central
24 Musa Vinoteca
25 Proyecto Nativa
26 Tierra

DRINKING & NIGHTLIFE
27 Café Mirador San Miguel
Kulturcafé Berlin (see 12)
28 La Ermita de San Francisco
29 Malaba
30 Terraza 625
31 Typica Café

ENTERTAINMENT
32 Alliance Française
Casa de la Cultura (see 26)
33 Centro Cultural los Masis
34 El Mercado de Kinsa Molle
35 Orígenes Bolivianos

SHOPPING
36 Alpaca Andina
37 Awaj Warmi
38 Chocolates Para Ti
39 Chocolates Taboada
Distrito (see 30)
40 Inca Pallay
41 La Recoleta Stalls
42 Sombreros Burcal

WHY I LOVE SUCRE

Michael Grosberg, Lonely Planet writer

Upon arriving in Sucre from elsewhere in the country, my heart rate and breathing slows and I feel like I've arrived home. There are few spots as pleasant as the city's Plaza 25 de Mayo to while away a few hours. Shaded by tall palms, immaculately groomed and punctuated by a large statue of Bolivian independence leader Mariscal Antonio José de Sucre, it's the perfect spot to watch a parade of *chuquisaqueños* go about their days, from breakdancing youngsters to a few newspaper-reading old-timers. Nighttime, when it's equally animated, I grab a gelato from a plaza-side *heladería* and return to a bench seat, amazed at the youngsters out and about with their parents in tow, wondering if my kids would behave so well so late.

MICHAEL GROSBERG/LONELY PLANET

Sucre, from roof of Prefectura de Chuquisaca

dream-like depictions of *khurus* – strange, demon-like figures – inspired by weavers' visions of a mythic underworld called Ukhu Pacha (Kai Pacha is the world of the living and Hanan Pacha refers to their analogue of heaven). It was only in the 1990s that *axsus* began to be designed and sold as tapestries, as a means of preserving the dying tradition and to provide income for Jal'qa women. Indeed, the entire museum celebrates these ancestral weaving practices, playing a role in their continued revitalization and community pride. It's open from 9am to 12:15pm and then 2:30pm to 6pm.

The adjoining store markets high-quality ceramics and weavings, but it can be a more satisfying experience to buy them direct from the villages where they're made.

Bird's-Eye Views

Appreciate the city from above

The city's whitewashed adobe walls and red-tile roofs stretch in an aesthetically pleasing unity to low mountains on the city's horizon. There's no shortage of spots where you can appreciate central Sucre's architectural uniformity.

For perhaps the best view in town, head inside the wedding-cake-like **Prefectura de Chuquisaca** *(entry B$15)* on Plaza 25 de Mayo next to the cathedral to access the

DRINKING IN SUCRE: BARS

Joy Ride Café: Gringo-friendly cafe, restaurant and bar has everything from dawn espressos to midnight vodkas, plus food. *7:30am-2:30am, to midnight Sun*

Kulturcafé Berlin: Most backpackers end up at this happening bar for a night or two. Outdoor patio seating, sports on the TV, game nights and live music. *8am-late*

Florín: Line up along the 13m-long bar to swill the owner's own Belgian-style brewed beers and Bolivian specialties like *aguardiente de coca*. *11:30am-2am*

Malaba: Great festive vibe, with live music, DJs and sometimes big-screen TVs showing soccer in the central patio. Excellent food menu as well. *4-10pm*

open rooftop and cupola (signage indicates it's called *mirador de la mansarda*). Note the murals depicting the struggle for Bolivian independence as you head upstairs. You can also skip the museum and head directly to the nearby *mirador* of the **Museo de la Catedral** (p209; *adult/child B$15/5*) for equivalent views. Only a few blocks away, the **Convento de San Felipe Neri** (*entry B$17*) offers 360-degree panoramic takes from its rooftop surrounding a large and pretty central courtyard.

Only a long block away from the northern corner of Plaza 25 de Mayo, is the early-17th-century **Iglesia de San Miguel's cafe**. There's a B$5 admission fee, or you can simply purchase a drink or bite to eat from its cafe for at least B$5 and grab a table on one of the spiral staircases' five floors of small landings. To appreciate the church's beautiful Moorish features inside, head to Mass, Monday to Saturday at 8am and 7:15pm; on Sundays there's an additional Mass at 11am.

To grab some sun in a chair with commanding views of the city, sipping a coffee, gobbling an enormous slice of cake or downing a beer, take the long uphill slog to **Café Time & Coffee** (*timeandcoffee.coffee*) at the top of Recoleta. After climbing the steep steps up Grau, turn right, pass the Museo de Arte Indigena, and the cafe sits just below the colonnaded walkway of Plaza Anzures.

At night, when the city turns into a reflection of the starry sky above, the best views are clearly from **Terraza 625** (*parador.com.bo/terraza*), a stylish bar on the roof of the Parador Santa María la Real. Grab a table that offers your preferred vantage – all are first rate – and drink to the fortune that brought you here.

Religious Instruction

Window onto convent life

It wouldn't be much of a surprise if the massive, rusted brass key used to open the wooden front door to the **Museo Convento de Santa Clara** (*admission B$20*) dates to the buildings origins in 1639. At its peak, an estimated 300 sisters spent their cloistered lives here and nearly double the number are said to have been buried under the floor and behind the walls of the convent's crypt. The still beautifully landscaped central courtyard garden must have appeared as a dreamy oasis. Guided tours (10am to 12:30pm and 4pm to 5:30pm Tuesday to Saturday), informally offered and at your preferred pace, also pass through a hall filled with religious art, including several, admittedly unremarkable, works that were taken when it was robbed in 1985. The highlight might be the chapel's pipe organ inaugurated in 1664. Still functional and an impressive sight, though now powered by electricity and only played on Christmas Eve.

It's a treat if you can make it to Sunday's 8am **Mass** when the sisters, all seated in the front row, lead the congregation in the singing of hymns, imbuing them with an undeniable spirituality.

TOP TIP

There's no shortage of good-value accommodationss, the majority in colonial buildings built around pretty central courtyards. Some midrange to upmarket places have boutique features in historic buildings. The cheapest places cluster near Mercado Central and along Ravelo and San Alberto.

CALENDAR OF FIESTAS

Pujllay: In March Tarabuco stages one of Bolivia's largest fiestas, commemorating an 1816 battle with a Quechua Mass and folk dancing.

Santa Veracruz Tatala: Farmers gather at a chapel 7km from Sucre in May to pray for fertile soil, along with folk music and dancing.

Fiesta del Señor Santiago: Torotoro village's July fiesta featuring sheep sacrifices, dynamite explosions and some light *tinku* (ritual fighting).

Fiesta de la Virgen de Urkupiña: For around four days in August the *chicha* flows and folkloric musicians and dancers perform in Quillacollo.

Fiesta de la Virgen de Guadalupe: Locals celebrate with songs, dances and a religious parade around Sucre's central plaza. in September.

PINK PALACE

Only 7km south of central Sucre, on the way to Potosí, keep your eyes peeled on the left for the fish-out-of-water **Castillo de la Glorieta**, built by silver mining magnate and business tycoon Francisco Argandoña Revilla and his wife Dona Clotilde Urioste. From 1898 until Revilla's death in 1910, the couple ruled La Glorieta as a principality – they were 'granted' the title by Pope León VIII.

The interior is mostly empty, and what remains isn't maintained (really, the only remarkable elements are the intricately carved coffered ceilings), so while you can visit, it's enough to appreciate the unusual mix of Gothic, Renaissance and Moorish syncretism from afar.

SAIKO3P/SHUTTERSTOCK

Casa de la Libertad

Origins of Independence

Tour the Casa de Libertad

The early 17th-century building anchoring the northwest side of Plaza 25 de Mayo has the architectural feel of a convent, which it was at its beginning. But its significance and fame are much more worldly. Rather than the proverbial 'shot heard round the world' of the US Revolutionary War, this is the site of the 'shout heard round the world' or the *'primer grito libertario de América'*, when the country declared its independence from Spain on August 6, 1825, the first anniversary of the Battle of Junín. The new republic was named Bolivia in Simón Bolívar's honor.

At the end of the guided tour (which lasts for less than an hour) through the various halls and courtyards of the museum galleries of **Casa de la Libertad** *(casadelalibertad.org.bo, entry B$30)*, you too will feel the temptation to cheer. Spanish-speaking guides especially are adept at communicating earnestly and passionately about the figures and events that contributed to Bolivian independence.

EATING IN SUCRE: OUR PICKS

Bienmesabe: Venezuelan/Bolivian-owned; menu of *arepas* (fresh corn pancakes), *cachapas* (sugar and cornmeal pancakes). *11am-2pm & 4-8pm Mon-Sat* $

Male Salteñería: Serves Sucre specialty of a few types of *salteñas* (B$8), as well as croissants and paninis. *8:30am-1:30pm & 6-10pm Tue-Sun* $

La Posada: Outdoor seating around a stone-flagged courtyard, with tasty fish and meat dishes and affordable *almuerzo* (set lunch). *7am-10pm* $$

El Huerto: In a secluded garden, with stylishly presented traditional plates and specialties like prawns, Bolivian fish and excellent wine. *11:30am-3pm, closed Mon* $$$

It has been designated a national memorial and is considered the birthplace of the nation. The first score of Bolivian congresses were held in the Salón de la Independencia, originally a Jesuit chapel. Doctoral candidates were also examined here. Behind the pulpit hang portraits of former presidents Bolívar, Hugo Ballivián and Antonio José de Sucre. Bolívar claimed that this portrait, by Peruvian artist José Gil de Castro, was the most lifelike representation ever done of him. The charter of independence signed on August 6, 1825 takes pride of place, mounted on a granite plinth. A fine, inlaid wooden ceiling and elaborate choir stalls are also noteworthy.

English- and French-speaking guides are available for groups of three or four minimum; you can, though, ask for free use of a tablet computer with text in English.

A Resting Place to Die For

Stroll Sucre's bucolic cemetery

Inequality doesn't die when we do. There's no better proof than Sucre's immaculately maintained **Cementerio Municipal** (Municipal Cemetery), where elaborately designed mausoleums of wealthy colonial families and their descendants are larger than most living residents' homes. Rows of above-ground, five-level vaults of the recently deceased, nearly all decorated lovingly with photos, flowers, letters and other personalized items, are closer to the entrance. The park-like setting includes arches carved from poplar trees, picturesque palms and wide pathways with benches for contemplation. Of the notable figures buried here are two past presidents: Antonio José de Sucre and Hilarión Daza.

At weekends it's jam-packed with families. It's easy enough to walk the eight blocks from Plaza 25 de Mayo south along Junín, or take a taxi or micro A.

Dinosaur Tracks

Ogle prehistory at Parque Cretácico

It seems that 65 million years ago the site of Sucre's Fabrica Nacional de Cemento SA (Fancesa) cement quarry, 5km north of the center, was the place to be for large, scaly types. When the grounds were being cleared in 1994, plant employees uncovered a nearly vertical mudstone face bearing about 5000 tracks of at least eight different species of dinosaur – the largest collection of dinosaur footprints in

SWEET TOOTH CITY

Far from the country's cacao growing region in the Amazon, Sucre nevertheless claims the title as Bolivia's Chocolate City. The historical explanation is simple: Sucre was on the trail between the Amazon and Potosí where wealthy mining magnates once enjoyed chocolate in liquid form. **Chocolates Para Ti** and **Chocolates Taboada**, the two brands competing for the chocolate crown, sit side by side on the northeast corner of Plaza 25 de Mayo. Undoubtedly, Para Ti has slicker advertising, shops scattered nationally and a **factory** in Sucre you can visit (no floor tours, but can view the machinery). Taboada, also sold in stores across Bolivia, is slightly less expensive. Both offer products flavored with local ingredients like amaranth and quinoa and the incredibly affordable by the pound rates make them excellent gifts.

EATING IN SUCRE: FINE DINING

Tierra: Beautifully presented vegetarian dishes like gnocchi in a creamy basil and peanut sauce. *noon-2pm & 6-9:30pm Tue-Sat, noon-3pm Sun* $

Proyecto Nativa: Regional flavors and ingredients. A la carte or fabulous 11-course tasting menu of complex yet unadorned dishes. *6:30-10:30pm Tue-Sat* $$

El Solar: Polished, eight-course tasting menu – every dish of elaborate and inventive design – in elegant, light-filled dining room. *noon-3pm & 6-11pm Mon-Sat* $$

Musa Vinoteca: Tapas, wood-fired pizza, pasta, and charcuterie boards paired with curated Bolivian and South American wines. *6:30-10:30pm Mon-Sat* $$

MICHAEL GROSBERG/LONELY PLANET

the world. You can see some of the prints from outside the chain-link fence of **Parque Cretácico** *(Cal Orck'o; facebook .com/ParqueCretacicoSucre; adult/child B$30/10)*, but of course you get a better panorama inside. The best light for photographs is during the afternoon. From the terrace, you can examine the tracks on the rock face opposite with binoculars, though the exposed prints are increasingly eroded with every passing winter. The best way to appreciate their size and array is on the guided 'footprint tour' (noon and 1pm, Tuesday to Sunday) that takes you down into the quarry for close-up views. Under 12s not permitted; no open-soled shoes.

Otherwise, the majority of Parque Cretácico is best for kids. Skip the long and uninformative introductory film. You're encouraged to join 20- to 30-minute guided tours that pass by a number of kitschy life-size models of dinosaurs, including a massive 36m by 18m titanosaurus. Disconcertingly, even this is dwarfed by a gargantuan concrete silo that looms just on the other side of the fence. There's a room with fossil displays; another with good explanatory text (in Spanish) on the various dinosaur species and the fossilization process; and a basic restaurant. Adults can run through these spaces quickly.

Micro 4 (B$1.50) runs from the city center past the site; tell the driver where you want to get off. Taxis are B$30 each way and the park runs transportationation (either a double-decker bus or small van depending on demand, B$10 each way) that leaves from in front of the cathedral at the southern corner of Plaza 25 de Mayo (9:30am, 11am, noon, 2pm and 3pm); it's worth taking for the views of the city and surrounding countryside from the top deck.

BEST CULTURAL SPACES

El Mercado de Kinsa Molle Gathering place for artists and intellectuals with readings, musical performances and screenings.

Orígenes Bolivianos Dinner theater featuring Bolivian folkloric dancing with elaborate costumes. Two performances a night from Wednesday to Saturday.

Centro Cultural los Masis Small venue hosting concerts, as well as classes to learn to play the *charango* and Andean instruments.

Casa de la Cultura Hosts *artesanía* exhibitions, music recitals and folkloric ballet shows (most often Fridays at 7pm).

Alliance Française French-language library; sometimes screens foreign films and puts on photo exhibitions.

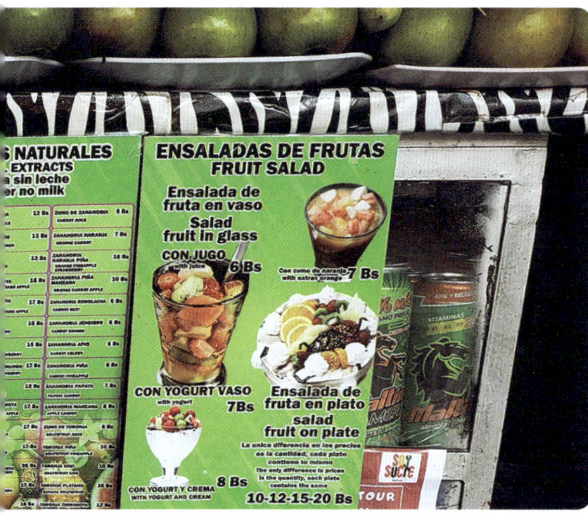

Juice stands in *Mercado Central*

Kaleidoscopic Market Stalls

Taste Sucre's flavors

Even if every *chuquisaqueño* (Sucre resident) were served a fruit salad daily there still would be a huge amount of leftovers considering how much is on display at the city's ***Mercado Central***. Entering the market off Aniceto Arce, there's a seemingly endless supply of ordinary and more exotic produce (vegetables are inside), from *cupuaçu*, *achachirú* (related to the mangosteen and indigenous to the Bolivian Amazon), rambutan, maracuya, tumbo and beyond. It's easy, and incredibly inexpensive to try a few varieties new to your palate. But it's even easier to head to the fresh juice stands (B$7 to B$15) located in the ground-floor open courtyard – the vendors and their blenders are arrayed in a colorfully delicious and nutritious mise-en-scène; try the *zumo verde* (green juice), a mix of nine ingredients, each advertised with a corresponding health benefit. Upstairs, above the clothing vendors, tasty, cheap meals (B$18) are fried up quick and served at picnic tables from morning to night. We enjoyed the spicy chorizo, but sensitive stomachs might want to pass. Groups can go full-on decadent for dessert by choosing one of the creamy, sugary cakes in mouthwatering displays downstairs, closer to the entrance on Av Ravelo.

Museum Central

A few of the best picks

It's quite natural that one of the country's most historically resonant cities also houses one of the highest concentrations of museums, most within a short walk from one another. Next door to Sucre's cathedral, the **Museo de la Catedral** *(adult/child B$30/5)* holds one of Bolivia's best collections

BEST SHOPPING

Awaj Warmi: High-quality, high-end textiles, sweaters, scarves and blankets.

Inca Pallay: A weavers' and artisans' cooperative with high-quality handmade crafts; returns a high percentage of profits to the weavers.

Alpaca Andina: Small, crowded shop crammed with souvenirs, trinkets, sweaters and tourist-oriented textiles and gifts.

Mercado Americano: Around the junction of Mujía and Reyes, will keep clothes lovers busy for hours.

Distrito: Entered via the Hotel Parador Santa Maria's lobby; very high-priced, top of the line Bolivian designer clothing, handbags and jewelry.

La Recoleta: Nearly a dozen stalls selling sweaters, souvenirs, etc, on Av Iturricha.

Sombreros Burcal: The place for high-quality sombreros.

THE COUNTRY'S NAMESAKE

Born in Caracas in 1783, Simón Bolívar, greatest of the Libertadores (liberators) of South America, died alone in Santa Marta, Colombia, on December 17, 1830. He began his military career commanding the Venezuelan independence movement. Battle followed battle until 1824. Establishing Gran Colombia (comprising modern-day Venezuela, Colombia, Panamá and Ecuador) was easy, but holding it together proved impossible. As the union slipped from his hands, he tried establishing a dictatorship. After surviving an assassination attempt in Bogotá, he resigned in 1830, disillusioned and in poor health. Almost at once, Gran Colombia dissolved and Bolívar was banned from his homeland. 'There have been three great fools in history: Jesus, Don Quixote and I,' he said shortly before his death.

of religious relics. The highlight comes in the Capilla de la Virgen de Guadalupe, which was completed in 1625. Encased in the altar is a painting of the Virgin, the city's patron. She was originally painted by Fray Diego de Ocaña in 1601, but the work was subsequently coated with highlights of gold and silver and adorned in robes encrusted with diamonds, amethysts, pearls, rubies and emeralds donated by wealthy colonial parishioners. The jewels alone are worth millions of dollars, making it the richest Virgin in the Americas.

On the other side of Plaza 25 de Mayo, housed in the impressive former Banco Nacional building, the **Museo Nacional de Etnografía y Folklore** *(musef.gob.bo; entry B$20)* brings together fascinating temporary exhibitions that vividly illustrate Bolivia's tremendous ethnic diversity. These have included native Bolivian fiesta masks, costumes and apparel, plus ceremonial ceramics, textiles and silverwork. Stays open to 10pm and has free admission first Friday of the month.

Wondering why millions labored for centuries under terrible conditions, and still do, including in mines around nearby Potosí in pursuit of precious metals and stones? Check out the privately run **Museo del Tesoro** *(museotesoro.com, admission B$30),* and its highly polished collection of precious metals and stones, and jewelry made from them, on display in one of the city's oldest buildings, circa 1560s. Guides, some English-speaking, add insight and provide excellent historical context.

South of the plaza, the relatively old-fashioned **Museos Universitarios** (*facebook.com/museocolonialcharcas; admission B$35*) has three separate halls housing colonial relics, anthropological artifacts and modern art. Most interesting are the cases filled with dolls dressed in traditional ethnic fiesta clothing and, for the more macabre, a collection of skulls and mummified remains. The permanent gallery of paintings are mostly dark and dour portraits of generals and politicians; you can pay for entry to each hall individually.

DRINKING IN SUCRE: CAFES

Typica Café: Spot to unwind with a journal or book in the back garden; varied menu of drinks and food (crepes, empanadas, pastries). *8am-10pm Mon-Sat, 10am-8pm Sun*

Coffee Bike Roastery: Sharing Villa Antigua's graceful inner courtyard, with coffees, paninis, salads, breakfast and more. *7:30am-10pm Mon-Sat, 8am-9pm Sun*

Augustina Tetería: Cozy up at this refined spot for decadent-sized cake slices and wide tea selection. *3:30-9:30pm Mon-Wed & Fri & Sat, 9am-5pm Thu*

La Ermita de San Francisco: Atmospheric spot occupying the ground floor and terrace of a church, with sandwiches, pastries and desserts. *9am-12:30pm & 3:30-9pm*

Beyond Sucre

Tarabuco's Sunday market and trekking opportunities abound in this mountainous region, with its one-of-a-kind geology and intriguing Jal'qa communities.

The imposing, serrated ridge forming Sucre's backdrop creates a formidable barrier between the departments of Chuquisaca and Potosí. Only a short drive heading northwest out of Sucre, roads carve their way around forested mountains, leaving modern Bolivian urban life far behind. Home to the Jal'qa people, this region of bizarrely shaped and multihued rocks and deceptively tall and remote peaks is a trekker's dream. Or you can head to villages in the countryside near Tarabuco, a small, predominantly indigenous village 65km southeast of Sucre that's famous for its textiles.

Places

Tarabuco

TIME FROM SUCRE: 1½ HRS

Shop the Sunday sprawl

Traditionally dressed *campesinos* (subsistence farmers) living in small villages from the surrounding mountains make a weekly pilgrimage to Tarabuco's colorful **Sunday market**. This otherwise ordinary, dusty town 64km southeast of Sucre comes alive from early morning to early afternoon when most of the commerce is finished, goods and people are hauled back to whence they came and Tarabuco once again lies eerily dormant. The streets and alleyways north and east from the central **Plaza 12 de Marzo** are crowded with vendors selling mostly ordinary goods of every stripe, from from kitchen utensils to batteries. Keep an eye out for low-hanging tarp coverings. Bulk sacks of cheap and appetizing fruit and vegetables are found in the covered *mercado campesino* (farmers market) at the far northeastern edge of town. Items like *charangos*, coca pouches, touristy ponchos and weavings featuring geometric and zoomorphic designs, and other souvenirs like stuffed llamas for the kids are sold on and close to the plaza. You'll be quoted an elevated price. Bargaining is expected. Best to go with ballpark prices you're willing to pay by checking out costs for similar items sold in Sucre before visiting. Despite the presence of other camera-wielding gringos, many in tour groups, always ask for permission before photographing people (it might involve a nominal payment).

GETTING AROUND

Of course, the best way to see this region is on foot. But you'll need transportationation to get out of Sucre to trailheads and villages to begin your hike. Most travelers arrive via private transportationation arranged by tour companies in Sucre. On public transportationation, the easiest way is probably to take a Potolo-bound *trufi* (shared car or minibus) from the Parada a Ravelo in Sucre to Chataquila.

THE JAL'QA

The Cordillera de los Frailes is home to the Quechua-speaking Jal'qa people, of whom there are some 10,000 in the area around Potolo and Maragua. They have traditionally made a living from farming potatoes, wheat and barley, and herding sheep and goats. They are also renowned for their weavings, called *axus*, meaning 'two colors', in reference to the red and black colors used to produce textiles. Along with other indigenous communities in the region, some still practice *trueque*, a non-monetary, non-capitalist system of exchange. Of the 'give me those beads and I'll give you some spices' sort.

SL-PHOTOGRAPHY/SHUTTERSTOCK

Sunday market, Tarabuco (p211)

Though undoubtedly large in terms of goods sold, even those moving at a slow and leisurely pace generally only need a few hours. Set aside time for an equally leisurely lunch at family-run **Pukara Wasi** *(7-185-2363)*, far and away the best place to eat in Tarabuco. It's a charming spot only a block from the southeast corner of the town plaza with a central stone-covered patio lined with potted plants, flowering trees and tables set with local textiles. *Almuerzos* (B$50) come with *cazuela da maní* (peanut soup, cooked with onions, potatoes and vegetables), seasonal fruit and a chicken or meat dish served with rice and salad. Several sandwiches are also on the menu for B$25. The bulk of tables are often reserved in advance by groups, so get there early for lunch on market days. Or contact them in advance for your own reservation.

For those interested in overnighting in otherwise somnolent Tarabuco (Saturday evening, pre-market could make sense), head to **Centro Ecológico Juvenil** (or Hostal Tarabuco) at the corner of Calles Azurduy and Murillo a block east of the plaza. A few large, well-kept rooms (B$70 per person) surround an attractive courtyard where breakfast and lunch are served.

Getting to Tarabuco from a quiet Sucre on Sundays is fairly straightforward and easy to do on your own. Get a taxi to the **parada a Tarabuco**, 2.5km from Plaza 25 de Mayo, as early as feasible. From here, buses and *trufis (B$10)* leave when mostly full; the latter is significantly quicker and if you snag the roomy front seat it can be more comfortable. The road is good and still undergoing improvement. You'll be dropped off only a few blocks south of the main plaza, which is where you'll go for the return journey to Sucre.

Cordillera de los Frailes

TIME FROM SUCRE: 1 HR

Hike Chataquila to Chaunaca

The rocky ridge at the top of **Chataquila** (3560m) operates as one of the more common starting points for hiking into the Cordillera de los Frailes. The spot's marked by a lovely stone chapel dedicated to the Virgen de Chataquila, a Virgin-shaped stone dressed in a gown and placed on the altar (it's concealed behind a wall). The chapel is built from the local rock, and, like the next-door amphitheater (used for fiestas), blends in with its surroundings. It's also the site where Tomás Katari, the leader of an indigenous revolt against the Spanish, was executed in 1781.

Look around on the south side of the road for an obvious notch in the rock, which leads into a lovely pre-Hispanic route that descends around 2300ft, sometimes steeply, for a quad-straining 6km to the Río Ravelo canyon and the village of Chaunaca, 41km from Sucre. Lots of good paved sections remain and it's easy to follow.

Chaunaca is a lovely spot, a patchwork of small corn and potato fields overlooking the Río Ravelo. There's a school, a tiny church and an interpretation and information center on the Jal'qa region. Beds are available in the information center, but you'll have to bring or source your own food. There's also a campsite and the renovated colonial hacienda, **Samay Huasi**, which offers comfortable accommodations with hot showers.

For a head start, *camiones* (flatbed trucks) run the route from Sucre to Chaunaca and Chataquila, departing from Av Juana Azurduy de Padilla. From Chaunaca you have the option of continuing west 15km direct to Potolo, or taking the very rewarding detour south via Maragua and Humaca. The latter will add an extra day to your hike, but takes in some sites of real geological and paleontological interest.

Some tour companies, however, provide transportation for hikers directly from Chaunaca to Maragua and end their day in the latter before returning to Sucre.

Rock paintings at Incamachay and Pumamachay

A worthwhile side trip from Chataquila or Chaunaca leads to two fascinating sets of ancient rock paintings estimated to be up to 2000 years old. At the first major curve on the road west of Chataquila, a rugged track heads north along the ridge. For much of its length the route is flanked by craggy rock formations, but it's relatively easy going until you've almost reached the paintings, where you face a bit of a scramble. The first set, **Pumamachay**, lies well ensconced inside a rock cleft between two stone slabs. The pictographs here depict humans and geometric shapes in monochrome black. A more impressive panel, **Incamachay**, is 15 minutes further along beneath a rock overhang that contains anthropomorphic, zoomorphic and geometric motifs painted in red and white. Guides at the entrance charge B$10 – you will need one to find the paintings.

PRACTICAL ADVICE FOR HIKING

The best time to go is the dry season, from April to November. Unless you're given explicit permission, never photograph people in the communities you visit. Hikes require a reasonable fitness level; most trips average 8km to 12km a day. Bring a hat, sunscreen and plenty of drinking water. Also, an insulating outer layer for chilly nights.

Camping on your own is possible; best to set up far from any habitation or ask permission in advance. If on your own, be sure to have a detailed topographic map and/or good GPS app or device.

HOW TO ORGANIZE

Despite Sucre's popularity with foreign travelers and the undeniable appeal of hiking in the Cordillera de los Frailes, there are few Sucre-based agencies that specialize in this. **Confort Tours** *(7-343-6986)* and **Greentrekkers** *(7-342-1645)* are two of the few.

Otherwise, ask your accommodations to point you in the right direction. La Paz–based agencies can also usually help. Try to book at least a few days in advance. The more people in the party, the lower the per-person cost. The average price is B$760 for a two-day hike. If you go with a tour group, cultural activities that can be organized include demonstrations of Pujllay dancing, folkloric music or a visit to a *curandera*, a traditional healer.

From Incamachay, you can continue downhill for a couple of hours until you hit the road at the Toma de Agua aqueduct, where there's drinking water and a campsite. From here, take the road 6km to the Chataquila–Chaunaca road, where you can either ascend to Chataquila or descend to Chaunaca from where you can find transportationation back to Sucre.

Surreal scenery at Crater de Maragua

The surreal, scallop-shaped cliff faces of Maragua make it one of the most visually striking places in Bolivia. This unearthly natural formation, sometimes called the **Ombligo de Chuquisaca** (Chuquisaca's Belly Button), features settlements scattered across an 8km-wide red-and-violet crater floor, and bizarre slopes that culminate in the gracefully symmetrical, pale green arches of the Serranías de Maragua. There's plenty to see, including waterfalls, caves and a picturesque cemetery in the middle of the crater that dates from pre-Hispanic times.

The village of **Maragua** (3100m) is an active weaving center. The weavers have set up a store and will take visitors into their homes where you can watch them creating the textiles. Maragua has three *cabañas* (cabins) and a campsite. A kilometer from the village, in Irupampa, is the lovely stone and red-tile-roofed **Samary Wasi**, with cozy and comfortable beds and, on request, after-dinner visits from village musicians. Camping is also possible here.

Keep in mind, Maragua is a sometimes challenging three-plus-hour hike, involving some steep, demanding stretches. If you'd prefer a lift, ask about shared 4WD taxis at one of the Sucre travel agencies

Maragua to Potolo walk

From Maragua, it's a spectacular walk to **Potolo**. You can get there in five hours, but there's plenty to see on the way to slow you down. In the area around Humaca you will find *chullpa* (funerary towers) and a paleontological deposit where embedded fossils are clearly visible in the rocks. Additionally, dinosaur footprints (around 100) at **Niñu Mayu** can be visited if you are prepared to add an extra hour or so to your hike. These places can be found most easily with a local guide. Ask around in the villages and negotiate a price that is fair to the community.

Another side trip from Humaca could take you to the **Termas de Talula** *(entry B$30)*, 5km away. You'll need to ford the Río Pilcomayo twice. The Talula hot springs issue into rock pools that have temperatures of up to 115°F (46°C). Camping is possible anywhere in the vicinity.

From Talula it's 500m to the constricted passage that conducts the Río Pilcomayo between the steep walls of the Punkurani gorge. When the river is low, you can cross over to the Potosí shore and see the many rock-painting sites above the opposite bank.

Weaving and traditional medicine in Potolo

Set in an undulating, ochre-colored landscape, **Potolo**, one of the region's larger towns, has some typically stunning

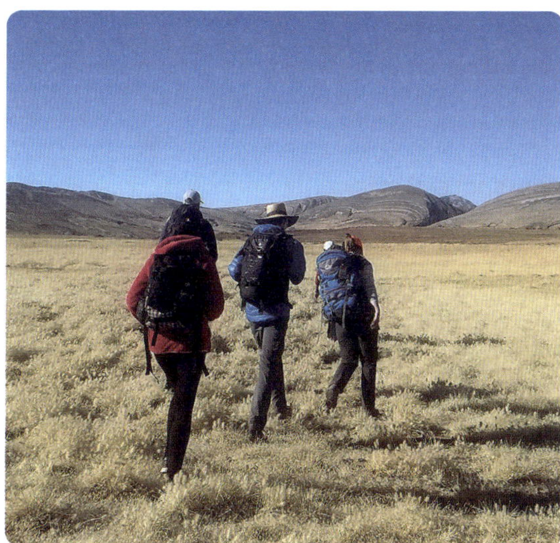

MICHAEL GROSBERG/LONELY PLANET

Hiking near Crater de Maragua

weaving going on in its workshops. It also has a little museum of traditional medicine, which demonstrates vernacular healing practices and other aspects of the culture. There are three *cabañas* here, a store and a campsite.

Camiones run infrequently to Potolo from Av Juana Azurduy de Padilla in Sucre via Chaunaca and Chataquila. They return to Sucre from Potolo when full.

Quila Quila

Beautiful **Quila Quila**, three hours southeast of Maragua by foot, is a formerly deserted village of largely mud buildings that is being slowly repopulated. The tower of the colonial church dominates the skyline and adjacent to it are the buried remains of the revered 18th-century indigenous leader Tomás Katari, who was murdered at the chapel in Chataquila in 1781. In 1777 Katari walked to Buenos Aires to confront colonial leaders and claim rights for the Aymara. He returned triumphantly with a document signed by the viceroy ceding to his demands and recognizing him as *cacique* (chieftain). Upon his return to Bolivia he was imprisoned, sparking a widespread uprising that eventually led to his death. A few kilometers away are the Marca Rumi monoliths with pictographs. The area is rich in pre-Columbian archaeological artifacts.

It's a challenging but doable hike from here to the summit of **Cerro Obispo**, at 3531m, one of the highest peaks in the area.

Daily *camiones* to Talula via Quila Quila (three to four hours) depart at 6:30am from Osvaldo Molina in Sucre, returning the afternoon of the same day. Alternatively, negotiate with a taxi driver.

OVERNIGHTING IN THE CORDILLERA DE LOS FRAILES

The Jal'qa have developed a series of accommoda-tionss, cultural centers and guiding services, all involving maximum community participation, with the villages receiving 100% of profits. Accommodationss and restaurant services have been set up in the villages of Maragua and Potolo. Sets of attractive thatched *cabañas* have been constructed using traditional methods and materials; they boast comfortable beds, hot water and attractive wooden furniture, and are decorated with local textiles. The cost is B$60 per person per night; for B$100 per person, meals and cultural displays are included. In Chaunaca, there's a camping area and some beds set up in the information center, but no restaurant service.

Potosí

COLONIAL ARCHITECTURE | ECCLESIASTICAL HISTORY | MINE TOURS

Cerro Rico, ominously known as 'the mountain that eats men', is a cone-shaped, ochre-colored, pock-marked mountain looming directly to the south of the city and has determined Potosí's history for hundreds of years. During it's long boom period starting in 1545, when its silver bankrolled the Spanish empire, Potosí became the Americas' largest and wealthiest city. Once the silver dried up, however, the city went into decline and its citizens slipped into poverty. Mining, if for other metals, still dominates the struggling economy. Nevertheless, the golden era's legacy survives in dozens of grand churches and elaborate, if fading, colonial architecture. It merits long strolls around narrow cobblestone streets past ornate doorways and pastel-colored facades. Because *potosinos* are generally tethered to traditions, if you can manage the altitude (4000m), visiting provides a window onto the lifestyles and customs of the Bolivian Altiplano.

GETTING AROUND

The fairly compact historical center of Potosí is best experienced on foot; however, it's a long uphill slope moving west to east. Taxis can be hailed and most trips within the city shouldn't rise above B$10. Traffic gets clogged on the city's extremely narrow one-way streets so leave plenty of time to get to the bus station for a timed departure.

The 'new' bus terminal is about 2km north of the center on Av Las Banderas and nearly all long-distance buses (except Uyuni) depart from here. Uyuni buses depart from the 'old' terminal, a 15-minute walk downhill.

TOP TIP

Regardless of daytime temperatures, there's usually a chill in the air in the evenings and it's commonly below freezing in June and July. Be sure to pack a hat and warm, insulated outer layer. Check if your accommodations has heating; if not, be sure you're supplied with several heavy blankets.

The Origin of Wealth

Casa Nacional de la Moneda

This is the source of the Spanish empire's economic engine, and where Bolivia's silver was converted from subterranean mineral to coin of the realm. That there was a 16th to 17th century phrase *'tan rico como Potosí'* ('as rich as Potosí') suggests how wealthy the city once was. And who knows how many of the rough and irregularly shaped *macuquina* (silver coins) minted here lie at the bottom of the sea? The 1622 wreck of the *Nuestra Señora de Atocha* off the coast of Florida, discovered in 1985, is proof of the treasure that once flowed from here.

The **Casa Nacional de la Moneda** *(National Mint, casanacionaldemoneda.bo, entry B$40)* is Potosí's star attraction and one of South America's finest museums. Potosí's first mint was constructed on the present site of the Casa de Justicia in 1572 under orders from the Viceroy of Toledo. This, its replacement, is a vast and strikingly beautiful building that takes up a whole city block. You don't have to be a numismatist (a coin collector) to find the history of the first global currency fascinating.

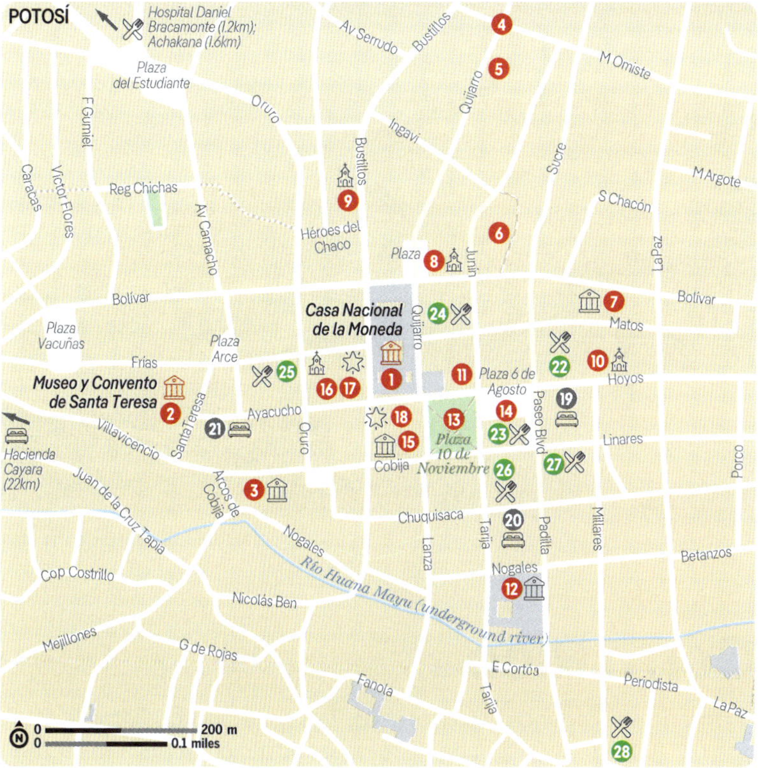

POTOSÍ

The building was construted between 1753 and 1773 to control the minting of colonial coins; legend has it that when the king of Spain saw the bill for its construction, he exclaimed 'that building must be made of silver' (expletive presumably deleted). These coins, which bore the mint mark 'P,' were known as *potosís*. The walls are more than a meter thick and, unsurprisingly, it has functioned not only as a mint, but also as a prison, a fortress and, during the Chaco War, the headquarters of the Bolivian army.

continues on p221

SL-PHOTOGRAPHY/SHUTTERSTOCK

Tin processing plant, Cerro Rico

TOP EXPERIENCE

Cerro Rico

El Dorado, the legendary city of gold, was never found. Potosí's 'rich hill' full of silver might be the closest approximation, and for the last 480 years, miners have labored to extract its mineral wealth. Guided visits are certainly memorable, an opportunity to witness how the beginning of the supply chain is built on the backs of workers scratching livelihoods out of grueling conditions.

DID YOU KNOW?

Between 12,000 and 15,000 miners still work Cerro Rico. Women are admitted to many cooperative mines, but only five are allowed in the mine's interior at one time.

Tin, zinc, copper and lead are now the primary minerals being extracted.

The Tour

You'll be transportationed from either your accommodations or the tour company's office to the miners' market at **Plaza el Calvario**, where miners stock up on acetylene rocks, dynamite, cigarettes and other essentials. You're encouraged to buy a handful of coca leaves, cigarettes, juice, soda, or pens and notebooks (for their children), which you'll later pass out to miners you encounter along the way underground. Photography is permitted.

Then you'll visit an **ingenio** (smelter), where the post-extraction process is explained. It's then another short drive along

PRACTICALITIES

- Tour departures: 8:30am and 1:30pm
- Tour are between four and five hours
- B$100 to B$200 per person

Cerro Rico's switchbacks before heading into Cerro Rico itself. Note that it's illegal for tour companies to give demonstrations of dynamite explosions, which destabilize the mountain and potentially threaten lives. Ask your tour-company vendor if a dynamite explosion is included. If they say yes, choose another operator.

Mine visits aren't easy and the low ceilings and steep, muddy passageways are best visited in your worst clothes. You'll feel both cold and hot at times, there will likely be some crawling and shimmying through narrow shafts, and the altitude can be extremely taxing – cases of acute mountain sickness (AMS) following a tour aren't uncommon. On some tours, you'll end up walking 3km or 4km inside the mountain. You'll be exposed to noxious chemicals and gases, including silica dust (the cause of silicosis), arsenic gas and acetylene vapors, as well as asbestos deposits. The plus side is that you can speak with the friendly miners, proud of their work, who are generally happy to share their insights and opinions about their difficult lot.

Working Realities

In the cooperative mines on Cerro Rico, all work is done with mostly primitive tools and underground temperatures vary from below freezing – the altitude is more than 4200m – to a stifling 115°F (46°C) on the 4th and 5th levels. Miners, exposed to all sorts of noxious chemicals and gases, normally die of silicosis pneumonia within 10 to 15 years of entering the mines.

Quite a few miners still hang on to the superstition that women underground invite bad luck, although, in many cases, the taboo applies only to miners' wives, whose presence in the mines would invite jealousy from Pachamama (Mother Earth). At any rate, lots of Quechua women are consigned to stay right outside the mines, picking through the tailings to glean small amounts of minerals that may have been missed.

When miners first enter the mine, they offer propitiation at the shrine of the miners' god Tata Kaj'chu, who they hope will afford them protection in the harsh underground world.

Since cooperative mines are owned by the miners themselves, they must produce the goods in order to scrape a living. The majority of the work is done by hand with explosives and tools they must purchase themselves, including the acetylene lamps used to detect pockets of deadly carbon monoxide gas.

Miners prepare for their workday by socializing and chewing coca for several hours, beginning work at about 10am. They work until lunch at 2pm, when they rest and chew more coca. For those who don't spend the night working, the day usually ends at 7pm. On the weekend, each miner (or a group of miners) sells their week's production to the buyer for as high a price as they can negotiate.

El Tío

Deep in the mines, visitors will undoubtedly see a devilish figure occupying a small niche somewhere along the passageways. Since hell (according to the traditional description of the place) must

FIESTA DEL ESPÍRITU

Dedicated to Pachamama (Mother Earth), regarded as the mother of all bolivianos, *campesinos* (subsistence farmers) bring their finest llamas to Cerro Rico's base to sell to the miners for sacrifice on the last three Saturdays of June and the first Saturday of August. As their sacrifice's throat is slit, the miners petition Pachamama for luck, protection and an abundance of minerals, and its blood is splashed around the mouth of the mine to ensure Pachamama's blessing.

TOP TIPS

- Sections of Mina Candelaria and Mina Rosario (B$130), both older mines are the most commonly visited.
- For a shorter, less claustrophobic experience tour a newly-opened section called Mina Kunti (B$100, 1½ hours), which at 4150m is also by far the lowest mine.
- For possibly the most intense and highest mine tour, ask to tour Mina Caracoles (B$200) at 4450m.
- If feeling panicky after covering only a short distance in the mine, speak up and ask to be escorted to the surface.
- Don't book on a tour if you're already dealing with symptoms of altitude sickness.

WARNING!

While medical experts note that limited exposure from a tour lasting a few hours is extremely unlikely to cause any lasting health impacts, if you have any concerns about exposure to asbestos or silica dust, don't enter.

Also, Cerro Rico has been hollowed out by centuries of mining and there's reasonable concern of collapse. Accidents can happen – explosions, falling rocks, runaway trolleys etc.

not be far from the environment in which they work, the miners reason that the devil himself must own the minerals they're dynamiting and digging out of the earth. In order to appease this character, whom they call **Tío** (Uncle) or Supay – never Diablo – they set up a little ceramic figurine in a place of honor.

On Friday nights a *cha'lla* (offering) is made to invoke Supay's goodwill and protection. A little alcohol is poured on the ground before the statue, lit cigarettes are placed in his mouth and coca leaves are laid out within easy reach. Then the miners smoke, chew coca and proceed to drink themselves unconscious. While this is all taken very seriously, it also provides a bit of diversion from an extremely harsh existence. It's interesting that offerings to Jesus Christ are only made at the point where the miners can first see the outside daylight.

Tour Companies

Plenty of Potosí tour operators offer guided tours through the mines. The best guides are ex-miners, who know the conditions and are friendly with the men at work. The safety standards are hit-and-miss; you really are going down at your own risk. We've either had a positive experience with or been recommended the following: **Koala Tours**, **Big Deal Tours** *(bigdealtours.blogspot.com)* and **El Mascarón Tours**.

Tour prices include a guide, transportationation from town and equipment (pants, waterproof jacket, helmet, rubber boots and lamp). Wear sturdy clothing, carry plenty of water and have a handkerchief/headscarf handy to filter some of the noxious substances you'll encounter. There is less activity in the mines on Sundays.

Silver miners, Cerro Rico

SL-PHOTOGRAPHY/SHUTTERSTOCK

continued from p217

As visitors are ushered into a courtyard from the entrance, they're greeted by the sight of a stone fountain and a freaky mask of Bacchus, hung there in 1865 by French artist Eugenio Martin Moulon for reasons known only to him. In fact, this aberration looks more like an escapee from a children's funfair, but it has become a town icon (known as the *mascarón*).

Apart from the beauty of the building itself, it contains a host of historical treasures. These include a fascinating selection of religious paintings from the Potosí school (especially remarkable are those by Melchor Pérez de Holguín), culminating in *La Virgen del Cerro*, a famous anonymous work from the 18th century, as well as the immense assemblies of mule-driven wooden cogs that served to beat the silver to the width required for the coining. The mules, which worked daily four to six hours with a life expectancy of only a few months, were replaced by steam-powered machines in the 19th century. Electricity became the power source in 1901 and the very last coins were minted here in 1953; the Bolivian coins you may have used to pay to enter the museum are made in Canada and Chile from cheaper materials like zinc and copper.

A change of pace from the mint-related galleries is a remarkably magnificent chapel, a composite of parts conserved, restored and relocated from other Potosí churches, including mestizo-style gold leaf from the Iglesia San Bernardo and the Iglesia de San Martin.

The excellent guided tour is long (1½ hours, starting at 9am, 11am and 2:30pm) and the temperatures inside can be chilly, so be sure to have a jacket on hand. Although there are also English and French tours available on request for groups of five or larger, the quality of the Spanish one is higher and the visit more comprehensive, so it's worth doing, even if your language skills aren't quite up to scratch. The building was scheduled to close for restoration work for six months from March 2025.

Religious Treasures

Tour these two convents

The desire for silence and meditation are easy to understand. The practice of self-flagellation, fleshed out, if you will, by the display of brutal looking tools, is more difficult to relate to. Whatever your spiritual beliefs, touring Potosí's two major convents provides a fascinating window onto this baroque and medieval world of renunciation. Guided tours of **Museo y Convento de Santa Teresa** (*facebook.com/museosantateresapotosi; B$25, 1¾ hours*) are best in Spanish, though English- and French-speaking guides are also available. They combine the merits of a primer on Carmelite religious practices circa the 1680s when the building was constructed, and a museum tour of a treasure trove of

LEY DE LA MITA

From the mid-16th century, so many workers died excavating Cerro Rico's silver that the Spanish imported millions of enslaved Africans to augment the labor force. In 1572, to improve productivity, the Viceroy of Toledo instituted the 'Ley de la Mita', requiring all enslaved indigenous and African people over 18 years old to work shifts so long underground that it was said that '10 Indians died for every peso of silver that was produced'.

Naturally these miners didn't last long. Heavy losses were also incurred among those who worked in the *ingenios* (smelting mills). It's estimated that over the three centuries of colonial rule (1545–1825) approximately eight million Africans and indigenous Bolivians died in these appalling conditions.

LEGEND OF CERRO RICO

The story begins in 1544 when a local Inca, Diego Huallpa, stopped to build a fire at the foot of the mountain known in Quechua as 'Potojsi'. The fire grew so hot that the earth beneath started to melt and shiny liquid oozed from the ground. Diego realized this was a commodity the Spanish conquerors craved. Perhaps he also remembered the Inca legend associated with the mountain, in which a booming voice instructed Inca Huayna Capac not to dig in Potojsi, but to leave the metal alone, because it was intended for others.

Whatever the truth, the Spanish eventually learned of the wealth buried here. In 1545, the Villa Imperial de Carlos V was founded beneath Cerro Rico and excavation began.

JORDISTOCK/SHUTTERSTOCK

Museo y Convento de Santa Teresa (p221)

paintings, silverwork and other valuable art. Some of the most striking pieces are the vividly maroon-colored *El Cristo de las cruces* (Christ with the Crosses), the mural depicting the 16th-century Battle of Lepanto and several prototypically *scuro* (dark and obscured) canvases by Melchor Pérez de Holguín. Don't miss the chapel's magnificent Mudéjar-style ceiling and stunning gold-leaf-covered pulpit, as well as the skull sitting in a bowl of dust in the middle of the dining room. The convent is open 9am to 11am and 2:30pm to 4:30pm Monday to Saturday and 3pm to 4:30pm Sundays.

Santa Teresa is still home to a small community of nuns, who have restored the sizable building and produce the sweet snacks for sale at the museum's entrance. The excellent guided tour explains how girls from wealthy families entered the convent at the age of 15, getting their last glimpse of parents and loved ones at the door (they were required to pay sizable dowries for the privilege). The darkness is alleviated by a stroll around two pretty courtyard gardens planted with plum, apple and cheery trees.

Similarly, guided tours of the **Museo y Convento de San Francisco** *(B$25)*, the oldest monastery in Bolivia, offer a mix of fine-art appreciation and religious-history education. The bonus comes at the end, when you're ushered up the tower and onto the roof for grand views of Potosí. A tour takes 1½ hours; English-speaking guides are unlikely.

POTOSÍ ARCHITECTURAL STROLL

Wend your way past the city's ornately carved doorways, facades and religious buildings to glimpse its richly textured architectural history.

START	END	LENGTH
Plaza 6 de Agosto	Arco de Cobija	2km; 1 hr

Begin in 1 **Plaza 6 de Agosto**, marked by a column celebrating the 1824 Battle of Ayucucho. Walk west on Hoyos to the stone and adobe exterior of the 2 **Iglesia Nuestra Señora de la Merced** (peek inside at its gorgeous ceiling).

North on Bolivar, the 3 **Casona de las Tres Portadas**, which once housed lay sisters of the Franciscan order, has widely spaced doorways with finely filigreed designs. Further north, walk to the intersection of Quijarro and Modesto Omiste, dubbed the 4 **Balcón de las Cuatro Esquinas** for its four colonial doorways. The 5 **Callejón de las Siete Vueltas**, an extension of Calle Ingavi, east of Junín, wends around a series of turns, displaying interesting architectural quirks along the way.

West along Bolivar is the 6 **Iglesia de San Agustín**, with massive wooden doorways within an elegant Renaissance facade. 7 **Calle Quijarro** winds between colonial buildings, many with doorways graced by old family crests.

The ornate Mestizo baroque portal of 8 **Iglesia de San Lorenzo de Carangas**, one of the most photographed in Bolivia, which has bas-reliefs carved by indigenous artisans in the 16th century. Backtracking south, the tower and doorway of the 9 **Torre de la Compañia de Jesús**, a Jesuit church completed in 1701, are adorned with Mestizo baroque ornamentation. Turn left on Oruro, then right at Armando Olmero. In the 18th century the 10 **Arcos de Cobija** archway marked the divide between Spanish and indigenous zones.

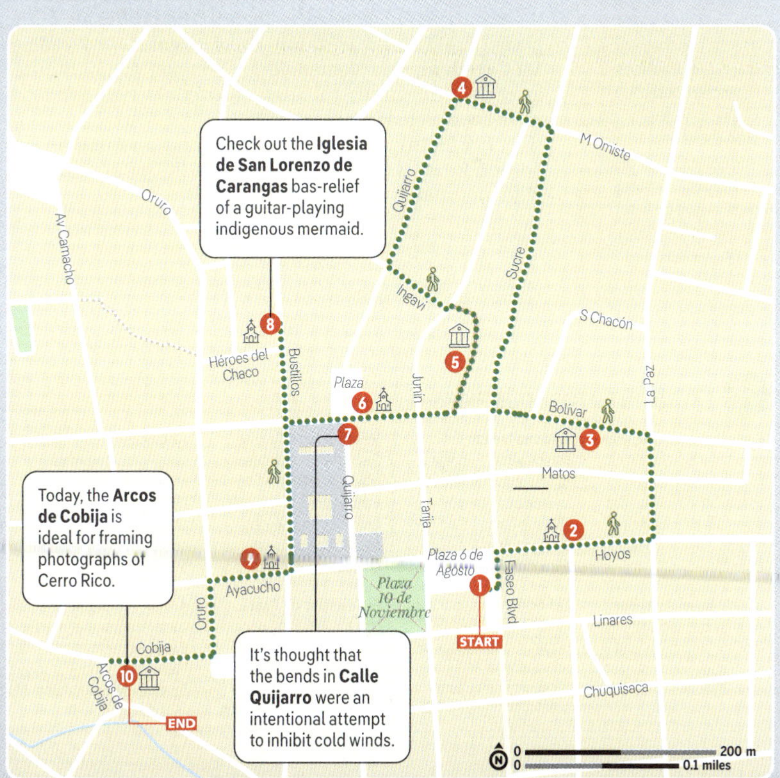

CONVENTS IN THE MODERN ERA

In the 1960s the Vatican declared that certain monastery conditions were inhuman and offered all cloistered nuns the world over the opportunity to change to a more modern way of life. Many of the nuns in Santa Teresa rejected the offer, having spent the better part of their life in the convent and knowing no different. Today most of the few remaining nuns are of advancing years and while the rules are no longer as strict as they once were, the practices have changed little. These days the cloistered lifestyle is understandably less attractive to young girls in an age where their families permit them to exercise their own free will.

Founded in 1547 by Fray Gaspar de Valverde, it was demolished in 1707 and reconstructed and enlarged over the following 19 years. The museum has a fine collection of religious art, including paintings from the Potosí school, such as *The Erection of the Cross* by Pérez de Holguín, various mid-19th-century works by Juan de la Cruz Tapia and 25 scenes from the life of St Francis of Assisi.

You also visit the catacombs, which have a smattering of human bones and a subterranean river running nearby.

A gold-covered altar from this building is now housed in the Casa Nacional de la Moneda (p216). The statue of Christ that graces the present altar features hair that is said to grow miraculously.

Monument Central

Relax in Potosí's central plaza

The epicenter of the city's social and cultural life, and ground zero of its historical heart, **Plaza 10 de Noviembre** offers voyeurism at Potosí's best. Something is often going on here, whether a festival (Carnaval and Independence Day might be most raucous) or demonstration, and it's frequently illuminated (including long before and after Christmas). Perhaps the most curious element is the mini Statue of Liberty circa 1926 honoring those who fought for the country's independence. Turn to the north side of the plaza to take in the elegantly neoclassical stone facade of **La Catedral**; this 'contemporary' version was built after an early-19th-century collapse; the original, begun in 1564, wasn't completed until around 1600. Occupying the western side, **Prefectura** (department administrative building) is housed in an elaborately designed 19th-century building with an ornately carved portal.

EATING IN POTOSÍ: OUR PICKS

Café la Plata: Chic and a good place to hang out. Espressos, magazines to read and wine by the glass. Pastas, cakes, salads, sandwiches. *1:30-11pm Mon-Sat* $	**Casona De La Pascualita**: Popular locals' spot for above-average *almuerzos* (B$30); has a salad bar. *11:30am-3pm & 6-10pm Mon-Sat, 11am-3pm Sun* $	**Restaurante Tambo Señorial**: Few tables, few dishes, including *k'alaphurca*, a stew of ground corn, onions, carrots, peas, beans and spices. *6:30-10:30pm* $	**Achakana**: Worth the taxi, Potosí fine-dining standout, beautifully plated vegetarian dishes and creative cocktails. *noon-3pm Wed-Sun & 6-11pm Wed-Fri* $
Oh My Bowl Acai Bar: Acai by the kilo with loads of toppings and even sugar-free versions. *8am-8pm Mon-Sat* $	**El Fogón:** This spacious, central restaurant is popular for its range of international and Bolivian food, including llama steaks. *noon-11pm* $$	**El Tenedor de Plata**: Brick walls and upscale vibe. Above-average chops, steaks and regional specialities. *noon-3pm & 6-10pm* $$	**4.060**: Popular with travelers looking for a night out at a spacious cafe-bar. Menu (over-priced) ranges far and wide. *4-11:30pm Mon-Sat* $$$

SAIKO3P/SHUTTERSTOCK

Plaza 10 de Noviembre

SO, SO TIRED...

That lethargy, panting and turtle-like pace isn't a soulfully weary ennui, but rather altitude sickness. One of the highest cities in the world (often ranked second only to El Alto), Potosí can take a toll on foreign travelers. If arriving after time in La Paz/El Alto you're less likely to be impacted.

If experiencing severe symptoms, get to a lower altitude as quickly as possible. Otherwise, in an emergency, try the **Hospital Daniel Bracamonte**, 2km northwest of the central plaza; an English-speaking doctor might be on hand. See p43 for more information.

Beyond Potosí

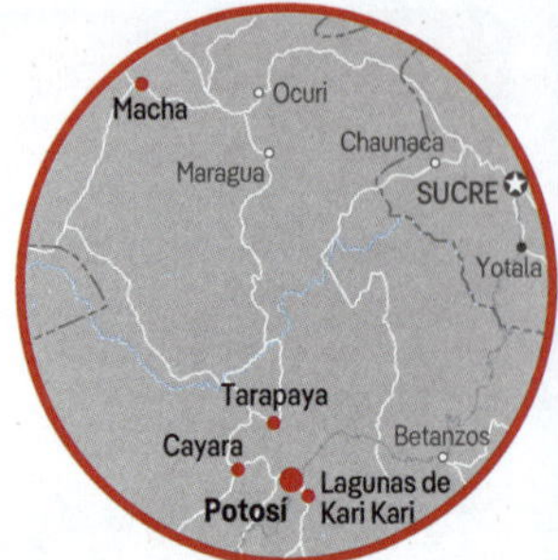

Warm, soothing waters, lunar-like hiking terrain and South America's oldest hacienda offer escapes into Potosí's countryside.

Places

GETTING AROUND

Camiones leave for Tarapaya (B$6) from Mercado Chuquimia near the old bus terminal in Potosí every 15 minutes from 6am to 7pm. Taxis cost about B$100 one way. The last *micro* from Tarapaya to Potosí leaves between 5pm and 6pm.

Access to Kari Kari is via public transportationation from Potosí. Or negotiate with a taxi driver for the day; you can ask them to follow the road to Tupiza before making a left onto a dirt road leading to Laguna San Sebastián.

Bulky Cerro Rico sits commandingly like a mothership over a lunar-like desolation. Even to the untrained eye, the unusual geologic formations and rocky outcroppings with shards glinting in the sun appear mineral-rich. Dust-covered heavy industrial buildings dot the landscape. But there's life to be found. The fertile, lower-elevation Cayara valley appears like a mirage. No wonder the first hacienda in the Americas was built here. Hot springs, imbued with legend, draw *potosinos* to their soothing thermal pools, and for those interested in off-the-track hiking with scenery, a system of reservoirs built in the late 16th century beckon to the south in the 5000m plus Cordillera Kari Kari.

Cayara

TIME FROM POTOSÍ: 1 HR

A historic hacienda

In 1557, one of the very first homes built by the Spanish in Bolivia was constructed at the head of a fertile green valley 25km northwest of Potosí. Only three families have owned the property and each has expanded and restored it close to its former glory. A number of patios centered around burbling fountains are surrounded by a maze of ranch style buildings with terracotta tiled roofs. An enormous 75-year old *patiño* tree guards the entry courtyard. Operating both as a house museum and a 16-room hotel retreat, visiting **Hotel Museo Cayara** *(hotelmuseocayara.com, entry B$50)* feels like time traveling back to an aristocratic past.

There are pieces of incalculable value, including Incan ceramics, an elaborately designed *bargueño* (carved writing desk from Spain) and the original sword and uniform of Marshal Antonio José de Sucre, who is said to have stayed the night before leaving to sign Bolivia's declaration of independence (the room where he stayed is preserved). The library, lined with 1500 books, ranging from religious and naturalist subjects and a complete collection of Voltaire, is an antiquarian's dream. You can hold (although should you?) one of the collections' most unique: an original 16th- century

JESSE KRAFT/ALAMY

Library in Cayara

Auto Sacramental Allegorical by Pedro Calderón de la Barca. Check out the piece of anamorphic art (a painting that's nearly indecipherable unless viewed through its reflection in a cylindrical mirror). Take a seat in the salon and gaze upwards at frescoes depicting the four seasons, five continents and four oceans known at the time. But the massive hall displaying weapons from the War of Independence and War of the Pacific is probably most impressive.

Allow yourself time to stroll through the small village of Cayara (named after a type of flowering cactus found here), its dirt roadways lined with poplar, willow and cedar trees aflutter with bird song.

Tarapaya

TIME FROM POTOSÍ: **30 MINS**

Soothing hot springs

Belief in the curative powers of **Tarapaya** (3600m), the most frequently visited hot springs area around Potosí (21km northwest of the city), dates back to Inca times. It even served as the holiday destination for Inca Huayna Capac, who would come all the way from Cuzco (now in Peru) to bathe. The most interesting sight is the 86°F (30°C) Ojo del Inca, a perfectly round, green lake in a low volcanic crater, 100m in diameter. If arriving by public transportationation, it's a 20-minute uphill walk along a dirt road. Warning signs and a caretaker strongly caution

VISITING CAYARA

Paola Cabrera, Hotel Museo Cayara manager *@hotelmuseocayara*

Cayara's town festival begins on the night of July 15th and continues the following day with native music and dance on the town square.

When visiting Cayara's dairy factory, check out the cows' names marked on an ear. If lucky to visit with the birth of a newborn calf, it can be baptized with your name.

The still-operating Cayara Hydroelectric Plant, only a short walk from the hotel, was built by Luis Soux in the early 1900s and is one of the first power plants in Bolivia.

La Estuquera Cayara at the entrance to La Palca, is one of the largest lime factories in the country. Its owner, engineer Juan Jorge Aitken, is also the owner of Hotel Museo Cayara, a descendant of Luis Soux.

CALENDAR OF FIESTAS IN POTOSÍ

Fiesta de San Bartolomé (Chu'tillos) is a rollicking celebration involving an ancient legend, on the final weekend of August or the first weekend of September. It's marked by processions, traditional costumes and folk dancing from all over the continent.

Exaltación de la Santa Vera Cruz on September 14 centers around the Iglesia de San Lorenzo de Carangas and the railway station, with dueling brass bands and dancing.

Festival del Charango is held the first weekend in December at Potosí's Teatro Modesto Omiste, with concerts of local and national artists featuring the 'Andean guitar'.

Día de los Compadres will be loud with brass-band music, dancing and dynamite! In February, before Carnaval, when miners transportation crosses down from Cerro Rico.

against bathing in the lagoon, citing fatalities from *remolinos* (whirpools). However, a rectangular stone-paved pool on the western edge is safe and soothing.

Along the riverbank below the crater are several very developed *balnearios* (resorts with bathroom facilities, changing rooms and food offerings) with medicinal thermal pools utilizing water from the lake. The largest, **Complejo de Tarapaya** *(entry B$10)* resembles an indoor water park with slides for kids. Weekends and holidays get very crowded.

Lagunas de Kari Kari

TIME FROM POTOSÍ: **30 MINS**

Remote hiking loop

Only 6km south of town, the landscape turns decidedly lunar-like: not especially pretty, but ruggedly and starkly impressive. From above, the **Lagunas de Kari Kari**, artificial lakes ranging from an elevation of 4500m to 5025m, appear as cerulean signs of life and hopefulness. Waterfowl also appreciate the incongruous surface water. The easiest way to visit the area is with a Potosí tour agency, which will charge about B$180 per person per day based on a group of three. If you prefer to strike out on your own, carry food, water and warm clothing. In a long day, you can have a good look around the lagunas and the fringes of the Cordillera de Kari Kari, but it may also be rewarding to camp overnight in the mountains (if fully kitted out with cold-weather gear). If choosing to go independently, be sure you have access to a good topographic map, hard copy or digitally. Nearby Cerro Kari Kari Central tops out at 5010m.

Constructed in the late 16th and early 17th centuries by 20,000 enslaved indigenous people to provide water for Potosí and for hydropower to run the city's 82 *ingenios* (smelters), only 25 of the 32 original lakes remain. Unfortunately, because of diminishing rains, and correspondingly diminishing water levels, there are serious concerns about their sustainability as source for Potosí's drinking water.

Macha

TIME FROM POTOSÍ: **3HRS**

Ritualized fighting

Akin to an open-air group MMA bout and native to the northern part of Potosí department, *tinku* fighting is deeply rooted in indigenous tradition and best interpreted as a type of ritualized means of discharging tensions between different indigenous communities. On May 3, festivities begin with singing and dancing, but celebrations soon erupt into mayhem and, frequently, violence, as emotions are unleashed in hostile encounters.

A *tinku* usually lasts two or three days, when men and women in brightly colored traditional dress hike in from surrounding communities. The hats worn by the men strongly resemble those originally worn by the Spanish conquistadors, but are often topped, Robin Hood–style, with one long iridescent feather. Alcohol plays a significant and controlling

NACHO CALONGE/ALAMY

Andean men perform a *tinku*, Macha

role. Most people carry bottles filled with *puro* (rubbing alcohol), which is the drink of choice; by nightfall, each participating community retreats to a designated house to drink *chicha* (fermented corn). This excessive imbibing inevitably results in social disorder. Roaming the streets, individuals encounter people from other communities with whom they may have some quarrel, either real or imagined, and may challenge them to fight.

On the first evening, the communities parade through town to the accompaniment of *charangos* and *zampoñas* (a type of pan pipe). Periodically, the revelers halt and form two concentric circles, with women on the inside and men in the outer circle. The women begin singing a typically repetitious and cacophonous chant, while the men run in a circle around them. Suddenly, everyone stops and launches into a powerful stomping dance. Each group is led by at least one person – usually a man – who uses a whip to ensure slackers keep up with the rhythm and the pace.

The situation rapidly progresses past yelling and cursing to pushing and shoving, before it turns into an almost choreographed form of warfare. This has been immortalized in the *tinku* dance, which is frequently performed during Carnaval in highly traditional Oruro, Potosí and other towns in the region. To augment the hand-to-hand combat, the fighters may also throw rocks at their opponents, occasionally causing serious injury or death. Any fatalities, however, are considered a blood offering to Pachamama in lieu of a llama sacrifice for the same purpose.

The best known and arguably most violent *tinku* takes place in the village of **Macha** during the first couple of weeks of May, while the villages of Ocurí and Toracarí, among others, also host *tinkus*.

Only some aspire to witness this private and often violent tradition, which categorically cannot be thought of as a

EARLY HYDROPOWER

In 1905, the French owner of Hacienda Cayara, an engineer who helped build the railroads in Chile, was also the first to electrify the property. Lights were powered by the first hydroelectric plant in Bolivia that he designed and built. Remarkably, it's still in operation, only a few kilometers from Hotel Museo Cayara. Two of the early 20th-century German generators remain in working condition; noteworthy, when you consider they were transportationed by mule overland from Lima, Peru. Perched on a hill just above the hydroelectric plant, **Cabaña la Rinconada**, owned by a third generation descendant of the family that owns Cayara, has several rooms with access to a fully serviced kitchen and living room.

TRADITIONAL FOOD SPECIALTIES

Misk'i Lawa: Todos Santos fiesta dessert made from boiled peaches in a thick and sweet sauce.

Thaya: Frozen dessert in various flavors, like oca (variety of sweet potato), sold by street vendors.

Phisara d'Quinua: Quinoa, cheese and regional vegetables in hefty, nutritious meal.

Tawa Tawas: Small strips of fried dough served with cane honey or sugar.

Kalapurka: Hearty, bubbling, corn-based stew, with potatoes or meat, served in earthenware bowl with a hot volcanic stone in the middle.

Ají de Achacana: Wild cactus root serves as the base of this dish served during Fiestas Chu'tillos and Todos Santos.

Ch'ajchu Potosino: Boiled, juicy pork in a red chili sauce with potatoes and onions.

FOTO ARENA LTDA/ALAMY

***TInku*, Macha (p228)**

tourist attraction; people who have attended insist they'd never do it again. For the terminally curious, however, **Big Deal Tours** *(bigdealtours.blogspot.com)* in Potosí conducts culturally sensitive visits to several of the main *tinku* festivities. Bear in mind that these traditional people most definitely do not want hordes of foreign tourists gawking at them and snapping photos; avoid photographing individuals without their express permission and do not participate.

Places We Love to Stay

$ Budget $$ Midrange $$$ Top End

Cochabamba

MAP p187

Running Chaski Hostal $ Best choice for budget-minded travelers in the city center. Wood-floored rooms have modern furnishings and the helpful staff can provide travel advice.

Hotel Boutique La Casa de Margarita $$ Family run with five homey rooms and a B&B feel in upscale Queru Queru cul-de-sac. Healthy breakfast and bucolic front garden.

Cesar's Plaza $$ For those interested in staying in the heart of downtown. Upscale in a bygone era, now faded.

Gran Hotel Cochabamba $$$ Cochabamba's top hotel is essentially attached to the Iglesia de la Recoleta. It's classy and elegant and has a wonderful patio.

Hotel Aranjuez $$$ Recoleta old-world classic with wonderfully decorated salons; not the place for those seeking contemporary style.

Torotoro

p194

Villa Etelvina $$ A garden oasis a five-minute walk south of town with modern, comfortable accommodationss, nice bathrooms with good hot water pressure, and delicious home cooking.

Cabañas Umajalanta $$ Remote and isolated, on an exposed slope with attractive stone and red-tile roofed cabins. Beds are comfortable and the views are fantastic.

Killa Rumi $$ Globe-shaped glamping tents off the road at the entrance to town.

Sucre

MAP p203

Kultur Berlin $ Sprawling and social, this is a big operation housed in a colonial-era building – ask for one of the uniquely configured and furnished upper-floor rooms in the back building.

Hostal CasArte Takumba $ Nicely furnished with wood floors, sunny courtyard, above-average breakfast and all manner of bedroom layouts.

Casa Verde $$ Solicitous Belgian owner encourages a relaxed, social vibe. Rooms arranged around a small courtyard with a pool.

La Posada $$ Low-key, classy property has tastefully furnished and comfortable rooms with an appealing colonial ambience and professional service. The courtyard restaurant, where breakfast is served, is recommended.

ON Hotel Boutique $$$ Possibly the country's most stylishly designed hotel. Nine unique rooms housed in a 16th-century building with beautifully restored antique furnishings.

Mi Pueblo Samary $$$ Samary has an ambitious concept – reproducing a traditional Chuquisaca village in hotel form. There's a plaza, a chapel and rooms adorned with Yamparaez textiles and replica rock carvings.

Potosí

MAP p217

Hostal La Casona Potosí $ An 18th-century colonial house with a handsome yellow and stone slab inner atrium. The private rooms have nice wood floors, heavy blankets and clean, hot-water showers.

Hacienda Cayara (p226) $$ There's no shortage of old-fashioned luxury at this historically significant sprawling property set amidst beautiful countryside west of Potosí.

Hotel Santa Teresa $$ On a quiet block by the convent of the same name, it's seen better days, but the small brown and green rooms are comfortably furnished; upstairs rooms have natural light.

Hostal Colonial $$ Whitewashed, well-kept colonial building near the main plaza with smallish rooms with windows onto a central courtyard; very helpful English-speaking staff.[1]

FAVIO ANTEZANA/SHUTTERSTOCK

Left: Carnaval, Tarija (p243); Right: Vineyard, Tarija (p246

Researched by
Brian Kluepfel

South Central Bolivia & the Chaco

HIGH TIMES, WINE AND ALTIPLANO ADVENTURES

This somewhat overlooked southern outpost of Bolivia is a warm place in culture and climate, host to good wines and food.

South Central Bolivia is a place of long memories – where the traditions of winemaking brought by the Spanish Jesuits 400 years ago are still alive, and the sting of the bitter Chaco War a century ago abides. The memories you make here will also be impactful: days sipping the wine and munching prize-winning hams, nights observing the crystal clear skies and stars, mornings idling away in Tarija's shaded cafes or pumping your adrenaline up a notch with Altiplano hikes or biking around torrid Villamontes.

The driving rhythms of twin violin and guitar will be fresh in your mind long after you've left this rough and ready corner of Bolivia behind. Your dinner plate is likely to be filled with fresh crayfish and crabs, and during summer's run of *sábalo* fish (streaked prochilod), you can join in the harvest on the banks of the River Pilcomayo.

There's no higher grape-growing region in the world, and the high from the hearty reds and intense burn from the eye-watering *singani* (grape brandy) will linger – as you should, in this oft-overlooked region. Indigenous encounters, flamingo-filled lakes and the largest reserve of cacti anywhere outside of Mexico, South Central Bolivia will stick to you months and years after you've departed.

ERICKDOCK/SHUTTERSTOCK

THE MAIN AREAS

TARIJA
Wine, dance, and high plains adventure. p238

VILLAMONTES
Torrid, placid, folksy frontier town. p251

Find Your Way

South Central Bolivia is remote, but not unreachable. Tarija's airport connects to both national and international destinations. Once in Tarija or Villamontes, you can walk most places; between the cities there is regular *trufi* (shared car or minibus) service.

Tarija, p238
The heart of the South Central, famed for its wine and warm climate and *chapaco (tarijeña)* culture.

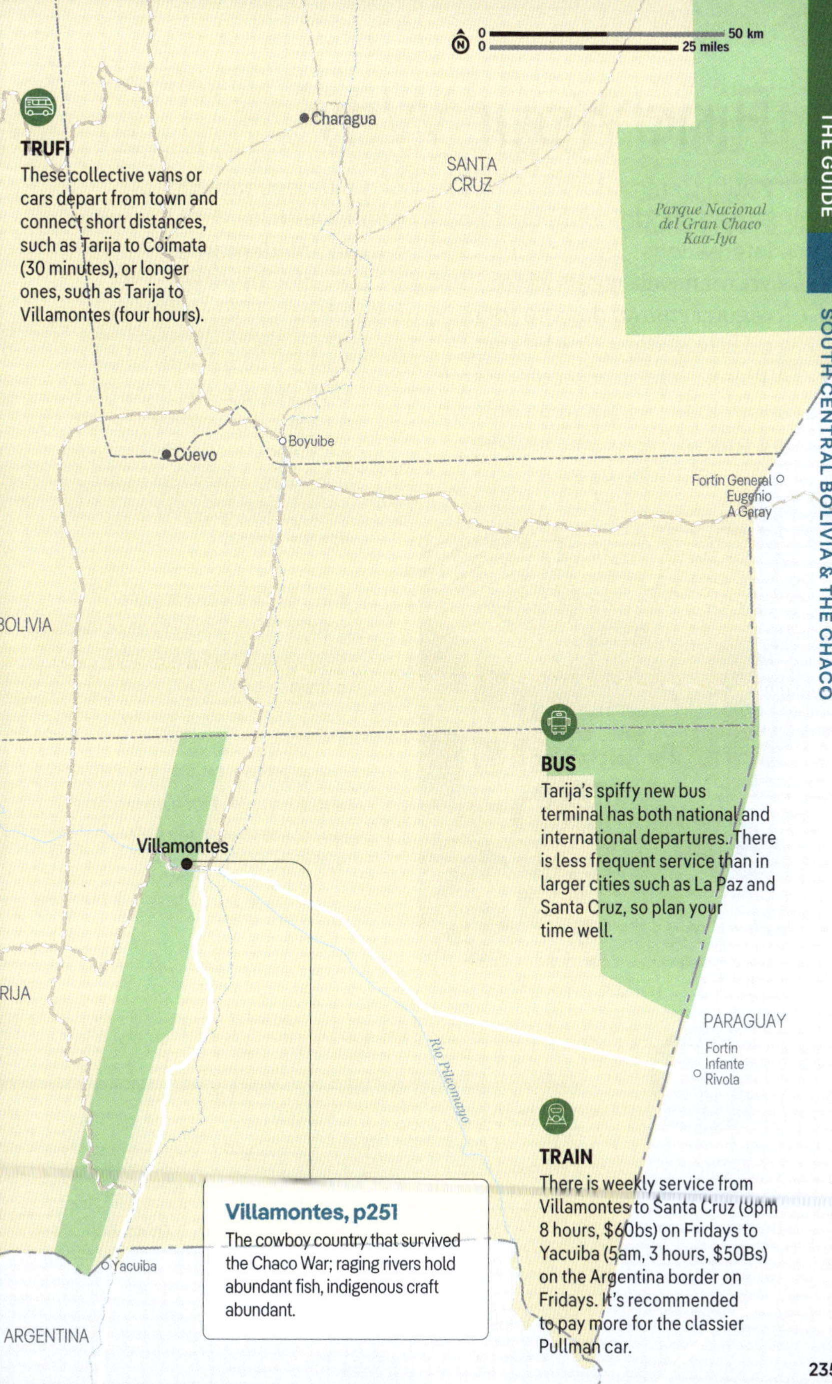

TRUFI

These collective vans or cars depart from town and connect short distances, such as Tarija to Coimata (30 minutes), or longer ones, such as Tarija to Villamontes (four hours).

BUS

Tarija's spiffy new bus terminal has both national and international departures. There is less frequent service than in larger cities such as La Paz and Santa Cruz, so plan your time well.

TRAIN

There is weekly service from Villamontes to Santa Cruz (8pm 8 hours, $60bs) on Fridays to Yacuiba (5am, 3 hours, $50Bs) on the Argentina border on Fridays. It's recommended to pay more for the classier Pullman car.

Villamontes, p251

The cowboy country that survived the Chaco War; raging rivers hold abundant fish, indigenous craft abundant.

Plan Your Time

Beyond the delicious wine, there's plenty to do here to fill a couple of days. The looming Altiplano has spectacular vistas and wildlife; just outside of town are refreshing rapids and star-filled night-time skies.

Mercado Central, Tarija (p244)

If You Only Have One Day

- If you only have one day in South Central, go for Tarija's wine. Start with breakfast at Tarija's splendid plaza **Habitat Cafe** (p243) and enjoy a stroll along Calle 15 de Abril, the city's main thoroughfare, before departing for a **half-day wine tour** (p247). Try to mix and match among the large-scale producers and the boutique, batch wine makers; also try to sample some *singani* brandy along with the vino.

- In the afternoon, have lunch or some charcuterie at one of the wineries before heading back to town.

- In the evening, just before sunset, hike up to one of the city's **miradors** (p245) for a memorable view of the landscape before a final dinner in Tarija.

Seasonal Highlights

In a place dependent on the mercy of Mother Nature, food-centric celebrations are crucial, and in a devout country like Bolivia many take on a Catholic tinge.

FEBRUARY

Carnaval allows Catholics to blow off steam before the general dourness of Lent.The Tarija celebration (Carnaval Chapaco) includes a parade of horses, the election of a carnaval queen and devils dancing.

MARCH

Vendimia (p241) holds court in the Valle de la Concepción, in Uriondo, Tarija. The event is hailed for its celebration of regional food, music, and dare we say...wine.

APRIL

San Lorenzo residents decorate their streets with decorative yellow flower displays (**Pascua Florida**) in honor of Christ's passion on Easter.

If You Have Three Days

- Do a full-day wine tour. Start day two at **Reserva Biológica Cordillera de Sama** (p249) and Lake Tajzara's birdlife. Lunch on the dunes; then head to the adjacent Parque de Cardon (cactus park). Take in an evening show at **Cacharpaya** (p243), featuring national music, big steaks and wine.

- Start the third day at Tarija's **paleontology museum** (p242), with its unexpected wealth of impressive artifacts. In the afternoon, lunch with locals at the **Mercado Central** (p246). Pick up some snacks for a quick trip to the swimming holes of Coimata.

- In the evening, switch it up with a dinner at one of Plazuela Uriondo's eateries like **El Fogón del Gringo** (p247).

A Five-Day Jaunt

- On the fourth day, catch an early *trufi* for the four-hour ride to Villamontes. In the afternoon, take a half-day bike trip or tour of the town's historic sites. In the evening, enjoy a meal of fresh fish or pork roasted on a large fire at one of the town's **rustic eateries** (p253).

- On day five, still in Villamontes, head up to the *angosto*, or narrows, for splendid views of the Río Pilcomayo.

- In the afternoon, have one last lunch before catching a *trufi* back to Tarija to arrive at sundown and check out the stars at the **country's only astronomical observatory** (p244), just outside of town. You'll be back in time for a late dinner and final glass of hearty red wine.

JUNE

The winter solstice on June 21 marks the **Aymara New Year** and is celebrated throughout the indigenous population; near Tarija these festivities are marked in the communities around Lake Pujzara on the altiplano.

JULY

Between May and August comes the legendary running of the *sábalo* on the Pilcomayo in Villamontes Community members of all ages gather on the riverbanks with nets to catch the popular and prodigious *pesce*.

AUGUST

August's **Fiesta de San Roque**, the city's patron saint, celebrants dress as *'chunchos'* or lepers, with face coverings and colorful costumes. Since 2021 this has been a UNESCO-recognized celebration.

DECEMBER

As in many Latin American countries, the **Christmas** celebrations begin before December 25 and extend to January 6. The town, and nation slow down and enjoy time with family.

Tarija

WINE & FOOD | ALTIPLANO ADVENTURE | SONG & DANCE

GETTING AROUND

Tarija is a very walkable city and if you use the principle 15 de Abril artery as your guide, you'll navigate the heart of the city easily – it connects the three main plazas: Uriondo, Luis de Fuentes, and Sucre. Taxis are abundant and cheap, and for out of town excursions to close-by places *trufis* are also a good bet.

TOP TIP

Although Tarija is mostly flat, it's also warm. Walk slowly, look for shade, wear a hat, and take time to relax on the benches in some of the sprawling plazas. Coffee and alcohol are diuretics; don't forget to hydrate.

While the Altiplano may be too cold and the Amazon too hot and steamy, gentle Tarija is in the words of the Goldilocks, "just right." Bolivia's southern city of a quarter-million residents offers shaded plazas bordered with cafes that provide perfect midday respites, and tours of the neighboring wineries, from boutique small-shop ops to industrial producers, are borderline obligatory. Its hams and cheese are legendary, as is the food stewing at the bustling Mercado Central, a must-stop for lunch. But beyond the culinary treats lie amazing Altiplano adventures just a short ride from town, where you can commune with camelids and trod the same pathways the Inca did centuries ago. The rarer condor and spectacled bear may make a surprise appearance; always be ready for wonder to be just around the corner on the high plains.

Meet a Former Bolivian President

Crunchy crabs, historic homes

In the tiny burg of San Lorenzo, you'll get to see the legacy of two Bolivian presidents: one dead, and one still living. The **Museo Moto Mendez** (Casa de Eustaquio Mendez, officially), just off the main square, is mostly a collection of weapons of warfare from one of the heroes of the Chaco, but the yard has some very interesting modern sculpture, worth the B$10 entry fee.

Just up the road, however, lies **El Picacho**, the residence of ex-president Jaime Paz Zamora (and once, of Moto Mendez, a local landowner and hero of independence from Argentina). Paz guides groups around his riverside home, with advance reservation *(B$25 Bs per person)*. The garden-filled river property (four hectares of rare trees and plants) is chock full of interesting tidbits such as mosaics with quotes from Miguel Cervantes, a laurel tree gifted to Paz by Pope John Paul II and an airplane wing that crashed in an assassination attempt on Paz; only he survived.

En route to San Lorenzo you'll pass the riverside stands of Tomatitos, all serving *cangrejitos,* the thumb-sized crabs caught in the Gauldaquivir, with a serving of *mote* (large kerneled corn).

TARIJA

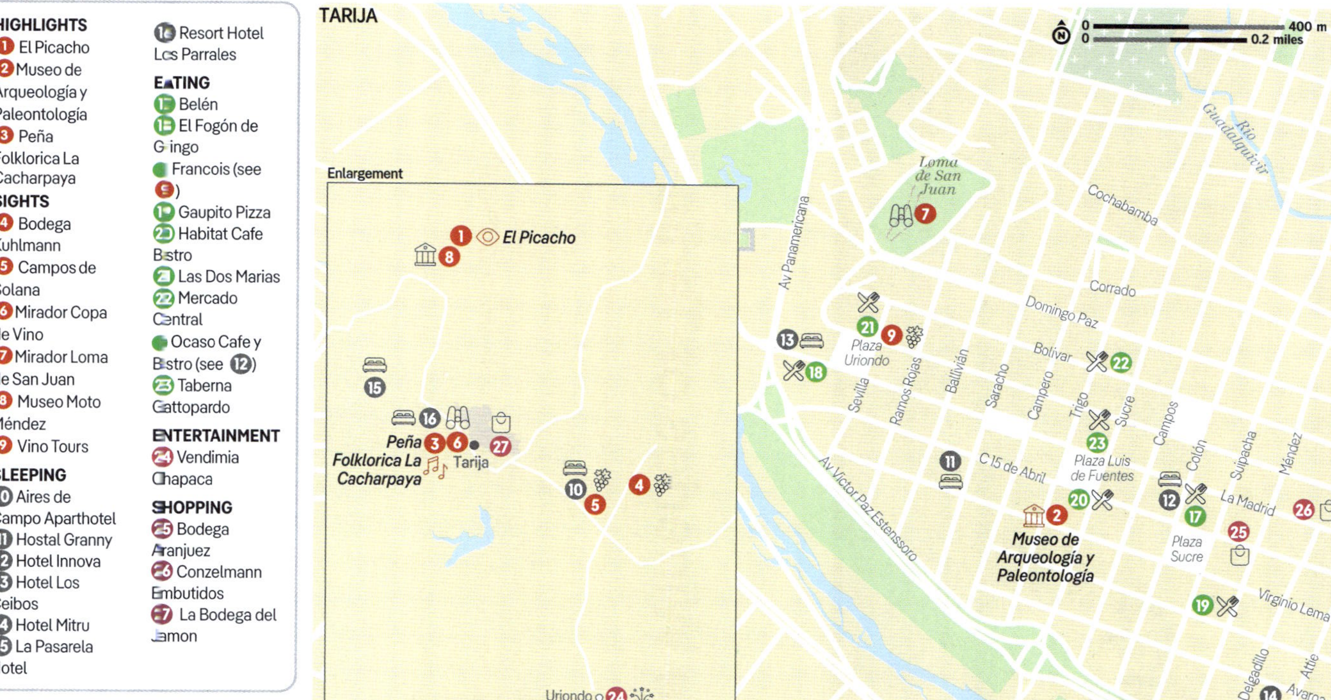

HIGHLIGHTS
1 El Picacho
2 Museo de Arqueología y Paleontología
3 Peña Folklorica La Cacharpaya

SIGHTS
4 Bodega Kuhlmann
5 Campos de Solana
6 Mirador Copa de Vino
7 Mirador Loma de San Juan
8 Museo Moto Méndez
9 Vino Tours

SLEEPING
10 Aires de Campo Aparthotel
11 Hostal Granny
12 Hotel Innova
13 Hotel Los Ceibos
14 Hotel Mitru
15 La Pasarela Hotel
16 Resort Hotel Los Parrales

EATING
17 Belén
18 El Fogón de Gringo
Francois (see 9)
19 Gaupito Pizza
20 Habitat Cafe Bistro
21 Las Dos Marias
22 Mercado Central
Ocaso Cafe y Bistro (see 12)
23 Taberna Gattopardo

ENTERTAINMENT
24 Vendimia Chapaca

SHOPPING
25 Bodega Aranjuez
26 Conzelmann Embutidos
27 La Bodega del Jamon

AIZAR RALDES/GETTY IMAGES

Bodega Kuhlmann

TOP EXPERIENCE

The Wineries of Tarija

Red, red wine. An eye-opening brandy called *singani.* Touring wineries and tasting these liquid refreshments is the motivation for most visits to Tarija, with good reason. Since the commercialization of vino really took off here in the 1970s, the unique Muscatel de Alexandria and other grapes from Tarija's high-altitude vineyards are producing something special. Just debuting on international markets, you'll get a unique peak at (and taste of) some strongly individual brands.

DON'T MISS

- Industrial producers
- *Singani* tasting
- Boutique wineries
- Wine and food pairing
- Guided vineyard walks
- Sunset tasting

Starting the Day

Your tour most often will begin with a hotel pick up, perhaps before breakfast or lunch. Remember, it's good to have something in your stomach before a couple of hours of wine-tasting.

Visiting the Big Three

A wine tour usually includes a visit to at least one of Tarija's 'big three' producers.

Campos de Solana is a modern winery that has spent a quarter century experimenting with US and German grapes at 1800m above sea level to produce a range of varietals, high in antioxidants. The secret lies in the rich clay soils and two malic acid fermentations in oak or bourbon barrels. Solana's Unico varietal has won 88 medals; it also produces a nice riesling and rosé. **Singani Casa Real** (part of Solana) grows lavender at its entrance, which helps with its gin-making, but the focus is on four million bottles of *singani* produced annually.

Bodega Kuhlmann's three fincas focus on *singani* and sparkling wine. They also have property in Sucre's Cinti Valley.

Vinos Aranjuez is one of the pioneers in the modern wine movement here, and the first to introduce Tannat grapes. With vineyards as high as 2000m above sea level, Milton has carried on his father Gerardo's legacy proudly.

Aro Aro: Chapaca Rap

One of the more entertaining parts of your wine tour may include a spoken-word performance by your vineyard guides. It's a Tarija oral tradition known as *aro aro* and involves spontaneous rhyming couplets, composed by the tour guides while the group gathers around. They are comic and playful in nature, and for the Spanish-speaking crowd, a great source of pleasure (if you don't speak Spanish, you'll probably get the gist, anyhow).

A few stops on tours also include musical performances on the patio or in the vineyard's bar.

Ham with That?

A few tours also include a musical performance on the patio or in the vineyard's bar. Some tours include a visit to the famed local serrano ham producers, the Ulloa family's grand estate 15 km outside of Tarija. You'll relish the magical combination of *jamon y vino*.

Getting Your Feet (& Hands) Wet

During Carnaval season from February to March, the smaller artesenal vineyards may introduce you to the art of *vino patero*, or wine made by stomping on the grapes. Visitors get individual tubs and can experience the ultimate in old-school winemaking.

You can also pick grapes during this season. Carnaval is also the time when **Vendimia**, the grape harvest festival, takes place.

WINE FROM ON HIGH

Large-scale wine production in Bolivia didn't truly begin until the 1960s and 1970s. Now the wine is marketed as 'wine from on high' and is marked by rich, deep colors ranging from red to violet, with notes of leather and tobacco and, after aging in oak barrels, characteristics of vanilla, honey and chocolate. It's said that the altitude allows the grapes to absorb more ultraviolet radiation than they would at other heights.

TOP TIPS

- Plan your wine tour in advance – some places simply will not open for drive-bys, so if you're out in the valley and fancy a glass, you might be out of luck.
- It's nice to have a mix of boutique and large-scale producers so you can feel and taste the difference.
- Try to include a *vino patero* (wine made by foot) experience in your day – the larger producers have beautiful verandas and classy tours, but there's nothing like the manual stomping of grapes.
- Talk to your tour planner about the best options for you, but note that you may be limited by what's open.

THE MILLIONAIRE'S MAST & BRIDGE

Flying the flag for economic solvency wasn't part of the plan, apparently. A giant flagpole (Hito Historico, or historic marker) sits nearly unused on the road to Tomatito, where it was placed to hoist the nation's largest flag. It cost nearly three-quarters of a million US dollars, money that, many lament, would have been better used funding basic services.

The original cost of the project was just under the five-million-boliviano limit (it cost about $720,000) for it to be vetted by authorities.

Already, some embarrassed citizens and politicians have proposed that the mast be replaced by a statue of the municipality's patron saint, San Roque.

Museo Nacional de Arqueologio y Paleontologico

Digging Deep at Tarija's Paleontology Museum

Far from just rocks and bones

Prepare to be amazed: Tarija's **Museo Nacional de Arqueologio y Paleontologico** *(ibolivia.org/museo-nacional-paleontologico-tarija; entry B$10)* seems unprepossessing from the outside on the corners of Calle General Trijo and Virginia Lema, but walk through the colonial-era doors and you're immediately steeped in the ancient history and prehistory of Bolivia and the continent, as told by various bones, rocks and other evidence (more than 11,000 pieces are in the museum's collection).

Most impressive are the megafauna fossils, many of which have been almost completely reassembled. These beasts from the Ice Age seem to come to life in the 1st-floor exhibit space, and show that once upon a time there was an alluvial plain twenty times the size of the modern-day Guadalquivir River that stretched across Tarija.

A complete mammoth skeleton, including impressively long tusks. A massive armadillo, head and all, completely reassembled (its tail is nearby, in a separate glass case). Skulls of equine ancestors. A 9ft land sloth. Five hundred of the 700 mammal fossils held here were found in the Cueva Cuaternaria outside of Tarija; about 200 date to the Paleozoic Era. But it's not the raw data or numbers of bones that impress – it's their size and completeness, giving visitors a striking impression of how these creatures appeared.

Yet more startling striking discoveries have been made in the region: in 2019 more than 600 dinosaur bones were uncovered outside of Tarija, some thought to date to the Jurassic Age. These are even older than Sucre's Cretacean specimens, and included more armadillos, sloths, and the legendary saber-toothed tiger (Smilodon).

The museum also holds a large collection of exhibits linked to our ancient relatives, including more than 5,000 ceramic pieces, bone arrows used to hunt the ancient mammals, and necklaces and other decorative pieces fashioned from bone and stone. The 2nd-floor Archaeology Museum is half-filled with a dazzling mineral collection, with a breathtaking range of colors and types of gems on display.

Alongside these rocks are skulls and other human remains, including the museum's most haunting sight: the mummy of a small child, still curled up in a blanket within its glass display case.

Set aside several hours at least to take in the two-floor collection and appreciate the comprehensive historic and scientific value on display here and the stories that this museum continues to tell.

Music & Dance of a Nation

Regional music in a big old barn

Large groups tend to fill the tables at **Peña Folklorica La Cacharpaya** *(facebook.com/LaCacharpayaTarija; entry B$70)*, a voluminous music hall on the outskirts of town whose dirt parking lot doesn't start to fill up until 10pm. You pay the B$70 entry fee and enter a zone worthy of an old Western film.

A sign here says 'our roots are expressed through our dance, our music, our songs and our food.' And that's what you'll get for as long as you wish to stay; weekend evenings extend 'til dawn.

A typical act may be like Beto and Chiky Vidal's five piece band featuring the rocking, staccato rhythms of *música chapaca,* bolstered by electric bass and twin violins dancing around the melody. Dry ice adds to the rock-and-roll arena vibe, but you're still in a club just steps from the stage.

The music isn't limited to bands, nor is it all live. Another typical performance may be a dance troupe from Santa Cruz, replete in costumes but playing to a pre-recorded soundtrack (this diminishes the vibe a bit, to be honest). More dry ice pours across the stage. The announcer asks the audience where everyone is from. La Paz? Cochabamba? Glorious shouts arise from the well-oiled clientele. The Bolivian nation is in the house.

A surprise guest rises from the seats: a violinist from Cordoba, Spain who performs a Celtic whirligig of a number, the equivalent, perhaps, of a Bolivian jig.

Here, wine goes by the bottle (B$40) and steak, by the yard, it would seem (B$70). The huge barn-like building and long wooden tables add to the communal spirit, and it's a great joint for a group meal. It's a tremendous *peña* (folk-music)

TARIJA'S SPECIAL VINTAGE

Edward Lara,
Llama Wines owner
@LlamawINES

I grew up in Northern California enjoying the amazing wines of Napa and Sonoma. I now go regularly to Bolivia to bring their best wines to the US.

The grapes are grown between 1700m and 3000m above sea level – the highest wine valley in the Americas. The vines work much harder at that altitude, which gives the grapes and wine a delicious complexity.

Campos de Solana has expanded its bodega at Casa Real to offer incredible estate tours, including the llamas in the vineyards.

To complete your experience, my vote for best restaurant in Tarija is Casona Del Molina. For a fun lunch in valley, Casa Vieja has delicious food and very sweet wines. In Valle de la Concepcion, check out the amazing murals.

EATING & DRINKING IN TARIJA: OUR FAVORITE CAFES

Ocaso Cafe: Old jazz, old radios, lovely blue-green sofas provide tranquility next to the Innova Hotel. *7am-10pm* $$

Habitat Cafe Bistro: On the main plaza with fab acai bowls and desserts such as the *beso chapaco* (chapaco kiss), and *lacayote* mousse. *8:30am-1pm & 4-9pm Mon-Sat* $$

Cafe Belén: Another fave on Calle Colon offering nice hot chocolate, two-fruit juices such as a mango-maracuya blend, and an *ensalada chapaca*. *8:30am-11pm* $$

Las Dos Marias: Quiet affair on a corner of Plaza Uriondo owned by two friends named – guess what – Maria. *8:30am-12:30pm & 4-10pm* $$

UFOS IN TARIJA?

On May 6, 1978, an unidentified flying object crashed into El Zaire, a remote mountain peak between Tarija and Argentina's Salta province.

The ground trembled. Windows broke 30 miles from the site. CIA agents were rumored to be on the ground. It crashed in Argentina. No, Bolivia. Authorities were keeping people away. It was a 'cylindrical, smoking object.' It was 15ft long and dented from the crash. Some even claimed that the United States sent a cargo plane to carry the remnants away.

There was an explosion, resulting in a massive crater. Was it a Russian satellite? Some space debris? Whatever happened, locals still talk about it.

ANDREAS WOLOCHOW/SHUTTERSTOCK

Mirador Copa de Vino

experience to catch a bit of the folkloric traditions from around the country.

Bolivia's Only Astronomical Observatory

Crystalline stars, thanks USSR

As you wander through the circular entryway to **Santa Ana's Observatorio Astronómico Nacional** *(facebook.com/OAN.Tarija.Bolivia; tour B$20)* a half-hour outside of Tarija proper, you'll perhaps want to pause for a moment and thank an unlikely sponsor for this stargazing opportunity: the Soviet Union (USSR).

Neither you nor the gaggle of schoolchildren who often attend the observatory's night tours may have been born during the Cold War, but it was crucial to the construction and location of this site. While much of South America was leaning to the right in the early 1980s, Bolivia was momentarily out of step and had a socialist president, Hernan Siles.

Bolivia and the Soviet Union signed a cooperative scientific accord in 1982 and in 1984 the Observatorio Astronómico Boliviano-Soviético opened. It remains the country's only astronomical observatory, aided by its location in the high, dry desert 14km from the city.

Your tour will be divided into two parts: the observatory, and the planetarium (also the country's only). You may choose to join the group with fewer children, although to be honest, it's a delight to see the students' innocent reactions to the marvels of the night skies.

From the observatory's massive telescope, which accesses the heavens via a very cool retractable roof, you might be lucky to see the moon, Mars, Jupiter, Venus, Saturn and Mercury, and stars such as Sirius and Antartes. Whether or not the night is clear, you'll have the chance to glance through the magnificent lens and witness how it turns on its mechanism for optimal viewing.

Crossing over from the observatory to the planetarium, you'll realize you're surrounded by local vineyards and their intoxicating smells – the observatory's land was donated by the Kohlberg wine-making family. Take a moment to look up at the Bolivian night sky, inky black, and imagine how the precolonial inhabitants viewed this scene, and what stories they created from it.

Ringing the serpentine corridors that lead to the 90-seat planetarium, you'll see mood-setting photos of planets, astronauts and other spacy memorabilia. The planetarium and its massive Mitsubishi screen were a gift from Japan in 2006.

The 20-minute planetarium show, unlike the observatory's, is not dependent on outside climatic conditions and is rather spectacular and comprehensive. It is not only the children in the audience who gasp in wonder at some of the material projected onto the two-ton screen.

Tarija's Prize-Winning Hams

Salt of the earth

What could be nicer with a glass of wine than a slice of quality ham? Tarija has been famous for its cured Serrano hams for decades, and the city's stores and producers provide ample opportunities to sample this local speciality.

In downtown Tarija, you can wander into Jamones Zenteno, also known as **La Bodega del Jamon** *(facebook.com/labodegadeljamontarija)*, where cured pork legs dangle from the wall like salty banjos. The family business, in this locale for two decades, also has a variety of cooked and raw pork products, like Chorizo Español, mortadella, *pernil* and bacon.

Also in downtown is the famed Mercado Central (p246), which has a ham kiosk right on the 1st floor of its massive hangar-like site. **Conzelmann Embutidos** (Calle La Madrid between Méndez and Delgadillo) sells a number of sausage and cooked ham products.

The biggest ham in town is Jaime Ulloa *(@jamones_ulloa_tarija)* who produces between 800 and 1000 hams per year on his ranch 15km outside of Tarija. Although Ulloa has no store of his own, you can visit the finca on tours; contact **Vino Tours** for a good option.

A combination of factors have led to Tarija ham's unique taste, which has garnered international prizes: the use of Bolivian salt from the Salar de Uyuni, Bolivia's famous salt flat, is crucial in the curing process. It's said to be similar to ocean salt, and has a good blend of nitrates and nitrites. Each year Tarija produces more than 3000 legs of ham. Most come from small-scale producers, yet are recognized on a global scale, with purchasers as far afield as France and Spain.

Two Most Excellent Lookouts

Panoramic vistas, contrasting viewpoints

As Tarija's most famous product is its wine, it's no surprise that one of its prominent promontories is a wineglass-shaped *mirador* (lookout) known as the **Mirador Copa de Vino** (aka Mirador de los Sueños). Just over the Puente San Martin from Plaza Uriondo, the neighborhood streets curve up and away

DRIVING OUT DEVILS: TARIJA'S CARNAVAL

Tarija celebrates Carnaval, the Catholic Lenten ritual, in its own unique way. It begins with a parade of women, short-skirted and twirling colorful *mantas* (short ponchos), spinning in groups, holding stalks of flowers. Next comes the *cabalgata* (horse parade), with chapaco cowboys and cowgirls riding high in the saddle, beating small hand-drums, astride lovely purebred horses equally decorated in fancy saddles and garlands of flowers.

Later comes the *soltado del diablo* (driving out the devil) where residents dress as frightening devil characters sporting horns and heart-stopping masks, while observers spray them playfully with water. Much food and merriment abides in this unique *tarijeña* custom.

At the end of Lent, San Lorenzo and neighboring towns celebrate Easter with Pascua Florida, decorating the streets with arches of bright yellow flowers.

FIESTA DE SAN ROQUE

Each August 16 thousands of pilgrims, or *chunchos* fill the streets of Tarija to honor the city's patron saint, San Roque, during the Fiesta de San Roque, or Grande Fiesta de Tarija. Outfitted in a colorful three-part ensemble, topped with a feathered turban, the *chunchos* represent lepers from past times, when leprosy and plague affected the area (hence the face coverings). They arrive beating drums, shaking colorful rattles, and playing traditional instruments such as wooden flutes, to ceremonially beg for provisions and a place to stay. Up to 50,000 people descend on the city for the event. The happening was declared a cultural event of importance by UNESCO in 2021.

FAVIO ANTEZANA/SHUTTERSTOCK

from the bridge, leading inevitably to the Copa. There are steep steps from the street on either side of the hill, but the wise go for the more central approach, hundreds of purple steps leading like a trail of spilled wine to the mirador.

It's a taxing climb; take it easy and reward yourself with a B$1 bag of water from the vendor near the top, if you haven't brought your own refreshment. The entire structure, of which you can clamber between levels until you reach the open-air topmost floor, is made of more than 1000 mirrors, and the 360-degree view is inviting, both the rooftops of the expansive city and the mountains in the far distance. An array of beautiful murals adorns the base of the hill where the Copa reigns, and is worth a slow walk of appreciation.

Opposite the Copa, uphill from Plaza Uriondo and Los Ceibos hotel, is the Mirador Corazón de Jesus (aka **Loma de San Juan**). The route around the top of this very Christian *mirador* follows a path of the Catholic Stations of the Cross, each panel depicting a scene from Christ's last day. From a certain perspective, the outstretched arms of Jesus may appear to be reaching across the divide toward the Copa de Vino. The pleasant gardens at the top are home to a bevy of orchids and roses, as well.

Mercado Central

Chowing down with the locals

Busy, friendly vendors milling around stacks of cheese and other local produce will be your first sights (and smells) as you enter Tarija's **Mercado Central** *(tarijaturismo.com/mercado-central)*. This vibrant building is where the city meets to shop, relax, talk, and of course, eat. Over three floors, there is a children's play area, a massage chair station, and tables and shelves stocked with dozens of fruits and sundries; but if you

Fiesta de San Roque

come around the lunch hour, head to the 2nd floor for some true Tarija flavor.

The imposing yellow-and-white building, which resembles a large airplane hanger with rings of stalls around its perimeter, is a relatively new addition to Tarija, replacing the older market in 2018. Like most Bolivian markets, it's a whirlwind of activity and raucous atmosphere – in addition to the visual and olfactory stimuli mentioned above, there is the auditory overload of dozens of vendors hawking their product.

A great array of freshly prepared items will tempt you in the 2nd-floor dining halls. A favorite here is *saice,* a rich stew of ground beef, onion, tomato, garlic and other spices, simmered for hours to reach just the right flavor. It's served with carbohydrates like pasta, potato and white rice and sits very nicely in your belly until dinner time comes around.

You may also try the popular *sopa de maní* (peanut soup) or *picante de pollo a la tarijena*, a chicken dish soaked in chilis and red wine. *Averjada* is a plateful of peas, french fries, onions and other condiments topped with an egg.

Desserts include *sopaipillas* (fried dough) drizzled in honey and rosquetes, a ring-shaped cookie smothered in white cream. Mainly, the Mercado Central is a fun, inexpensive place to try local dishes while mingling with everyday *tarijeñas*, who will delight in seeing you enjoying their culture.

EATING IN TARIJA: OUR PICKS

Gattopardo: Nice outdoor/indoor joint on the plaza, nice sandwiches, salads and mains with an attentive staff. *7:30am-11pm* $$

Gaupito Pizza: Ever tried a pizza topped with *charque de llama* (llama jerky)? That's just one reason to stop at this cozy corner eatery. *6-10:30pm Mon-Sat* $

Francois: A wine lover's dream. Excellent food with an attention to detail and hospitality that exceeds all expectations. *9am-11pm Tue-Sat, 11am-10pm Sun* $$

El Fogon del Gringo: High-level Argentine-style steakhouse; digest your meal in nearvy Plaza Uriondo afterwards. *noon-3pm daily, 6:30-11 Mon-Sat* $$

Beyond Tarija

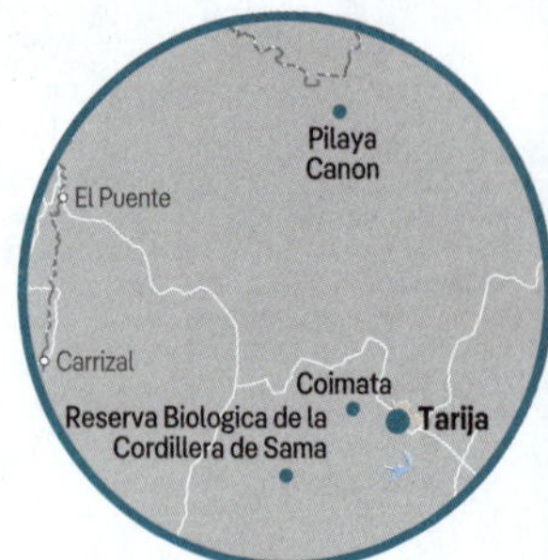

Just beyond the outskirts of town, a short taxi or bike ride away, are rustic roadside eateries, refreshing springs and waterfalls.

Places

A handful of nearby sights are just a few kilometers away, including the San Jacinto Dam, Coimata, Tomatitos, and San Lorenzo. These are places away from the closed-in streets and traffic of Tarija where locals go to breath more freely, swim, eat and be with family. For this reason, it may to avoid them on weekends if you're looking for a relaxing outing, because Bolivians go in great numbers. Easily accessible by public transportation (or even bike), these *pueblitos* will give you a moment or two to completely unwind, country-style.

GETTING AROUND

You can rent a bike to get to these places, but keep a close eye on it (bike rentals come with locks – use them). There are also regular *trufis* (shared cars or vans). Taxis are many, and relatively inexpensive, especially if you combine two destinations. On a good day, these sites are even walkable, but remember to protect yourself from the sun.

San Jacinto

TIME FROM TARIJA: **30 MINS**

Munching on crabs, sipping on wine

Just a short cab or *trufi* ride 7km outside of Tarija city is an interesting sideshow known as Represa San Jacinto (San Jacinto Dam). It was constructed in a 1978 engineering government project to generate hydroelectric power, and to irrigate nearby farmlands (some of the Bolivian wine boom of the 1970s owes a debt to the dam). Most cars park on the near side, and you'll get out and walk across the dam – it's a very steep drop on one side; stomach-churning, in fact. On the other side is Lago San Jacinto, created by the dam, filled with small rowboats (yes, you can rent one) and dotted with purple water hyacinths.

Crossing to the far side of the dam you'll arrive amidst a small market economy based on very few things: two of them are the crunchy, crispy crabs *(cangrejos)* that are stirred up in a pot and seasoned and the toe-curlingly sweet red wine, served in glasses that couldn't be filled any further to the brim. You can also purchase home-made *humintas* (corn cakes) *chirriadas* (corn tortillas) and a few different local fish, all roasted over wood fires. As you dine at one of the lakeside tables you'll notice swallows and swifts making an aerial show, popping in and out of their nests in the dam's many crevices.

Locals love to come and walk here, and if you stick around until sunset you'll often get a nice one over the mountains to the northwest. There are also motorized watercraft across the lake if a rowboat's too tame for you.

The drive or *trufi* ride from town takes 15 to 30 minutes. If you're fit, it's a decent bike trip, but mind your transport, as some have 'walked off' when unattended.

Reserva Biologica de la Cordillera de Sama

TIME FROM TARIJA: **2 HRS**

Tour and flamingos at Lago Tajzara

Visiting **Reserva Biologica de la Cordillera de Sama** independently or with a tour company from Tarija *(facebook.com/surbikebolivia; park entrance B$10, tours B$180-230 per person)*, the city turns to town turns to Altiplano village at 14,000ft above sea level.

Leaving Tarija, you'll pass San Lorenzo's iconic church. You'll then drive through the village of Izcayachi, then after crossing dry highland landscape with outcroppings of onion, garlic and potato, turning off the main highway, reach Tajzara.

You'll proceed further to Copacabana's Plaza de Integracion; oriented so that the light hits the Puerto del sol and Puerta del luna (gate of the sun and moon) on the June solstice, an Aymara sacred day. Take lunch at the nearby dunes, where you might sample local *charquican* (llama jerky) or *trucha* (trout).

You'll next visit the village of Pasajes, where a *capilla* (weatherworn chapel of orange-red clay) seems to emerge from the terrain itself, topped by two crosses. Take a 30-minute walk to Lago Tajzara (pronounced 'tax-ah-rah'), where you may be gifted with the sight of a flock of Andean flamingos. Sometimes they appear in the hundreds; for the fortunate traveler, they may come by the thousand. You may also see Andean ducks, Andean gulls, avocets, ibis and the ubiquitous coot.

From Tajzara you can walk a short distance to the smaller Laguna Pujzara (Pook-sah-rah) and the village of Pinos, from where independent travelers can catch transport back to Tarija; you may need to wait several hours for such transport to appear. Consult with the Sernap office in Tarija for maps and conditions if you decide to visit independently.

Bolivia's magic cactus park

A possible side trip for those visiting Lago Tajzara is an excursion to the adjacent Parque Natural y Área de Manejo Integrado El Cardón. This is the largest cactus reserve in Latin America, after Tehuacán in Mexico, home to 12 species of cacti not known elsewhere, 14 overall, all topped by red, yellow, white and green flowers and fruits. There are green, yellow, fox's tail, and *champú* cacti, and the towering 12ft toothpick cactus is known as one of the species that contains the psychoactive substance mescalino.

PLAZA DE INTEGRACIÓN: CULTURAL LANDMARK

Just down the road from its ancient adobe Catholic church is a plaza with as much significance to the Copacabana community on the shore of Lago Pujzara: the Plaza de Integración. The open-air rectangular monument contains wall carvings of indigenous heroes, as well as natural life of the high desert – camelids such as llamas and alpacas, and local birds such as flamingos, grebes, condors and emus. Crucially, this is the spot framed by the portals of the sun and the moon, where the Aymara New Year is celebrated on the winter (June 21) solstice, with the burning of ritual incenses and other salutes to Pachamama, or Mother Earth.

BEST SWIMMING HOLES & WATERFALLS NEAR TARIJA

Coimata: Coimata has a series of *pozos*, or swimming holes, quite popular locally. Lots of pop-up restaurants to choose from, too.

Coimata Falls: To escape potential crowds, walk 40 minutes from the Coimata entrance to these gushing 60m falls.

Rincon de la Victoria: Some 6km southwest of Tomatitas; features a swimming hole and waterfall.

Chorros de Jurina: Two interesting waterfalls 26 km from Tarija proper; one flows over white stone, the other over black. Walkable from San Lorenzo.

Tomatitas: Just 5km from Tarija, the natural swimming holes where three rivers meet are local favorites.

Pilaya Canon

TIME FROM TARIJA: **2 HRS**

Cycle to the world's sixth-deepest canyon

This guided tour from **Tarija with Sur Bike** *(facebook.com/surbikebolivia; B$180 per person)* will take you through old-use farmland and up steep hillsides to a vantage point over one of the deepest canyons in the world.

After summitting the dirt path – aware always of the cacti, blooming yellow and white flowers, and other blooming trees on the way – it almost feels like you could fall into the abyss. This is Pilaya Canyon, the sixth-deepest canyon in the world. At 3030m deep, it plumbs depths some 900m deeper than the US Grand Canyon.

Far below is the raging Pilaya River, a tributary of the Pilcomayo – so forceful are its waters that you can hear it up here. Across the canyon is another set of mountains and Chuquisaca, the Aymara name for Sucre province. You are on the border between states, and perhaps frightened to get too close to the edge.

On a fortunate day the strong, warm winds called thermals may bring a magnificent sight – that of the soaring Andean condor, the world's largest flying bird with a wingspan up to 9ft. The trademark white collar decorates a black body, wings also edged in white, a buzzard-ish red head atop. These birds hardly ever flap their wings, using the air currents to hover for minutes, sometimes hours, scouring the landscape for carrion. You may even be lucky enough to see them nesting in the cliffsides.

If you want to get even deeper into the experience, stick around, and Ademar from the resident Yumasa community, will guide you into the canyon for B$110.

Coimata

TIME FROM TARIJA: **30 MINS**

Coimata's calming waters

If Tarija has left you a bit hot and bothered, there's no cure like the *pozos* (water holes) of **Coimata** *(tarijaturismo.com/la-poza-del-pato; entry B$2)*, just a short drive, hike or bike from Tarija. Getting here is easy – there are frequent **micros** from Bolivar and Campo in Tarija, and a taxi (B$60 round trip) isn't too expensive. It should take a half-hour or less to arrive, passing fields of sunflowers. If you walk to the site, you'll tread on cobblestone pathways. The B$2 entrance fee brings you onto a plaza replete with snacks, grilled foods, and cold drinks for sale.

But you might want to save that for after a dip in the cool waters. Clamber over a rock and get yourself situated, or take a walk under the aquatic punch of the waterfall. On weekends, expect this spot to fill up, but during the week you may be in blissful solitude. You can also hike around on the trails above the river for a bit of birding or other nature appreciation. A 30- to 40-minute walk beyond the main plaza gets you to some even cooler – and cooling – waterfalls.

Villamontes

OUTDOORS | INDIGENOUS EXPERIENCE | HISTORY

If you head south from Tarija, red sandstone cliffs carved by years of erosion form the barriers of the Tarija–Villamontes Road. Incredible vistas are framed by goats, indigenous walkers, dogs and chacalaca birds. Your vehicle passes under the ominous shadows of the Angosto de Villamontes, staring into the unguarded abyss. You know you're headed into the country where memories of the last century and the brutal Chaco War are as fresh as yesterday, as are the legends of the Guarani tribesmen, and where fisherfolk work the river with nets that their fathers owned. This torrid territory is ruled by the whims of nature and locals understand the rhythms of life and obey them. Villamontes is not just a passing-through point, though – spending time here gives you an appreciation of an 'other' Bolivia, indigenous, independent and proud.

GETTING AROUND

Trufis (shared cars or vans) handle most of the traffic between Tarija and here; locally it's taxis and *toritos*, the little bike-car combos. Villamontes is a walking town but it's also nice to see by bike; renting a car isn't necessary. You can get bike rental (and other tour) information from Eduard at the Ecohotel Gota del Chaco (p255) or at Vanessa Pizzaro's small crafts store called Punto Debil.

A Lost Cause & Historic Wound

A 1930s military tragedy

The Chaco War – in which 100,000 lives were lost in a military stalemate with Paraguay between 1932 and 1935 – is still alive in the memories of southern Bolivia, particularly in Villamontes where one of the last stands of the conflict was made. Entering the **Museo Historico Militar Heroes del Chaco**, *(gotadelchaco.com/villamontes/atractivos/museo-historico-militar-heroes-del-chaco, in Spanish; entry B$5)* one feels a certain heaviness, even sadness, in the air, as young Bolivian soldiers, the same age as many of those who died, offer to guide you around.

As a museum, the small colonial house is comprehensive: uniforms, documents, and munitions from both sides show the somewhat primitive technology of a century ago. One can almost feel the sweat soaking through the heavy cloth uniforms as the combatants trudged through the heat of the Chaco summer and shivered through the wind-whipped desert nights.

TOP TIPS

Villamontes is the hottest place in Bolivia; prepare yourself. Ambitious though your plans may be, take things moderately, hydrate, and wear proper clothes.

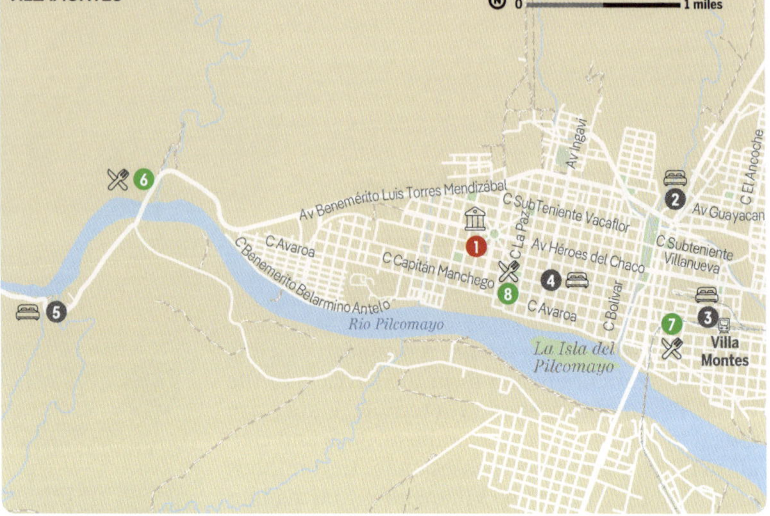

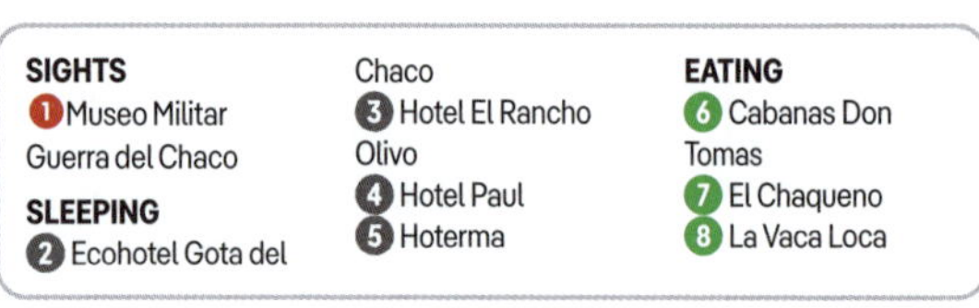

VILLAMONTES PUBLIC STATUES

Leaping Fish: A symbol of Villamontes' fishing bounty, this giant *sábalo* leaps out in the town center.

Indigenous Fisherfolk: Holding the nets of their ancestors, this realistic representation of the technique is one of many attractive statues in Parque 24 de Julio.

Sombrero Chaqueno: Nothing is more representative of the Villamontes man than this massive hat.

Toucan: Plaza 24 de Julio is host to many statues honoring local wildlife, and this is one of the more attractive.

Mate Drinker: Massive hands lift a boiling kettle to make a hot cup of mate, traditional drink of the chaqueno cowboy.

Photos tell you another story: the darker faces of the Bolivian troops show that their conscripts were highland indigenous youth, ill-prepared for the blistering sun and freezing winds of the Chaco climate. There is a reason it's called the 'War of Thirst' – it was for lack of water that many soldiers died.

You can stand behind the machine guns or gigantic field glasses and imagine some made-up enemy in the distance. Feel the weight of the gun in your hand. Look at the photos on the wall and imagine that nearly 100,000 of those fellows never came back home: was the oil and natural gas discovered eight decades hence worth the price?

A Ride Through Local History

Passing geographic and historic milestones

A great way to get an overview of what Villamontes offers is the half-day 'Ruta Pilcomayo' 4WD tour *(gotadelchaco.com/villamontes/que-hacer/ruta-pilcomayo, website is in Spanish; B$180 per person)*. You'll start your day driving to the Puente Pilcomayo (Pilcomayo Bridge). Then you'll go to KM 0, where the city of Villamontes proper begins, and learn a bit about its history. Next, you'll hit the historic Puente Ferrocarril, which connects Villamontes to Argentina and was actually inaugurated by legendary Argentinian first lady Eva Peron in 1957. You'll journey on to the indigenous community of

Tuntey, learn about their way of life, and have the opportunity to buy handwoven baskets, decorations and food products. These are the Weenhayek, who have lived along the banks of the river for centuries.

Now comes the adventure. Crossing the Puente Ustarez, you'll climb the unforgiving road that parallels the river below, an incredibly steep canyon with no guardrails – not for the faint of heart. A stop at the **narrows at Angosto de Villamontes** allows you to appreciate the power of the mighty, deep river below, and also to see cute parrots and swallows swoop in and out of clandestine openings in the clay cliffs. You can stop for views at several *miradors* (lookouts) before reaching the aptly named Boca del Diablo (the Devil's Mouth) – the narrowest point of the canyon – and walking the narrow suspension bridge at Tucainti.

This final nerve-wracking adventure will no doubt work up an appetite, and you'll finish at a riverside restaurant for some freshly roasted fish, straight off the spit to your plate.

ANGUISH IN THE ANGOSTO

From the edge of the Angosto de Villamontes ('the narrows') you wonder how vehicular traffic ever passes below the ominous overhangs. Large *camiones* (flatbed trucks) crawl around the hairpin curves, ever vigilant of shifting cargoes. In the chasm below flows the deep, powerful Pilcomayo. Some groups run white-water rafting trips from Sucre to Villamontes here, rapids ranging between Class III and Class IV until a hairy bit called Chorro Grande that escalates to Class V.

You'll be reminded of this passageway on your ride up to Tarija – and perhaps sorry that you peeked over the edge! The drop to the river is 450m in some places, and there are no guardrails.

A Visit with the Chimeo

Step into indigenous ancestry

Sharing a half-day with the Chimeo community on the outskirts of Villamontes is both charming and educational. It may blow away your perceptions of how the indigenous live in the 21st century, and provide a primer on the natural and cultural history of the region.

The origin of the name Chimeo is interesting: previously the indigenous peoples referred to themselves as Tïnguïu, the name of a local bird. They later changed it, according to a local historian, because many people had difficulty pronouncing it.

You'll drive out to the community in the morning. Since the Chimeos are located just 8km from Villamontes, note that you can also come here as part of a local **bicycle tour** *(gotadelchaco.com/villamontes/guias-artistas/vanessa-pizarro, website is in Spanish)*. It is neither wholly modern nor entirely rustic; mostly small brick homes and small animal enclosures. About 200 families live in the community, of which 30 participate in the tourism activities.

First, it's breakfast time, and you'll dig into a serving of *huminta* (corn cakes), *witimimbo* (bread) or *chirriada,* pancakes also made from *choclo,* or large grained corn, covered with honey.

A musical performance follows, along with a traditional dance. The women wear incredibly bright and beautiful

EATING IN VILLAMONTES: RUSTIC RESTAURANTS

La Vaca Loca: Local photographer and birder Cesar is also a whiz at making pizzas, and you'll be wowed by his wildlife photography. *4:30-11pm Mon-Sat* $$

Cabañas Don Tomas: This champion fisherman and mountain cyclist roasts awesome fresh fish – whatever is in season – using the simplest ingredients. *10am-4pm* $$

El Chaqueño: Forty-year tradition of *parrilladas* with seemingly endless supplies of flame-broiled steaks and hearty sides. Save your appetite. *9:30am-2pm Sat & Sun* $$

El Criollaso: If you're tired of fish, the house specialty here is fresh-roasted pig *(chancho)*, and it's spectacular. *11:30am-2pm daily & 6pm-11pm Mon-Sat* $

SURUBÍ AND CHAMPION DON TOMAS

Guarani legend has it that two friends came to a loggerheads over one's possession of a prized jaguarundi-pelt hat. One night on a fishing expedition, they drank too much, argued, and, naturally, the jealous non-hat-owner killed his friend. For this, God turned him into a *surubí*, or catfish.

Just along the Pilcomayo, beneath the ominous Angosto, is a local fishing hole called the Cueva de Surubí (*surubí's* cave), a stronghold of the deep-dwelling whiskered fish. Local boating tours will take you there and afterward you'll dine with another local legend at **Cabaña Don Tomas**, whose eatery along Route 11 bordering the river is renowned throughout the province.

OSCAR LOZA UGARTE/SHUTTERSTOCK

Old railway bridge, Villamontes

full length gowns of pink, yellow and blue. Inside a small **museum** *(gotadelchaco.com/villamontes/atractivos/museo-verde-chimeo)*, an elder recites the history of the *pueblo*; here, oral history is still a well-preserved tradition.

You'll hike up to the *represa* (dam), which is topped with a cross, symbolic of the native acceptance of Christianity. On your return, there's another lunch, and a chance to purchase some artisan goods.

The walk can get hot, so bring a hat, sunscreen and mosquito repellant.

Cycling Around Villamontes

A guided bicycle tour

This 26 km, half-day **spin around Villamontes** *(gotadelchaco.com/villamontes/guias-artistas/vanessa-pizarro; B$180)* will test your stamina and give you perspective on this city's natural history. A 4km level ride along the city's *ciclovía* (bike path) gives way to more natural vistas; reaching Puente Usterez you'll have a vantage point to check out the rocky river below. Another 2km further and slightly uphill alongside the Pilcomayo, there's an optional stop at Hotermas and a soak in hot-spring fed tubs. As you continue another 5km you'll slightly gain in altitude and in anticipation of the impressive – and rather scary – overlook of El Angosto.

The route then takes you 5km back into town on the Camino Viejo, stopping at a *mirador* (lookout) before you hit shady Plaza 6 de Agosto, dominated by a modernistic fountain. Finally, you'll reach Plaza 24 de Julio, the heart of chaqueño culture, with monuments to the toucan, the *quirquincho* (the beloved armadillo), indigenous fisherfolk as well as a giant teapot pouring out *mate* into a gourd(!).

Places We Love to Stay

$ Budget $$ Midrange $$$ Top End

Tarija

MAP p239

Hostal Granny $ Right for the price, this budget bargain has a friendly staff and fine breakfasts. Nothing fancy, but a solid choice.

Hotel Mitru $$ A few blocks distant from the hum of the main plazas makes this rustic establishment a quality option.

Hotel Innova $$ A modern, clean and quiet option smack in the middle of town. Steps from the main plaza and many eating, drinking and cultural activities.

La Pasarela Hotel $$ A tranquil oasis in Coimata, near the waterfalls and pools, also featuring trails and expansive terrace for lingering morning coffee breaks.

Aires de Campo Apart Hotel $$ Country living in classy *cabañas*, with rustic activities such as horseback riding and fishing on-site.

Resort Hotel Los Parrales $$$ A quality resort on a river bend outside of town. Good for families – includes a children's playground, a spa, restaurant and an enormous outdoor pool.

Hotel Los Ceibos $$$ A large hotel next to the Plaza Uriondo, with a swimming pool, fitness club and modern rooms – but try to avoid booking the same night as they're hosting a party in their ballroom.

Uriondo

Hosteria Valle d'Vino $ As eccentric as its owner, this shabby-looking vineyard is one of the only wineries to offer accommodations.

Kiwi Casita Apart-Hotel $$ A few blocks from Uriondo's central plaza, with vineyard views. The DIY decor is charming, with repurposed grape crates as shelves.

Villamontes

MAP p252

Ecohotel Gota del Chaco $$ Good location and friendly owner make this newer hotel a fine choice.

Hoterma $$ Named for its location on the Pilcomayo opposite steaming underground waters, these are funneled into baths onsite. Rooms are named for native trees.

Hotel Paul $$ A solid choice in the center of town, just across from the Mercado Central; newly built as of 2024.

Rancho Olivo $$$ A modern five-star option opposite the historic train station. Rustic, with modern touches everywhere, and attentive staff. Vines dangle from the shade trees in the expansive courtyard.

Researched by Alexis Averbuck

Santa Cruz & Gran Chiquitania

ABUNDANT LOWLANDS STEEPED IN HISTORY

Roam out from booming Santa Cruz to discover Jesuit missions hidden in Chiquitania forests and Andean foothills with Inca ruins and a wildlife-rich national park.

The Bolivian Oriente spreads in a vast wing along the country's eastern lowlands, in stark contrast to the towering Andes. This tropical region, the country's most prosperous, nevertheless remains less visited than its highland neighbors and its people have a palpable desire to differentiate themselves. The region's robust agriculture and industry yield incomes and a standard of living unequaled by any other province. It's also home to the majority of Bolivia's 80,000 Guaraní people, comprising around 20% of the region's population.

The capital, Santa Cruz de la Sierra, is Bolivia's most populous city with plenty of urban sprawl, yet its central old quarter retains a small-town atmosphere and residents are remarkably relaxed.

To the east lies Gran Chiquitania, undulating swaths of farmland cut from the Chiquitania dry forest – a zone defined by verdant jungle-like vegetation in the wet season (November to February), and fire-prone landscapes at other times of year. Don't miss this area's stunning carved-wood Jesuit missions from the 1700s, centered around sweeping squares and steeped in a turbulent history.

West of Santa Cruz, climb into forested foothills for miles of hikes and abundant wildlife in the Parque Nacional Amboró, the 'elbow of the Andes' where the ecosystems of the Andes, Chaco and Amazon Basin meet. Use Samaipata as a base, tour Inca ruins at El Fuerte and embark on a revolutionary pilgrimage to where Che Guevara died, near Villegrande.

POSZTOS/SHUTTERSTOCK ©

THE MAIN AREAS

SANTA CRUZ DE LA SIERRA
Modern city with a small-town feel. p260

SAMAIPATA
Cool highland village with magnificent Inca ruins. p267

JESUIT MISSION CIRCUIT
Resplendent 1700s churches in remote towns. p278

For places to stay in Santa Cruz & Gran Chiquitania, see p290

IMAGEBROKER/MICHAEL RUNKEL/GETTY IMAGES

Left: Santa Cruz de la Sierra (p260); Right: San Miguel de Velasco (p283)

Find Your Way

Fly into Santa Cruz's **Viru Viru International Airport**, 15km north of the center, if you're arriving from sea level and don't want to acclimatize to altitude in La Paz. The city is well-connected to the region.

Santa Cruz de la Sierra, p260
Rejuvenate in a bustling city with modern hotels and international restaurants, while soaking up the center's laid-back old-town vibe.

Samaipata, p267
Breathe fresh mountain air on the edge of the Amboró National Park in this village popular with travelers.

Jesuit Mission Circuit, p278
Thrill at sumptuously decorated, centuries-old churches in distinctive Chiquitania villages.

CAR

While the priciest option, a guided tour or hired car and driver guarantees access to remote regions on your own schedule. Negotiate for your price, including petrol and food and lodging for the driver.

BUS & MICRO

Long-distance bus (*flota*) and *trufi/micro* (shared minibus) services crisscross the region to all major destinations. These are more commonly used than the infrequent trains *(www.fo.com.bo)* trundling south to Argentina and east to the Brazilian Pantanal.

BRAZIL
BOLIVIA
PARAGUAY
Carmen Ruiz
Espiritu
San Ignacio
Ascencion
San Javier
Iglesia de San Xavier
Iglesia de Santa Ana
San Miguel
San Ramón
San Julian
Santa Rosa del Sara
Mineros
Villa Germán Busch
Montero
Jesuit Mission Circuit
Parque Nacional Amboró
Santa Cruz de la Sierra
Basílica Menor de San Lorenzo
San José de Chiquitos
San José de Chiquitos Mission Church
San Juan de Taperas
Saipina
Mairano
Bermejo
Samaipata
El Fuerte
Iguazurenda
Parque Nacional del Gran Chaco Kaa-Iya
Chochis
Roboré
Aguas Calientes
Postrer Valle
Pucara
Cabezas
Fortin Ravelo
El Carmen
Puerto Suárez
0 200 km
0 100 miles

MIGUELANGHELO/SHUTTERSTOCK

El Fuerte (p269)

Plan Your Time

Get your bearings in Santa Cruz then prepare for wildly different experiences: from the flat Chiquitania Jesuit Mission Circuit to the Andean foothills around Samaipata and Amboró National Park.

Pressed for Time

- Travel can be time consuming in expansive eastern Bolivia, so you'll have to pick: a quick jaunt to the Jesuit Mission Circuit, perhaps stopping off in **San Xavier** (p278) and **Concepción** (p282) to see UNESCO World Heritage churches, or a day or two in **Amboró National Park** (p272), using **Samaipata** (p267) for a base and ogling the giant carved-rock ruin of **El Fuerte** (p269).

Five Days to Travel Around

- Soak up city life for a day in Santa Cruz, then loop through the whole **Jesuit Mission Circuit** (p278). Next, decide whether to pair **Samaipata** and **Amboró National Park** or do something even wilder, like overnight at a wildlife sanctuary – **La Paraba Frente Roja Lodge** (p277) and **San Miguelito Jaguar Conservation Ranch** (p288) – or visit Che Guevara's mausoleum (p277).

Seasonal Highlights

MARCH–MAY

Carnaval lights up Santa Cruz and Vallegrande. Catch the **Festival de Música Misiones de Chiquitos** (p284) in even numbered years.

JUNE–AUGUST

Visit Chiquitania from May to August to avoid the worst heat. June 21 is winter solstice (seasons are reversed from the northern hemisphere) and **Aymara New Year**, celebrated at El Fuerte.

SEPTEMBER–NOVEMBER

In October, join the faithful at **Vallegrande's Che Festival**, in memory of the revolutionary leader who died near here.

DECEMBER–FEBRUARY

The quiet 'low' season falls during the wettest weather, from November to February. Catholic pilgrims walk from Santa Cruz to Cotoca on December 8 by candlelight.

Santa Cruz de la Sierra

PLAZA LIFE | ART HUB | NATURAL ADVENTURES

GETTING AROUND

Santa Cruz is Bolivia's most connected city by air. The **bimodal terminal**, 1.5km east of the center, has an information booth and combines long-distance bus (*flota*, some with fully reclining seats) and train station. On the other side of the tunnel is the *micro/trufi* (minibus) terminal for some regional services (others leave at diverse spots across town). City buses and *micros* buzz all over Santa Cruz (download Cruzero app for routes). Taxis (call one with the Easy Taxi app) are cheap but you must negotiate price in advance. Typically a daytime trip for one person within the first/second *anillo* is about B$15/20.

Bolivia's largest city sprawls across a region of flat farmland and industry. The edges thrum with modernity, from massive tractor dealerships to office and residential towers in the swanky Equipetrol district. But as you make your way to its heart, you slip into a smaller-town feel in the *casco viejo* (old quarter). Suited businesspeople sip *chicha* (fermented-corn drink) at street stalls, restaurants close for siesta and little stores line arcaded colonial buildings, some in crumbling disrepair. It all radiates out from the bustling palm-lined central square, a bastion of relaxed tropical vibes. Join *cruceños* (Santa Cruz residents) lounging on benches listening to *camba* (eastern lowlands) music, watching the world go by.

You'll notice the area's great diversity, from overall-wearing Mennonites strolling past Goth kids, to the Japanese community, Altiplano immigrants and fashionable *cruceños* cruising the tight streets in their SUVs. Spend a day or two, eating at international restaurants and absorbing the unique way of life.

Join the Central Square Stroll

Enjoy the plaza's people-watching *paseo*

To feel the pulse of the city of Santa Cruz, head to the center of town in the evening. People of all ages make their way to the shady tree-lined central square, **Plaza 24 de Septiembre**, walking, gossiping, flirting and playing. Slip into the people-watching buzz, as coffee sellers in cream-colored uniforms circulate with their trolleys, kids fly paper airplanes and everyone unwinds. From here, it's an easy stroll around, to sip a fruit juice in one of the city's many cafes, a beer from a bar terrace, or to browse one of the nearby artisans' markets.

Explore the Luxurious Cathedral

Santa Cruz's religious heart

Rising impressively on the southern side of the Plaza 24 de Septiembre, the **Basílica Menor de San Lorenzo** remains a magnet for nightly services and flower-festooned baptisms, and it defines the central skyline of old Santa Cruz. The original cathedral was founded in 1605, and the present structure dates from 1845. Wander inside (if dressed respectfully, covering your shoulders) to examine its elaborate ceiling woodwork and glistening silver altar. The church's small **Museo de Arte Sagrado** *(B$10)* showcases religious icons, vestments and medallions, or for sweeping city views, climb the **bell tower** *(B$3)* – both from 9am to noon and 3pm to 6pm Monday to Friday.

Art-Hop at Central Culture Hubs

Free exhibitions in the *casco viejo*

The vibrancy of Santa Cruz and its arts and culture scene are on easy offer – for free! – around the central **Plaza 24 de Septiembre** (p260). On its southern edge, **Manzana Uno Espacio de Arte** *(manzanauno.org.bo; free)* fills several floors and outdoor patios with excellent exhibitions, such as international photography.

Meander a block east to the **Casa Melchor Pinto** *(facebook.com/CasaMelchorPinto; free)*, in the impeccably restored family home of Dr Melchor Pinto Parada, an influential *cruceño* doctor-politician, to discover multiple galleries hosting temporary exhibitions and regular concerts as well as activities such as tango classes. And just one block south of the square, **Espacio Fundacion Patiño Cultural Centre** *(patino.org; free)* fills a modern cultural space with exhibits and events for all ages, plus a small shop.

Shop for Local Handicrafts & Treats

Markets and boutiques in central Santa Cruz

Santa Cruz is eastern Bolivia's shopping hub. You'll find carvings unique to the area made from tropical hardwoods *morado* and more expensive *guayacán*. Relief carvings on tari nuts make good, portable souvenirs. People also craft beautiful macramé *llicas* (root-fiber bags), embroidered textiles and other easy-to-carry arts and crafts. While llama- and alpaca-wool goods are also sold, prices are higher than in La Paz, since many are brought from there.

Head five blocks southwest of the central square to find the finest *artesanías* (locally handcrafted items) at **Artecampo** *(artecampo.com.bo)*. This outlet for the work of 1000 rural *cruceña* women and their families offers truly inspired and innovative pieces from leatherwork, hammocks, weavings, handmade paper and greeting cards to natural-material lampshades.

continues on p264

TOP TIP

Santa Cruz is laid out in *anillos* (rings) forming concentric circles around the old town (*casco viejo*) center within the *primer anillo* (first, innermost ring). *Radiales* (spokes) connect the rings. To the northwest, Av San Martín in Barrio Equipetrol teems with restaurants, bars and late-night clubs. Get city info at *vivasantacruz.bo*.

NATIONAL PARKS IN EASTERN BOLIVIA

Parque Nacional & Área de Uso Múltiple Amboró: The highlight, it's easily accessible from Santa Cruz, Samaipata and Buena Vista.

Parque Nacional Noel Kempff Mercado: Virtually closed to tourists, with campsites in disrepair. Rough 4WD road takes over seven hours to approach; most fly in.

Parque Nacional Kaa-Iya del Gran Chaco: In the remote south, Latin America's largest park, a wild domain of jaguars. Largely inaccessible, requiring permits and guides with all supplies for survival. Adventure companies **Misional Tours** (p265) and **Nick's Adventures** (p265), can put together a (pricey) expedition.

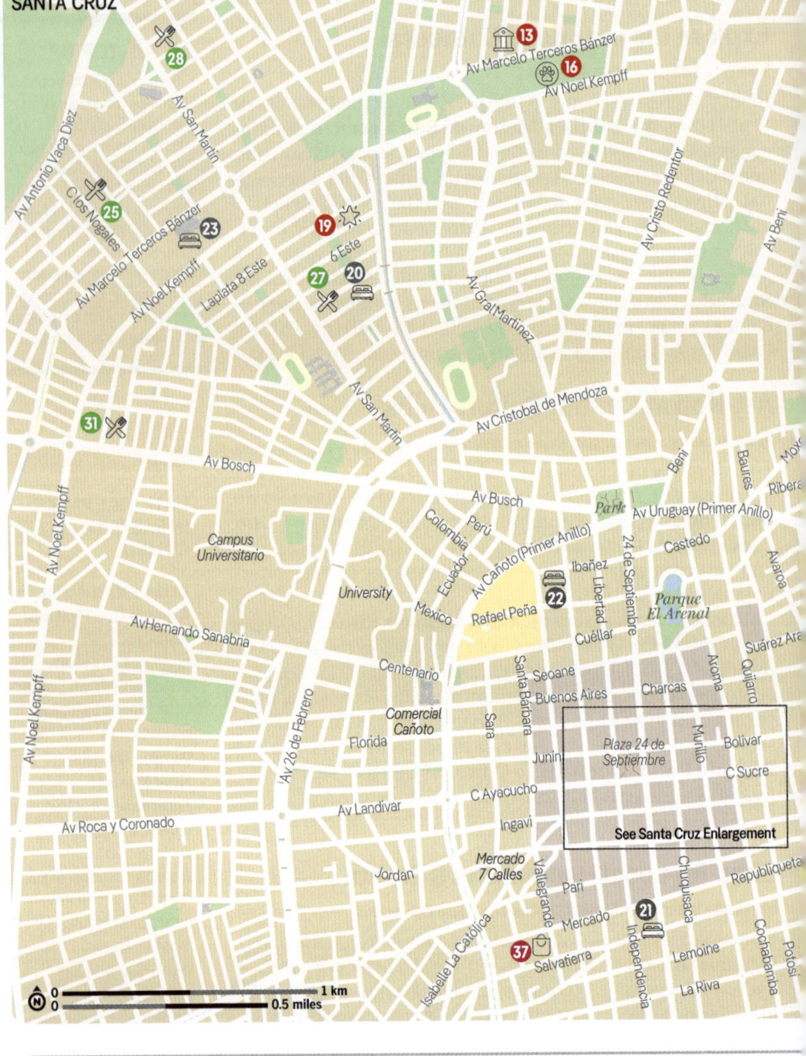

HIGHLIGHTS
1 Basílica Menor de San Lorenzo
2 Historico Militar Heroes del Chaco
3 Plaza 24 de Septiembre

SIGHTS
4 Bell Tower
5 Casa Melchor Pinto
6 Espacio Fundacion Patiño Cultural Centre
7 Jardín Botánico
8 Lomas de Arena
9 Manzana Uno Espacio de Arte
10 Museo de Arte Contemporáneo
11 Museo de Arte Sagrado
12 Museo de Historia Regional
13 Museo Guaraní
14 Santuario de la Purísima Concepción de Nuestra Señora de Cotoca
15 Tapekuá
16 Zoológico Municipal Fauna Sudamericana

ACTIVITIES, COURSES & TOURS
17 Biocentro Güembé
18 Misional Tours
19 Nick's Adventures

Av Tercer Anillo Interno
Av Alemana
Yomomo
Av Trinidad
Plaza B Mercado
Av Argomosa (Primer Anillo)
Chiquitos
Bimodal Terminal (1.2km)
Oruro

SLEEPING
20 Alfonsina
21 Cosmopolitano
22 Hotel Lido
23 Hotel Los Tajibos
24 Nomad Hostel

EATING
25 Chalet La Suisse
26 El Aljibe
27 El Arriero
28 Jardín de Asia
29 Ken
30 La Casa del Camba
31 Michelangelo
Pizza Noi (see 5)
32 Rincón Vallegrandino

DRINKING & NIGHTLIFE
33 Citronelle
34 Colors Coffee
35 Duda Bar

ENTERTAINMENT
36 Casa de la Cultura Raúl Otero Reiche

SHOPPING
37 Artecampo
38 Artisans Market
39 El Ceibo
40 magazine & book kiosks
41 Mercado Nuevo
42 Paseo Artesanal La Recova

MUSEUMS & GARDENS

Museo de Historia Regional: Museum in a 1920s home, dedicated to local personages, pre-Columbian history in Chiquitania, Jesuit missions and masks.

Museo de Arte Contemporáneo: Breezy central patio surrounded by contemporary art exhibitions by Bolivian artists.

Museo Guaraní: Region's important Guaraní culture, from animal masks to *tinajas* (clay pots) for brewing *chicha* (fermented maize drink).

Casa de la Cultura Raúl Otero Reiche: Arts center on the plaza hosts a year-round program of exhibitions, performing arts and film festivals.

Jardín Botánico: Rustic parkland, 12km east of the city, with woodland trails, lake, labeled fruit trees and elevated viewing platform.

ROAMING PICTURES/SHUTTERSTOCK

Plaza 24 de Septiembre (p260)

continued from p261

Closer to the square, **Paseo Artesanal La Recova** is an alleyway packed with kiosks selling both handmade and factory-produced handicrafts. Or, rummage through the **Magazine & Book Kiosks** on the southwest corner of the square for vintage print matter. You'll often also find an **artisans market** between the cathedral and Manzana Uno Espacio de Arte.

For Bolivian chocolates, **El Ceibo** *(elceibo.com)* is your place, and for other fun food browsing, explore the **Mercado Nuevo**, four blocks east, where empanadas and other stuffed breads are cooked up on the spot.

Toucans, Monkeys & Jaguars, Oh My!

Take the kids to the zoo

Weekends thrum at Santa Cruz's zoo, **Zoológico Municipal Fauna Sudamericana** *(facebook.com/ZooMunicipal; adult/child B$10/5)*, when families come to check out the native birds, wildcats and reptiles kept in pleasingly humane conditions, although the llamas are a bit overdressed for the climate. Keep your eyes open for free-ranging sloths and squirrel monkeys in the trees.

EATING AROUND CENTRAL SANTA CRUZ: OUR PICKS

El Aljibe: Easygoing restaurant specializing in *comida típica* (traditional food), served in a charming colonial house and courtyard. *noon-3pm & 7-11:30pm Mon-Sat* $$

Noi: Buzzy, mod eatery in the Casa Melchor courtyard, mixing excellent cocktails (try the pisco sour) and serving pizza with handmade crust. *8:30am-11pm* $$

Ken: Low-key Japanese restaurant with massive *yaki soba* (stir-fried noodles) laden with chicken and cashews. *11:30am-3pm & 6-11pm Tue-Sun* $$

La Casa del Camba: Sprawling landmark for *cruceño* dining experiences. Juicy grilled meat sizzles while singers belt out tunes. Now a local chain. *11am-11pm* $$

Weekend Getaway to a Market Town

Visit Cotoca's street market

Join a popular weekend tradition and head for the day to **Cotoca**, 20km east of Santa Cruz. Radiating out from its central **plaza** and the church of the **Santuario de la Purísima Concepción de Nuestra Señora de Cotoca**, the streets are thronged by market stalls, with all manner of trinkets and plastic goods. Just wander the pedestrianised streets taking it all in, then let the day culminate with a lavish meal of barbecue pork *(chancho al palo)* at one of its weekend restaurants. If you're there on a Sunday, you'll see many people bring their new cars to be blessed at the church.

Adventure in the Sand Dunes

Play in the Lomas de Arena desert

The strange, striking dunes of **Lomas de Arena**, 12km south of Santa Cruz, make for a wild half-day adventure. Tour companies, such as **Nick's Adventures** (p324), offer 4WD or dune-buggy outings, some including sandboarding. It's a good spot for bird-watching and you may see sloths. Bring sunscreen and water.

It's also possible to come by taxi *(about B$200)*, but unless you have a 4WD you'll need to walk a long, hot 4km to 7km to reach the sand, depending on the muddy road conditions.

Escape to a Butterfly Farm with Pools

Marvel at orchids and forests

If you're feeling like a great day trip from Santa Cruz, take a taxi 12km west of the city to **Biocentro Güembé** *(biocentroguembe.com adult/child B$150/50)* where you can play on a butterfly farm, examine orchid exhibitions, or cool off in 15 natural pools. Fish and hike in the surrounding forest. There's a restaurant, cabins and a campsite, too. If it's a hot day get here early: the place fills up fast!

Graze Weekend Honey, Fruit & Vegetable Markets

Honey and barbecue pork around La Guardia

Folks in the lowland appreciate great food, using their abundant local ingredients. On a weekend, join *cruceños* jaunting 18km southwest to **La Guardia** when **honey producers** set up stands along the street, selling fresh honey and honey-based

TOUR COMPANIES

Nick's Adventures: Excellent tour company with a strong ethos of social responsibility and promoting conservation through tourism. Especially good for wildlife tours, including tours to the **San Miguelito Jaguar Reserve** (p288) and the Pantanal. *(nicksadventuresbolivia.com)*

Misional Tours: One of Santa Cruz's most well-organized and reliable tour operators. Specializes in the Mission Circuit, but just as good for other attractions across Bolivia. *(misionaltours.com)*

Bird Bolivia: Professional birding and wildlife tours with expert guides for those with a special interest in nature. Based in Santa Cruz but without a public office; arrange tours by phone or email. *(birdbolivia.com)*

DRINKING IN CENTRAL SANTA CRUZ: OUR PICKS

Colors Coffee: Excellent strong brews, juices and cookies, plus shares space with vegan restaurant Buddha Bowls and bar Ganesha. *10am-10pm Mon-Sat, 3-9pm Sun*

Citronelle: Elegant cafe with a shady interior courtyard, good coffee, tea and cakes. On weekends, happy families dig into brunch. *8am-11pm*

Tapekuá: Casually upscale Swiss- and Bolivian-owned place. Live music most nights from 10:30pm *(B$40 cover)*, and serves good, earthy food. *7pm-midnight Wed-Sat*

Duda Bar: Colorful bar in an historic building. Under plaster arches you'll find retro furniture and bric-a-brac. *9:30pm-2am Tue-Thu, to 3am Fri & Sat*

EASTERN BOLIVIAN DRINKS

Thanks to abundant sunshine, heat and moisture, eastern Bolivia produces all manner of special food and drink. Favorite tipples include:

Achachairú Juice: Spicier cousin to the purple mangosteen fruit.

Copoazú Juice: Relative to the cocoa tree with a tangier flavor.

Té de Muña: Tea made from a minty-flavored healing herb that dates to the Incas.

Somó: Drink made from a white corn called *frangollo*, cloves and cinnamon – you'll see street sellers.

Té de Carbón: Tea brewed from charcoal, typical of San José de Chiquitos.

Rimpolio: Cream liqueur from Vallegrande, like Baileys.

DANYLLO FRANCO/SHUTTERSTOCK

Butterfly at Biocentro Güembé (p265)

desserts. Top off the outing with *chancho al palo* (barbecue pork, literally 'pork on a pole') at one of the weekend restaurants. Other specialties include *patasca,* a soup made from pig's head and corn, and *mani* (peanut) soup, typically including meat – which you can also find at **El Aljibe** (p264), **La Casa del Camba** (p264) and **Rincón Vallegrandino**. Vegetarians, stop instead at **El Torno's weekend market** of regional fruit and vegetables, 14km south of La Guardia.

Splash in Lavish Waterfalls

Cool off in cascades and pools at Los Espejillos

The green waterfalls and natural swimming pools at **Los Espejillos**, 42km southwest of central Santa Cruz, make for a refreshing dip, with water sparkling over polished rock formations. The falls are only accessible in dry weather (November is usually the best month) – roads become dangerous when it rains. While it's easiest to book a tour from Santa Cruz, you can self-drive via Porongo, north of Hwy 7, when the river is lowest, or take the bus to San José, where 4WD *trufis* can take you up for around B$100.

EATING IN EQUIPETROL: HIGH-END INTERNATIONAL

El Arriero: Local favorite for the country's best steaks. The portions are huge and the service excellent. *11:30am-11pm Tue-Sat, to 9pm Sun* **$$$**

Jardín de Asia: Bolivian ingredients with Asian flavors create original dishes.Candlelit setting and delicious cocktails. Book ahead. *noon-3pm & 7pm-1am Mon-Sat* **$$$**

Chalet La Suisse: Swiss restaurant with a refined yet easygoing vibe. Book ahead – it's perennially packed. *noon-2:30pm & 7pm-midnight Mon-Fri, 7pm-midnight Sat* **$$$**

Michelangelo: Tops for a romantic evening or some Italian self-indulgence. Pastas are homemade and there's a good wine list. *noon-2:30pm & 7-11pm* **$$$**

Samaipata

BOHO VILLAGE | MOUNTAIN AIR | WILDLIFE & WILDERNESS

Quaint Samaipata has developed into one of the top tourist spots in eastern Bolivia, but don't let that put you off. This sleepy village in the foothills of the Cordillera Oriental has held on to its tranquil feel, with low-slung adobe houses and pavement tapering off into dirt roads. Since it's now brimming with well-run hostels and restaurants, you can enjoy international foods and rich coffee accompanied by stunning views of the verdant landscape.

Samaipata is the main jumping-off point for forays to **Parque Nacional Amboró** (p272) and local operators specialize in park trips. It's also a popular weekend destination for *cruceños* (Santa Cruz residents) who wind their way up Hwy 7 (the old road to Cochabamba) through the foothills to reach Samaipata, where the Quechua name, meaning 'Rest in the Highlands,' is spot-on. Save time to explore the Inca site of El Fuerte and nearby coffee plantations and wineries.

GETTING AROUND

Trufis (shared car or minibus) run throughout the day when full between Santa Cruz and Samaipata *(B$30, three hours)*. From Samaipata, services depart from the main plaza. Buses to Sucre leave from opposite the gas station on the main road. Samaipata itself is mostly walkable, but if you want a hand, a quick and easy way to go is by ***moto taxi***, some of which hang around near the market. Expect to pay around B$4 one way.

Shop for Crafts & Coffee

Support local artists and producers

The tourist-friendly streets of Samaipata radiate out from its leafy central plaza, and are studded with handicraft shops, great for a browse. Many also sell locally produced coffees and wines. For example, **Mucho Mundo** offers all manner of arts and crafts designed by resident artists. You can also explore the small **artisan's market** that sets up on the street in front of the food **market**.

TOP TIP

Take care when choosing your tour operator for outings to Amboró National Park and nearby attractions. Seek accredited, responsible guides such as locally-run, excellent **Samaipata Tours** *(samaipatatours.net)* or **Kaleidoscope Travel** *(kaleidoscope-travel.com)*, run by a Dutch couple. Samaipata's helpful sites are samaipata.info and facebook.com/visitsamaipata. There's no official tourist office in town.

Watch Hummingbirds Feeding on Native Plants

Visit a hummingbird eco-sanctuary

On the way up to El Fuerte, stop off at the immersive **Refugio de Colibríes** *(adult/child $B35/15)*, where 25 hectares

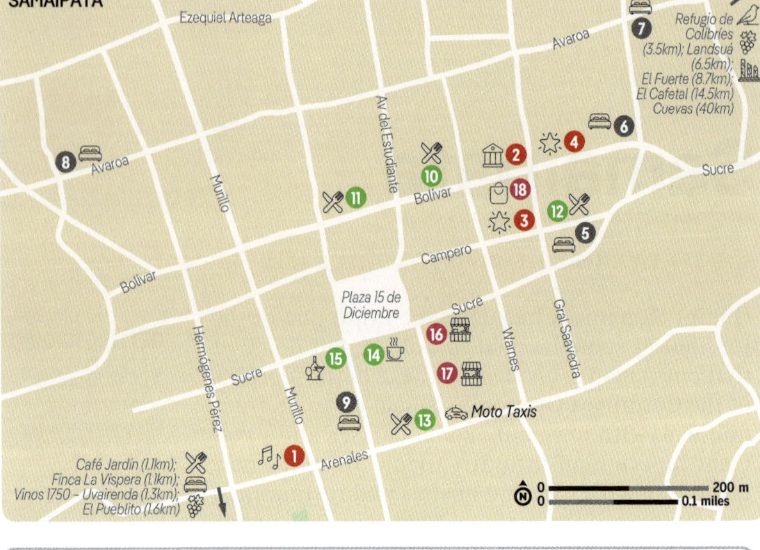

of organically grown native plants create the ideal home for 21 species of hummingbirds. Their seasons and feeding times differ, so during an average visit to the gardens and viewing platforms you're likely to witness about nine species. The friendly biologist-owner Elva Villegas, keeps the sanctuary open year-round, from 8am to 12:30pm and 2pm to 7pm.

EATING & DRINKING IN SAMAIPATA: OUR PICKS

La Pizzeria: Great-value, thin-crust pizzas are served hot from the oven at this cozy little joint opposite the market. *5:30-9:30pm* $

La Cocina: Cheerful burger and nacho place with a few vegetarian options, accompanied by tasty, fresh french fries. *6:30-10pm Tue-Sat* $$

Humos: Cheese platters, small plates and ceviches are the order of the day, with homemade lemonade. *noon-3:30pm & 7-10:30pm Fri-Sun* $$$

Café Jardín: Admire Finca La Víspera's garden from its alfresco veggie cafe with all-day breakfasts and lunches. *8am-4pm Mon-Thu, to 6pm Fri-Sun* $$$

Caffé Art: Coffee, juices, cakes and more at this cafe-art gallery, with gorgeous painted tables. *3-7:30pm Wed-Thu, 8:30am-11pm Fri-Sun*

Coffee Agape: Grab a table out front at this cafe on the square for local coffees and bodacious sweets and snacks. *8am-8pm*

La Boheme: Bumping bar with food and many beers, like El Fuerte IPA, to sip on the starry roof terrace. *5-11pm Tue-Thu & Sun, to 2am Fri & Sat*

Melody Park: A block southwest from the plaza, Melody Park hosts occasional live music and always has bawling karaoke. *hours vary*

TOP EXPERIENCE

El Fuerte

The mystical site of **El Fuerte** exudes such pulling power that visitors from all over the world come to climb to these remains of the Incas' eastern outpost. A designated UNESCO World Heritage Site since 1998, the giant carved rock temple and its accompanying ruins occupy the crown of a hill 9km east of Samaipata, and offer breathtaking views across the valleys.

Origins

The site of El Fuerte was first occupied by diverse indigenous groups as early as 2000 BCE. It wasn't until 1470 CE that the Incas, the most famous tenants, arrived. By the time the Spanish came and looted the site in the 1600s it was already deserted. The remains of over 500 dwellings have been discovered in the immediate vicinity.

Carved Stone Sanctuary

You'll ascend about 200m up a dirt track and stairs to reach the main site. Here, the 100m-long carved stone slab is almost certainly of religious significance (p270). The many sculpted features include seats, troughs and *hornecinos* (niches), which are believed to have held idols or funerary urns. Seven steps leading up to the main temple represent the phases of the moon. Zoomorphic designs include reliefs of pumas and jaguars (representing power) and serpents (representing fertility). *Chicha* (fermented corn) and blood were poured into the snake designs as an offering to Pachamama (Mother Earth). Erosion is making the designs difficult to discern.

Transport

Round-trip taxis from Samaipata, including a 1½-hour wait at the ruins, charge B$100 for up to four people. On the approach look for **La Cabeza del Inca**, a rock formation resembling the head of an Inca. Watch, too, for condors and, in November, parrots nesting in rock faces.

TOP TIPS

- Samaipata's small **archaeological museum** (p270) displays El Fuerte finds and provides information about the site.
- Allow 1½ hours to fully explore, and take sunscreen, water and a hat. Snack kiosk on-site.
- It's well-signed in English and Spanish.

PRACTICALITIES

- Tickets cost B$50
- A guide costs B$100
- Site is open from 8:30am to 4:30pm daily.

WHAT WAS EL FUERTE USED FOR?

The purpose of **El Fuerte** (p269) has long been debated. The conquistadors, in a distinctly combative frame of mind, assumed the site had been used for defense, hence its Spanish name, 'the fort.' In 1832, French naturalist Alcide d'Orbigny proclaimed that the pools and parallel canals had been used for washing gold.

In 1936, German anthropologist Leo Pucher described it as an ancient temple to the serpent and the jaguar. His theory, incorporating worship of the sun and moon, is now the most accepted. In fact, the celebrations for the Bolivian winter solstice (June 21), which is the Aymara New Year, bring people from far and wide to witness the dawn and dance.

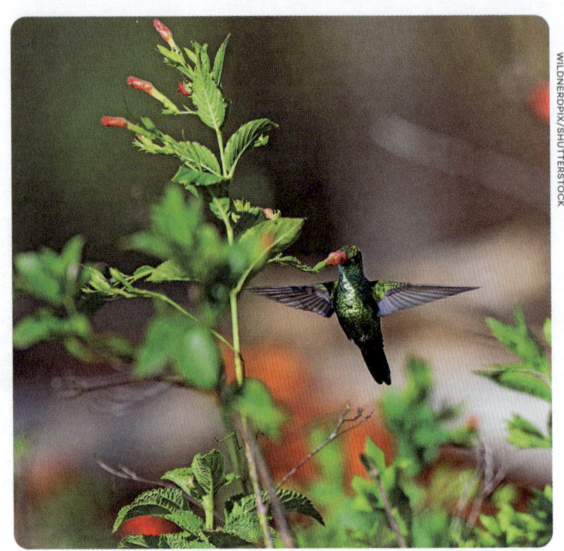

WILDNERDPIX/SHUTTERSTOCK

Hummingbird at Refugio de Colibríes (p267)

Visit Coffee Plantations & Wineries

Follow the coffee and wine routes

The lush hills, river-laden valleys and temperate climate around Samaipata make it tops for coffee and wine production. Local tour operators like **Samaipata Tours** (p267) offer outings to coffee plantations such as **El Cafetal** and **Cuevas Coffee**, near the hamlet of Cuevas (p276), where you can taste local brews and learn about growing. Then hit the wineries **Vinos 1750 - Uvairenda** *(vinos1750.com; tour & tasting from B$40 per person)* and **Landsuá** *(bodegaslandsua.com; tastings & tours B$50 per person)*, located beneath El Fuerte.

Learn about Local History & Archaeology

Examine finds at the archaeological museum

Samaipata's small **Museo Arqueológico** *(entry B$5, combo ticket with El Fuerte B$50)* displays pieces excavated from El Fuerte and provides background for the site. It's worth stopping in before visiting the ruins. You'll explore five well-arranged rooms with artifacts from different peoples and periods, accompanied by good explanations. It's open from 8am to noon and 2pm to 6pm from Monday to Friday.

Beyond Samaipata

Hike lush Andean foothills, explore a wild national park and haunt the historic site of Che Guevara's last days.

Samaipata is blessed with a temperate setting nestled in the foothills of the Andes, and it's surrounded by winding valleys and verdant forests with hidden lagoons and refreshing waterfalls. By far the biggest attraction in the region is the wildlife-rich Parque Nacional & Área de Uso Múltiple Amboró, which sits just north of town and calls for days of exploration.

To the south, the pretty town of Vallegrande's claim to fame is that it was the spot where famed revolutionary Che Guevara's body was exhibited before its burial, and it's the main base for the Che Trail, a community-based tourism project that follows Che's final movements through the hills where he was captured near La Higuera.

Places

Refugio Jacha Inti

TIME FROM SAMAIPATA: **10 MINS**

Support a wildlife refuge

The charming and responsible little **Refugio Jacha Inti** *(facebook.com/jachaintisamaipata; adult/child B$20/10)* is a sanctuary for rescued wild animals. The refuge is run by volunteers who can lodge for free in exchange for their labor (one month minimum), and there's an attractive wooded campsite if you fancy spending a night among the animals. You can reach it on a pleasant 3km walk south from Samaipata.

Empinado

TIME FROM SAMAIPATA: **2 HOURS**

Camp out at the La Pajcha waterfalls

Hire a local guide to take you on the long day trek to **La Pajcha**, a fabulous series of three waterfalls on a turbid mountain river that plunge 45m into a dreamy tropical lagoon. It has a sandy beach for swimming and inviting campsites where you can stay if you want to break up the trip.

It's 42km south of Samaipata, toward San Juan, where there is a turnoff that leads 7km to the falls. You access it via a tough 4WD dirt road and a five-hour hike up and down. If you go on a tour, they can combine it with a condor sanctuary and visits to ceramics producers along the way.

continues on p276

GETTING AROUND

Trufis from Samaipata run to Santa Cruz (via Cuevas) and Vallegrande, but to explore the national park, go with a 4WD and a guide familiar with unmaintained, unmarked roads. From Samaipata to Vallegrande, a taxi costs around B$300 for a carload. Vallegrande's bus and *trufi* terminal is 1km north of the center and services run every couple of hours to Santa Cruz *(B$35 to B$60)*, passing Samaipata. There's also a bus to Cochabamba *(B$50, 11 hours)*.

JUAN PABLO BUENO/SHUTTERSTOCK

TOP EXPERIENCE

Parque Nacional & Área de Uso Múltiple Amboró

The abundant 637,600-hectare **Parque Nacional & Área de Uso Múltiple Amboró** lies in a unique geographical position at the confluence of three distinct ecosystems: the Andes, the Amazon Basin and the Chaco. This range of rich habitats attracts both highland and lowland species from elusive spectacled bears, jaguars, tapirs and peccaries to monkeys, and over 900 birds species, including the endangered horned curassow.

DON'T MISS

- Bosque de Helechos Gigantes
- Los Volcánes
- Jardin de las Delícias Waterfalls
- Río Macuñucu Route
- Laguna Verde
- Mairana Area Cloud Forests
- Swimming in Río Surutú

Samaipata Access Points

The town of Samaipata sits just outside the southern boundary of the Área de Uso Múltiple Amboró and provides the best access point for the Andean lowland section of the park. There's no real infrastructure, or any public facilities, in this part of the park, and you are required to enter the park with a guide. Hire one in Samaipata (p267) or Santa Cruz (p265), and plan also to pay park entrance fees.

Bosque de Helechos Gigantes (Giant Fern Forest)

A highlight of this part of the park is the popular day hike through an ancient cloud forest famous for its giant ferns, some of them

PRACTICALITIES

Visit the official park website (*https://sernap.gob.bo/amboro*) to download maps and information. Park entrance fees from B$20 to B$100.

more than 4m high, called the **Bosque de Helechos Gigantes**. It's easiest to book a tour from Samaipata with transport included *(from B$175 per person)*, then you'll walk an 11km trail that starts 17km north of Samaipata, just past the community of Chorolque.

Mairana Area Cloud Forests

Tough to access, and once again, requiring a guide, this trek near the Mairana area takes you 7km uphill to **La Yunga**, at 1800m. This is a particularly lush region, surrounded by tree ferns and other cloud-forest vegetation. From La Yunga, a 16km forest traverse can connect with the main road near Samaipata.

Comarapa Rainforest

You can also reach a little-used entrance to the park, 4km northwest of **Comarapa**. After the road crosses a pass between a hill and a ridge with a telephone tower, you'll follow a minor road turning off to the northeast at the settlement of **Khara Huasi**. Continue uphill to verdant stands of cloud forest, which blanket the peaks. The big payoff here is the **Laguna Verde**, a striking green lake with interpretative trails and the chance to see caimans.

Los Volcánes

The beautiful region known as **Los Volcánes** features an otherworldly landscape of tropical sugarloaf hills, right on the edge of the park boundary. It's marked by a hulking slab of red rock known as **El Portón del Diablo**, which is flaking and chipping into natural arches. An ideal overnight plan is to stay at **Refugio los Volcánes** (p290) where activities on offer include bird-watching and guided hikes through wonderfully wild landscapes, with pools for swimming.

The access point is the village of Bermejo, 41km east of Samaipata and 85km southwest of Santa Cruz, and a jeep from Refugio los Volcánes can be booked to meet you and take you in.

Near here are other comfortable accommodations and some good hikes. For example, **Laguna Volcán** is an intriguing crater lake 6km up the hill north of Bermejo. A walking track climbs from the lake to the crater rim; it begins at the point directly across the lake from the end of the road. At the time of writing the hotel there, Hotel Laguna Volcan Eco Resort, was closed due to a change in ownership – check ahead.

Jardin de las Delícias Waterfalls

It's well worth the two-hour drive in a 4WD *trufi* from **El Torno** to reach the magnificent **Jardin de las Delícias** waterfalls. They pour over a sheer bowl-shaped rockface into a refreshing pool, and you can climb to the vertiginous top to look down.

Buena Vista Access Points

Buena Vista is a nice little town two hours (103km) northwest of Santa Cruz, and is the staging point for trips into Parque Nacional Amboró's forested lowland section. Access to this eastern part of the reserve requires crossing the Río Surutú, in a vehicle or on foot. Depending on the rainfall and weather, the river may be anywhere from knee- to waist-deep. Inexperienced

AMBORÓ UNDER THREAT

The location of Parque Nacional Amboró is a mixed blessing – although it's convenient for visitors, it's just a few hours from Santa Cruz's urban sprawl and squarely between the old and new Cochabamba–Santa Cruz highways. Conservation groups are keen to avoid the destruction of the region's natural treasures, but are also fully aware of the needs of the human population, who are allowed to live around the edges of the park.

TOP TIPS

- Beyond Samaipata, there are also good lodges near Cuevas and Bermejo, on the road from Samaipata to Santa Cruz.
- North of the park, Buena Vista is the place to stay.
- Boycott any restaurant offering wild game as it isn't legal.
- Going with a well-qualified guide helps you identity flora, from palm trees to cacti; and fauna, from spider monkeys to boa constrictors.
- The park altitude ranges from 300m to 3500m, so depending on where you go you'll need everything from mosquito repellant to woolly sweaters.
- Dry season (April to October) is the ideal time to visit, with better road conditions and fewer insects.

USING BUENA VISTA AS A BASE

Though most foreigners prefer Samaipata for national-park exploration, the Buena Vista area has excellent spots to observe wildlife and birds, plus see local traditions. The downside is a more humid climate and significantly less choice on where to stay and eat.

If you go, be sure to pop in if its **Iglesia de los Santos Desposorios** is open. This Jesuit mission was founded in 1694 (its current form dates from 1767), and each year on November 26, the saint's day features food stalls and general merrymaking.

hikers should not attempt any of the treks in this part of the park without a guide.

The Buena Vista tourist office in the **Casa Municipal de Turismo y Cultura** on the southwest corner of the plaza can be helpful, supplying names and contact numbers for guides. **Servicio Nacional de Áreas Protegidas** a block south of the plaza has information on the park. A useful online resource about the town is buenavista.com.bo.

Swimming near Buena Vista

Residents here love taking a dip at the **Río Surutú**, where there's a pleasant sandy beach ideal for picnics, swimming and camping during dry season. From Buena Vista it's an easy 3.5km walk southwest to the **Villa Aquiles** river bend nearest town. The opposite bank is the national park boundary.

You can walk an hour from town to the lovely swimming hole at **El Cairo**. Head downhill from the plaza past the *alcaldía* (town hall) and follow the road as it curves to the right. After about 2km, take the unpaved left fork and cross a bridge. El Cairo is further down, on the right.

Río Macuñucu Route

The Río Macuñucu route is one of the most popular treks into Amboró. To reach it, go to **Las Cruces**, 35km southeast of Buena Vista and continue 7km to the Río Surutú (you must drive or wade across). Just beyond the opposite bank you'll reach **Villa Amboró** where you can overnight at its **campsite**. Villagers may charge an entrance fee en route to Macuñucu, regardless of whether you intend to stay there or not – avoid unpleasantness and pay.

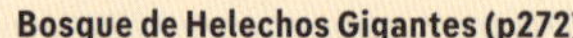

Bosque de Helechos Gigantes (p272)

MATTHIAS KESTEL/GETTY IMAGES

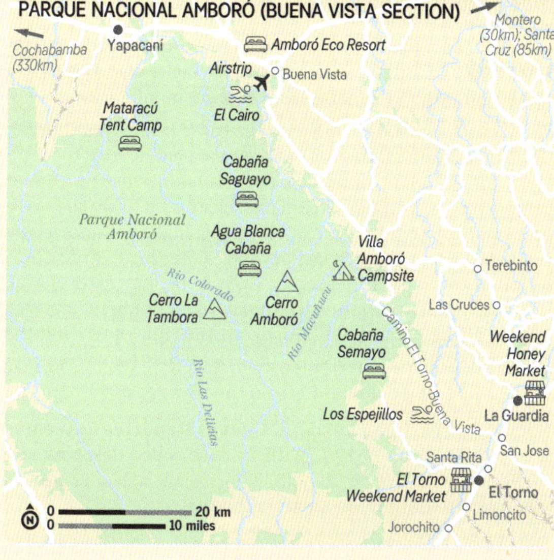

From the campsite, the trek follows the banks of the **Río Macuñucu** through thick forest. You can do a portion of it as a day hike, or after about four hours continue through a narrow canyon to a rock overhang, beyond which the trek becomes increasingly difficult and the terrain more rugged en route to beautiful waterfalls and another campsite. Take a guide if you are doing the full hike.

Mataracú Area

From near **Yapacaní**, on the main Cochabamba road, a 4WD-only track heads south across the Río Yapacaní into the northern reaches of the park. After a rough 18km, you'll roll up to the former **Mataracú Tent Camp** (closed as of writing), surrounded by woodland, waterfalls and hiking trails where you might get lucky and spot a giant sloth.

Río Isama & Cerro Amboró

The Río Isama route turns off at the village of **Espejitos**, 28km southeast of Buena Vista, and provides access to the base of 1300m **Cerro Amboró**, the bulbous peak for which the park is named. It's possible to climb to the summit, but it is a difficult trek and a guide is essential.

Transportation & Tours

By far the easiest and safest way to visit the park is by guided tour in a 4WD vehicle with one of the recommended agencies in Santa Cruz (p260) or Samaipata (p267). Roads and paths are not regularly maintained and an experienced guide is essential for knowing the way around. From the Buena Vista side all routes require a crossing of Río Surutú.

LIVING IN THE PARK?

When Parque Nacional Amboró was created in 1973, its charter forbade settlement and resource exploitation. Nonetheless, hunters, loggers and *campesino* (subsistence farmer) settlers continued to pour in – many displaced from the Chapare region by the US Drug Enforcement Agency. By 1996, with conflicts increasing over the park, it was redesignated as the Área de Uso Múltiple Amboró, which effectively opened parts of it up for settlement.

CHE GUEVARA'S ARRIVAL IN BOLIVIA

Fresh from revolutionary success in Cuba (and frustrating failure in the Congo), iconic revolutionary Ernesto 'Che' Guevara de la Serna heard about the oppression of the Bolivian working classes by dictator René Barrientos Ortuño's military government. Strategically located at the heart of South America, Bolivia seemed like the perfect place from which to launch socialist revolution on the continent.

Che first established his Bolivian base in 1966 at the farm Ñancahuazú, 250km southwest of Santa Cruz. He hoped to inspire *campesinos* (subsistence farmers) to rebellion, but was surprised to be met with suspicion. A cunning move by Ortuño granting *campesinos* rights to their land had earned their support and all but doomed Che's revolution before it began.

continued from p271

Cuevas

TIME FROM SAMAIPATA: **30 MINS**

Swim beneath Las Cuevas waterfalls

You'll easily see the entrance to the three lovely **Las Cuevas** *(B$15)* waterfalls 20km east of Samaipata on the road to Santa Cruz, among plant nurseries, coffee plantations (p270) and campgrounds. Walk upstream on a clear path to reach two of the waterfalls, spilling into swimmable lagoons bordered by sandy beaches. About 100m beyond is the third, largest waterfall. It gets busy at weekends. Taxis from Samaipata charge B$100 with a two-hour wait. Alternatively, jump on a bus or *trufi* heading toward Santa Cruz. At the time of writing the falls were temporarily closed – make sure they have reopened.

Soar through the air

Get your adrenaline coursing at **Cuevas Deportes Extremos** *(7-295-6664; from B$100)*, with intense roped descents and thrilling ziplines, or gentler but inspiring aerial ladder climbs. You can also dare to do an aerial biking route.

Hike the remote Codo de los Andes

Your work to reach the wilderness area and trail known as **Codo de los Andes** will reward you with its dramatic forested peaks and sweeping beauty, plus the chance to spot condors. Agencies in Samaipata and Santa Cruz offer guided hikes, and you can camp overnight to spread out the five to seven hours trekking and add a stop at a waterfall.

You'll find the area from a turnoff on Hwy 7 near Cuevas, but if you're going on your own check locally first to make sure it is passable.

Mataral Area

TIME FROM SAMAIPATA: **1½ HOURS** 

Examine ancient wall paintings

Hire a guide in Samaipata, like **Samaipata Tours** (p267), to take you to see the region's ancient *pinturas rupestres* (wall paintings). There are sites near Mataral, Mairana, El Buey and Vallegrande in caves and on rocks with depictions of maps and animals. Usually you just pay someone in the local community to let you look at them (no organized site). To learn more about this fascinating slice of Bolivian history, look up the books of Professor Roy Querejazu Lewis, who has championed the study and preservation of this heritage, and the website of the Bolivian Rock Art Research Society, SIARB (*siarb-bolivia.org*).

La Paraba Frente Roja Sanctuary

TIME FROM SAMAIPATA: **3 HOURS** 

Visit an endangered bird sanctuary

For a unique bird-watching getaway and to support the vital work of NGO **Armonía** *(armoniabolivia.org)* in preserving the endangered red-fronted macaw (Ara rubrogenys), known locally as *paraba frente roja*, visit their remote reserve close to the town of Saipina. Found only in dry inter-Andean valleys in the Vallegrande area, this handsome bird has a world population of just 1000. The superb and comfortable nonprofit **La Paraba Frente Roja Lodge** *(room including meals US$200)* supports the conservation work and the local Quechua population.

You'll recognize the red-fronted macaw in its red, green and yellow plumage – the colors of the Bolivian flag, and it's only one of about 300 species in the area. Look out for the raucous cliff parakeet and somber Bolivian blackbird, too. For an English-language guided birding tour contact **Bird Bolivia** (p265).

Vallegrande

TIME FROM SAMAIPATA: **2½ HOURS**

Pay tribute to a legendary revolutionary on the Che Trail

Vallegrande, a little market town in the Andean foothills, is the main base for the Che Trail following Che Guevara's final days around La Higuera and the sites in Vallegrande where his body was brought and later buried (though now his body is in Cuba). The **Ruta del Che City Tour** *(B$40)*, is a two-hour guided Vallegrande walking tour from the **tourist office**, on the east side of the plaza, to the laundry at **Hospital Señor de Malta** where Che's body was displayed for the world's press. You'll continue to La Fosa de los Guerrilleros, where fellow fighters are buried, and the Che Guevara Cultural Center, containing Che's **mausoleum** and the simple **Museo de Che**. The town also celebrates an **Che Guevara festival** on October 17.

Vallegrande has a lovely temperate climate, and is ideal for unwinding and walking in the hills. In the morning at **Mercado Samuel Villazón** vendors arrive with huge baskets of freshly baked corn bread and pallets of local cheese and whiz up fruit smoothies.

Day trip to La Higuera, where Che was killed

At the **Quebrada del Churo**, 5km north of the isolated village La Higuera, a steep path leads down to the clearing where Che Guevara and 16 fellow guerrilla fighters evaded capture for 10 days until, on October 8, 1967, they were surrounded by troops and a gun battle ensued. In La Higuera, wounded Che was held prisoner in a schoolroom before being executed. It's just off the plaza and is now **Museo Comunal La Higuera**. You'll also see statues of the revolutionary around the Plaza del Che.

Reaching La Higuera independently is difficult so it's cheapest to go with a tour from Vallegrande – ask at Vallegrande's tourist office for a taxi or guide *(from B$250 per car)*.

CHE'S DEATH

Che Guevara wrote *Bolivian Diary* during the final months of his life. Despite minor setbacks he considered things to be moving along nicely and in his last entry on October 7, 1967, 11 months after his arrival in Bolivia, he wrote that the plan was proceeding 'without complications.' The following day he was captured near La Higuera by CIA-trained Bolivian troops and was shot in the legs, neck and shoulder. Just after noon on October 9, he was executed and his body was flown to Vallegrande, where it was displayed in the hospital laundry room to prove to the world that 'El Che' was finally dead. His body was re-discovered in 1997 and sent to Cuba for burial.

Jesuit Mission Circuit

INCREDIBLE CHURCHES | RURAL VILLAGES | RICH FORESTLAND

GETTING AROUND

As recently as 2024, it required a three- to five-day journey to complete the circuit (San Xavier, Concepción, San Ignacio, San Miguel, Santa Ana, San Rafael and San José), with horribly rough dirt roads, sometimes impassable in wet season. In 2025, a seven-year endeavor to pave the circuit (except for roads to Santa Ana), was completed, making self-driving possible (p281). Easiest is a guided tour from Santa Cruz (around US$500 per person for a four-day package with **Misional Tours** (p265). *Micros* connect all of the towns, and *flotas* (buses) from Santa Cruz to the largest towns usually travel in the evening (after 8pm).

Dry forest and farmland in Gran Chiquitania harbor spectacular, unusual treasures: the seven-town *Circuito de Las Misiones Jesuíticas* (Jesuit Mission Circuit). Some of Bolivia's richest cultural and historic sites, dating to the 1700s, these remote mission towns and their elaborate churches were forgotten by the world for centuries...allowing them to survive with minimal interference. Through decades of painstaking work from the 1970s to the '90s, directed by architect Hans Roth (1934-1999), these unique churches were restored to splendor. The immense value in their synthesis of Jesuit and native Chiquitano (Guaraní) cultures resulted in UNESCO declaring the region a World Heritage Site in 1991.

The 1986 Palme d'Or winner *The Mission* replayed the last days of the Jesuit priests (p283) in South America (with Jeremy Irons and Robert de Niro leading missions in Argentina and Paraguay). Now, each town and church has its own flavor, and newly paved roads open them to the world as never before.

The Soaring, Cream-Colored San Xavier Mission

The region's oldest mission town

The first (or last, depending on which way you travel) settlement on the circuit, San Xavier (also spelled San Javier), founded in 1691, is the oldest mission town in the region. It's a favorite holiday destination for wealthy *cruceño* (Santa Cruz resident) families. The village sits on a lovely, forested ridge with a great view over the surrounding low hills and countryside.

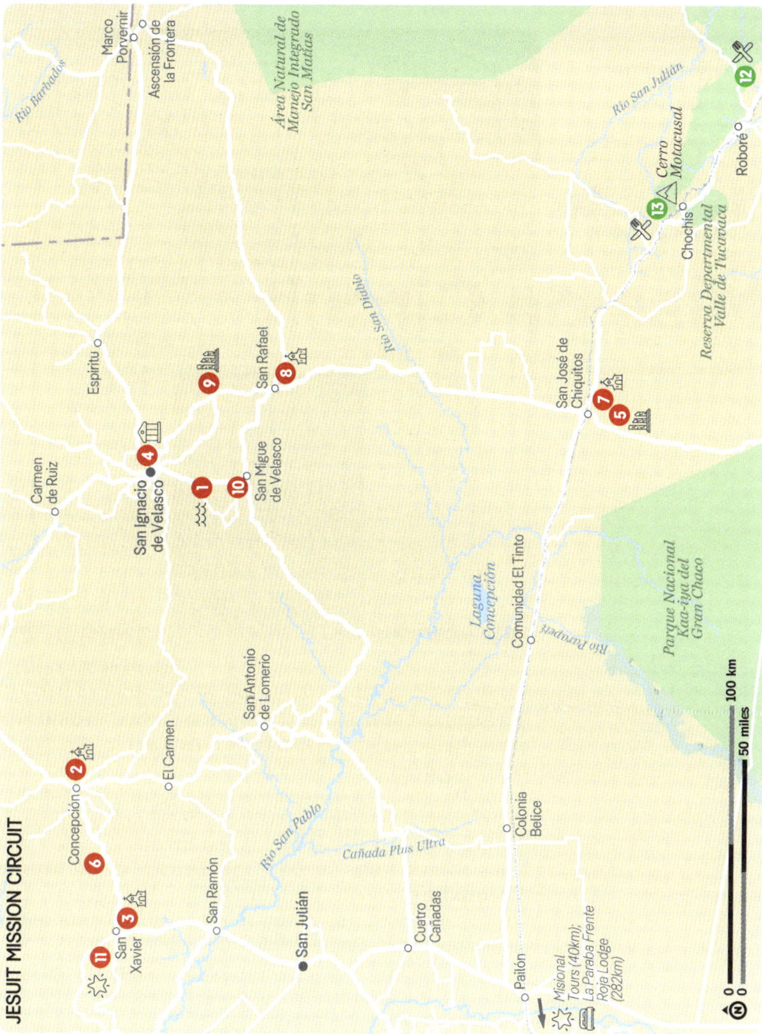

SIGHTS

1 Capybara Lagoon
2 Catedral de Concepción
Iglesia de San Ignacio (see 4)
3 Iglesia de San Xavier
Iglesia de Santa Ana (see 9)
Mirador de Ñuflo de Chaves (see 5)
Mission Museum (see 7)
Museo Casa Natal Germán Busch (see 3)
Museo Misional (see 2)
Museo Misional (see 3)
4 Museo Misional de Ignacio de Velasco
Museo Santa Cruz la Vieja (see 5)
5 Parque Histórico Santa Cruz la Vieja
6 Piedras de Paquio Rock Formation & Lagoon
7 San José de Chiquitos Mission Church
San Miguel de Velasco Mission Church (see 10)
8 San Rafael de Velasco Mission Church
9 Santuario Arqueológico El Viborón
10 Taller Obispo Nicolás Castellanos
Valle de la Luna (see 5)

ACTIVITIES

11 Aguas Calientes
Sendero Montañeta Forest Walk (see 5)

EATING

Chinoly (see 4)
Dolce Capricho (see 3)
El Buen Gusto (see 2)
12 El Tacú del Buen Sabor
Heladeria Ame Tauna (see 4)
Las Palmeras (see 8)
Pascana (see 3)
Pizzeria Napolitano (see 4)
Restaurant Turubó (see 7)
13 Restaurante Camping Las Piedras
Restaurante El Tacu (see 9)
Tatiana (see 4)

INFORMATION

Tourist Office (see 4)

TOP TIP

The mission circuit is busier on weekends in dry (high) season (May to October). Some restaurants reduce hours or close in wet season. The best hotels are in San José, San Ignacio and Concepción (which also have ATMs). In smaller villages, there's little choice and rooms are basic. Most churches open 8:30am-noon & 2-6pm.

JESS KRAFT/SHUTTERSTOCK

Iglesia de San Xavier

Swiss priest Martin Schmidt (p284) arrived in 1730 and founded and designed **Iglesia de San Xavier**, which was constructed between 1749 and 1752. Restoration work was completed in 1992 to beautiful effect, and the soaring cream-colored interior, inscribed with sienna patterns, is distinct from other missions on the circuit.

Outside mass times, access to the church is via the **Museo Misional** next door. Schmidt founded the region's first music school here, and a workshop crafting violins, harps and harpsichords, some of which are displayed inside. Look, too, at original carvings, bells and ceramics, plus read mission and Chiquitos history (mostly in Spanish). You can also buy carvings at its shop.

At the northeast corner of the plaza, **Museo Casa Natal Germán Busch** *(admission free)* was the home of former president and Chaco War hero Germán Busch (1903-1939) and also contains the **tourist office** *(open 8am to noon and 2pm to 6:30pm)*.

EATING IN SAN XAVIER, CONCEPCIÓN & SANTA ANA: OUR PICKS

Pascana (San Xavier): Home-cooked, good-value family food on the square. Breakfast, lunch and evening empanadas (stuffed, savory pastries). *7am-8pm* $

Dolce Capricho (San Xavier): Head here for fresh cakes and ice cream, the perfect dessert after a market lunch (two blocks east). *1-11pm Tue-Sun* $

El Buen Gusto (Concepción): Take a seat in the leafy, quiet patio for generous portions on the north side of the plaza. *8am-10pm* $$

Restaurante El Tacu: (Santa Ana de Velasco): Call ahead *(6-781-4229)* to eat at outdoor tables shaded by fruit trees (used for juices). *By appointment* $

DRIVING THE MISSION CIRCUIT

The newly paved road around the Jesuit Mission Circuit invites exploration of a formerly remote region

START	END	LENGTH
Santa Cruz de la Sierra	San José de Chiquitos	670km; 2-3 days

The hardest part of the four-hour drive on paved roads from Santa Cruz to San Xavier is getting out of the urban sprawl. From there, the flat landscape opens to verdant jungle in the wet season and fire-prone forest in the dry season. You'll notice entry lanes to Mennonite settlements (p289), granaries and grazing local breeds of white cattle rising to palm-topped hills as you approach ❶ **San Xavier** (p280). It's a further one hour to ❷ **Concepción** (p282), and 2½ hours to ❸ **San Ignacio de Velasco** (p282), the natural hub for overnighting.

On day two, you can complete the circuit if you drive 50 minutes to ❹ **San Miguel de Velasco** (p283) through anthill-studded farmland. After San Miguel, it's 35 minutes to ❺ **San Rafael de Velasco** (p284), and then two hours to ❻ **San José de Chiquitos** (p285). You'll notice newly-built hamlets on this stretch – some homes of Guaraní people, and others of people form the Altiplano relocated here by the government with the advent of the new road.

If you have more time, add on the rural outpost of ❼ **Santa Ana** (p285). It's 1½ hours on rutted dirt roads from San Ignacio or San Rafael to Santa Ana – keep an eye out for toucans and monkeys along the way.

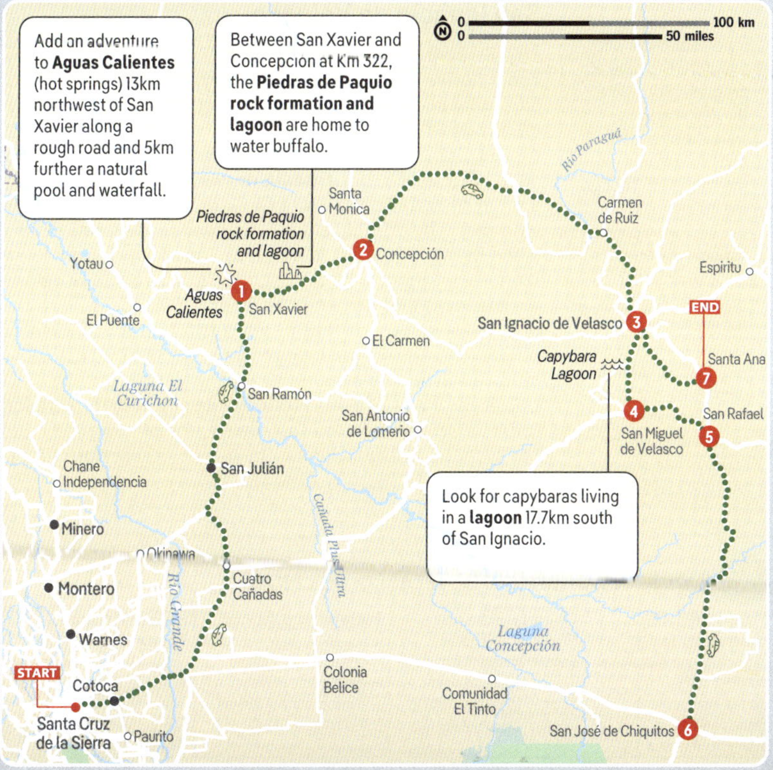

Add an adventure to **Aguas Calientes** (hot springs) 13km northwest of San Xavier along a rough road and 5km further a natural pool and waterfall.

Between San Xavier and Concepcion at Km 322, the **Piedras de Paquio rock formation and lagoon** are home to water buffalo.

Look for capybaras living in a **lagoon** 17.7km south of San Ignacio.

JESUIT BOLIVIA

In 1609, the Jesuits established an autonomous religious state in Paraguay. From there they fanned out into territories previously unexplored by Europeans, founding missions in Argentina, Brazil and Bolivia. Keen to co-exist with the numerous indigenous peoples they encountered, Jesuit *reducciones* ('mission settlements') were headed by two or three priests and a council of eight indigenous representatives who monitored community progress. For a time, the Jesuit armies were the strongest and best trained on the continent. Though the indigenous populations were supposedly free to 'choose' whether to live within the missionary communities, the reality was that those who chose not to were forced to live under the harsh Spanish feudal system or in outright slavery.

Immerse in Original Jesuit Carvings in Concepción

Gilded art restoration center

'Conce' (pronounced con-chay), as Concepción is known, is a wee village with a friendly atmosphere and a particularly abundant central plaza, in the midst of an agricultural and cattle-ranching area. It's the center for all the mission restoration projects and one of the most visited missions because its picture-perfect church is so elaborate.

Built in 1709, **Catedral de Concepción** will stun you with its overhanging roof supported by 121 huge carved-tree-trunk columns and its ornate bell tower. You'll be wowed by gilded baroque designs depicting flowers, angels and the Holy Virgin. Outside mass times, access the church through its small museum displaying interesting photos from before, during and after the church was restored in the 1970s.

If the church museum is closed, ask at **Museo Misional** *(entry B$25)* on the plaza's south side. Leave time, too, to browse this museum, packed with intricate art-restoration work, fine original Jesuit carving – the most on the circuit – and models of mission churches.

Get into the Action in San Ignacio de Velasco

The mission circuit's largest town

You'll notice right away that the thriving commercial hub, San Ignacio de Velasco, is the largest town on the mission circuit, with a real buzz about the place. It's a natural spot to overnight with its good restaurants and hotels.

It's hard to tell, but **Iglesia de San Ignacio** is actually a modern reconstruction of the largest of all the mission churches. The original church, founded in 1748, was demolished in the 1950s and replaced by a modern church. Realizing they'd made a huge mistake, the architects razed the replacement and designed an impressive facsimile of the original structure. It retains a beautiful altar and wooden pillars from the original church and overlooks an extensive and well-pruned plaza.

Visit the small **Museo Misional de Ignacio de Velasco** *(admission free)*, across the square, for photographs and background information on the missions. The **tourist office** is here.

EATING IN SAN IGNACIO DE VELASCO: OUR PICKS

Pizzeria Napolitano: Seems every family in town is vying for an outdoor table to eat pizzas, pasta, meat dishes and more. *6pm-midnight Tue-Sun* $$

Chinoly: Extremely simple, but all home-cooked changing roster of lunch recipes, from *sopa de maní* (peanut soup) to occasional souvlaki. *11am-3:30pm* $

Tatiana: Popular spot for beer, fresh-squeezed juices and fancy cakes, or a full menu of Bolivian and international dishes. *7:30am-11pm Tue-Sun* $$

Heladeria Ame Tauna: It's tough to choose between ice cream sundaes, trifles and other frozen treats on a cool patio streetside. *4-10pm Tue-Sun* $

NORADOA/SHUTTERSTOCK

Iglesia de San Ignacio

Hear the Bells Ring in San Miguel de Velasco

Authentic mission with deluxe bells

Sleepy San Miguel hides in farmland, 37km south of San Ignacio. Its **church** *(open 9am to noon and 3pm to 5pm Monday to Friday and 9am to noon Saturday)* was founded in 1721 and is, according to restoration architect Hans Roth, the most accurately restored of all the Jesuit churches. Look for its superb spiral pillars, carved wooden altar with flying San Miguel, golden pulpit, original frescoes and elaborately painted facade.

Unique to San Miguel are the seven bells in its charming bell tower, which ring in patterns to communicate: the largest bell rung with two others signals the departure of a dignitary, rung alone it's the baptism of a child, while a special bell calls the faithful to prayer.

Go a block west of the plaza to **Taller Obispo Nicolás Castellanos** to see if the craftsman is in, working on ironwood (*cuchi*) pillars, like those in his front garden.

THE JESUIT EXPULSION FROM BOLIVIA

In the mid-1700s, political strife in Europe escalated into a power struggle between the Catholic Church and the governments of France, Spain and Portugal. When the Spanish realized the extent of Jesuit wealth and influence in South America they decided to act. In 1767, swept up in a whirlwind of political babble and religious dogma, the missions were disbanded and King Carlos III signed the order of expulsion, which evicted the Jesuits from the continent and threw the lives of indigenous people into further turmoil. In the wake of the Jesuit departure the settlements fell into decline.

FOR BIRD LOVERS

To see the rare red-fronted macaw, make the pilgrimage to the **La Paraba Frente Roja Sanctuary** (p277) northwest of Samaipata.

BAROQUE MUSIC HISTORY & FESTIVAL

The Jesuit settlements reached their peak under the untiring Swiss priest Father Martin Schmidt (1694-1772), who not only built the missions at San Xavier, Concepción and San Rafael de Velasco, designed many of the altars and published a Spanish-Chiquitano dictionary, but also founded music schools, created musical instruments and workshops, and acted as chief composer.

Now, a 10-day biennial **Festival de Música Misiones de Chiquitos** *(festivalesapac.com)* in even-numbered years, celebrates the area's baroque musical tradition. Concerts are held in Santa Cruz and the Jesuit mission towns (which carry on the musical training) sometime in late April to early May. Be sure to book your lodging in advance during this time.

San José de Chiquitos

Visit San Rafael de Velasco's Resplendent Church

Understated magnificence

San Rafael de Velasco, a rural outpost 132km north of **San José de Chiquitos**, was founded in 1696, and the magnificent mission remains this village's main draw. *(hours vary)*, constructed between 1743 and 1747, is particularly beautiful inside with intact original paintings and woodwork. Notice shimmering mica covering the pulpit and spiral pillars carved from *cuchi* (ironwood) logs. Look, too, for the lavishly decorated sacristy. The church retains the original style of roof, with cane sheathing. If the church is locked, look on the main door for the key holder's phone number.

EATING IN THE SOUTHERN JESUIT MISSION CIRCUIT: TRADITIONAL FARE

Las Palmeras, San Rafael de Velasco: No-frills restaurant-pension on the square; soups and Bolivian mains such as *milanesas* (breaded cutlets). *7:30am-9pm* $

Restaurant Turubó, San José de Chiquitos: Fare is straight-up Bolivian, and well prepared, the best of the squareside options. Burgers, too. *6-11pm Mon-Fri* $

Restaurante Camping Las Piedras, Chochís: Omelets, fish and steak with rice, plantains and potato served in thick jungle alongside a campsite. *7:30am-7pm* $$

El Tacú del Buen Sabor, Santiago de Chiquitos: One of several low-key eateries around the square. Food varies, from sausage to cutlets. *hours vary* $

Off the Beaten Path in Santa Ana de Velasco

Really remote, rustic church

Of all the villages on the mission circuit, tiny **Santa Ana de Velasco** is the most peaceful and perhaps the most charming. Reached by a rutted dirt road (from San Ignacio or San Rafael), it feels barely connected to the modern world. The tranquility of the large high-grass square is interrupted only by free-roaming chickens and the occasional sounds of children's music practice.

Iglesia de Santa Ana, with its wooden altar and reed roof, is the least adorned mission church, evoking a sense of the very first churches the Jesuits constructed upon arrival. Plain walls shine with mica from local quarries. Don't miss the **organ**, which dates from 1754, in the loft alongside an historic harp. The caretaker, Antonia, who you can find one block east of the main square, may even turn it on for you.

Discover an Ancient Snake Sanctuary

Santa Ana's giant rock serpent

Bushwhack a few blocks east of the plaza to reach the **Santuario Arqueológico El Viborón** *(free)*, where a roof protects an ancient 25m-long rock-hewn serpent. It's over 2000 years old and sits on a north-south orientation – a reminder that many of the mission churches were founded on indigenous sanctuaries and incorporate their motifs.

Marvel at the San José de Chiquitos Stone Facade

Explore a grand stone-built complex

Stroll the welcoming, arcaded sidewalks in San José de Chiquitos and you'll encounter plenty of mom-and-pop restaurants and comfortable hotels. With an enormous, handsome plaza shaded by *toboroche* (thorny bottle) trees, the most accessible Jesuit mission town is also the easiest stay in. It's particularly beautiful at sunset, glowing pink across the mission church.

That **mission church** *(church & museum entrance B$20)* is the only one made from stone. The intricate, carved-wood main altar resembles those in other missions but the reason behind its exceptional exterior remains unclear. The looping stone silhouettes are reminiscent of some of California's mission churches such as San Diego, Santa Barbara and Carmel, built by the Franciscans.

Fully explore the sprawling church compound's four principal buildings arranged around a courtyard and occupying an entire city block. Construction – as with the other missions, done by the Chiquitano people – began prior to 1731, and the bell tower was finished in 1748, the *funerario* (death chapel) in 1752 and the *parroquio* (living

MISSION ARCHITECTURE & URBAN PLANNING

The Jesuit's *reducciones* (mission settlements) in Bolivia all established a vast central square with the mission church on one side and low-lying residential buildings radiating out in a grid formation. All of the churches but San José (which is built from stone) utilized materials accessible locally, like ironwood for the gigantic carved columns, cane for roofs and mica (in Santa Ana and San Rafael) to add shimmer to stucco work. Look closely and you'll notice the many ways decorative motifs incorporate indigenous symbols (sun and moon) and vegetation (corn and jungle flowers) alongside Jesuit themes (cherubs). Sundials featured in all of the churches' courtyards, dictating when to ring the bells for services.

CARNAVAL & THE ABUELO CHIQUITANO MASK

If you're in Santa Cruz during **Carnaval** (in February or March, one week before Lent), you should make for the paintball-plagued center and join in the collective chaos. As dancers create elaborate choreography in the streets (during other festivals, too), or if you visit San José de Chiquitos, you'll notice ubiquitous *abuelo chiquitano* masks. A white-painted caricature with bright red cheeks and a saucy black mustache, these masks are believed to be a mockery of Spanish settlers, created by the indigenous people. You can learn more about the masks and how they are made as part of **Ruta de SaborArte** (p286) in San José de Chiquitos.

area) in 1754. Take half an hour to walk the mural-adorned rooms of the church **museum** to learn more about all of the Jesuit missions.

Immerse at Local Arts & Culinary Workshops

Go deeper on the Ruta de SaborArte

Book ahead for a special organized culinary and cultural tour, **Ruta de SaborArte** *(rutasaboreartechiquitos.com; from B$160/80 per adult/child)*. Tours include a guided visit to the mission church and museum, but the real highlights are numerous workshops to choose from: hammock maker, mask maker (see sidebar), weaver, cheese producer, or a cooking demonstration. Along the way you can taste *somó* (corn beverage, p266), and learn how to make *té de carbón*, specialty tea brewed from charcoal. Tours can incorporate **Parque Histórico Santa Cruz la Vieja** (p286) and a walk in **Montañeta forest**.

Walk among the Ruins of Historic Santa Cruz

Visit Parque Histórico Santa Cruz la Vieja

Go south of San José toward a low escarpment and 2.5km outside town you'll find **Parque Histórico Santa Cruz la Vieja** *(admission free)* – the site of the original city of Santa Cruz de la Sierra, founded in 1561. Wander its evocative ruins, wild birds stalking through, where Ñuflo de Chávez (commemorated with a statue on the site) consolidated indigenous peoples and made them work the area, until he was murdered in 1568. The settlement of Santa Cruz was ultimately expelled west, twice, until it established its current location in 1622. **Museo Santa Cruz la Vieja** *(museosantacruzlavieja.org; B$20)*, 2km south of town, describes more of this history.

Stretch Your Legs with Great Views

Viewpoints and hidden valleys

From Parque Histórico Santa Cruz la Vieja drive or hike 2.7km uphill to **Mirador de Ñuflo de Chaves** for sweeping views across town and the Chiquitania forests. Continue 550m to reach **Valle de la Luna** where a short walk will take you to this hidden valley of forested rock formations. When we were there we saw the rare red-fronted macaw. Area residents come here to walk the stations of the cross during Easter.

Also up here is the **Sendero Montañeta forest walk** (p286), but it's easy to get lost. You can go with a guide from the tourist office or as part of **Ruta de SaborArte** (p286).

NORADOA/SHUTTERSTOCK

Courtyard of San José de Chiquitos (p284)

Beyond the Jesuit Mission Circuit

Roam the Gran Chiquitania planes to discover rock spires and hidden valleys for hikes to waterfalls, springs and jaguars.

Places

GETTING AROUND

Buses ply the asphalt highway from Santa Cruz to Puerto Quijarro at the border with Brazil, passing the mission town of San José de Chiquitos and Roboré. The road is in decent condition so is self-driveable. The train line *(www.fo.com.bo)* runs parallel to Hwy 4 from Santa Cruz to Puerto Quijarro, and trains also stop in San José and Roboré, though they run infrequently. Check at the nearest station for current schedules. *Micros* connect each of the smaller towns.

The Jesuit Mission Circuit sits smack in the middle of the Gran Chiquitania, which spans from the tropical Amazon Basin in the north to the frontiers of the thorny Gran Chaco in the south, bounded by Brazil and Paraguay. The region takes its name from the indigenous Chiquitano (meaning 'little people'), a term coined by the Spanish who were surprised by the low doorways to their dwellings.

Hwy 4 cuts through the region, running along the train line from Santa Cruz and San José de Chiquitos east to Brazil. The flat Chiquitania farm and forest is broken by unexpected monolithic mountains and red-rock spires at Chochís, offering superb hiking there and around hillside hamlet Santiago de Chiquitos.

Route 39 Countryside

TIME FROM SAN MIGUEL DE VELASCO: 3½ HRS

Go in search of jaguars

Bolivia's once-thriving jaguar population has become threatened as people convert forests to soy farming and ranchland, and demand for illegally poached teeth and skulls soars. Plan ahead to get out to **San Miguelito Jaguar Conservation Ranch** *(wildlifeconservationtour.com)*. Most of the forest surrounding San Miguelito has been cleared for agriculture, leaving a pocket of protected wetland densely populated with jaguars: it's often possible to see them. It's also home to pumas, ocelots, margays, Geoffrey's cats and jaguarundi. You're required to go by tour (minimum two-night stay), which includes hikes to check cameras, canoeing on Río San Julian and bird-watching. Contact **Nick's Adventures** (p265) or **Misional Tours** (p265) in Santa Cruz.

Chochís

TIME FROM SAN JOSE DE CHIQUITOS: 1¼ HRS 

Hike red rock spires to grand views

The flatlands of the Chiquitania rise to towering red rock spires and jagged cliffs around tiny **Chochís**, 93km east of San José de Chiquitos. Wind your way 3km uphill from the hamlet to **Santuario Mariano de la Torre** *(B$10)*, a religious sanctuary and memorial to the victims of a 1979 flood (designed by Hans Roth, restorer of the Jesuit Missions), at the base of the imposing red rock known as La Torre. Walk up its flank, or local guides can take you to waterfalls, hidden natural pools and stunning viewpoints atop surrounding cliff faces. Chochís has a couple of decent campsites and pensions.

Santiago de Chiquitos

TIME FROM SAN JOSÉ DE CHIQUITOS: **2 HRS**

Hike to waterfalls, springs and caves with rock art

Set in the hills at 622m, **Santiago de Chiquitos**, 20km east of Roboré, provides a welcome break from lowland heat. Peep into its **mission church** (though it's not included in the UNESCO site). Really, though, you'll find the highlights to be the great hikes: a 3km walk to **La Colina,** a refreshing tall waterfall, or trek to **Las Pozas de Santaigo** natural pools, 3.5km south of town.

Another longer walk takes you to **Las Cuevas de Miserendino**, caves that contain wall paintings; for this one, it's best to visit with a guide (guide fees B$180 to B$200; ask at *hostal* **Churapa** (p291).

Behold stony spires in the Valle de Tucavaca

One of the best hikes from Santiago, requiring a guide (ask at hostal Churapa), is north of town to a rocky hilltop with dizzying views of the **Tucavaca Valley**, where jagged rock fingers jut skyward. It's all part of **Reserva Departmental Valle de Tucavaca**. The three-hour round-trip from town is particularly lovely in late afternoon when the light hits the rocks.

Quick dip into rock art

Surprisingly close to Hwy 4, **Parque Ecorupestre El Manantial** *(parqueecorupestreelmanantial.com; B$20)* is an easy spot to look at 6000-year-old rock paintings on an open-air cliff face. There's also a series of small springs (30 minutes on foot) for a cool dip.

Take a hot soak at Aguas Calientes

Ready for a Bolivian favorite? Go 25km east on Hwy 4 from the turnoff to Santiago de Chiquitos to reach **Aguas Calientes**, a village based around shallow, kid-friendly natural hot springs in the forest. Multiple camping/barbecue hangouts, like **Los Hervores** *(B$30/15 per adult/child, camping B$50)*, offer facilities for picnicking, food kiosks and camping out for a moonlit soak. Bring repellant – when you're not soaking, there are sand flies.

MENNONITES IN BOLIVIA

Traveling in eastern Bolivia, you likely see horse-drawn buggies, the transport of the Mennonite community. Numbering only 189 in 1959, and 70,000 in 2013, they now have a population of over 150,000. With roots in Prussia and Ukraine, Bolivian Mennonites have been migrating here, by way of Canada and Latin American countries, attracted to the open farmland and relative lack of governance. Their insulated settlements lie deep in the interior and adhere to strict rules. They speak Plautdietsch (a German dialect) and Spanish. The book *Women Talking* by Miriam Toews, made into a 2022 movie by Sarah Polley, detailed abuses in the Manitoba community, midway between Santa Cruz and San José de Chiquitos.

BORDER CROSSINGS

The Brazil border crossing at the eastern terminus of the railway line and Hwy 4 is Puerto Quijarro, with Corumbá, the gateway to the Brazilian Pantanal, on the other side. For more on the more common entries to Bolivia by air, see p332.

Places We Love to Stay

$ Budget $$ Midrange $$$ Top End

Santa Cruz de la Sierra

MAP p262

Nomad Hostel $ One of the city's best budget options, right on the edge of Plaza 24 de Septiembre in the old town.

Hotel Lido $$ Solid midrange option with comfortable rooms and restaurant, near Parque El Arenal.

Cosmopolitano $$$ Contemporary design in the city center around a central courtyard with a small pool. The great cafe is worth visiting in its own right.

Alfonsina $$$ Excellent small hotel in Equipetrol, with a pool and central to restaurants and nightlife. It's also got a cafe of its own, and rich breakfasts.

Hotel Los Tajibos $$$ Grand resort in Equipetrol with huge pool and tropical gardens, patrolled by peacocks – a family-friendly getaway.

Samaipata

MAP p268

Hostal Andoriña $ Tidy little hostel with a communal kitchen, pretty hill views and a relaxing courtyard.

Posada Guasu $$ Super-central near the main square, this guesthouse has clean, comfortable rooms around a courtyard with a friendly owner.

La Vida Es Bella $$ This villa sits several blocks from the center and has spacious rooms and expansive grounds – a lush getaway.

Hotel Colibri $$ Minimalist whitewashed rooms, some with private bathroom, are set around the standard shady courtyard.

Nómada $$ Care has been taken to make this hostel a welcoming and relaxing place. Rooms are cozy and decorated with local fabrics and original artwork, and there are gorgeous gardens with fruit trees. On-site cafe.

Finca La Víspera $$$ Relax on an organic farm with commanding valley views: camping, rooms with shared kitchen, and guesthouses are all among the accomodations.

El Pueblito $$$ Luxe hillside resort comes complete with its own church, plaza and pool. Dripping with creativity.

Around Samaipata

p268

Balneario Mama Pascuala $ This campground is on the road to El Fuerte with natural pools *(B$10 for non-guests)* for cooling dips.

Samaiwasi $ Verdant gardens surround this guesthouse and campground perched riverside in Aguas Ricas, near Cuevas.

Refugio los Volcánes $$$ Ecofriendly, solar-powered *cabañas* are a gateway to the national park. Meals are included and they program activities in Los Volcánes (p273).

Buena Vista

MAP p275

Villa Amboró Campsite (p274) $ A community-run campsite with good facilities inside the park, gives easy access to trails.

Hostal Buena Vista $ Clean simple rooms surround a courtyard in the village, and the owners will occasionally cook.

La Casona $ This is a colorful place on the western corner of the plaza, with a friendly owner and a nice patio with sagging hammocks. The rooms are simple with good beds.

Hacienda El Cafetal $$$ Set up to support Bolivian coffee growers and their families, this hacienda 5km southwest of town has stylish, self-catering *cabañas* (cabins) and suites, all with good views.

Vallegrande & Higuera

p277

Hostal Juanita $ People love this family-run hostel just two blocks southwest of the Vallegrande plaza.

Casa del Telegrafista $ Cobbled patio and tasteful rustic rooms fill an historic house in La Higuera. The place also uses solar power and offers camping.

Plaza Pueblo Hotel $$ Two and a half blocks uphill from the Mercado Campesino, Plaza Pueblo has rather plain, motel-style rooms and friendly, helpful staff.

San Xavier & Concepción

p278

Hotel Suite El Escondido, Concepción $ Well-maintained, simple rooms surround a rich garden, six blocks northwest of the plaza.

Gran Hotel Concepción, Concepción $$ This charming, mission-inspired hotel has a pool, quiet patio and a garden, right on the plaza.

Residencial de Chiquitano, San Xavier $$ Pension with toucan motifs on the main road.

The terrace has killer views of the hills.

San Xavier Quinta Eco-Resort, **San Xavier** $$$ This property is an ambling favorite for its pool, *cabaña*-style rooms and tasty restaurant.

San Ignacio de Velasco

p282

Parador Santa Ana Chiquitos $$ Friendly and helpful owners distinguish this pretty pension, a block from the square.

Apart-Hotel San Ignacio $$ This is a family-friendly choice, with hammocks, a verdant courtyard, pool and large rooms with a refrigerator, plus, of course, family rooms.

Hotel La Misión $$$ Embrace a bit of luxury, on the east side of the plaza, where chic rooms surround a little pool and opulent suites include one with church views.

San Rafael & Santa Ana

p284-5

Pascana Rafaeleña $ Meters from the church, only choose this bare-bones pension if you're forced to stay in San Rafael de Velasco.

Hotel Museo Misional Santa Ana $ The village museum has three simple rooms and food, too, but try to call ahead to let them know you're coming.

San José de Chiquitos

p285

Hotel La Casona Chiquitana $ Comfortable, with pretty central garden and hammocks for chilling, one block south of the plaza.

Hotel Villa Chiquitana $$ Spacious rooms 800m south of the plaza with pool, palm garden with orchids and tropical birds. Good restaurant-bar.

Hotel Misiones de Chiquitos $$$ Slick hotel on the plaza. Rooms, around a pool, have flat-screen TV and luxe bathrooms. Roof terrace bar with views, and gym.

Las Churupas $$$ Shady terraces surround a pool, and rooms are spacious, some kitted out for families or with bunk beds. You'll find it just west of the center.

Santiago de Chiquitos

p289

Churapa $$ Complex of comfy rooms around a lush garden, with a guests-only restaurant. Friendly staff can connect you with trail guides.

Hotel Cachuelitas Santiago de Chiquitos $$ Clean rooms and a friendly welcome go well with a good night's sleep and breakfast to match.

Casa Del Telegrafista

For places to stay in the Amazon Basin, see p328

Left: Blue-throated macaws, Rurrenabaque (p298), Right: Capybaras, Río Mamoré (p3

Researched by
Vesna Maric

Amazon Basin

ENTER THE RAUCOUS REIGN OF THE RAINFOREST

The Bolivian Amazon is one of the country's largest and most mesmerizing regions, yet it is also its least traveled.

Wildly underrated on the world's radar of unforgettable places to visit, it is a place that will truly enrich anyone's experience of life and the planet. The Amazon Basin offers the chance to learn about and stand in awe of the simultaneously fragile, yet robust, ecosystems of our world. Experience wandering around the humid selva, guided by an experienced local, and uncovering the mysteries of the forest's flora and fauna, all the while learning about the richness of indigenous cultures, traditions and languages that exist throughout the region.

The main town for visitors is cute Rurrenabaque, with its mossy hills and steaming Río Beni, which gives the province of Beni its name. Most people's first point of entry into the region, Rurrenabaque is the main base camp for visits to the fascinating Parque Nacional Madidi, home to a fully fledged ethno-ecotourism industry established by and in aid of the local communities – your money here is well spent. Further out, San Ignacio de Moxos has the most colorful and raucous July village fiesta; Trinidad, the region's transportation-ation hub on the road to Santa Cruz, is encased by steaming wetlands. North of here are the remote towns of Riberalta and Guayaramerín, touching the border with Brazil. Travelers in the region seldom come this far.

AIZAR RALDES/AFP VIA GETTY IMAGES

THE MAIN AREAS

WESTERN BOLIVIAN AMAZON
One of the world's biodiversity gems. p298

EASTERN BOLIVIAN AMAZON
See Trinidad's pink river dolphins. p312

CHAPARE REGION
Rainforest treks and wildlife refuges. p318

NORTHERN BOLIVIAN AMAZON
Remote wildlife reserves and acai-producing communities. p322

Find Your Way

The Amazon Basin is Bolivia's largest region, and getting around is not without its challenges. Flights can be canceled at the last minute, bus journeys can take long in the rainy season, road blocks can halt you, and boats are slow going.

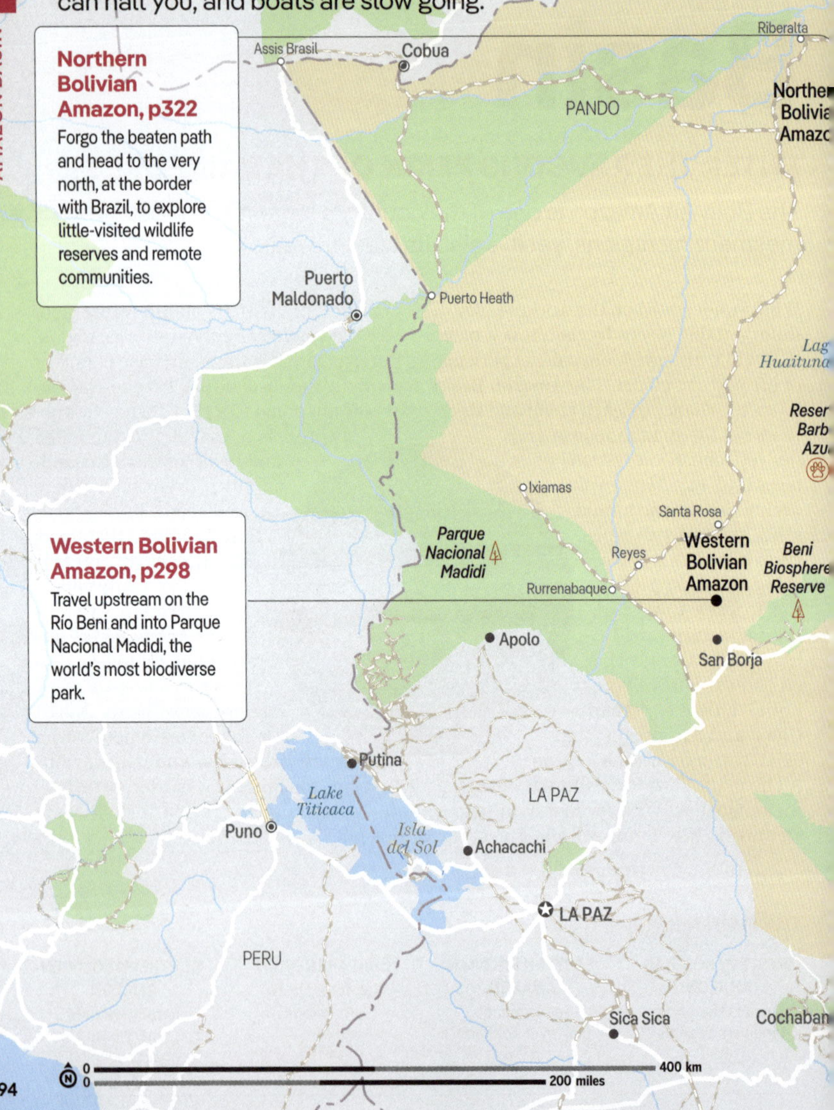

Northern Bolivian Amazon, p322

Forgo the beaten path and head to the very north, at the border with Brazil, to explore little-visited wildlife reserves and remote communities.

Western Bolivian Amazon, p298

Travel upstream on the Río Beni and into Parque Nacional Madidi, the world's most biodiverse park.

PLANE

Both **BoA** and **EcoJet** fly to the region. Though handy and much quicker than buses, flights are frequently canceled – last minute – during inclement weather or because of airplane maintenance. Be very flexible.

BOAT

Riverboat travel isn't for everyone: it's relaxing but slow going, and there are no real schedules. Passenger comfort is the last thing cargo-boat builders have in mind – Bolivian boat accommodations are quite basic.

BUS

Even though most roads have been asphalted in the last decade, the rainy season still presents problems for bus and car journeys – the road can get flooded and your bus may take twice as long as you thought it would.

Abunã
Esperanza
BRAZIL
Guajará-Mirim
Guayaramerín
Parque Nacional de Pacaás Novos
Forte Príncipe da Beira
Reserva Extrativista Pedras Negras
San Joaquín
San Ramón
Magdalena
Baures
Piso Firme
Santa Ana del Yacuma
Parque Nacional Noel Kempff Mercado
Eastern Bolivian Amazon
Santuario Chuchini
Trinidad
San Ignacio de Moxos
BOLIVIA
Asención de Guarayos
Concepción
San Javier
Portachuelo
Parque Nacional Carrasco
Chapare Region
Parque Nacional Amboró

Eastern Bolivian Amazon, p312

Get onto a boat tour in Trinidad, and float down the serene Río Ibare to view the elusive and endemic pink river dolphins.

Chapare Region, p318

Take a tour to visit the fascinating Parque Nacional Carrasco or engage in some Amazonia-light at the local wildlife reserves.

Plan Your Time

This fascinating region remains one of the least visited parts of the country. It is a prime destination for the adventure traveler, with incredible opportunities for wildlife spotting, bird watching and boat travel.

GASTON BRITO MISEROCCHI/GETTY IMAGES

Fiesta de Moxos (p306)

Pressed for Time

- If you only do one thing, head straight for **Rurrenabaque** (p298), having booked a two-night tour into the jungle of **Parque Nacional Madidi** (p296) – it's unmissable and the best of Bolivia's Amazon. Replete with wildlife endemic to almost all of Bolivia's ecosystems, from tropical rainforest and savanna to cloud forest and alpine tundra, it is one of the most biodiverse places on the planet and a once-in-a-lifetime opportunity to witness such a remarkable range of species. Stay at the highly regarded, community-run **Chalalán Ecolodge** (p302) for the ultimate jungle experience. You can also organize a tour from Santa Cruz, La Paz or Cochabamba.

Seasonal Highlights

Traveling in the dry season between May and October is the best time. Wildlife is easier to spot and the Amazon's wildest fiesta takes place in San Ignacio de Moxos in July.

JANUARY

This is the rainiest month of the year, making some activities and getting around more difficult, but river travel is a breeze.

FEBRUARY

Carnaval takes place across the whole country, and the Amazon Basin inhabitants get to put their masks, costumes and feathers on. Easter Week sees more solemn street processions.

MARCH

The Semana Santa (Easter Week) also sees street processions, but this time they're solemn and religious.

A Week of Amazon Wildlife

- After **Parque Nacional Madidi** (p296), spend a couple of days checking out the pampas in **Rurrenabaque** and the town's tropical charm.

- A three-hour bus ride away from here is the sleepy town of San Borja, from where you can head to the little-visited **Reserva de la Biosfera y Estación Biológica del Beni** (p309) to see amazing wildlife and birds, and visit indigenous communities. Stay in San Borja and visit the park daily, or if you're really tough, stay in the park and go horseback riding. From San Borja, get a bus to **Trinidad** (p313), the transportationation hub. Spend a day checking out this tropical town, then embark on the legendary two-day boat journey **La Ruta del Bufeo** (p312) to view pink river dolphins.

Two Weeks to Travel Around

- Those with more time can board the fancy two-, three- or four-day boat tour in Trinidad, with the **Flotel Reina de Enin** (p316), and watch the dolphins from a deck, drink in hand. Back in Trinidad, visit the **Santuario Chuchini** (p315) to get an eyeful of a wildlife sanctuary that sits on the remains of an ancient civilization.

- After Trinidad, get on a further three-hour bus ride to **San Ignacio de Moxos** – make sure your visit is at the end of July, for the not-to-be-missed **Fiesta de Moxos** (p306).

- Alternatively, bird lovers can get on an organized tour from Santa Cruz, to see the rare blue-throated macaw at the **Reserva Barba Azul** (p324) or any of the Amazon's more far-flung national parks.

JULY

High season, more tourists and the end-of-July **Fiesta de Moxos** (p306), the biggest party in Beni. Outrageous costumes and street parties.

SEPTEMBER

The end of the high season and the start of the rainy season, with humid days and warm nights.

OCTOBER

At the end of winter (and the high season), rainfall spikes. It's tougher to generally be outdoors. It'll stay rainy until April.

DECEMBER

One of the hottest months of the year in the lowlands, with humid days and warm nights. Very low tourist season, with many agencies closed until spring.

Western Bolivian Amazon

EPIC BIODIVERSITY | MYSTICAL RAINFOREST | INDIGENOUS CULTURE

GETTING AROUND

Rurrenbaque's airport is 4km north of town. There are twice-weekly flights from La Paz with **EcoJet** and **BoA**, but beware of last-minute cancelations. The flight from La Paz is an affordable way of avoiding the arduous 10- to 12-hour bus journey. The main bus terminal is across from the airport and a moto-taxi ride from town.

The route to Trinidad (10 to 13 hours) goes via San Borja (three hours) and San Ignacio de Moxos (seven hours). It may take longer in the rainy season. Access the Reserva de la Biosfera y Estación Biológica del Beni via San Borja.

Visiting the western part of the Bolivian Amazon is unforgettable. While it's still not as popular as other parts of Bolivia, it is one of country's most beautiful and interesting areas. And frankly, it's not for everyone – you have to be up for some slow and sometimes uncomfortable travel. Here, you're visiting a land where nature rules and you are just a guest.

Spend time in Rurrenabaque, a sleepy Amazon town, then float down the river into Parque Nacional Madidi, one of South America's (and the world's) most precious wilderness gems. Encompassing a spellbinding range of habitats, from Andean mountains to steamy lowland rainforests, the park has an astonishing array of wildlife. Take it all in on guided rainforest walks and boat trips on the river, staying at a community-run ecolodge. Then, if you're visiting at the right time of the year, party with the locals at the annual Fiesta de Moxos, in the indigenous village of San Ignacio de Moxos, before calming down again in the lushness of the Reserva de la Biosfera y Estación Biológica del Beni.

Town at the Edge of the Rainforest

Knockin' on jungle's door

This is where it all starts for most people visiting the Bolivian Amazon: in sleepy **Rurrenabaque**, affectionately known as Rurre.

Cleaved by the deep Río Beni and surrounded by mossy green hills, Rurrenabaque has mesmerizing sunsets that turn the sky salmon, and a foaming morning mist that sneaks down the river among the lush, moist trees. In the evenings, the surrounding rainforest comes alive with croaks, barks, buzzes and roars, giving you a sense of all the life unfolding inside the woods. In many ways a typical jungle town, with

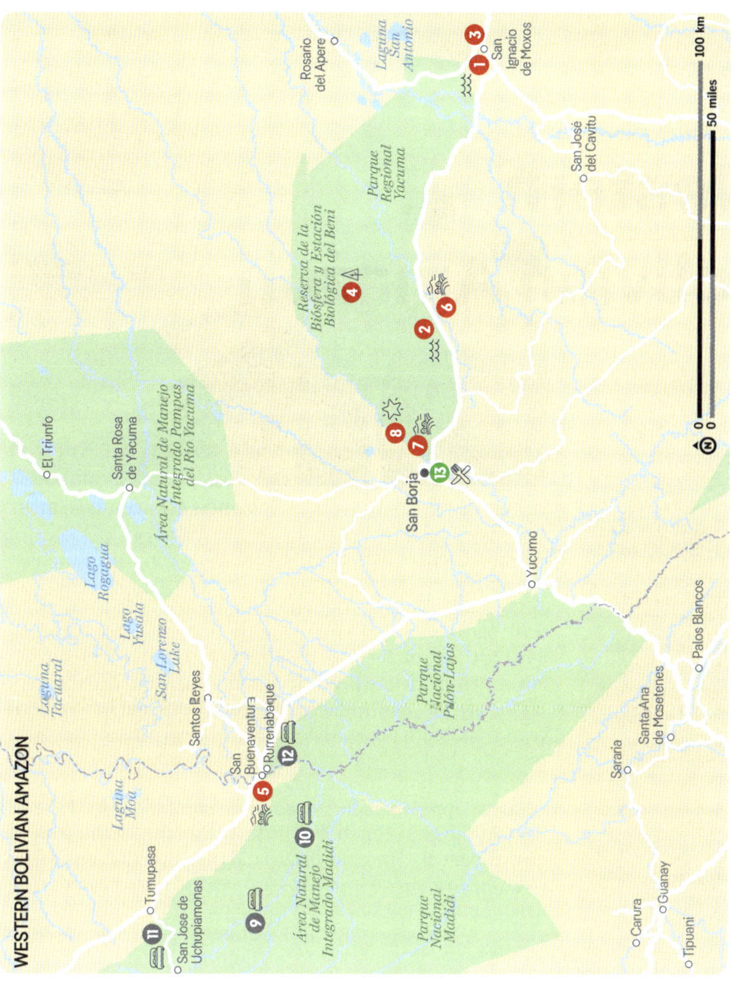

SIGHTS

- Iglesia Parroquial de S.I. (see 3)
- 1 Laguna Isirere
- 2 Laguna Normandia
- 3 Main Plaza
- Museo de Mojos (see 3)
- 4 Reserva de la Biosfera y Estación Biológica del Beni
- 5 San Buenaventura
- 6 Totaizal
- 7 Tsimané Communities

ACTIVITIES

- Bala Tours (see 5)
- El Chorro (see 5)
- El Porvenir (see 2)
- 8 Río Maniqui

SLEEPING

- Albergue El Porvenir (see 2)
- 9 Chalalán Ecolodge
- Chalalán Ecolodge Booking Office (see 5)
- Hotel Maya (see 5)
- 10 Madidi Jungle
- Madidi Jungle Booking Office (see 5)
- 11 Sadiri
- Sadiri Booking Office (see 5)
- 12 San Miguel del Bala
- San Miguel del Bala Office (see 5)

EATING

- Bakery Rurre (see 5)
- Big Burger San Borja (see 13)
- Casa de Campo (see 5)
- City Rock (see 13)
- 13 Hanna Pastelería y Repostería
- Juliano's (see 5)
- Kiosko Dulcetti (see 13)
- La Cabaña (see 5)
- La Pascana del Gordo (see 3)
- La Perla de Rurre (see 5)
- Luz de Mar (see 5)
- Market (see 5)
- Moxos Social Club (see 3)
- Panadería París (see 5)
- Roots Cafe (see 5)

DRINKING & NIGHTLIFE

- Jungle Bar Moskkito (see 5)
- Luna Lounge (see 5)

SHOPPING

- Centro Cultural Tacana (see 5)
- Clothing Stalls (see 5)
- La Cambita (see 5)
- Pampas Supermercado (see 5)

INFORMATION

- Parque Nacional Madidi Sernap Office (see 5)
- Sernap (see 13)

TRANSPORTATION

- EcoJet (see 5)

WHAT'S IN A NAME

The area's original people, the Tacana, are responsible for Rurrenabaque's name. It was derived from 'Arroyo Inambaque,' the Hispanicized version of the Tacana name Suse-Inambaque, the 'Ravine of Ducks.' The Tacana people have preserved their own, eponymous, language, though not all Tacana speak it today. Subject to Jesuit missions and enforced Christian conversions in the 17th century, the Tacana used to make their living from extracting rubber and working with cinchona, a medicinal tree. In contemporary times, the Tacana were crucial in developing a territorial management programme to significantly reduce forest loss in large areas of South America. The Centro Cultural Tacana in San Buenaventura is the place to see their cosmovision.

Río Beni, Rurrenabaque (p298)

low-built houses and an easy vibe, it's where you will most certainly spend a day or three while exploring your excursion options into the jungle and the pampas. And what a pleasant little place it is – prepare to lounge in hammocks, eat some local fish and/or deep-fried caiman's tail, and meet some fellow travelers, before heading out into the wild. Backpackers fill the streets, and while restaurants, cafes and hotels often cater to Western tastes, there's a ton of local eateries too, with roasting chickens and smoky barbecues catering to Rurrenabaque's friendly inhabitants.

Rurre's appeal is in its surrounding natural beauty. Take an hour in the morning to huff your way up the 295-step staircase two blocks from the plaza, and then up a dirt-and-stone pathway to a *mirador* (lookout) and finally to a big cross (La Cruz) overlooking town and the Beni. On very hot days, you can spend the afternoon at **El Chorro**, an idyllic waterfall with a series of pools apt for swimming. You'll find it at the end of Calle Santa Cruz, following a well-worn trail 500m upstream into the jungle. It's popular with local families, but you should still be sure to watch your belongings. You can do a bit of Amazonian souvenir shopping in **La Cambita**, which sells chonta-wood plates, jipijapa baskets and organic coffee from Pilón Lajas.

Continues on p308

EATING IN RURRENABAQUE: OUR PICKS

Luz de Mar: Charming restaurant, bar and cafe, near the main square with patio seating and a street-side terrace. Decent lunch menu. *7:30am-10:30pm* $

La Cabaña: By the riverfront, this is the spot for inventive fish dishes and simple lunches. The tropical terrace gets busy at lunchtime. *11am-10:30pm daily* $

Juliano's: Good fish dishes and the only imported Peruvian shellfish in town. The crème brûlée is particularly popular. *5-11pm* $$

Casa de Campo: Rurrenabaque's freshest, most delicious food – but you'll have to order at least half a day, if not a full day, in advance. *noon-3pm & 7-10pm* $$

TOP EXPERIENCE

Parque Nacional Madidi

Madidi National Park is part of one of the largest protected areas in the world, and it is a lucky traveler who gets the chance to visit. Add to that the opportunity to meet local, indigenous peoples and contribute to their community's wellbeing by staying in an ecolodge, where they also guide you around the jungle, and it really is an experience of a lifetime.

Yellow monkeys, Parque Nacional Madidi

Enormous Biodiversity

The 18,000 sq km Parque Nacional Madidi is one of South America's most intact ecosystems, taking in a range of habitats from steaming lowland rainforests to 6000m Andean peaks. It is also one of the most significant protected areas in Bolivia, hosting an astonishing variety of Amazonian wildlife: 44% of all mammal species in North and South America, 38% of neotropical amphibian species and more than 1000 species of bird. According to some scientists, it is one the most biodiverse places on earth. Comprising of 272 species of mammals, 213 species of amphibians, 204 species of reptiles, 496 species of fish, 1254 species of birds and over 120,000 species of insects, you will certainly be able to see some animals on your visit, and you will definitely feel some insects.

While visitors long to spot a jaguar, sightings of these shy cats are very rare. You are more likely to see tapir, capybara and caiman in Chalalan lake, as well as many types of bird – the park is a birders' paradise, with more species discovered each year. Overall, the wildlife count equates to a staggering 14% of the 9000-plus identified species worldwide.

Indigenous Communities

Around 50 indigenous communities inhabit the park, including Leco, Tacana, Araona, Esse Ejja, T'simane and Mosetene peoples. These communities have always been strong custodians of the park's ecosystems and many have turned to ecotourism. Incorporating walks in the rainforest with visits to indigenous communities, where you can peek into local lifestyles and traditions, is a great way to respectfully learn about how these communities combine ancient traditions and modern life.

TOP TIPS

- Dry season (April–November) is the best time to visit. Transportation is easier and wildlife congregates around rivers, making it easier to spot.
- During wet season (December–March), paths can be soggy and mosquitoes abound. Heavy rainfall may impact activities and flights.

PRACTICALITIES

See *madidiid.org* for information on the park. Tour prices vary by length and operator; see p302.

Ecolodges at Parque Nacional Madidi

Most tourists visiting Madidi will spend a couple of nights at one of the park's unique ecolodges. Accessible only by boat, the isolated lodges are located deep within the jungle, making them perfect bases for exploring the park's natural wonders. Both comfortable and environmentally friendly, the ecolodges also help to improve the lives of the park's local people, who both benefit from a sustainable income and also have a large say in how the park's tourism impacts their pristine environment. They have very basic amenities; luxurious options will have en-suite bathrooms and may have some hot shower water, while more regular rooms will share bathrooms and have tepid showers.

Which Lodge is Right for You?

Established, Successful & Elegant

Chalalán Ecolodge *(chalalan.com; adult from US$150 per night)* is the oldest and most successful community-based ecotourism project, with simple and elegant wood cabins situated around the idyllic oxbow lake, Laguna Chalalán. Set up in the early 1990s by the inhabitants of remote San José de Uchupiamonas, it has become a lifeline for villagers, and has so far generated money for a school and a small clinic.

Built entirely from natural rainforest materials by the enthusiastic San José youth, the lodge surrounds you with lovely flora and fauna. You will see it on day and nighttime walks on the 30km of trails, or during boat excursions on the lake.

Bird-Watchers' Heaven

The only project created and sustained 100% by the indigenous people of the park is **Madidi Jungle** *(madidijungle.com; 1-day tours from US$110 per person)*. All-inclusive trips here include bird-watching, night hikes and boat excursions. The project also organizes handicraft workshops and river tubing, all within the 210,000-hectare stretch of land belonging to the San José de Uchupiamonas community. You'll sleep in comfortable thatch-roofed cabins set by the Río Tuichi.

The Cool Highlands

Sadiri Lodge *(sadirilodge.com; adult from US$150 per night)* has six luxury cabins in dense foothill rainforest in the Serranía Sadiri, with a unique highland location (elevation between 500m and 950m) and cooler temperatures. The cooler climate brings in a whole new set of animals, the dozens of species of glittering tanagers being a delight to bird-watchers.

The lodge was created by local conservationists and the indigenous people of San José de Uchupiamonas, who favoured the long-term benefits of this sustainable tourism project over the advances of forestry companies. Meals are served on a terrace flanked by hummingbird feeders and with some of the most incredible views over the national park.

On Madidi's Doorstep

A shorter boat journey (40 minutes upstream from Rurrenabaque) is with **San Miguel del Bala** *(sanmigueldelbala.com; 1-day tours US$60)*, a glorious ecolodge in its own patch of paradise right on Madidi's doorstep. Hosted by the indigenous Tacana community, you will witness its traditional agricultural methods, weaving and wood carving. Along with the several guided walks, you can visit the small San Miguel community. The three-day/two-night arrangement includes a day's visit deep into Parque Nacional Madidi.

STRUCTURED VISION/SHUTTERSTOCK

Tapir, Parque Nacional Madidi (p301)

HOW TO

When to go
The dry season between April and November is the best time to spot wildlife, with the least mosquitoes.

Book ahead
These community lodges have offices in Rurrenabaque, but they can be difficult to find open. You're best off booking in advance, via their websites.

What to bring
Good waterproof shoes and, in the rainy season, a raincoat. Insect repellent is a must, regardless of season. Good binoculars and a camera.

Budget
Established projects have a two-night minimum stay. They're well worth the daily fee (around US$180 per person), which includes transportation, accommodations, full board and knowledgeable guides.

How Long to Stay

You can choose between a one-day tour and a longer stay over one or more nights – the lodges that are further up inside the park offer stays that are two-nights minimum, because the boat journeys are much longer. **Madidi Jungle** and **San Miguel del Bala** offer one-day and half-day river tours and walks, which include no overnight stays, and are more affordable. **Chalalan Ecolodge** and **Sadiri Lodge** projects are more immersive, and take you deep into the jungle. In all cases you'll be taken on rainforest walks, lake swims and bird-watching expeditions by local guides, who are invaluable for their knowledge of the diverse native wildlife.

If you decide to stay for multiple days, three meals a day are included in all stays, as well as a snack for the (longer) upstream boat journeys. All trips involve a boat trip up the Beni and Tuichi rivers, where you will be able to spot birds and some mammals along the way.

Electricity is drawn from solar panels (when there are solar panels installed) and is only available at certain times of the day (normally at dinner time and up to bedtime, or around 10pm) and running water is limited, so don't expect steamy hot showers. There is no internet or phone reception anywhere in the park.

Choosing a Jungle or Pampas Tour

Jungle and pampas tours are Rurrenabaque's bread and butter, but it's extremely important to choose a tour responsibly. The quality of service provided by the numerous agencies varies considerably, and some operators are much less responsible than they ought to be. Equally, travelers need to understand that the rainforest and the pampas are not tourist commodities, but living ecosystems that must not be interfered with. Consider the following carefully before you hand over your cash.

Which Company to Choose If You Like...

Pampas Tours

It's easier to see wildlife in the wetland savannas northeast of Rurrenabaque, but the sun is more oppressive and the bugs can be worse, especially in the rainy season. Some of the most exciting activities are horseback riding and night-time canoe trips to spot caiman. Guides are forbidden from feeding, handling or disturbing animals. If your guide offers to capture anacondas, caiman or other animals, object.

Always opt for one of the community-run ecotourism ventures, which, although more expensive, are definitely worthwhile since they aim to help sustain communities and preserve the richness of the rainforests for the generations to come. Talk to other travelers about their experiences and boycott companies that break the rules. Be responsible in your own expectations.

One of the best pampas tours options is **San Miguel del Bala** (p303; *sanmigueldelbala.com; 1-day tours from US$120)*, who run pink dolphin and anaconda sighting tours, which range from one-day to 3-day packages. You'll be hosted by the indigenous Tacana community.

Jungle Tours

Jungle tours can be one-day long or you can stay for almost an entire week, depending on your time, budget and preference. When going on a jungle tour your guixde will be the most important aspect of your excursion, and it's important that they're respectful and professional when it comes to handling their visitors, and the animals and environment. Remember, there are no guarantees of spotting wildlife. Any company, or guide, that offers them is likely to be breaking the rules. Guides are forbidden from feeding, handling or disturbing animals. If your guide offers to capture anacondas, caiman or other animals, or do piranha fishing, object and explain why. A great option for ensuring your stay is professionally organized is to book with **America Tours Bolivia** *(america-ecotours.com; tours starting at US$170 per person per day)*, an agency run by David Ribalde and his wife Jasmin. David is a biologist who trains Madidi and pampas guides – always local, indigenous people – and they organize tours (some tailored) into the jungle, the pampas and down the Yacuma river. All their guides use only operators authorized by the **Servicio Nacional de Áreas Protegidas** (Sernap), as only they can legally enter Parque Nacional Madidi.

Foreigners must be accompanied by a local guide, but not all speak good English. If this is a possible concern, ask to meet your guide.

Boat Tours

All tours will involve some length of boat travel, either along the Beni, Tuichi or Yacuma river. **Bala Tours** *(71245281; 1-day tours from US$60)* is a reputable Rurrenabaque-based agency with its own jungle camp, Caracoles, on the banks of the Yacuma River. It's a comfortable pampas lodge on the river bank that also runs a forest lodge in Tacuaral, near the eponymous lake. Boat trips include spotting monkeys, birds and larger mammals, such as the capybaras, with the highlight being the sighting of pink dolphins. River boat trips are interspersed with some walking inside the rainforest.

SCOTTIEBUMICH/GETTY IMAGES

Capybaras in The Pampas

HOW TO

When to go
The pampas are full of mosquitoes all year round, but the dry season (April - November) is a little easier to bear. Always carry insect repellent.

Book ahead
Booking ahead is helpful especially in the high season, to ensure you have your spot saved.

What to pack
Bring binoculars, a good flashlight, extra batteries and plenty of mosquito repellent, especially for the pampas, where the bugs are rife.

Budget
Pampas tours start at US$60 per person for a day, while jungle tour prices start at US$110 per day.

How Long to Stay

Half-day and one-day tours are good if you're short on time, although staying at least one night and waking up to the sounds of the wildlife is a treat that you should not miss, if at all possible. One-night and two-day tours are quite popular, while two nights and three days will offer you a wonderful chance to take longer boat trips and see more wildlife. Staying an entire week inside the jungle is a great way to really get under the skin of the selva.

All trips involve a boat ride up the Beni and Tuichi Rivers, while some pampas tours will go on the Yacuma River. Try **Bala Tours** (*71245281; 1-day tours from US$60*) for a single-day pampas tour, or a multiday package, or **America Tours Bolivia** (*america-ecotours.com; tours starting at US$170 per person per day*) for a three-day boat tour up the Yacuma River, with rainforest walks and wildlife spotting on the river.

In all cases, food is included on the tours – sometimes snacks are included for half-day trips. Three meals a day are included in the multiday tours, as well as drinking (bottled) water and snacks for the boat trips.

GASTON BRITO MISEROCCHI/GETTY IMAGES

TOP EXPERIENCE

Fiesta de Moxos

The village of San Ignacio de Moxos normally has a quiet, workaday atmosphere, with little appeal for travelers. But come the last week of July, and La Ichapekene Piesta Inasianuana, or the Fiesta del Santo Patrono de Moxos, sees the villagers let their hair down and their feather headgear up, with everyone drinking, dancing and letting off fireworks for three days.

DON'T MISS

Día de la Fiesta de Santiago (25 July)

Macheteros, *achus* and musicians (30 July)

Procession of returning the images of San Ignacio

Fireworks

Achus with firecrackers spectacle

Eating fish

VIPs parading around

Pre-Festival Week Processions

The pre-festival mood begins on July 22, when the small statue of Santiago is paraded from the church and worshipped each evening until July 25, **Día de la Fiesta de Santiago**. Somewhat confusingly for outsiders (but hey, who's counting) the same statue is then worshipped as an image of San Ignacio for the rest of the fiesta.

During this time each family in the village brings an image of San Ignacio to the church and places it there in his honour. These solemn processions take place over four days prior to the beginning of the festival. Take a peek at **Iglesia Parroquial de San Ignacio**, on the main plaza, which was

PRACTICALITIES

If you want to see the Moxos community developments and news, check out its Facebook page, at facebook.com/GAMSANIGNACIO.

restored and rebuilt from 1995 to 2003, with its Jesuit-style wide roof supported by wooden columns. There's a colorful Amazonian mural on the facade. If you get a small group together, one of the church workers will take you around inside for a small fee.

Macheteros, Achus & Musicians Parade

On July 30, a procession leaves the church, incorporating *macheteros* (local youths dressed in white with radial headdresses traditionally made from macaw feathers) and *achus* (village elders with wooden masks and hats bearing fireworks). Musicians beat and blow out Moxos music with drums, enormous bamboo panpipes and flutes. The procession visits every house in the village, returning the images of San Ignacio that had been deposited in the church and receiving food and drink in return. The winding route ends at the church, where the participants attend Mass, after which the festivities begin.

Fabulous Fireworks & Fizzing Firecrackers

The evening of the first day of the fiesta starts with huge fireworks let off by two rich local families outside the church, who 'compete' with each other through the lavishness of their displays. Then it's over to the *achus* – men and women wearing large, high-topped leather hats with lit firecrackers on top – who run through the crowd while everyone shrieks and runs away from them, laughing and screaming. Children have a particularly good time. Fresh river fish is eaten in abundance, plenty of drinking takes place (as you'll see by the number of booze casualties sleeping in the streets) and local handicrafts are displayed around the village.

Processions, VIPs, Dancing & Bulls

On the morning of the second day another mass is held. The small statue of San Ignacio is returned to the church and a larger statue of the same saint is extracted for the first time to lead a second procession, this time accompanied by local politicians, religious authorities, invited dignitaries and others VIPs. Once the formalities are dispensed with, it's party time again. The second and third days are filled with lots of dancing; there will also be bull-teasing, when the (drunk) locals attempt to get the bulls' attention by waving bright pink capes in front of their faces and generally harassing the frightened animals.

BAROQUE MUSIC TRADITION

Inscribed in UNESCO's Intangible Cultural Heritage of Humanity list, the Ichapekene Piesta of San Ignacio de Moxos has the unexpected element of featuring baroque music – a leftover of the Jesuit missionaries who founded the village. Apart from being able to hear some here, April or May of even-numbered years see a **Baroque Music Festival** *(festivalesapac.com/musica)* take place across more than 20 former missions, including San Ignacio de Moxos.

TOP TIPS

- Book your accommodations in advance if you're coming to the festival.
- To learn more about local culture, go to the **Museo de Mojos**, where you can view both the Ignaciano and Moxos cultures, including the *bajones*, the immense flutes introduced by the Jesuits. You can also learn about the legacy of baroque music here at the Archivo Musical.
- The festival kicks off on July 22 with church processions, but the real party takes place on July 30 and 31.
- Outside festival time, the village isn't a huge draw.

ILLEGAL MINING AND THE FOOD CHAIN

Illegal mining companies have been sifting the waters of the Río Beni for gold, and there are wide reports of mercury poisoning being found in aquatic life. Mining in Mayaya, a community in the northern La Paz municipality of Teoponte, affects the waters of Madidi National Park and Manuripi National Amazon Wildlife Reserve. Unlicensed boats dump mercury in the water as they operate, and the toxic element works its way up the aquatic food chain, eventually reaching the indigenous communities that catch and eat the contaminated fish. Researchers at the Higher University of San Andrés (UMSA) also carried out a study on mercury contamination in the Beni River Basin, determining that 74.5% of people tested had high levels of the heavy metal.

CRETAN NOMAD/SHUTTERSTOCK

Amazonian fish cooked in banana leaves

Continued from p300

Across the bridge over Río Beni sits sleepy **San Buenaventura**, a Rurrenabaque neighbourhood, watching all the busy goings-on, but content with its own slower pace. You can see the area in less than an hour. Located on the southwest side of the main plaza in San Buenaventura is the **Centro Cultural Tacana** handicrafts store, where you can see crafts and souvernirs made by Tacana artisans.

Try Amazonian Dishes

Taste the fish

Eating in Rurrenabaque will give you the opportunity to try some Amazonian delights. In addition to the Beni standard, *masaco* (mashed yucca or plantains, served with dried meat, rice, noodles, thin soup and bananas), try the excellent *pescado en dunucuabi* (fish wrapped in a rainforest leaf and baked over a wood fire) – you'll mostly need to order this dish some hours in advance. There is also the excellent *pescado al ajillo* (fish cooked with lots of garlic), which you should make sure you try. The *cola de caiman*, deep fried caiman's tail, is worth tasting. If you didn't know what it was, you'd easily mistake it for fleshy fish. The best place to taste these in Rurrenabaque is at the Luz de Mar (p300), and at

EATING IN RURRENABAQUE: SNACKS

Sunday market: Get your Brazil nuts and 100% Beni chocolate here, as well as fruit juices, empanadas and baked goods. *6am-8pm* $

Panadería París: A great spot for breakfast before you hit your tour, the French baker makes really great croissants! *6am-12:30pm* $

Bakery Rurre: Breakfast options and bread rolls to take away, with cute street side seating. *8am-8pm* $

Pampas Supermercado: Pre-tour snacks and water bottles, as well as sun block and insect repellent, can all be found here. *7:30am-9pm* $

La Cabaña (p300), where they specialize in fish dishes. The Sunday **market** along the riverfront is another foodie stop, attracting local farmers with all their wild and wonderful produce and some 100% Beni chocolate.

Pit Stop in San Borja

A necessary stopover before the reserve

San Borja is one of those places that you might get stuck in during the rainy season, waiting for transportation between Trinidad and Rurrenabaque; it's also an obligatory stop on the way to the Reserva de la Biosfera y Estación Biológica del Beni. Buses arrive at the station 2km southwest of town from Rurre and, more frequently, from Trinidad. As well as a transportation hub, San Borja is the location of the Sernap office (p310) where you must stop to register and plan out your trip into the reserve, including booking tours and activities. Anyone headed that way will have to spend at least a few hours here, and some spend a night in one of the very basic hotels.

Besides that, there's not much to do in town, besides a stroll in the tropical main square and refueling at one of the many restaurants before continuing your journey.

Wildlife Spotting in the Beni Biosphere Reserve

See some critters

Created by Conservation International in 1982 and run by Servicio Nacional de Áreas Protegidas (Sernap), **Reserva de la Biosfera y Estación Biológica del Beni** *(sernap.gob.bo; free entry)* is a highly diverse park composed of forests, rainforests and savannas, and is home to a staggering array of wildlife. There are around 80 species of mammals, 412 types of birds and 55 species of reptiles. The jaguar, savanna deer and black caiman are among the rare species here, and there are also pink dolphins, puma, toucan and various types of parrots. In 2020, the reserve was certified as an Area of Importance for the Conservation of Bats – it is home to 43 species of bats in Bolivia, out of a total of 138 species. You'll have opportunities to see many different species on a tour in the park, but if you want to spend two weeks in the area volunteering (check via Sernap), there are opportunities during the nesting season for Amazon river turtles (mid-August to mid-September).

TOP TIP

If you want a hammock of your own, the **clothing stalls** along Pando street are a good place to pick up *hamacas* and finely woven cotton and synthetic *mosquiteras* (mosquito nets). You can also get *chubasqueros* (raincoats) and rubber boots, for rainy season visits.

LUCKY ESCAPE

The 400-plus black caimans that you will see at Laguna Normandia are the descendants of reptiles originally destined for the fashion industry, bred for their leather by a company producing shoes and bags. The business eventually failed, and the animals were left behind, many sadly perishing in the wild. Other endangered species that can be found at Laguna Normandia are the turtles, which have been hunted for their skin, shells, fat and meat, and the beautiful olive green anacondas, whose skin is also much coveted for leather products.

EATING IN SAN BORJA: OUR PICKS

Big Burger San Borja: Choose between American, Spanish, Italian, Mexican or Amazonian burgers – the locals love this place. *6-11pm* $

Kiosko Dulcetti: Get all your sugar rushes in one at this little kiosk that sells cookies and acai-based desserts. *3:30-9pm* $

City Rock: A very popular diner with local dishes – fish with plantain, yucca and rice – and a big, busy terrace. *3-11pm* $

Hanna Pastelería y Repostería: A popular spot for sweet rolls, muffins and other portable snacks. *9am-8pm* $

SEEING MARVELLOUS WILDLIFE

Jasmin Caballero Garcia, Head of America Tours Travel & Ecotourism Consultants; america-ecotours.com

Any traveler that comes to Bolivia must visit Madidi National Park and take a tour to **Chalalan Ecolodge**, a prime location to see several wild macaws, diverse species of monkeys, and explore a beautiful lake and occasionally find giant otters. This experience can be combined with a visit to the Bolivian neotropical savanna/pampas where you will see the endemic pink dolphin, capybaras and caimans. While staying in Rurrenabaque, I would recommend the Hotel Maya (p328) and La Perla de Rurre for Bolivian food. For international cuisine, Juliano's (p300) is my place to go.

TRISTAN BARRINGTON/SHUTTERSTOCK

Black caiman

Visiting the park is rewarding only for those travelers who enjoy basic provisions and accommodations – the area is rich in wildlife, but demands physical resilience and flexibility. The **Sernap** office in San Borja organizes everything in the reserve: accommodations, food, guides and horseback riding. The best way to observe wildlife is to organize a guided hike, though the heat might be easier to take if you hire a horse. The ranger station at **El Porvenir** has a very basic 40-bed *albergue* (guesthouse) that it offers to visitors free of charge. Should you want electricity and gas, you'll need to pay a small fee of about B$80 at the Sernap office. All these need to be booked ahead. Theoretically you could use the El Porvenir station as your base for tours, but keep in mind that tours are quite difficult to arrange during the wet season.

Laguna Normandia – a savanna lake 2km from El Porvenir – is the Beni biosphere reserve's most popular destination. Here you'll be treated to a truly spectacular sight: one of the world's largest populations of crawling, rare black caimans. There are at least 400 on this savanna lake. It's safe to observe the caimans but keep an eye out for snakes!

DRINKING IN RURRENABAQUE: OUR PICKS

Roots Cafe: Rurre's best new cafe and bar, with speciality Bolivian coffee and some great cocktails. It also serves food. *7am-9pm Mon-Sun, 3-10pm Sat*

Luz de Mar (p300): People come here for the delectable daiquiris and some great pisco sours. *7:30am-10:30pm*

Luna Lounge: Good lighting, lots of cocktails, a pool table, table football and a good atmosphere in the high season. *6pm-2am*

Jungle Bar Moskkito: Don't expect a wild night, but you can play darts and pool, plus there's a DJ, lots of drinks and good vibes. *4pm-3am*

There's also the eight-hour (20km) round-trip hike to the rainforests near the Marimono ranger station and its many monkeys. Bird lovers can take the **Loro tour** on foot or horseback to see spectacular macaws and parakeets – you may also see them in the palm trees at El Porvenir.

Note that it is essential to stop by the Sernap office in San Borja to register and plan out your trip, including booking any of these tours.

Visit Totaizal's Indigenous Community

Witness local life

Totaizal, the closest village to the reserve, is a 40-minute walk from El Porvenir station. It's worth the trek for the chance to experience a slice of daily life for inhabitants of this village of 300, and their neighbors from Cero Ocho who make the four-hour walk here to sell bananas and other goods. You can also set off from here on horseback rides and canoe trips, both of which provide ample opportunities for wildlife observation. Tours to and around the village are arranged at the Sernap office in San Borja.

Get to Know the Tsimané

Learn about local crafts

For an in-depth look at indigenous life in the Amazon, hit the Sernap office to arrange a trip to the remote **Tsimané communities** along **Río Maniqui**, some 35km upriver from San Borja. Two-day, one-night ranger tours operate out of the Campamento Los Petos ranger station. It is reached by boat in the wet season or taxi the rest of the year. The Tsimané, traditionally a nomadic forest tribe, have faced danger of expulsion from their ancestral lands by lumber companies and highland settlers, and there are around 1200 people living here now in scattered villages. The Tsimané people are generally skilled hunters, and they have a fascinating way of fishing, using natural poisons to kill their prey. They co-exist with their environment in ways that allow them to collect wild honey without harming or disturbing the bees.

A tour gives you the chance to observe the Tsimané people's daily life and see their artisans at work, weaving straw and making utensils. You can also hike up into the riparian forests or along the river to view pink dolphins and Amazonian turtles.

SAN IGNACIO DE MOXOS HISTORY

Originally founded by the Jesuits in 1689, the village of San Ignacio de Moxos suffered pestilence in 1749 and had to be shifted to its present location on healthier ground. The indigenous Moxos population, known as *los mojeños*, speaks an indigenous language known as *ignaciano*, and have unique traditions and food. The rich character of the community – a mixture of the indigenous Moxos traditions and the colonial Christian Jesuit customs, as is the case with many of Bolivia's indigenous communities – really comes alive when the huge fiesta starts.

EATING & DRINKING IN SAN IGNACIO DE MOXOS: OUR PICKS

La Pascana del Gordo: A local favorite ideal for tasting traditional Moxos dishes. *8am-2pm* $

Moxos Social Club: A popular lunch spot off the main square, where you can get soup and a main, in a big, local social club. *8am-3pm* $

Main Plaza: Grab a drink from a shop and get to the main square – it's a super spot to chat to locals. *6-8pm* $

Laguna Isirere: Get some sandwiches and have a picnic lunch at this beautiful little lake, watching the sunset. *12-3pm* $

Eastern Bolivian Amazon

RIVER CRUISES | NATURAL PARKS | TROPICAL THOROUGHFARE

GETTING AROUND

Departing air travelers must pay B$15 for use of the Teniente Jorge Henrich Arauz airport, which is just outside the northwest corner of town *(taxi/moto-taxi B$20/10)*.

BOA has six flights weekly to La Paz, and daily flights to Santa Cruz and Cochabamba.

EcoJet has daily flights from Trinidad to Cochabamba, Guayaremerín and Riberalta, and regular flights to La Paz and Santa Cruz.

The **bus terminal** is a 1km walk or B$25 taxi ride east of the centre. Daily buses go to Santa Cruz, Rurrenabaque and San Borja.

While no traveler to Bolivia will make their way to Trinidad just for the city itself, if you're heading from Santa Cruz to Rurrenabaque on land, you'll have to make a stop here. It's a busy thoroughfare with the typical easy air of a tropical town, some colonial architecture and a main square dotted with eateries where a traveler can while away a few hours watching the town go by. Adventure travelers wanting to take a trip down the long and deep Río Mamoré also head for Trinidad.

Originally constructed on the banks of the Río Mamoré, 14km from its present location, the city of La Santísima Trinidad (the Holiest Trinity) was founded in 1686 by Padre Cipriano Barace as the second Jesuit mission in the flatlands of the southern Beni. It was was relocated in 1769 to its current location on the Arroyo de San Juan, which now divides the city in two.

Glide Down the River on la Ruta del Bufeo

Dolphin viewing

One of the most popular activities in the Trinidad region is taking **La Ruta del Bufeo**, a one- or two-day boat journey through the Área Protegida Municipal Ibare-Mamoré to view the pink Amazon river dolphins – known as *bufeos*. Departures are typically from Puerto Ballivián, 8km from Trinidad, the entry to the Protected Area of the Ibare-Mamoré rivers.

The pink dolphin species is unique to the Bolivian Amazon. Like with other wildlife, it is very important that tourism does not disturb the animals, who are usually fishing or mating when sighted. To go on a tour, try **ECOTerra** *(7281-8317; ecoterra.srl@bolivia.com; full-day tours from B$400)*. Another company that can take you on a river tour is **Turismo Moxos** *(7113-0122; facebook.com/moxosviajes; Av 6 de Agosto 114; tours start from B$400)*. Apart from the one- to

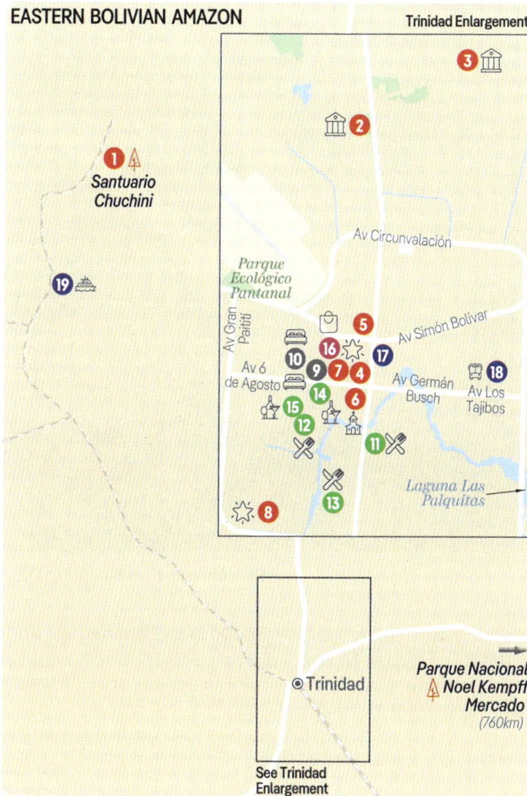

HIGHLIGHTS
1 Santuario Chuchini

SIGHTS
2 Museo Etnoarqueológico del Beni Kenneth Lee
3 Museo Ictícola
4 Plaza Gral José Ballivián
5 Plazuela Natuch
6 Trinidad Cathedral

ACTIVITIES
7 Bici Tour
Conservación Loros Bolivia (see 7)
8 Flotel Reina de Enin
Turismo Moxos (see 7)

SLEEPING
9 Hostal El Tajibo
10 Hotel Colonial

EATING
11 Churrasquería La Estancia
12 El Tábano
13 Pescadería Don Pedrito
Sabor Brasil (see 7)

DRINKING & NIGHTLIFE
14 Cafe Pub Palo Diablo
La Terraza del Club (see 4)
15 Magic Club

SHOPPING
16 Chocolates Para Ti

TRANSPORTATION
17 BOA
18 Bus Terminal
EcoJet (see 7)
19 La Ruta del Bufeo

three-day dolphin cruises on the Río Ibare, it also has three-day survival courses, visits to Sirionó indigenous villages, four-day canoe safaris into the jungle and day trips on horseback into remote areas. English-language guides cost extra.

Spend a Day in Trinidad

Walk or bike around town

Take a day to explore Trinidad, before heading on to pastures new. The town's loveliest feature is **Plaza Gral José Ballivián**, with its tall, tropical trees and lush gardens – it's the spot where locals gather to hang out and chat. Have an ice cream and watch hundreds of motorcycles orbiting around.

On the south side of the plaza is Trinidad's mustard-yellow and white **cathedral** *(free entry)*, built between 1916 and 1931 on the site of a Jesuit church. Further north is **Plazuela Natuch**, with lively Beni wall murals depicting indigenous people on river boats, and wooden statues of local wildlife. Check out the stalls selling local *artesanía* (handcrafted items) for some Beni souvenirs.

TOP TIP

If you're happy to go about town on a bike, motorcycles are a great way to while some time away – you can hire a bike for an hour or a full day and explore. Pick one up from outfits north of the main square. You'll need your driver's license.

BEST TOURS IN TRINIDAD

La Ruta del Bufeo: One or two days on a boat through the Área Protegida Municipal Ibare-Mamoré for pink Amazon river dolphin-spotting (p312).

Conservación Loros Bolivia: The foundation's director José Antonio Díaz is a super bird lover and will organize guides for you.

Flotel Reina de Enin: Multiday river cruises down Río Ibare into Río Mamoré on a comfortable hotel boat (p316).

Turismo Moxos: Dolphin cruises, survival courses, visits to Sirionó villages, canoe safaris and horseback riding.

Bici Tour: Bike rentals and guided city tours (some in English). Also offers nature-focused bike trips to nearby lakes.

YANN HUBERT/SHUTTERSTOCK

Pink Amazon river dolphin (p312)

Further north of the centre is the **Museo Etnoarqueológico del Beni Kenneth Lee**, with artifacts from the Trinidad region including traditional instruments and tribal dress. It was closed at the time of research with no scheduled reopening, but it's considered to be the city's top cultural attraction, so check if it has reopened while you're there.

See an Amazon Aquarium

Weird and wonderful denizens of Río Beni

About 1.5km north of the town centre, along Cipriano Barace and part of the Universidad Autónoma del Beni is the **Museo Ictícola** *(museoicticola.uabjb.edu.bo; free entry)*, an extensive aquarium featuring species of Amazonian fish. Some are preserved, others still swimming – in any case, it's fascinating stuff and sometimes a bit creepy, considering all the unknown creatures in the Río Beni! It's a B$7 moto-taxi ride from town.

EATING IN TRINIDAD: OUR PICKS

Churrasqueria La Estancia: Trinidad's favorite BBQ spot. Sit on the terrace and get your meat prepared on a coal fire – it's delicious. *11am-3pm & 7pm-midnight* $$

El Tábano: Try the *cola de caiman* (caiman tail) here, deep fried and crunchy. Alternatively, get a garlicky fish. Good for drinks too. *11am-3pm & 7pm-midnight* $$

Pescadería Don Pedrito: Try *chicharron de cola de caiman* – bits of caiman tail, deep-fried. Otherwise choose fried, grilled, or ceviche fish. *11am-3pm & 7pm-midnight* $$

Chocolates Para Ti: Choose from a selection of Sucre's most delicious chocolates, wrapped with love – excellent gifts or for self indulgence. *9am-12:30pm & 3-7:30pm Mon-Sat* $

See Ancient Bikinis at the Santuario Chuchini

Take a walk in the Jaguar's Lair

The **Santuario Chuchini**, or 'Jaguar's Lair', *(chuchini.org; entry fee B$30, half-day visit incl meal & boat ride B$120; all-inclusive overnight stay US$146)* is a wildlife sanctuary and camp that sits 14km north of Trinidad, on an 8-hectare *loma* (artificial mound) of the ancient Paitití civilization. It's a rare, easily accessible site and has an archaeological museum displaying articles excavated from the *loma*, including a piece that appears to be a female figure wearing a bikini (it's actually thought to be an identification of, and homage to, specific body areas rather than an article of clothing).

After seeing the museum, you can take short walks in the rainforest to lagoons with caimans, other larger animals and profuse birdlife. There are pedalo boats to go on the lake. The lookout tower is a good place from which to watch the birds. The camp has shady, covered picnic sites, trees, children's swings and a variety of native plants, birds and animals. You can bring your own food to have as a picnic, if you're visiting for a day. There are also overnight stays, and one- to four-day organized excursions available.

Should you wish to, you can volunteer here for one week at the minimum. Otherwise, you can enter by organizing a guided tour, which will include transportationation and museum entry. A moto taxi driver will charge around B$20-25 for the journey from Trinidad, or you can scoot over on a rented bike.

Take a Boat Trip into the Rainforest

Adventure, mystique and solitude

If you want to get to the heart of the Bolivian Amazon, go on a river trip along the **Río Mamoré**. This is best done during the dry season. It's an incredibly relaxing journey, mostly because you have to surrender to the river's and the boat's slow pace. The diversity of plant and animal species along the shore will keep you busy – watch the forest darkness and scan the riverbanks for signs of wildlife. Bring good binoculars.

A DIY trip means you should bring your own hammock (which you can buy in Trinidad), a sleeping bag or a blanket in case nights get cold – winter humidity can be surprisingly frisky. Make sure you also have a mosquito net. Carry some snacks and water, or water purification pills; the boat food is pretty basic but decent. Organizing your own trip will require

BEST NATIONAL PARKS & RESERVES IN THE BOLIVIAN AMAZON

Parque Nacional Madidi: The Amazon's best spot for wildlife viewing, community projects and learning about the jungle (p301).

Reserva de la Biosfera y Estación Biológica del Beni: Explore the less-frequented *cerrado* savannas, observe rare wildlife species and see life in indigenous communities (p309).

Reserva Barba Azul: Home to one of the world's rarest parrots – the blue-throated macaw – that's thankfully made a comeback from the endangered species list (p324).

Parque Nacional Noel Kempff Mercado: The virtually unexplored forests of this remote park have the most dramatic scenery (p317).

Parque Nacional Carrasco: Some of Bolivia's most easily accessible cloud forest is to be found here, in the lowlands of the Chapare Region (p320).

DRINKING IN TRINIDAD: OUR PICKS

Cafe Pub Palo Diablo: A big cocktail menu and Saturday night live music make this a busy weekend spot for Trinidad's youth. *6pm-1am*

La Terraza del Club: An ample terrace with lots of different cocktails, martinis, Bolivian wine and beer. Upmarket-ish. *7pm-2am*

Sabor Brasil: Lots of fresh tropical juices, acai bowls and desserts in this cafeteria, plus good coffee. *4-11pm Sat-Thu*

Magic Club: If you want to mingle with the locals in a bar/club setting, this is one of the most popular for drinking and dancing, Trinidad-style. *6pm-3am*

ANCIENT CIVILIZATIONS

The area of Llanos de Moxos, near San Ignacio de Moxos, has delighted archaeologists who discovered hundreds of *lomas* (artificial mounds), embankments and prehistoric earthworks depicting people and animals – one such anthropomorphic figure is over 2km from head to toe! The region was previously considered to be a total wilderness, save for a few dispersed tribes who lived in the woods, but these discoveries show that it was populated by a large, advanced civilization of farmers and artisans, whose society was highly organized and sophisticated. According to archaeologists, the very amount of pots indicates the complexity of this lost society. Learn more at Santuario Chuchini (p315).

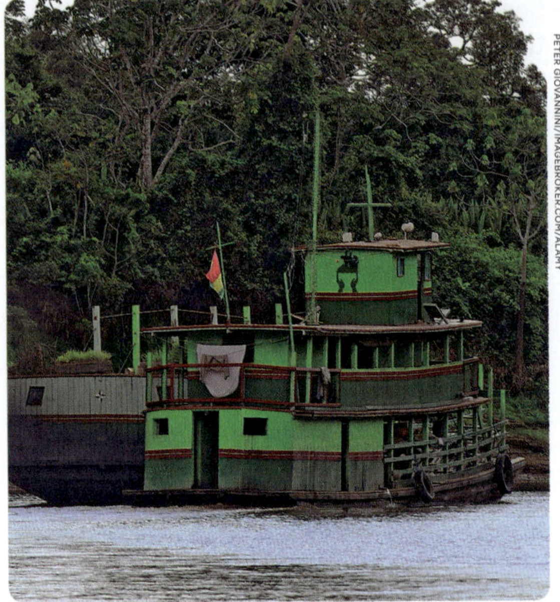

PETER GIOVANNINI/IMAGEBROKER.COM/ALAMY

Río Mamoré (p315)

resourcefulness and patience. Ask around at the Capitanía in Puerto Almacén, 8km southwest of Trinidad, or Puerto Ballivián, 8km to the northwest, and be sure to discuss sleeping arrangements before committing to a boat.

An easier and more comfortable way to cruise the river is on the lovely **Flotel Reina de Enin** *(reinadeenin.com; overnight night tours US$162; 3-day tours US$564)* from Puerto Ballivián, on the outskirts of Trinidad. Accommodations are in good, comfortable bunk beds and activities include looking for dolphins or caimans and stopping for walks through the jungle to view prehistoric *lomas*. The boat has a hammock deck and a river-fed pool. It floats down Río Ibare and into the widths of the Río Mamoré.

TOP EXPERIENCE

Parque Nacional Noel Kempff Mercado

Home to a vast number of Amazonian wildlife in wide-ranging habitats, from savanna to dense rainforest, the far-flung Parque Nacional Noel Kempff Mercado is a UNESCO's World Heritage site and a national park of global significance. It is administered by Sernap (*sernap.gob.bo*) and every visitor must register their trip in a park-information office in **La Paz** or **Santa Cruz**. Your tour agency can also register you.

Waterfalls & Rivers

This is some of the most dramatic and beautiful scenery in northern Bolivia – expect rivers, rainforests, waterfalls, plateaus and rugged 500m escarpments. This national park is one of the largest and most intact parks in the Amazon Basin, with an altitudinal range of between 200m to almost 1000m, giving it an incredible wealth of habitats. These include evergreen rainforests, palm forests, *cerrados* (savannas), swamps, gallery forests, and semideciduous dry forests.

Tours normally take five or six days, starting in Santa Cruz and spending the first and last nights with the Piso Firme community. A 10-hour boat ride up Itenez and Pauserna Rivers takes you into the depths of the park. The accommodations are in campsites, near waterfalls and lakes – it's truly magical. There are long treks (five to six hours on average) around the many waterfalls in the park; local guides will help you spot wildlife and tell you about different aspects of the fascinating flora and fauna.

Ancient History & Species Galore

The park's geography dates back over a billion years to the Precambrian period. The *cerrado* habitats found on the Huanchaca Meseta have been isolated for millions of years, giving scientists an incredible opportunity to study this unique environment.

TOP TIPS

- The park remains an off-the-beaten-track option for adventurous travelers.
- Visiting is by organized tours only, which are booked in Santa Cruz. An attempt to generate a tourist trail to the park has so far failed.

PRACTICALITIES

- There is no real infrastructure here.

Amboró Tours (*amborotours.com; tours starting from US$300 per person*) run reliably good tours.

Chapare Region

RICH RAINFOREST | WILDLIFE REFUGES | CLOUD FOREST

GETTING AROUND

Getting to the Chapare is relatively easy, as the region lies on the main highway between Cochabamba and Santa Cruz. Catch a regular bus or *micro* from Cochabamba from the dedicated bus stop to the Chapare region. The first bus sets off around 6am, and subsequent vehicles depart every couple of hours. Buses take four hours and charge B$20, while *micros* take three hours and charge B$30 for a ticket.

TOP TIPS

Bolivians from Cochabamba love visiting Villa Tunari on weekends, hence the modern hotels, many with swimming pools, and relatively high prices. The town is popular with local families and kids. Accommodations – and general appeal – is much more basic in Puerto Villarroel.

The Chapare Region leaves the last peaks of the Andes behind as these bare, dry mountains are replaced by the lush rainforest and verdant valleys of the Amazon. Descending the road between Cochabamba and Villa Tunari, as it twists around the high peaks and mountain lakes then drops steeply into deep, steaming tropical valleys, you'll have no shortage of spectacular landscapes to behold.

The two towns, Puerto Villarroel and Villa Tunari, have tried hard to encourage tourism, and the latter has some mildly interesting things to do such as visiting wildlife refuges and a few outdoors activities. The regional highlight is taking a tour inside Parque Nacional Carrasco. This region is also the controversial *cocalero* land, where the strong coca growers' unions and former Bolivian president Evo Morales have their home base.

Get Active in Villa Tunari

Raft and hike

If you want a tame introduction to the Amazon, Villa Tunari is it. Stretched along the Cochabamba–Santa Cruz highway, the town is a base for truck drivers, who stop here to eat and rest on their way from Cochabamba, while Bolivian weekenders also flock here for a break.

This, oddly, makes the town (relatively) more expensive than other places in the Amazon. If you do end up here, the best thing to do is visit the wonderful Parque Nacional Carrasco (p320) or do some hiking. You can also take a tour with the long-established agency **Ranabol** *(ranabol.com)*, for 10 or 20km rafting trips, fishing trips, or more serious seven- to 10-day rafting and trekking expeditions that connect Cochabamba and Coroico. It also offers multiday community-based trekking adventures.

If you just want to relax, there is a series of natural swimming holes known as *las pozas* that can alleviate the tropical heat. For those visiting during the first week of August,

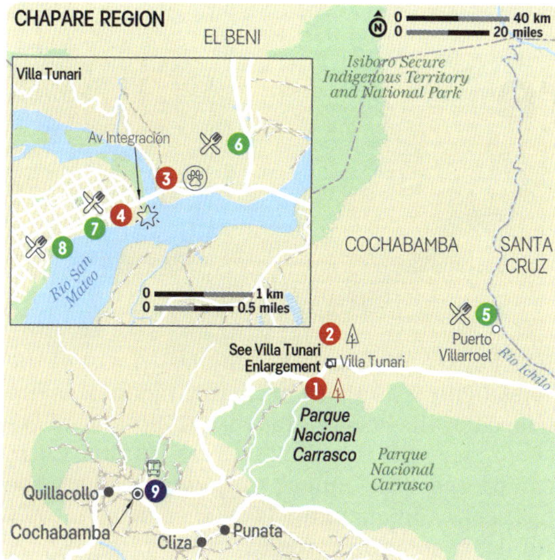

HIGHLIGHTS

1 Parque Nacional Carrasco

SIGHTS

2 Centro de Preservación La Hormiga
3 Parque Machía

ACTIVITIES

4 Ranabol

EATING

5 El Cliper
6 Las Lomas
7 Restaurant San Silvestre
8 Revollo

TRANSPORTATION

9 Micros & Buses to Chapare

there is the **Feria Regional del Pescado** – the regional fish fair – where you can try all the Amazonian fish specialities.

Glide down the Río Ichilo

Muddy tropical port

Puerto Villaroel is a little river port town with very little appeal except going on a cruise down Río Ichilo to go bird-watching and spot pink river dolphins. Ask in **El Cliper**, a three-story open-air wooden tower by the port, to see if they can organize day-long fishing or camping trips to nearby river beaches, as well as visits to one of the six indigenous communities located within the territory: Yuki, Yuracaré, Trinitario, and Movima peoples. El Cliper is the one-stop shop for food, local crafts and tourist information, so you can have lunch or dinner here while attempting to arrange a boat trip down the Río Ichilo.

Visit or Volunteer at Animal Refuges

Pet or help

A day can be spent visiting popular animal refuge centres at Villa Tunari. One is the **Parque Machia** (*intiwarayassi.org; entry B$7; open 9.30am-4pm Tue-Sun*), where you can see more than 200 free-range poached or injured critters, and another 300 or so in enclosures. Those who run free (mostly monkeys) make cameos on the 1km hike up to a scenic overlook. If you fancy volunteering, this is a great place – the minimum commitment is 15 nights – see the website for more information.

SACRED PLANT

Erythroxylum coca is the scientific name for coca, a plant native to northwestern South America. In Bolivia the plant grows primarily in the Yungas and in the Chapare region. Its leaves are widely used by the locals as a mild stimulant, akin to coffee – it's very good for aliviating altitude sickness. The locals 'chew' it, or drink it as *mate* (tea), as a general pick up.

Most Westerners are likely to have heard of coca as the base for the narcotic cocaine. The illegal drug is made with the addition of kerosene, hydrochloric and sulfuric acids and other hard chemicals; for most Bolivians, the resulting drug has nothing to do with their sacred plant, which has been safely used for centuries.

CONTROVERSIAL COCA

The Chapare Region is prime farming land for highland *campesinos* (subsistence farmers). They emigrated here in the 1970s and made the region into Bolivia's main coca growing fields. Unlike the Yungas coca leaf, which is used by Bolivians in their traditional chewing and tea practice, this is known as the type of coca used for the manufacture of cocaine. The US Drug Enforcement Administration (DEA) made the region unstable by trying to destroy coca fields. Morales' government expelled the DEA in 2008. While critics argue that Morales' policies have enabled a huge black market for illegal cocaine production in Bolivia, Morales' supporters claim that life conditions and the infrastructure of the Chapare Region have much improved thanks to Morales' governance.

ERLANTZ P.R/SHUTTERSTOCK

The **Centro de Preservacion La Hormiga** (*villatunari.gob.bo; entry B$40; open 8am-5.30pm daily*), is a small park/wildlife garden 11km from Villa Tunari featuring a variety of bromeliads and other plant life, as well as some (caged) local fauna. A taxi will take you from Villa Tunari (20 minutes), wait while you tour the site (one hour), then take you back to town for B$90.

Explore the Parque Nacional Carrasco

Night birds and bats

This **national park** (*globalnationalparks.com/es/bolivia/carrasco)* sits along a large portion of the road between Cochabamba and Villa Tunari, and a large lowland area of the Chapare. Created in 1988, it has some of Bolivia's most easily explored cloud forest. The rainforest hides a vast variety of mammals, a huge variety of birds, reptiles, amphibians, fish and insects. Some 180 mammal species, 12 of them endemic, have been registered, as well as 750 species of birds. Among the 3000 species of plants, there are over 300 species of orchids, 50 of which are endemic.

The best way to visit is to take a Chapare tour with Cochabamba-based agency **El Mundo Verde Travel** (*elmundoverdetravel.com; tours starting at US$200 per*

Bats, Parque Nacional Carrasco

person per day), which will lead you on a wonderful hike through the jungle, taking you to the deep and narrow Guacharo cave to see the weird, nocturnal *guáchero* (oil-bird) and six bat species.

Warning: access to the rest of the park is much more difficult and potentially dangerous. The once-popular trek descending from 4000m to 300m along the old Cochabamba–Chapare road was allegedly being used by drug traffickers and is now deemed unsafe for tourists. Independent access to the park is not recommended, for the dual risks of getting lost and of coming across these alleged drug routes.

EATING IN VILLA TUNARI & PUERTO VILLAROEL: OUR PICKS

San Silvestre: The town's best restaurant, hands down. If you're there with company, order the enormous *pique macho. 9:30am-10pm* $$

Revollo: Fish, rice, plantain: the Amazon standards are abundant in this simple but decent-quality eatery. *9:30am-10pm* $$

Las Lomas: A little out of the centre, with a terrace overlooking Parque Machia, a standard Amazon menu of fish and rice, and lots of cold beer. *10:30am-6pm* $

El Cliper (p319): A one-stop shop for food, local crafts and tourist information in Puerto Villaroel. *9:30am-10pm* $

Northern Bolivian Amazon

COWBOY TOWNS | DUSTY STREETS | RIVER CRUISES

GETTING AROUND

Frequent minibuses take four to six hours between Trinidad and Santa Ana de Yacuma – they depart every two hours. Get your ticket on board. While they operate year-round, the journey can be complicated in the wet season as vehicles often easily get stuck halfway. Riberalta's airport is a 15-minute stroll south from the main plaza. Flights to Cobija are by *avioneta* (light aircraft) and will only depart when full.

The north begins in the cowboy town of Santa Ana de Yacuma, where everything revolves around cattle and travelers stop on their way to the spectacular Reserva Barba Azul, a birdwatchers' heaven where the rarest species of parrot fly about and are easily seen. Going further up north, towards Riberalta, Guayaramerín and Cobija, the country's and the Amazon's northernmost part, is to reach Brazil's doorstep, an area where only those heading over the border on land normally end up – and those are few and far between these days, since flying to Brazil is much more common. In Riberalta, there is bird-watching and wildlife spotting at the Area Protegida Municipal Aquicuana and some lush nature along Río Beni. If you do head up this way, you'll be one of the rare travelers that visit this remote region – make sure your Spanish is good, and that you have plenty of time for long bus journeys.

Admire the Cattle at Santa Ana de Yacuma

Cows and more cows

Santa Ana de Yacuma is proper cattle land, with ranchers, farmhands and, well, cows. The first town on the way to northern Bolivia, and the Brazilian border, Santa Ana is the cattle capital of Bolivia. This profile means that the town has one of the highest standards of living in the Bolivian Amazon, and some good steak. There isn't much to do in town and you are only likely to land here en route to the nearby Reserva Barba Azul (p324), for macaw viewing. There are a few burger shops and some half-decent spots for a steak – ask locally for what's hot.

Touch the Brazilian Border in Guayaramerín

Dusty border town

Knocking on Brazil's door, Guayaramerín has a twin town across the Río Mamoré, which is called, funnily enough, Guajará-Mirim.

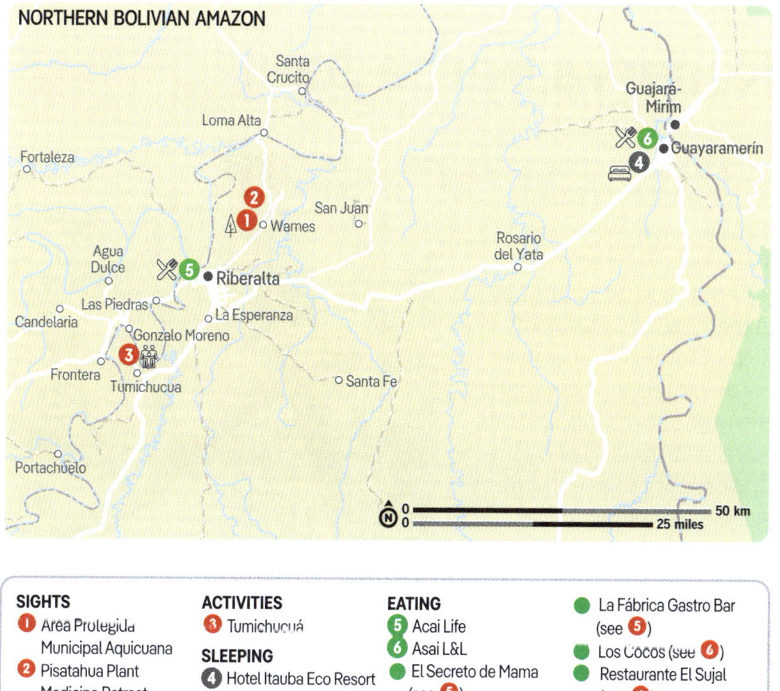

There's not much to do in the town itself except walk the dusty streets and look at the cheap goods in the many markets. But north of town you can follow *la ruta del caucho* (the Rubber Trail) to **Cachuela Esperanza**, a town that was once the centre of the so-called 'rubber fever' from the late 19th to the early 20th century. The Brazilian city of Manaus was at the centre of this phenomenon, but Guayaramerín was the centre of these activities in the Bolivian Amazon. Indigenous communities were used as cheap workforce and subjected to terrible treatment. Cachuela Esperanza, a scenic spot near the rapids of the Río Beni, was the grandest city in the Bolivian Amazon during that period (for those profiting from the trade), but today virtually nothing remains of its former opulence.

Back in Guayaramerín, you can spend the day (if you're not staying here) on the edge of a private lagoon, canoeing and fishing, at **Hotel Itauba Eco Resort**, where you can also eat lunch in a lovely thatch-roofed restaurant.

TOP TIP

Flying to most of these destinations is your best option and you will not regret the extra expense, but mind that flights can get canceled easily, especially in the wet season.

TOP EXPERIENCE

Reserva Barba Azul

This amazing reserve was formed to protect the largest congregations of blue-throated macaws known in the world. An estimated 480 of these birds remain in the wild, and lovers of flying feathery friends will be delighted to know that the numbers of this species have stabilized. Having the opportunity to see this rare species, endemic to the unique and fast-disappearing Beni savannas, is truly a treasure.

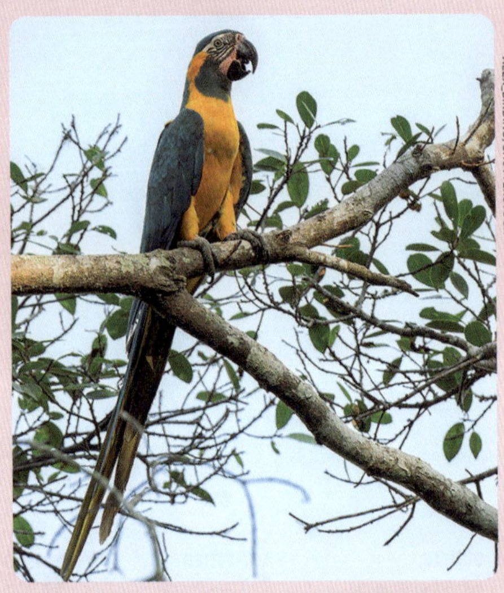

ALEX_BIRDING/SHUTTERSTOCK

Blue-throated macaw

TOP TIPS

- March to September is the best time to visit, when waterbirds congregate at the reserve.
- Armonía can help organize transportation, which is not included in the cost. It's quickest and safest (and priciest) to fly in on a private jet, which has room for five passengers.

PRACTICALITIES

Your visit should be arranged in advance through conservation NGO **Armonía**: (*armoniabolivia.org; turismo@armonia-bo.org; reservations@armonia-bo.org*)

Rare Bird Spotting

Thanks to the efforts of the conservation NGO **Armonía**, the endangered blue-throated macaw or *barba azul,* has become something of a regional celebrity in the Bolivian Amazon. Unlike most of the surrounding savanna, the open grasslands here are completely intact and the birds can be seen relatively easily along with a plethora of threatened birds and mammals such as the giant anteater, marsh deer and the rarely seen maned wolf, ocelots, pumas, jaguars and armadillos.

Logistics demand a minimum three-night stay, with a memorable trip costing US$200 per person per night, including food, access to a motorboat and horseback riding. Accommodations are in one of the four wooden cabins, with private bathrooms, and meals are served in the central canteen space. Each cabin has views of the Omi River, and you can relax in the hammocks after the wildlife walks.

Alternatively, contact **Nick's Adventures** *(nicksadventuresbolivia.com; tours from US$200 per person per night)* for a guided tour.

More Feathery Friends

Birdwatchers will be in heaven: the reserve attracts over 140 species of birds. Aside from spotting macaws, you might see savanna critters such as greater rhea, cock-tailed tyrant, sharp-tailed tyrant, streamer-tailed tyrant, black-masked finch, seedeaters, and migrant bobolink. Marshland birds include orinoco goose, plumbeous ibis, jabiru and migrant buff-breasted sandpiper.

ALEXANDRE LAPRISE/SHUTTERSTOCK

Cow, Riberalta

Riberalta: Enter the Real North

Nuts and sunsets

This remote northern town is large, but sees very few foreign tourists. The only thing to do here is nibble on Brazil nuts and watch the sunset and the circling motorcycles around the plaza. **Riberalta** is one of the world's top Brazil nut production sites, which is basically the engine of the local economy. Acai is another important produce here and those interested in either of these can go on agro tours.

You can see wildlife at the reserves on the periphery of town – the **Paseo Turístico La Costanera**, an abandoned walking path on Riberalta's river bluff, which was showing signs of being upgraded when we visited, overlooks a broad, sweeping curve of the Río Beni with views of the water and rainforest.

Tumichucuá is a small community about 25km south of town, reached most easily by a moto-taxi (B$30). There is a lake for swimming and a forested island with walking trails. If you want to stay here, there are **cabins** with five beds and a deck.

THE BLUE-THROATED MACAW

Known to the Bolivians as *barba azul* – bluebeard! – the gorgeous blue-throated macaw (Ara glaucogularis) is endemic to the Beni savannas. As of the end of 2024, it numbers between 420 and 480 mature adults in the wild. The population trend has changed from endangered to stable thanks to successful conservation programs.

Bolivia has 12 of the world's 19 macaw species, and the blue-throated macaw only exists here. Protecting the forest's motacú palm nuts is essential to the bird's survival, since that is its favorite food. The use of their tail feathers for ceremonial purposes was also a threat to the species, but the local community now fashions artificial feathers from palm fronds.

EATING IN GUAYAMERÍN: OUR PICKS

Restaurante El Sujal: Thatch-roofed restaurant on the main street serves good steak, chicken, and *surubí* catfish in coconut milk. *11:30am-3pm & 7-10pm Tue-Sun* $$

Los Cocos: Grilled everything can be found in this sizeable restaurant – meat, chicken and fish, and some veggies too. *11am-3pm & 6:30-11pm* $$

Asai L&L: A good place for a snack – there are acai shakes, burgers, hot dogs and quick sandwiches. *7am-7pm Mon-Sat, to noon Sun* $

Hotel Itauba Eco Resort: On a small lake near the bus terminal, this resort has a good restaurant serving Amazonian fish specialities. *11am-3pm & 6:30-11pm* $

THE MIGHTY NUT

Riberalta's specialty is its famous *nueces de Brasil* (Brazil nuts; $B10 per packet), which are roasted in sugar and cinnamon and sold at bus terminals and the airport. When not coated in sugar, the Brazil nut is a nutritional treasure, recognized for its anti-inflammatory properties due to its high selenium content, an important antioxidant that controls inflammation, thyroid function and immune health. This mighty nut also contains ellagic acid, which, according to research, may offer anti-depressant effects. And finally, their mono and polyunsaturated fatty acids are good for the heart and they're full of fibre and minerals, making Brazil nuts good for anyone with cholesterol issues. What's not to like? Get munching!

Bird-Watching at Area Protegida Municipal Aquicuana

A far-flung forest reserve

Some 22km north of Riberalta is the jungle reserve **Area Protegida Municipal Aquicuana** *(sustainablebolivia.org/es/reserva-aquicuana; entry B$10)*, a great spot for wildlife watching, including all kinds of birds. The communities of San José and Warnes run the park, and locals work as guides. They mostly speak only Spanish, so if you're not proficient bring a phrasebook. You should be sure during tours that no wildlife is disturbed or handled.

There are volunteering opportunities at the reserve, where you can help with maintenance, research and youth programs. Applications are online, via the organization's website. There is also the **Pisatahua Plant Medicine Retreat** (*pisatahua.org/retreats*), which works with traditional plant-based wellness treatments.

The Sleepy Border Town of Cobija

Hot and sweaty

A former rubber-production centre that now sits forgotten, Cobija is the capital of the remote Pando Department and Bolivia's wettest and most humid spot. It sits on a sharp bend of the Río Acre and rambles over a series of hills, giving it a certain desultory charm. If you spend a day here on your way across the border, take a look at the remaining tropical wooden buildings in the centre and the lovely avenues of royal palms around the plaza.

EATING IN RIBERALTA: OUR PICKS

Acai Life: Ultra-healthy breakfasts of acai bowls, fresh jungle juices, empanadas, and even waffles. *7:30am-noon & 4:30-10pm* $

El Secreto de Mama: Salty treats are empanadas, *cuñapes* (cheese and yucca balls) and *sonso* (cheesy yucca bread). Hot chocolate is Beni-grown cacao. *4-7pm Mon-Fri* $

El Tropical: Remarkably expensive, with enormous portions of meat, chicken and fish, Ribearalta's fanciest restaurant is near the airport. *7-11pm Mon-Sat* $$$

La Fábrica Gastro Bar: This place packs it all in: burgers, fish, smoothies, beer, mojitos – you name it, it's served. *6pm-12am* $$

CHEAP GOODS GALORE

As with many other border towns, a lot of 'goods' make it across one way or another. As you'll no doubt witness in Guayaramerín, the town's markets specialize in counterfeit electronic goods, brand-name shoes and clothes, so if you want to get yourself some Klevin Kleins, this is the spot. The fake electronics may not be such a great investment. Formerly a duty-free zone, Guayaramerín is basically a black market for goods from Brazil. In theory, it's a shopping hub, but there's little of real interest.

J.CHIZHE/SHUTTERSTOCK

Brazil nuts

Places We Love to Stay

$ Budget $$ Midrange $$$ Top End

Rurrenabaque p298

Hostal El Lobo $ A cut above the rest of the region's hostel accommodations, with private rooms, dorms, a swimming pool and a wonderful, breezy hammock-strewn terrace that looks at the river.

Hostal Turístico Santa Ana $ The most beautifully lush garden with communal seating and hammocks, and a shared kitchen. The rooms are clean and it's good value.

Hotel Los Tucanes de Rurre $ Clean and simple rooms can be found here, but the biggest draw is the big garden and the roof terrace from which to take in the views.

Casa de Campo (p300) $$ Rurre's best home-away-from-home option. Comfortable and elegant rooms with kitchenettes, air-conditioning and amazing breakfasts.

Hotel Maya $$ At the town entrance, this 'boutique hotel' has en-suite rooms with air-conditioning, eclectic decor and a large lawn-garden with swimming pool.

Hotel Takana $$ Hefty wooden furnishings, hot tubs and a swimming pool – right on the main square. Good views of the Río Beni.

La Isla de los Tucanes $$ An eco-cabin complex 1km north of town with thatched bungalows, pool tables, an international restaurant and two swimming pools.

Parque Nacional Madidi p301

Chalalan Ecolodge (p302) $$$ Accommodations are simple and elegant – jungle luxury. Thatched bungalows, all en-suite, with comfy beds, and the sounds of the jungle to (maybe) put you to sleep.

Madidi Jungle (p302) $$$ Comfortable, incredibly atmospheric thatch-roofed cabins are set by the Río Tuichi. Lush in every way.

Sadiri (p302) $$$ Six jungle cabins with comfortable beds and good bathrooms at this fantastic location in the Madidi highlands.

San Miguel del Bala (p302) $$$ Closer to Rurrenabaque, this lodge has cabins all decked out in wood and floors made out of glorious mahogany. The bathrooms are outside.

San Ignacio de Moxos p306

Hotel San Ignacio $ The town's best budget option, with large rooms, en-suite bathrooms, air-con and breakfast.

Residencial Don Muñeco $ Mr Toy's *residencial* has basic rooms, a big porch with hammocks and outdoor seating.

Residencial Don Joaquín $ Very basic, with clean and simple rooms, conveniently located at the corner of the plaza near the church.

San Borja p309

Hotel Jatata $ Pretty, centrally located, the Jatata owners are really welcoming and the rooms are comfortable and clean. Good breakfasts and patio with hammocks.

Hotel San Borja $ Sitting right on the main plaza and occupying a whole corner, this large hotel has spacious, basic rooms that have seen better days, but will do for a night or two.

Trinidad p313

Hostal El Tajibo $ A decent budget option, with good, clean rooms and comfortable beds. Some rooms have balconies. Breakfast is included, and air-conditioning optional.

Hotel Colonial $$ Once a treat, this hotel is now expensive and slightly dated (but this is Trinidad, and accommodations options aren't great). But it does have a pool, decent rooms, wi-fi and breakfast.

Villa Tunari p318

Hotel Los Cocos $ This is a good budget option in Villa Tunari. The rooms are clean and tasteful with en-suite bathrooms, and everyone loves the pool.

Hotel de Selva El Puente $$ By far the best place in the (wider) region, in the rainforest 4km outside Villa Tunari. It has good, spacious cabins around a courtyard and a big swimming pool.

Hotel Las Palmas $$ Good views of the river, a refreshing swimming pool and big but basic rooms. On the south side of the main road.

Riberalta p325

Hotel Colonial $$ Riberalta's fanciest hotel is an old colonial home, with rooms decked out with antiques and hammocks. The garden is beautiful, and eating breakfast here is very peaceful.

Hotel Jomali $$ A really lovely, quality hotel, with well-kept, clean rooms that are spacious, comfortable and elegant, concentrated around a lush patio.

Guayaramerín p322

Hotel Itauba Eco Resort $ A 10-minute walk from the bus terminal, this is a fantastic little resort with a lagoon and thatched cabins in the greenery, and a good restaurant. You can even camp here.

Hotel Santa Ana $ A decent budget option with clean, spacious rooms and fans. Some rooms have no windows, so check yours does before committing!

ARAPI
TikTok
NONI
DIABETIZAN
MEGA
COLAGENO
MAGNESIO

TOOLKIT

The chapters in this section cover the most important topics you'll need to know about in Bolivia. They're full of nuts-and-bolts information and valuable insights to help you understand and navigate Bolivia and get the most out of your trip.

Mercado de las Brujas, La Paz (p65)

NATALIYA DERKACH/SHUTTERSTOCK

Arriving

Most visitors fly into one of Bolivia's two main international airports – Santa Cruz's **Viru-Viru International Airport** and **El Alto International Aiport** in La Paz. Landing in El Alto, be aware that you'll most likely be hit by some degree of altitude sickness as you get off the plane.

Visas

US citizens need a visa to enter Bolivia. Citizens of most European countries do not need a visa. Visas are available on arrival, but some airlines will refuse to let you board without one.

ATMs

There are ATMs at most airports and it's simple and easy to get your Bolivianos out. There is not much difference between ATMs here.

Vaccination Requirements

Generally, unless you're arriving from a yellow-fever hot spot, travelers are not required to provide vaccination proof.

Customs

There is a loosely enforced duty-free allowance of 200 cigarettes and 1L of alcohol per person. In general, you can bring most articles into Bolivia duty-free, providing they are for personal use.

Getting to the Center of Town...

	La Paz	Santa Cruz
TAXI	B$80 per person	B$80 per person
MINIBUS	B$5 per person	B$8 per person

ALTITUDE SICKNESS

Altitude sickness may develop in those who ascend rapidly to altitudes greater than 2500m (8100ft), and in Bolivia this includes La Paz (altitude 4000m). Symptoms usually include headache, increased heart rate and shortness of breath. There may also be nausea, insomnia and loss of appetite. This will clear up the longer you stay, but if you find your symptoms worsening, the best treatment is descent to lower altitudes. Relief may be found by taking the so-called 'sorojchi' pills – containing 125mg or 250mg acetazolamide – twice daily, starting 8 hours before arrival. Keep hydrated and eat regularly. Chewing coca leaves, or drinking coca *mate* (tea) is effective – you can buy it at the airport (B$4 for a cup).

Altitude sickness should be taken seriously; if it is severe, it can be life-threatening.

FROM LEFT: ADWO/SHUTTERSTOCK, BENNIAN/SHUTTERSTOCK, GOGLIK83/GETTY IMAGES

Getting Around

Road infrastructure has vastly improved. However, road closures caused by protests, construction or landslides are common. Two main airlines, BoA and Ecojet, provide flights (often delayed, sometimes cancelled) across the country.

TRAVEL COSTS

Internal Flights
US$100-150 one way

Minibus
B$4 per person

Taxis in La Paz
Around B$20 for a ride

Air

Flights are great for saving time, but are obviously more expensive than buses. If you do fly inside Bolivia, make sure you confirm your flight via a message, to ensure the flight is still going (airlines use WhatsApp for communicating with customers). Expect delays. Cancellations are also common. When weather-related disruptions occur, planes eventually get through, even during summer flooding in northern Bolivia.

Bus

Buses are the country's most popular type of transport. Long-distance bus services are called *flotas*, large buses are known as *autobuses*. Put any valuables into your day pack and keep them close to you on the bus. Reserve tickets in advance, at the bus station you're traveling from. Better companies offer *semicama* (half-sleeper, with seats that recline a long way and footrests) and *cama* (sleeper) services. Sleepers are more expensive, but your back will thank you.

TIP

Many buses depart in the afternoon or evening and arrive in the early hours of the morning. Daytime departures are available on most major routes. Bus schedules can be found at the main bus stations.

CYCLING IN BOLIVIA

For cyclists who relish cold winds, poor road conditions, high altitudes and steep terrain, Bolivia is a paradise. Mountain bikes are common on Bolivia's many dirt roads. Steep cliffs and large vehicles pose problems. Carry ample food and water if cycling in remote areas – many prefer to leave organizing a circuit and provisions to a tour company. Get good travel insurance.

Cable Car in La Paz

The 11 lines of the **Mi *Teleférico*** cable car system are the best way to get around La Paz and to El Alto. Silently gliding over the city, you'll avoid traffic jams and the price is only nominally more expensive than the *micros* and minibuses. The views are breathtaking. Refillable cards for multiple-day use cost B$30, with B$15 in credit. You can buy them at any *Teleférico* station, and then refill when it runs out.

Micros & Minibuses

Micros (half-buses) and minibuses are Bolivia's cheapest form of public transportation. They follow set routes, with the route numbers or letters usually marked on a placard behind the windshield. They can be hailed anywhere along their route. When you want to disembark, get to the front and tell the driver where you want them to stop. Pay at the window.

Taxis

In cities and towns, taxis are affordable. Few are equipped with meters, but in most places there are standard fares for short hauls. In some places, taxis are collective and charge a set rate per person. If you have three or four people all headed for the same place, you can usually negotiate a reduced group rate. You can hail a taxi and negotiate the price before getting in. Hotel staff can also arrange a taxi.

DRIVING ESSENTIALS

Drive on the right

You must be over 25 to rent a car

US$50 per day for small car rental

4WDs start at US$120 per day

In La Paz, those going uphill have right of way at intersections

Money

CURRENCY: BOLIVIANO B$

Exchanging Money

Change currency at *casas de cambio* (exchange bureaus) and at some banks in larger cities. US dollars are much coveted. *Cambistas* (street money changers) operate in most cities but only change cash dollars. They're convenient, but beware of rip-offs and counterfeit notes.

Cash

Bolivianos are divided into 100 centavos. Cash is the best way to pay your way around – always carry cash with you, and have B$20 notes handy.

ATMs

Sizeable towns have *cajeros automáticos* (ATMs), but service can be unreliable. Don't rely on your card in rural areas – always carry cash to cover your Accommodations, food and transport costs.

Card & Contactless Payment

Visa, MasterCard and (less often) American Express may be used in larger cities at the more upmarket hotels, restaurants and tour agencies. Contactless payment can be used in larger cities, especially Santa Cruz and La Paz, but definitely don't count on it anywhere more remote.

HOW MUCH FOR A ...

Micro fare
B$4

Museum entry
B$5-20

National park tour (including food, guides and Accommodations)
From US$165 per day

HOW TO... Tip

Restaurant service is not usually included, so leave 10% to 15% of the total bill. Tip any locals who might help you with Accommodations or transport. When using taxis, tipping is not expected, but most people round up the price.

Remember to tip tour guides; they'll be grateful, and 10–20% is the norm. Their pay is often much lower than the tour price.

Even though this is not always the case, you may find that higher-end hotels, travel agencies and tour operators will quote their prices in US dollars. You can, of course, always pay in bolivianos.

BOLIVIANOS, PESOS OR DOLLARS?

Bolivians will often refer to their currency as bolivianos or pesos – the currency was changed to bolivianos in 1987, but some people still say pesos. Many Bolivians use US dollars for savings, and if you want to exchange or pay in US dollars, make sure your notes are in good shape, otherwise they won't be accepted.

Bolivianos are extremely difficult to exchange once you leave Bolivia. Change or spend them before you leave.

Accommodations

Camping

There are few organized camp sites, but you can pitch a tent almost anywhere outside populated areas, especially along trekking routes and in remote mountain areas. If you camp in the highlands, make sure you have a sleeping bag intended for sub-zero temperatures. If possible, ask for permission and check locally whether a certain area is safe for camping.

Hostels

Hostels are a very popular Accommodations options for travelers to Bolivia, both for the price and the promise of socializing. Hostelling International is affiliated with a network of Accommodations in different parts of Bolivia. Common areas, bunk beds in shared rooms, shared bathrooms with or without hot water, book exchanges and wi-fi are the norm.

Hostales & Hotels

Bolivia has some comfortable hotels in the midrange and top-end bracket, but mostly in larger cities and in Uyuni. Generally, you'll get a good breakfast, private bathrooms with 24/7 hot showers, wi-fi and color TV; many places in the Amazon have swimming pools. Booking ahead can mean a better deal. You can also arrange an airport pickup through your hotel.

Posadas, Alojamientos, Residenciales

Residenciales, *alojamientos* and *posadas* are synonymous and cheap places to stay. While they can be *really* cheap, they can also be quite low on hygiene, and sometimes there are issues with dangerous electrics and suspicious clientele. Make sure you take a quick look around and check the state of the communal bathrooms. Note that usually there's no heating or hot water.

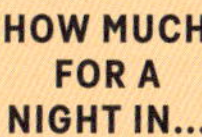

HOW MUCH FOR A NIGHT IN...

A mid-range hotel
B$620

An eco-lodge
B$1140

A casa de huéspedes
B$100

Casas de huéspedes

A ***casa de huéspedes*** – literally, guest house – can sometimes offer a more midrange, B&B-like atmosphere, with breakfasts and en suite showers. Ask to see a couple of rooms before committing, keep your valuables in a safe when possible and make sure you always check the sheets for bedbugs.

ACCOMMODATIONS: RENTAL TIPS

If you're traveling to any area where festivals or the carnaval are taking place, make sure you book well in advance. Room availability can be a serious problem in smaller towns, where you can end up with nowhere to stay, miles away from the next town. Book early on weekends if you're traveling to popular weekend getaways. Also, some things will make room prices higher (and are worth it): heat and hot water in the Altiplano, and air-con and fans in the sweaty lowlands.

CLOCKWISE FROM TOP LEFT: ANDRZEJ ROSTEK/SHUTTERSTOCK, NDSIGN/SHUTTERSTOCK, IHORL/SHUTTERSTOCK

Family Travel

While not many people travel with small children to Bolivia, if you choose to visit this incredible country *alla famiglia*, you'll reap great rewards. There are some great environmental challenges – think altitude or tropical heat, mosquitoes and long drives – but you'll experience the incredible local culture, mind-blowing landscapes, and boat trips through steamy jungles.

Plan for the Unexpected

While families can and do visit Bolivia, be prepared to cope with a number of potential obstacles. These include high altitude, the sometimes inhospitable climate (either very cold or very hot and humid), poor levels of hygiene and a general lack of predictability – you may run into floods, snow and *bloqueos* (road blocks caused by political protests). Travel to Bolivia is all about being flexible.

Eating Out

Choose restaurants carefully (try to assess hygiene levels and go for places that have a lot of trade, since their ingredients are bound to be fresher) as food poisoning and diarrhea are common. Bakeries selling fresh bread, buns and cakes are usually a delicious and safe option for kids' snacks. Restaurants will often offer a child-sized serving at a lower price, or will let two kids share an adult meal. Stock up on snacks and bottled water at city supermarkets before venturing into rural areas.

Road Trips with Kids

Although most of Bolivia's roads have been (largely) paved, road surfaces are often bumpy, and cars may swerve to avoid potholes, which may trigger car sickness! Buses rarely have toilets, can be cold and road traffic accidents are frequent. Roadblocks are also common.

Accommodations

Bolivians travel with families on weekends and many hotels have family rooms. Remember that nights at high altitude are freezing cold, so be sure to check your hotel room has heating. In warmer, lowland areas, you may want air-conditioned rooms.

BEST ATTRACTIONS FOR FAMILIES

Mi Teleférico (p58)

Children will be delighted with La Paz's 30km-long cable-car system.

Parque Cretácico (p208)

Trace the largest collection of dinosaur footprints in the world, near Sucre.

El Fuerte (p269)

Spacious pre-Inca ruins where your children will learn about fascinating history.

Senda Verde Wildlife Sanctuary (p132)

Fascinating place to see Bolivia's wildlife in their element.

Pipiripi

La Paz's children's museum, where you can play Giant Scrabble, among other things.

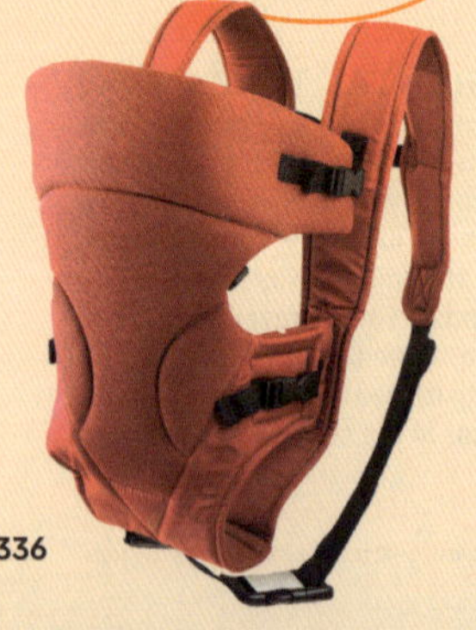

BOLIVIA PLANNING WITH KIDS

Make sure you get informed about treating altitude sickness in children, since it is particularly important to consider when traveling to the Altiplano. As much as possible, ascend slowly, allowing time for acclimatization. Descending to a lower altitude is the fastest and safest cure.

If you're using a tour operator, make sure they have the necessary standards of safety – you'll know a reputable agency by the fact that they will be happy to show you their equipment and discuss the safety measures they have in place. If you have a baby, bring a baby carrier, because strollers can be hard to use.

Health & Safe Travel

HEALTH INSURANCE & HEALTHCARE

Make sure you get comprehensive travel insurance for Bolivia, before you travel. The quality of medical services depends on where you are in the country: good medical care is available in the larger cities, but may be difficult to find in rural areas. Bolivian pharmacies are generally well equipped, and you'll find everything you need.

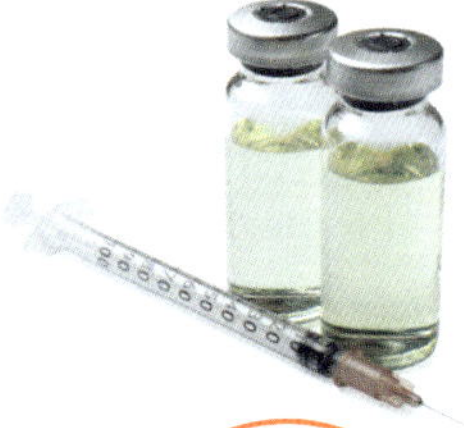

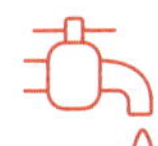

Tap Water

Tap water is not safe to drink anywhere in Bolivia. Bottled mineral water is cheap and freely available. If you are going anywhere remote, take a good supply with you. It's a good idea to pack some water purification tablets. Remember that vigorous boiling for one minute is the most effective means of water purification. At altitudes over 2000m (6500ft), boil for three minutes.

Infectious Diseases

Hepatitis A is the second most common travel-related infection (after traveler's diarrhea). It's a viral infection of the liver that is usually acquired by ingestion of contaminated water, food or ice. Most cases resolve themselves. Try not to pet, handle or feed any animal. Any bite or scratch should be promptly and thoroughly cleansed and local health authorities should be contacted immediately.

INSECT BITES & STINGS

Prevent mosquito bites by wearing long sleeves, long pants, hats and shoes. Bring good repellent and sleep in a mosquito net.

FOR JUNGLE VISITS

Wear ankle-high boots

Use insect repellent

Have your own mosquito net

Vaccines

Yellow fever is a life-threatening viral infection transmitted by mosquitoes in forested areas. Yellow fever vaccine is strongly recommended for all those visiting areas where this illness occurs, including the departments of Beni, Cochabamba, Santa Cruz and La Paz. Proof of vaccination is required from all travelers arriving from a high-yellow-fever-risk country in Africa or the Americas.

MALARIA

Malaria occurs in nearly every South American country but is rare. It's transmitted by mosquito bites at night. Taking malaria pills is only recommended for areas below 2500m (8202ft) in the departments of Beni and Pando, where the risk is highest, though it is absent in the cities. Falciparum malaria, which is the most dangerous kind, occurs in Beni and Pando.

FROM LEFT: MARCELO TRAD/SHUTTERSTOCK, NEW AFRICA/SHUTTERSTOCK, PIXEL-SHOT/SHUTTERSTOCK

Food, Drink & Nightlife

When to Eat

Desayuno (breakfast; 7am to 9am) Depending on the part of the country, breakfast can be a *salteña* (pasty), fresh fruit, toast, and fruit smoothies.

Almuerzo (lunch; noon to 3pm) The main meal of the day. A restaurant almuerzo usually offers a no-frills set meal with soup and fish or meat.

Cena (dinner; 7am to 9pm) Budget diners offer roast chicken and potatoes and salad; fancy restaurants offer fine dining.

Where to Eat

Markets The cheapest and most adventurous place to eat, but make sure you peel all fresh fruit and veg before ingesting.

Restaurants Bolivia's restaurants range from basic home cooking to fine dining spots with high prices.

Cafes Increasingly popular, especially for serving Bolivia's specialty coffee, but found mostly in cosmopolitan towns and cities.

Comedores (simple diners) This is the most common type of restaurant in rural areas, aimed at working families, with simple set menus.

MENU DECODER

Sopa (soup): Bolivians love soup, which can be vegetarian, meat or grain and corn based.

Sopa de maní: Gooey peanut soup, widely served at lunchtime – important to note for those suffering from nut allergies.

Asado (barbecued) or a la parrilla (grilled): How some meat and vegetables dishes are prepared.

Choclo (corn): A side dish on the Altiplano. There is also *mote* (rehydrated dried corn kernels).

Yucca or plantain: A side served with everything in the tropics.

Pollo (chicken): Comes either *frito* (fried) or *asado* (roast on a spit). Cheap chicken restaurants are ubiquitous in Bolivia.

Palta: In Bolivia, this is the word for avocado.

Pique macho: Ubiquitous on Bolivian menus (and huge) combining beef, sausage, eggs, peppers and onions piled over potato fries.

HOW TO...

Street Snack Like a Local

As you travel through Bolivia, you'll come across endless snack sellers and their mini stands parked on pavements, as well as many food stalls in local markets. It can be hard to know what's what, and street snacks vary regionally. The most ubiquitous yellow-orange empanada in La Paz is a *salteña*, although you'll come across it all over Bolivia. It comes stuffed with meat, fish or vegetables. Look out for cornmeal dough, which is filled with llama meat, it's called *tamales de charque*. Cheesy bread rolls known as *cuñapé* are also sometimes known as *chipá*. Grilled mashed yucca with cheese is called *sonso de yuca*, and is particularly popular in Tarija. In Santa Cruz, look out for *pan de arroz* – delicious rice flour rolls, filled with tapioca and cheese, and baked in a banana leaf. *Api de maíz morado* is a hot drink made with ground purple corn, cinnamon, sugar and cloves. It's popular in the Altiplano, and sold mainly at markets of La Paz, Oruro, Potosí and Cochabamba.

Basic set menu lunch
B$15–20

Fancy three-course dinner for two with wine
B$600

Cafe breakfast
B$12–25

Fruit juice at a street stall
B$2–4

Cup of specialty coffee
B$15–20

Coca mate
B$10

Chuflay cocktail
B$40

HOW TO... Navigate Bolivia's Food by Region

Bolivia's food scene is as diverse as its peoples and landscapes.

The best culinary scene is in La Paz, Cochabamba and Santa Cruz. The restaurant scene in La Paz is ever evolving and the city has some amazing spots serving haute cuisine and focusing on local-only ingredients cooked in creative ways.

Cochabamba has some of the best food in the country. Whatever you try here will be good, be it street food or in a high-end restaurant. Local specialties include *silpancho* (meat on rice and potatoes), *lomo* borracho (beef cooked in beer) and *picante de pollo* (spicy chicken). *Ranga-ranga* (peppers, onions and minced beef) is delicious and has a great name.

The best food in Santa Cruz is international – there are some high quality Japanese and Peruvian restaurants, and there's very good grilled meat.

Don't miss the Altiplano *trucha* (trout) – it's incredibly popular and quite delicious. Potosí offers a really interesting soup known as *k'alaphurka*. It is made of corn and bacon and – this is very exciting – is heated by dropping a hot volcanic stone into the bowl!

In Oruro, they love grilled meat. Make sure you taste the typical local dish, called *charquekan*, made with dried llama meat and served with egg, corn, cheese and hot sauce. The Amazon Basin has an abundance of river fish, cooked in palm leaves or bamboo, and tropical fruits.

Inca Potato Chips

Rural areas close to Oruro specialize in making ***chuño*** – potatoes left out to freeze then thaw over several days and nights, turning into freeze-dried potato chips. This technique was developed by the Incas some 800 years ago.

DRINKS IN BOLIVIA

One of the most popular non-alcoholic drinks in the Altiplano is the *mate de coca* – an infusion of water and dried coca leaves. It tastes like green tea, with a grassy, earthy fragrance. Another popular tea is *trimate* – a blend of chamomile, coca and anise, which is common in hotels and restaurants.

Fresh fruit juices are fantastic and juice stalls are ubiquitous, particularly in the tropics, but also on the Altiplano. There is orange and lemon juice, papaya juice, prickly pear juice (delicious!), and squeezed watermelon.

The specialty coffee scene is booming, especially in Santa Cruz. Beans are grown in the Yungas, specifically Caranavi, and the coffee is mind-blowingly good. Prices can be high, though.

Bolivia's favorite *cervezas* (beers) are the Paceña, Huari, Sureña, Taquiña, Potosina and Tropical Extra.

The real draw for wine lovers in Bolivia is the southern regions of Tarija and Cintis valleys. This growing and high-quality wine industry has 200-year-old vines, ancient vineyards and unique local grape varieties. Eating some good beef, accompanied by a rich Tarija red, is a total treat.

If you like cocktails, don't miss the most Bolivian of drinks: Chuflay – a mix of *singani* (grape brandy), ginger ale, and lime juice, with plenty of ice.

Chicha is fermented alcohol popular in the countryside. It can be made from corn, peanut or quinoa, depending on the region.

Responsible Travel

Climate Change & Travel

It's impossible to ignore the impact we have when traveling; Lonely Planet urges all travelers to engage with their travel carbon footprint, which will mainly come from air travel. While there often isn't an alternative, travelers can look to minimise the number of flights they take, opt for newer aircrafts and use cleaner ground transport, such as trains. One proposed solution—purchasing carbon offsets—unfortunately does not cancel out the impact of individual flights. While most destinations will depend on air travel for the foreseeable future, for now, pursuing ground-based travel where possible is the best course of action.

The **UN Carbon Offset Calculator** shows how flying impacts a household's emissions

The **ICAO's carbon emissions calculator** allows visitors to analyze the CO2 generated by point-to-point journeys

Even a little Spanish - such as greetings and thanks - will be a huge help in Bolivia. If you can, take some classes before you travel.

Plants in the Amazon should not be disturbed or cut - when a vine is cut in the rainforest to demonstrate the water it contains, this tree will likely die.

Choose Indigenous-run Community Eco Lodges

Wherever possible, choose ventures run by local communities. Particularly in the Amazon Basin, there are many eco-lodges where all the proceeds go towards funding community infrastructure, such as medical centers and schools. The **Bolivian Network of Community and Solidarity Based Tourism** (boliviandando.com) supports a number of community-run tourism initiatives across the country.

Don't Be Cheap

Before booking a tour, inquire with your agency about the wellbeing and treatment of their staff. Guides and drivers may be poorly paid or forced to work long hours, they may be unqualified and basic health and safety may be lacking. Any responsible operator will welcome your interest and will be able to answer the questions you have satisfactorily.

Bargaining

Gentle bargaining is usually fine at markets, but bear in mind that many Bolivians have limited funds in comparison to tourists, so arguing over a dollar or two isn't worth it.

Volunteering

There are hundreds of voluntary and nongovernmental organizations (NGOs) working in Bolivia, making this a popular country to volunteer. From animal shelters to language teaching, you can find a suitable spot; there is always a minimum time commitment.

Check out **Volunteer Latin America** (volunteerlatinamerica.com) for general opportunities.

Sustainable Bolivia (sustainablebolivia.org) is a Cochabamba-based not-for-profit with a variety of volunteering programs, both short- and long-term, through 22 local organizations. Also offers Spanish language classes.

WWOOF (wwoof.net) sets you up with volunteer opportunities on organic farms.

Help by Eating

Support Bolivia's youth and the country's cuisine by eating at the wonderful **Gustu** (p82) restaurant, in La Paz. The owner, Claus Meyer, runs the Melting Pot Foundation (meltingpotfonden.org), which has around 14 cooking schools across La Paz's poorest districts, training underprivileged youths in skills which will gain them jobs in the tourism industry. The foundation and the restaurant are all about reviving Bolivian gastronomy and tradition, using indigenous ingredients and techniques. It's an amazing place to eat and your money goes to the best of causes.

Wildlife

While it may be cute to consider feeding bananas to the monkeys, or seeing a wild animal close up, know that this is very much the biggest no-no in the wild. Refuse any agency or guide that offers handling wild animals.

Photography

Be respectful of local people and don't take photographs without asking permission, no matter how attractive their traditional attire may be. A smile and a compliment with a polite photo request will be welcomed.

Littering remains a serious problem in Bolivia, despite many government educational projects to raise awareness.

Don't opt for the cheapest tours and guides - this usually translates into low pay for the staff, and signals poor social or environmental commitment.

A Biodiverse Gem

As one of the most biodiverse countries in the world with 1415 bird and 5000 plant species, Bolivia is a major force in global conservation efforts.

Don't Visit Prisons

Prison tours are illegal and dangerous - if someone offers to take you around San Pedro Prison in La Paz, in particular, remember that this can get you into trouble.

National Park Entrance Fees

Make sure you're paying the entrance fee to any national park you may be visiting. Check with your agency or guide. When you pay your entrance fee, you are directly contributing to park conservation.

RESOURCES

bolivia.com
News and cultural information in Spanish.

bolivianexpress.org
English-language magazine focusing on cultural coverage.

boliviaentusmanos.com
News, culture and tourism site, in Spanish.

LGBTIQ+ Travelers

Bolivia's 2009 constitution is one of the first in the world to expressly ban discrimination on the basis of sexual orientation or gender identity. Both male and female same-sex sexual activity and same-sex civil unions are legal in Bolivia. All this being the case, Bolivia is a very traditional country and there is still plenty of prejudice regarding non-heteronormative sexuality.

Hotels and Sharing

In general, you should have no problem traveling in Bolivia. Sharing a room, especially in higher-end hotels, is hassle free. La Paz and Santa Cruz are tolerant of international gay couples, though you might get looks in smaller towns – remember that this is a conservative country with a lot of religious ideology, and legislation is slow to change mindsets in more provincial areas. There are no designated gay areas in any of Bolivia's cities or towns.

QUEER RESOURCES

La Paz is known for **La Familia Galán**, the capital's most fabulous collective of drag queens, who aim to bring awareness around issues of sexuality and gender through performances. **Mujeres Creando** (mujerescreando.org) is a feminist activist group based in La Paz that promotes the rights of oppressed groups, led by the legendary and formidable María Galindo. **@maricas_bolivia** tracks the gay and trans community initiatives in La Paz and El Alto.

Bolivia's LGBTIQ+ Venues

LGBTIQ+ bars and venues as well as rights lobby groups are only found in larger cities, especially Santa Cruz, La Paz, and Cochabamba, although there are no designated hotels and places to stay that are marked as gay-friendly.

BOLIVIAN PRIDE

Santa Cruz was the first place in the country to have a Pride march, back in 2001. The country's most progressive city for diverse sexuality is Santa Cruz. The *orgullo* – Pride – march is well-attended in Santa Cruz, La Paz and Cochabamba.

GENDER IDENTITY

A local documentary, titled *Nacer*, meaning 'to be born', traces the background for the Gender Identity Law in Bolivia in 2016, which protects transgender people's right to legally change their gender. You will need Spanish language skills to follow it (it is available online), but it's a great way to hear local voices who campaigned for the implementation of this groundbreaking legislation.

Queer and Indigenous

For a unique insight into the experience and challenges of being an indigenous gay person in Bolivia's public spaces, check out the film *Callejear una nacion imposible: india y marica*, by Movimiento Maricas Bolivia.

NITO/SHUTTERSTOCK

Accessible Travel

Bolivia's infrastructure is ill equipped for travelers with disabilities, and owing to its extreme and varied terrains, those with accessibility concerns will find it very hard to travel around, though it is not impossible.

Top Tip

Traveling around Bolivia in a wheelchair will need careful planning. Your best bet is Uyuni and its high-end hotels and transport options.

Airport

El Alto, La Paz International and Viru Viru, Santa Cruz airports have wheelchair assistance and assistance for travelers with visual impairment or low vision.

Accommodations

High-end and luxury hotels have wheelchair access rooms and bathrooms, but midrange and budget options are sadly lacking in any provisions.

RESOURCES

The Hidden Disabilities Sunflower (hdsunflower.com) has a Bolivian website branch where you can find places that collaborate with this network. It's a simple tool for you to voluntarily (and silently) indicate that you may need a hand, more time in shops or on transport, as well as in public spaces, by wearing a sunflower badge.

HI (hi.org/en/country/bolivia-and-andean-states) is an independent and impartial aid organization with a Bolivian branch, that works in collaboration with local incentives and government initiatives to improve the conditions for disabled and vulnerable populations in the country.

LA LUCHA

Bolivian filmmaker Violeta Ayala's film about a groundbreaking disability rights protest in 2016, called La Lucha (lalucha.red), was instrumental in bringing about change for people with disabilities. The protest and the subsequent film resulted in the legislation of monthly pensions for disabled Bolivians.

Challenges

Travelers with mobility issues will find it impossible to visit and get around the National Parks in Bolivia, because of the extensive walking requirements on difficult surfaces.

Outdoors

Most hiking and outdoor activities are off-limits to travelers with mobility impairments, because of the difficult terrain and high altitudes.

SOLO & WOMEN TRAVELERS

Women traveling through the country alone will find midrange to top-end hotels safer. Take the usual precautions, and make sure your guide is trustworthy for any wilderness excursions.

The **GoodMaps app** – available at Santa Cruz's Viru Viru airport in Bolivia, and inside the US – helps guide travelers with visual impairment around this airport.

Mestiza Dress

One of the most distinctive features of the Altiplano that visitors marvel at is the traditional clothes worn by indigenous Aymara women. The incredible range of colors, tasteful combinations, the petticoat skirts, long, connected coal-colored braids, knitted shawls, and carefully balanced bowler hats are an impressive sight – with a surprising history.

The Spanish Imposition

Believe it or not, the characteristic dress worn by many Bolivian indigenous women is a leftover from the Spanish colonizers. It was imposed on them in the 18th century by the Spanish king and Viceroy of Toledo, when they banned the use of Inca clothing and ordered women to wear clothing typical of the mountains in Spain – including the middle parting of the hair. After parting their hair in the middle, the women normally braid their hair into two long plaits that are joined by a tuft of black or brown wool known as a *pocacha*.

Petticoats & Skirts

Petticoats became popular and sought after, along with the traditional shawl of Madrid, garments that today are an essential part of the Aymara girls' traditional dress. The so-called pollera skirts they wear are constructed of several horizontal pleats, and worn over multiple layers of petticoats, giving the impression of olden-day court dresses. Traditionally, only a married woman's skirt was pleated, while a single woman or girl's was not. Today, most of the synthetic materials for these brightly colored polleras are imported from South Korea.

Fashion dictates subtleties, such as the length of both the skirt and the tassels on the shawl, or the fact that the women used to wear boots but now prefer flat shoes.

Lovely Layering

Layering is where the real art lies for these outfits. The women wear a stunning combination of factory-made blouses, woollen *chompas* (sweater/jumper), a short vest-like jacket and a cotton apron. Usually, they throw over their shoulders a knitted shawl, known as a *manta* (blanket). Some wear the distinctive bowler hats in dark green, brown or black, balanced either on top of their heads or tipped to the side, while others opt for wooly knitted hats, often in a beautiful nut brown.

Many don an *aguayo* (also spelled *ahuayo*) across their backs, the rectangle of traditional handwoven cloth in bright pink with colorful horizontal stripes. It's used as a carryall and is filled with everything from coca to groceries or wares for sale at the market, and often, very cute babies.

The Quechua Attire

The clothing of the Quechua on the highland valleys is equally colorful, but not so universally recognized. While they style their hair with the same middle parting and long plaits, their hats, called a montera, are wider and flat-topped, made of straw, a bit like sun hats. Others wear hats made of finely woven white wool. These are often taller and broader than the bowlers worn by the Aymara. The women here wear skirts that are usually made of velour and are shorter in length.

The felt montera hats of Tarabuco – also called *morriones* – were modeled after Spanish conquistadores' helmets. Worn by both men and women, these strangely helmet-shaped hats are decorated with pink and green wool tassels, and are absolutely beautiful.

Wear it With Pride

The distinctive ensemble of the Mestiza dress – also known as *cholita paceña* – is both colorful and utilitarian, and is pretty much Bolivia's defining image. And while it once denoted membership of a marginalized and poor section of Bolivian society, the last two decades have seen an emergent indigenous middle class, and fashion ventures now sell entire Aymara outfits at very high prices. Combined with golden jewelery to complement the clothes, wearing the full traditional garb – which car only really be witnessed at weddings and private functions – increasingly symbolizes confidence and a higher income.

CULTURAL CHANGES

For centuries, Bolivia's indigenous peoples had very little access to mainstream society and wearing a pollera or a poncho to any official function was unthinkable. The 2006 election of Evo Morales, Bolivia's first indigenous president, changed this. O of his main aims was to raise the sense of cultural pr and dignity for Bolivia's indigenous communities, as well as facilitating political representation for indigenous people. He has done this with remarkabl success – Morales himself only ever wore traditiona knitted alpaca jumpers, never suits. In the two deca since, wearing a pollera for indigenous women has become a matter of pride, with indigenous fashion a modelling ventures cropping up.

Nuts & Bolts

OPENING HOURS

Whatever business you might have to do in person, make sure you do it on weekdays – almost everything is closed on weekends. Nearly all businesses close for lunch, usually from noon to 2:30pm.

Banks Standard hours 9am–4pm or 6pm Monday to Friday.

Shops Weekdays 10am–7pm but sometimes close for lunch noon–2pm. Open 10am–noon or 5pm Saturdays.

Restaurants Generally open for breakfast (8am–10am), lunch (noon–3pm) and dinner (6pm–10pm or 11pm) daily. Many are open all day.

Smoking

Smoking is banned in all public spaces, transport, restaurants, cafes, bars, offices and hotel rooms.

SIM Cards

Getting a local SIM card will save you from killer roaming prices.

Toilets

Buses have no toilets. Smelly *baños públicos* (public toilets) charge about B$2, providing a square of paper.

Time Zone
Bolivia Time (GMT/UTC -4)

Country code
+591

Ambulance
118

Fire
119

Population
12,413,315 (2024)

Electricity

220V AC/ at 50Hz

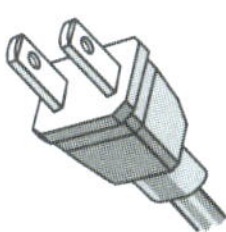

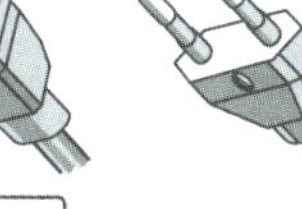

Type A
120V/60Hz

Type C
220V/50Hz

PUBLIC HOLIDAYS

Banks, public offices and some private businesses close on these public holidays.

Año Nuevo (New Year's Day) January 1

Día del Estado Plurinacional (Celebrates new constitution) January 22

Carnaval February/ March

Semana Santa (Easter Week) March/ April

Día de los Trabajadores (Labor Day) May 1

Corpus Christi May/ June

Año Nuevo Andino Amazónico y del Chaco (Andean New Year) June 21

Día de la Independencia (Independence Day) August 6

Día de los Muertos (All Souls' Day) November 2

Navidad (Christmas) December 25

Language

Spanish is one of Bolivia's 37 national languages, the other 36 being Indigenous languages such as Aymara and Quechua. All are recognized in the country's constitution. Knowing some basic phrases is not only courteous but also essential, particularly when navigating rural areas. Influenced by Indigenous languages, Latin American Spanish varies slightly from country to country, especially when it comes to vocabulary.

Basics

Hello. Hola. *o·la*
Goodbye. Adiós. *a·dyos*
Yes. Sí. *see*
No. No. *No*
Please. Por favor. *por fa·vor*
Thank you. Gracias. *gra·syas*
Excuse me. Con permiso. *kon per·mee·so*
Sorry. Perdón. *per·don*
What's your name? ¿Cómo se llama usted? *ko·mo se ya·ma oo·ste*
My name is ... Me llamo ... *me ya·mo ...*
Do you speak English? ¿Habla inglés? *a·bla een·gles*
I don't understand. Yo no entiendo. *yo no en·tyen·do*

Directions

Where's ...?
¿Adónde está ...? *a·don·de es·ta ...*
What's the address?
¿Cuál es la dirección? *kwal es la dee·rek·syon*
Could you please write it down?
¿Podría escribirlo? *po·dree·a es·kree·beer·lo*
Can you show me (on the map)?
¿Me puede mostrar (en el mapa)? *me pwe·de mo·strar (en el ma·pa)*

Signs

Abierto Open
Cerrado Closed
Entrada Entrance
Salida Exit

Time

What time is it? ¿Qué hora es? *ke o·ra es*
It's (10) o'clock. Son (las diez). *son (las dyes)*
It's half past (one). Es (la una) y media. *es (la oo·na) ee me·dya*
morning mañana. *ma·nya·na*
afternoon tarde. *tar·de*
evening noche. *no·che*
yesterday ayer. *a·yer*
today hoy. *oy*
tomorrow mañana. *ma·nya·na*

Emergencies

Help! ¡Ayúdame! *ah·yoo·dah·meh*
Go away! ¡Váyase! *va·ya·se*
I'm ill. Estoy enfermo/a. *es·toy en.fer.mo/a*
I'm lost. Estoy perdido/a. *per·dee·do/a* (m/f)
Call ...! ¡Llame a ...! *ya·me a ...*
a doctor un doctor. *oon dok·tor*
the police la policía. *la po·lee·see·a*

Eating & Drinking

Can I see the menu, please?
¿Puedo ver la carta, por favor? *pwe·do ver el car·ta, por fa·vor*
What would you recommend?
¿Qué me recomienda? *ke me re·ko·myen·da*
Cheers! ¡Salud! *sa·lood*
The bill, please. La cuenta, por favor. *la kwen·ta por fa·vor*

NUMBERS

1 **uno** *oo·no*
2 **dos** *dos*
3 **tres** *tres*
4 **cuatro** *kwa·tro*
5 **cinco** *seen·ko*
6 **seis** *seys*
7 **siete** *sye·te*
8 **ocho** *o·cho*
9 **nueve** *nwe·ve*
10 **diez** *dyes*

DONATIONS TO ENGLISH

Numerous – you may recognize armada, aficionado, embargo, fiesta, machismo, patio, plaza...

DISTINCTIVE SOUNDS

Note that *kh* is a throaty sound (like the 'ch' in the Scottish loch), *v* and *b* are like a soft English 'v' (between a 'v' and a 'b'), and *r* is strongly rolled.

To lisp or not to lisp

If you're familiar with the sound of Castilian Spanish, you'll notice Latin Americans don't 'lisp' – ie the Castilian *th* is pronounced as *s*.

False friends

Warning: some Spanish words look like English words but have a different meaning altogether! For example, *suburbio* is 'slum district' (not 'suburb', which is *barrio*).

Where the @!*# is it?

Spanish-language and English-language keyboard layouts differ because the two alphabets aren't quite the same. This shouldn't generally be a problem, but for one pesky – all too useful in the age of email – key. The @ ('at') symbol – in Spanish this symbol is called *la arroba* (la a·ro·ba) – isn't necessarily labeled on keyboards or may not be accessed by simply pressing the keys you're used to. Try the F2 key, use an ALT code – or ask for help:

Where's the @ key? *¿Dónde está la arroba?* (don·de es·ta la a·ro·ba)

Regional variations

There are some variations in spoken Spanish across Latin America, the most notable being the pronunciation of the letters ll and y – depending on where you are on the continent, you'll hear them pronounced like the 'y' in 'yes', the 'lli' in 'million', the 's' in 'measure' or the 'sh' in 'shut'.

This is also true for day-to-day vocabulary, such as the term for petrol/gas station. The word *gasolinera* (ga·so·lee·ne·ra) is the standard term for 'petrol/gas station', and will be understood throughout Latin America. However, in Bolivia, the term *surtidor* (soor·tee·dor) can also be used.

LATIN AMERICAN PLACE NAMES

Many Latin American place names are linked to historical events. Bolivia is named after Simón Bolívar, the famous revolutionary general who helped liberate many Latin American countries from Spanish rule, then became Bolivia's first president.

THE BOLIVIA

STORYBOOK

Our writers delve deep into different aspects of Bolivian life.

Oruro Carnaval (p154)
CURIOSO.PHOTOGRAPHY/SHUTTERSTOCK

A HISTORY OF BOLIVIA IN 15 PLACES

Bolivia's history goes back millennia. The through line, nay fault line, has always been territorial conflict. Several pre-Columbian civilizations grew powerful; the Spanish arrived, exploiting the indigenous population; and after independence, the story continues in a complex, never-ending quest to blend the country's disparate regions, peoples and cultures into a unified whole. By Michael Grosberg

LOCATED AT THE geographic heart of the South American continent, Bolivia has been at the crossroads of civilizational currents for thousands of years. Empires, both regional and global, have prospered and declined. The rise and fall of the Inca empire that would truly define the pre-Columbian period was followed by the Spanish who gained their economic foothold through the country's mineral wealth.

Agriculture, trade and geographic advantages jumpstarted the Andes' emergence as the cradle of South America's highest cultural achievements. Nomadic tribes in the lowlands, farmers in the Yungas, organized societies such as the Tiwanaku and Inca in the high plateau all played their part. Between 1476 and 1534 the Inca extended their influence over the Aymara Kingdoms around Lake Titicaca, pushing their empire far from its seat of power in Cuzco. By the late 1520s, internal rivalries began to take their toll. When Atahualpa, the victorious scion of Inca Huayna Capac, was captured by the conquistador Francisco Pizarro, ransomed and eventually beheaded, the power vacuum paved the way for the Spanish to conquer and control.

Missionaries showed up in the 18th and 19th centuries around Santa Cruz and Tarija, altering the cultural landscape of the region. During the early 20th century wealthy tin barons and landowners controlled Bolivian farming and mining interests, while the peasantry was relegated to a feudal system of peonage. Civil unrest brewed. After a series of territorial wars with neighboring countries from the late 19th century to the early half of the 20th, Bolivia has experienced nearly uninterrupted political instability.

1. San Ignacio de Moxos

ANCIENT AMAZONIAN CIVILIZATION

This village's indigenous residents in Beni province, known as *los mojeños*, are descendants of an ancient culture that cultivated the Amazon more than 2500 years ago. Archaeologists, beginning in the early 20th century, have uncovered an extensive system of earthen work structures called lomas (operating as homes, fields for crops, animal husbandry and sites for rituals), aqueducts, canals, even lagoons (scientists speculate these were developed for fishing), as well as finely designed pottery. The discoveries have proven that the region was inhabited by developed, flourishing, even 'semi-urban' societies long before the arrival of the Spanish and Jesuit missionaries.

For more on San Ignacio de Moxos, see page 306.

2. El Fuerte de Samaipata

PRE-INCA HILLTOP MYSTERY

First occupied by diverse ethnic groups as early as 2000 BCE, it wasn't until 1470 CE that the Incas, the most famous tenants, first arrived. By the time the Spanish came and looted the site in the 1600s it was already deserted. The purpose of El Fuerte has long been debated, but the prevailing theory is that it was an ancient temple to the serpent and the jaguar, incorporating worship of the sun and moon. There are no standing buildings, but the remains of 500 dwellings have been discovered in the immediate vicinity and ongoing excavation reveals more every day.

For more on El Fuerte, see page 269.

3. Tiwanaku

BIRTHPLACE OF ANDEAN CIVILIZATION

By 700 BCE, the time of the European Iron Age, Tiwanaku was a thriving metropolis with an extensive system of roads, irrigation canals and agricultural terraces. From 500–900 CE the Tiwanaku expanded throughout the Andean region. Around 900, Tiwanaku's power began to wane, the population dispersed and the ceremonial site became largely abandoned – possibly because of climate change (drought), an earthquake or foreign invasion by the warlike Kollas (also known as the Aymara) from the west. When the Spanish arrived they were told an Inca legend about a battle between the Kollas and 'bearded white men' on an island in Lake Titicaca.

For more on Tiwanaku, see page 70.

4. Cerro Rico, Potosí

FIGHTING OVER SILVER

During the initial stages of the Spanish conquest of the Americas, infighting between Spanish factions was common and the fate of Bolivia – a political backwater until the discovery of silver – was subservient to the more powerful political centers in Cuzco and Lima. Potosí's mine was the most prolific in the world and its silver underwrote Spain's international ambitions, enabling the country to conduct the Counter-Reformation in Europe, and supporting the extravagance of its monarchy for centuries. But not all wealth left the region and cathedrals sprung up in Potosí and across the Altiplano; indigenous people who were dragooned into working the mines paid with their lives.

For more on Cerro Rico, see page 218.

Iglesia de San Xavier, Chiquitos Missions (p280)

JOSE ARCOS AGUILAR/SHUTTERSTOCK

5. Chiquitos Missions

JESUIT INFLUENCE

Venturing into territories previously unexplored by Europeans, the Jesuits established settlements, known as *reducciones* that essentially operated as autonomous theocracies. The indigenous were given a 'choice': live within the missionary communities with strict regimes of work and prayer or under the harsh *encomienda* (Spanish feudal system) or, worse, outright slavery. Under Swiss priest Father Martin Schmidt, the settlements, including those he built at San Xavier, Concepción and San Rafael de Velasco, reached their peak. By the mid-1700s, amidst political strife in Europe, the missions were disbanded and King Carlos III signed an order evicting the Jesuits from the continent. The settlements fell into decline, their churches standing as mute testimony to their existence.

For more on the Jesuit missions, see page 278.

6. Casa de Libertad, Sucre

BOLIVIA DECLARES INDEPENDENCE

In 1558, Alto Perú gained its autonomy from Lima with the placement of an *Audiencia* (Royal Court) in Sucre. Fast forward to the early part of the 19th century, when the French Revolution, Napoleon's wars in Europe and British support for Latin America's independence movements created a ferment for the overthrowing of monarchies. By May 1809, Spanish America's first independence movement was well underway in Chuquisaca (later renamed Sucre), with other cities following suit. With both Argentina and Peru eyeing the prize of the Potosí mines, Antonio José de Sucre declared the country's independence from Peru and, in 1825, the new Republic of Bolivia was born here. And the museum tells the story.

For more on Casa de Libertad, see page 206.

7. Isla del Sol, Lake Titicaca

WHERE SACRED LEGENDS ARE BORN

The origin stories of more than one Andean civilization, including pre-Inca peoples, can be traced to the shores of Lake Titicaca, high in the Altiplano. They believed that the sun was birthed on Isla del Sol, and their bearded white god-king, Viracocha, and the first Incas, Manco Capac and his sister-wife Mama Ocllo, had risen out of the lake's mysterious depths nearby. Trails run through spectacular ruins and past oddly shaped rock features, mystical and sacred sites to pilgrims, and to many of the indigenous communities that call the island home, tangible proof of the veracity of their legends.

For more on Isla del Sol, see page 96.

8. Palacio Portales, Cochabamba

AGE OF THE TIN BARONS

In the late 19th century the demand for tin exploded and Bolivian tin barons anointed. Perhaps, the biggest tycoon was Simón Patiño, who by 1930 controlled more than 60% of the global supply. His Cochabamba mansion, a testament to his standing as one of the wealthiest people alive. Oruro, its mountains chock-a-block of the commodity, was a boom town for decades. Miners' demands for better working conditions were met with violence, but eventually the radical union that formed as a result led to wide scale reforms and the nationalization of the mines in the 1950s. In the 1980s, as the economy was liberalized, tin prices plunged, decimating the industry.

For more on Palacio Portales, see page 191.

9. Museo Héroes de la Guerra del Chaco

THE FIGHT OVER THE CHACO

After a major loss of the rubber-tree-rich Arce territory to Brazil in 1903 and two separate territory losses to Argentina (first, Argentina annexed a large slice of the Chaco in 1862; then, in 1883, the territory of Puna de Atacama went to Argentina), Bolivia was desperate to have the Chaco, an inhospitable region beneath which rich oilfields were supposed to lie, as an outlet to the Atlantic via the Río Paraguay. Between 1932 and 1935, a particularly brutal war was waged between Bolivia and Paraguay over the territory. No decisive victory was reached; however, peace negotiations in 1938 awarded most of the disputed territory to Paraguay.

For more on Museo Historico Militar Heroes del Chaco, see page 251.

10. Vallegrande

REVOLUTIONARY INSPIRATION

Because of its central location and René Barrientos Ortuño's oppressive military government, Argentinian Ernesto 'Che' Guevara, the iconic figure of the South American revolutionary spirit, identified Bolivia as the ideal place to launch the continent's socialist revolution. However, after failing to inspire the *campesinos* to rebellion, Guevara was executed in the tiny hamlet of La Higuera by a CIA-backed military squad in 1928. His body was displayed in Vallegrande and secretly buried under the town's airstrip; in 1997 it was exhumed and reburied in Cuba. A museum and cultural center draws like-minded spirits to the sights for a Che pilgrimage.

For more on Vallegrande, see page 277.

11. Museo de la Revolución Nacional, La Paz

OVERTHROW OF THE OLIGARCHY

During the early 20th century, the most significant development was the emergence of the Movimiento Nacionalista Revolucionario (MNR) political party. It united the masses behind the common cause of popular reform, sparking friction between peasant miners and absentee tin bosses. Under the leadership of Víctor Paz Estenssoro, the MNR prevailed in the 1951 elections, but a last-minute military coup prevented it from taking power. Serious combat followed, ending with the military's defeat and Paz Estensorro's rise to power in what's been called the April Revolution of 1952. He immediately nationalized the mines, evicted the tin barons and put an end to *pongueaje* (a feudal system of peonage).

For more on the Museo de la Revolución Nacional, see p66.

12. Chapare Region

COCA WARS

In the mid 1990s, reforms, namely economic liberalization and privatization of state-owned enterprises, were overshad-

El Alto (p68)

owed by violence and unrest surrounding US-directed coca eradication in the Beni and Chapare regions, where coca generated, and still generates, substantial income for the growers and traffickers. About 1.2 million kilos of coca leaf are consumed monthly in Bolivia. The government faced swelling public discontent over the drug wars, as well as increasing gas prices, a serious water shortage and economic downturn. A decade later, President Evo Morales would make it a personal mission to highlight the difference between coca, a plant sacred to the highland indigenous cultures, and cocaine, the narcotic.

For more on the Chapare, see page 318.

13. Sorata

THE RISE OF MORALES

In October 2003, during the dying days of President Sánchez de Lozada's government, the town of Sorata was the scene of roadblocks and violent clashes between police, the military and *campesinos* (subsistence farmers) protesting the selling of the nation's natural resources and mistreatment of the indigenous population. After a military mission was launched to 'rescue' more than 100 tourists trapped during demonstrations, six people were killed during violent clashes. The fallout led to Sánchez de Lozada's resignation and ultimately to the election of Evo Morales of Movimiento al Socialismo (MAS) in December 2005, the country's first indigenous president and a former *cocalero* (coca grower).

For more on Sorata, see page 138.

14. El Alto

URBANIZATION

Bolivians have been moving from rural areas to cities at a rapid pace since the mid 2000s. Nowhere else has this internal migration been more impactful than El Alto, the sprawling city, largely Aymara, sitting on a high plateau above La Paz. Once only an informal 'satellite' town of La Paz, now more populous, partly a result of climate change's continuing consequences, El Alto's both a stronghold of the country's leftist politics with frequent blockades and demonstrations, but also an example of Bolivia's modernization in the form of the *teleférico* (cable car) linking it with La Paz below.

For more on El Alto, see p68.

15. Plaza Murillo, La Paz

THWARTED COUP

When troops entered La Paz's Plaza Murillo in June, 2024, it marked the 191st attempted coup d'état in Bolivia's tumultuous political history. The economy had waxed and waned since Evo Morales was reelected with a majority of 60% in 2014. Seeking to extend his presidency beyond 2020 and run for a fourth consecutive term, amid scandals and corruption charges, Morales lost a referendum in 2016 to revise the constitution. Under pressure, the courts later flip flopped, twice, and two term limits were reinstated. Undeterred, Morales announced his intention to run for a fourth term again in 2025, likely against his one time ally, now rival, President Luis Arce.

For more on Plaza Murillo, see page 67.

MEET THE BOLIVIANS

Bolivians are proud of their roots and enjoy showing visitors the traditions and festivals that mark the social and cultural life of the country. Maria Silvia Trigo introduces her people.

AT FIRST GLANCE, some people in Bolivia may seem blunt to visitors, but in general, you will find people who are proud of their identity and eager to show the world the traits of their culture, their music, and their gastronomy. Although Bolivians have a reputation for being unpunctual and not very formal, they are kind and hospitable to guests.

Spanish is spoken throughout the country, but each region has its own particular idioms and accents, especially those of people who speak an indigenous language as their mother tongue. In the west of the country, the Aymara and Quechua heritage can be distinguished in the way of speaking, in the lowlands the population usually omits the 's' at the end of words, and in Tarija, in the south of the country, conversations sound like a sweet melody similar to the Cordoban accent of Argentina.

For Bolivian families, the dining table is a meeting place. Lunchtime is very important to them: it's when they gather to eat together before they go back to their activities in the afternoon, so it's not surprising that cities, except for the largest ones, seem sleepy and frozen in time after midday. Bolivians will unquestionably gather as a family for annual celebrations linked to religious holidays, such as Christmas or All Saints' Day, when those who are far away return home to share family traditions.

Main squares remain the centers of social activities, especially in small and medium-sized towns and cities. People come to meet friends, enjoy street attractions, or simply watch time pass by.

A Vast Country

Bolivia is home to 11.3 million people – a geographically vast country with 11 inhabitants per sq km. Although the majority of the population is *Mestizo*, Bolivians are very proud of their indigenous roots.

Bolivians love to party and have many reasons to celebrate. Carnaval and 'folkloric parades' are very popular, and it is not unusual to find streets cut off by a parade or local party with a magnificent display of Bolivian music and dance. However, excessive drinking is common and can spoil a nice experience.

When Bolivians are asked how they define themselves, they respond that they are hard-working, happy people who love their country. All of this can be seen in their streets full of shops, in the numerous annual celebrations, and in the pride they feel when talking about their country.

I GREW UP IN TARIJA & LIVE IN SANTA CRUZ

I come from a Bolivian family with Irish origins. Although I was born in Argentina, I spent my childhood and youth in Tarija, a city in the south of Bolivia that I consider my home; then I lived in La Paz, where I fell in love with the city's Andean culture and mysticism; and I currently live in Santa Cruz. It's the most populated and cosmopolitan region, with the largest number of national migrants and where all the traits of Bolivia can be found.

My Irish heritage is not very common in Bolivia. Besides Spanish, the main foreign ancestry, there are communities of African origin in Los Yungas in La Paz and Japanese-origin communities in rural Santa Cruz. People of Arab descent, mainly from Syria, Palestine and Lebanon, are quite common across the country, as are people with Croatian, Jewish and German backgrounds, who began to increasingly migrate to Bolivia over the last century.

Indigenous people, Tiwanaku (p7
LINA CHERO PHOTOGRAPHY/SHUTTERST(

APPROACHING INDIGENOUS CULTURES

Bolivia is a multicultural country where tradition blends with modernity. By Maria Silvia Trigo

BOLIVIA DID NOT acquire its official name – the Plurinational State of Bolivia – by coincidence. This country is home to 36 indigenous nations, each of which enriches the culture with their music, traditions and different ways of understanding the world. An approach to these peoples is an ancestral journey through different colors, textures and sounds that have persisted throughout the centuries.

Population

Bolivia's two largest indigenous peoples are the Quechua and the Aymara, who live in the western Andes. In the eastern lowland regions of the country, the

Chiquitano and Guaraní peoples predominate, but their numbers are much smaller than the indigenous population in the highlands. All across the country, there are other peoples whose populations have dwindled and who are in danger of disappearing – the Weenhayek, for example, or the Tapiete, of whom only a handful of families remain, living in the Chaco region in the south.

These populations face several threats, including the environmental destruction of their territory and illegal economic encroachments, such as gold mining or the expansion of coca leaf plantations. Nevertheless, it is possible to find authentic expressions of indigenous cultures, especially in the Andean region.

According to data from the 2012 census, 41% of the population considers themselves to be of indigenous origin, but *Mestizos* (a mixture of Spanish and indigenous blood) are by far the country's largest demographic group. One of the first things that visitors notice when they arrive in La Paz is the particular way of coexistence between the Creole and the indigenous; in this city you still find traditional clothing, patronal festivities that take place in the streets and markets offering ancestral rituals.

The Quechua and Aymara cultures are very obvious in the west and the valleys of the country, but in the lowlands, the characteristics of local indigenous cultures aren't so apparent in the cities, where the quirks of the *Mestizo* and modernity predominate. For an authentic experience, it is worth traveling into rural areas and visiting places such as the surroundings of Madidi Park (in the north of La Paz) or Chiquitanía (in Santa Cruz).

FOR AN AUTHENTIC EXPERIENCE, IT IS WORTH TRAVELING INTO RURAL AREAS AND VISITING PLACES SUCH AS THE SURROUNDINGS OF MADIDI PARK (IN THE NORTH OF LA PAZ) OR CHIQUITANÍA (IN SANTA CRUZ).

Rurrenabauqe **(p298)**

TONIFLAP/SHUTTERSTOCK

Cultural Diversity

One thing that characterizes the indigenous populations in Bolivia is the perseverance of their cultures, which they have maintained since before colonial times. Visitors won't necessarily find the signs of this culture in the country's monumental ruins or other significant historic landmarks, because the strength of these people lies not in their urban expression but in enduring cultural and social modes of organization that have survived over the centuries.

In each region, the indigenous and authentic have their own characteristics. A common feature among them is the symbolic expressions that are present in dance and music; these in turn are linked to the agricultural calendar and to Catholic festivities that took root here during the colonial era.

Textiles also have an important symbolism for indigenous populations. The differences between peoples are manifested in the style of the textiles, the techniques applied in producing them, the materials and colors, as well as the use that is made of them. The finest and most appreciated are those made with wool from the *vicuña*, a camelid from the highlands, which is woven into luxurious, soft and durable fabrics.

Inclusion in Political Life

Most of the indigenous population has historically been marginalized and excluded from the country's public and political life. Although in practice there is still a very evident ethnic inequality in Bolivia, the arrival of former president Evo Morales to power in 2006 certainly marked a before and after in Bolivia.

Cholitas (p69)
DIEGO GRANDI/SHUTTERSTOCK

Morales, considered the first president of rural and humble origin, concretized some historical demands of indigenous peoples, such as their constitutional recognition, and laws began to take into account the indigenous particularity, allowing them to maintain their means of social organization and an autonomy based on their customs.

However, there are critics who think that this recognition was only a symbolic one designed to obtain political benefits. Certainly, despite the advances accomplished in terms of inclusion, the road to active participation in national development is still long and steep.

'Cholitas' - a Symbol of Blended Cultures

One of the distinctive signs of La Paz is the presence of women with a special outfit that features a colorful skirt made up of several layers covering them from the waist down, a colored cloak over a knitted sweater and a small bowler hat, black or brown, that rests delicately on their heads. These women, known as cholitas, braid their hair in two threads and some wear on their backs an aguayo, a traditional fabric from the highlands in which they carry their babies or some special luggage such as food or coca leaves.

This style of dress, which today characterizes the women of western Bolivia, is a direct result of the influence of Spanish-origin clothing from the 18th century.

Authentic Experiences

You will find options in various cities to learn about the cultural expressions of indigenous communities; however, it is best to make sure that they are as authentic as possible. One such authentic experience is found 62km from Sucre in the municipality of Tarabuco, where every Sunday locals, vendors and visitors gather at a traditional market. Here, you can appreciate the culture of the place through clothing, the way of commerce and the variety of handcrafted textiles. The market is best experienced on the second Sunday of March, the date of Pujllay, a dance and music festival of the Yampara culture that was designated as an example of the Intangible Cultural Heritage of Humanity by UNESCO in 2014.

A must-see to understand the indigenous culture of the lowlands of Bolivia is a visit to the communities around the Madidi National Park, in the Amazon region of the country. As well as appreciating the lush and little-explored nature, travelers here will gain insight into the daily life of the Tacanas, who are used to receiving visitors thanks to community tourism projects that they manage themselves.

RHYTHMS & SOUNDS OF BOLIVIA

This is a country thriving on diverse music and constant movement. By Maria Silvia Trigo

THERE ARE THREE strands of traditional Bolivian that play a remarkable role in the country's music scene: pure indigenous music played in rural communities without foreign influence; Mestizo dances expressed through popular folklore; and African-Bolivian dances.

Folk Music

The styles of traditional music in Bolivia's highlands, valleys and eastern regions differ along with the ethnic origins of these areas' populations, but they do share some elements: the different styles have indigenous roots, with musical traditions mostly linked to patronal festivities or agricultural periods and with songs usually played by musical groups.

The greatest musical expression of the country is folk music, which developed through the cultural syncretism of the colony, drawing from both indigenous and European musical styles. Varieties in the Andean region include caporales, morenada, kullawada, diablada and tinku; each accompanying dance has its own special choreography, with dancers dressed in colorful costumes.

In the region of Los Yungas in La Paz, the saya, a musical style emanating from African-Bolivian communities, constitutes one of the country's main artistic expressions. Traditional in valleys, the cueca's lighthearted rhythms accompany a dance in which men and women wave white handkerchiefs, symbolizing the flirtation between couples. In the eastern plains, higher-tempo, festive rhythms such as the chovenas and taquiraris predominate. Some writers say these are influenced by the Catalan sardana.

Between the 1960s and '70s, a boom in folk music brought the rise of emblematic bands such as Los Kjarkas or Savia Andina, whose compositions became anthems for many Bolivians and have transcended the country's borders. This era also saw the emergence of female composers, among whom Matilde Casazola and Gladys Moreno stand out as milestones in the country's musical history.

Where to Experience Bolivian Folk

You can discover the diversity of Bolivian music at a *peña folklórica*, a kind of folk club that is very popular in La Paz, Cochabamba, Tarija and other cities. Patrons can enjoy dinner and appreciate several music bands and native instruments on nights that sometimes turn into big parties, stretching into the early hours. Likewise, folkloric parades take place

PERCUSION
PERCUSION

in towns and cities throughout the year, with streets along extensive routes closing to allow musicians and dancers to process through, normally commemorating some patronal festivity. Oruro's Carnaval, the Gran Poder of La Paz, and the Urkupiña Virgin Parade in Cochabamba offer great opportunities to get to know the diversity of Bolivia's folk music.

Emerging Music

Beyond these persistent Creole sounds, folk music has undergone mutations in recent years. A new trend emerged around the beginning of this century that some experts call neo-folklore or folk-pop: universal rhythms played on traditional Bolivian instruments, fusion sounds that have further diversified the Bolivian musical scene.

Contemporary Bolivia has seen a period of amazing creativity with young artists bringing innovative new styles into urban genres. Aided by the internet and social media, pop, indie, trap, hip hop, cumbia, and rock bands have been creating new local audiences for their respective genres. The new scene spans everything from Aymara women rappers to singers with influences from northern Mexico such as Luis Vega, a TikTok sensation turned venue-filling live performer.

CONTEMPORARY BOLIVIA HAS SEEN A PERIOD OF AMAZING CREATIVITY WITH YOUNG ARTISTS BRINGING INNOVATIVE NEW STYLES INTO URBAN GENRES.

Charango (p200)

A Quechua Voice that Sounds Like Birds

Possibly the most universal of Bolivia's traditional music artists is Luzmila Carpio, whose songs tell of the life and ancestral culture of the northern Potosí indigenous community she was born in. Carpio plays the *charango*, a stringed musical instrument like a small guitar originally made from an armadillo shell; she is known especially for the tones she reaches with her voice. Music experts have compared these to birdsong, earning her the nickname 'Nightingale of the Highlands.' Carpio, who lives in France, has released 25 albums in her native language, Quechua, and was recognized as an icon of Latin folk music in 2023.

Baroque Music from the Lowlands

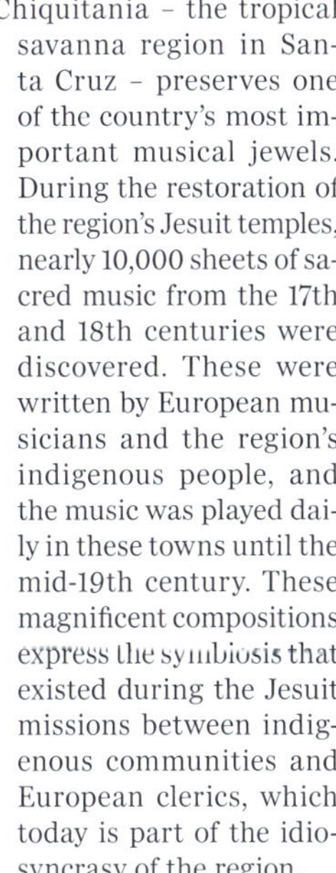

The Bolivian Chiquitania – the tropical savanna region in Santa Cruz – preserves one of the country's most important musical jewels. During the restoration of the region's Jesuit temples, nearly 10,000 sheets of sacred music from the 17th and 18th centuries were discovered. These were written by European musicians and the region's indigenous people, and the music was played daily in these towns until the mid-19th century. These magnificent compositions express the symbiosis that existed during the Jesuit missions between indigenous communities and European clerics, which today is part of the idiosyncrasy of the region.

Every two years the International Festival of Renaissance and Baroque Music 'Misiones de Chiquitos' is held among eastern Bolivian rural communities, which open their old churches to offer concerts by local and international orchestras, something that has begun to encourage the emergence of the lowlands as a tourist destination focused on history, music and art.

Music is profoundly connected to Bolivians' daily lives. There is no cultural, religious or agricultural event that is not enhanced with its particular rhythms and melodies. To understand the country and fully appreciate its diversity, it is essential to sense the 'soundtrack' behind every celebration.

Dancers, Oruro Carnaval (p154)

THE DIVERSE & WONDERFUL WILDLIFE OF BOLIVIA

Bolivia's geography is almost without equal in its diversity; so too is the wildlife that lives here. By Vesna Maric

BOLIVIA'S LANDSCAPES AND wildlife are some of the most diverse in the world. Apart from the heights of La Paz and the salty flats of Uyuni, which are known worldwide, the Bolivian region encompasses an incredible range of altitudes – from 130m in the Amazon Basin to 6542m on the peaks of the arid Andes. The Altiplano, the central highlands and the Amazon Basin, form a cycle of humidity and rainfall, and keep the country's – and the world's – ecosystem intact. Travelers will certainly feel this as they move through this incredible land, and their bodies cope with adjusting to the vast variations of climates and altitudes!

And it's not just the landscapes – Bolivia has some of the most diverse wildlife on the continent. The country has 1415 bird species and 5000 described plant species, numbers that are hard to match in the rest of the world. It's also among the neotropical countries with the highest level of endemic species (those that exist only here), with 21 birds, 28 reptiles, 72 amphibians and 25 mammals found nowhere else on earth. The distribution of all this wildlife is dictated by the country's geography and varies considerably from region to region.

Unfortunately, the Bolivian environment is under constant threat from destruction by economic exploitation and the country is struggling to balance the tireless demand for economic progress with the need to sustainably and responsibly benefit from its natural resources.

Pictured clockwise from top left: Black capped squirrel monkey; Armadillo; Llama with baby, Southern Altiplano (p145); Leaves of coca plant (p319)

The Animals of the Altiplano

The Altiplano is home to vicuñas, llamas, flamingos and condors. The most threatened wildlife in the highlands are a little-known deer called the North Andean huemul, the Andean hairy armadillo and the endemic short-tailed chinchilla, which is hunted for its luxurious fur. The windswept lakes of the Southern Altiplano are the exclusive habitat of the rare James flamingo, while the charming Cochabamba mountain finch has a total range of just 3500 sq km and is endangered by its proximity to Cochabamba's urbanity. One of the weirdest-looking endangered species is the incredible Titicaca giant frog, named after the lake on which it lives. It is hunted by locals who consume it for its supposed aphrodisiac effect.

Amazonian Beauties

The Amazon Basin takes up more than half of Bolivia's entire territory and contains the richest density of species on earth, featuring an incredible variety of reptiles, parrots, monkeys, hummingbirds, butterflies, fish and insects. The tropical rainforest sits in the western section, while it's mostly the flat cerrado savannahs that occupy the east. In the country's southeastern corner is the Gran Chaco, mostly impenetrable forest and the country's hottest spot.

While the Amazon Basin is famous for its pink river dolphins, the blue-throated macaw (*barba azul* in Spanish) is one of its unsung heroes! This species was once considered critically endangered but thanks to preservation efforts its numbers seem to have stabilised – there were 430 adult blue-throated macaws counted in the wild in 2024.

Travelers long to spot the majestic yet shy jaguar, the continent's top predator, which is notoriously difficult to see. The elephant-nosed tapir (anta) and the lolloping giant anteater are also incredible sights, but are easier to find. Those traveling up and down rivers will see cute capybaras, cool caiman (close relatives of alligators) and playful river dolphins. There are also anacondas and piranhas in the rivers of Beni, but neither should be disturbed, handled or fished, since it's imperative that their environment is left intact for their survival.

Botanical Beauties

The wealth of Bolivia's altitudes means that there is a wealth and diversity of flora and endemic species.

The globally threatened Polylepis shrubs, which grow on the Altiplano, form dense, low forests at altitudes of up to 5300m, making them the highest growing arborescent plants in the world. Much of the vegetation in the highlands grows slowly and is endangered, because of overgrazing.

The less harsh highland hills and valleys, such as the area around Samaipata, are particularly rich in endemic plants, thanks to the more temperate climate of that region. Here one can find the the world's highest growing palm, the gigantic Bolivian mountain coconut (Parajubaea torallyi).

The Yungas are characterised by lush dwarf forest, which is suitable for growing tropical plants and produce such as coffee and coca. Across the slopes of the cloud forest, the trees grow larger and the vegetation gets thicker, until they turn into the rainforest that covers so much of the humid lowlands. The rainforest is punctuated with vast wetlands and cerrado savannahs – no fewer than 895 plants only grow here, including 16 species of passion-fruit vines and at least three genera of orchids.

The Flames of El Chaqueo

All this natural beauty faces many dangers in our modern world, and one of the particular and consistent issues is posed by the annual fire setting, locally known as *el chaqueo.*

El chaqueo takes place every year between July and September, when farmers slash and burn the savannahs and some forest for the purposes of agriculture and grazing. While some justify this destructive practice with their belief that smoke from the fires transforms into rain clouds, in reality the clouds are formed by the release of water vapour produced by the forest canopy, and not due to fire. As global warming turns the dry season longer and drier each year, these fires engulf increasingly vast areas, growing beyond control and devastating parts of the rainforest – 2024 brought some of the worst fires the Amazon Basin has yet seen. This fire-setting harms wildlife and local life as well as the forest, also ruining the hydrological cycle and aggravating respiratory issues among Bolivians.

Gateway of the Sun, Tiwanaku (p71)

INCA VS TIWANAKU

Centuries before the Inca arrived in modern day Bolivia, another ancient civilization burned brightly on the shores of Lake Titicaca. By Joe Sills

THE MORNING AIR is thin in Tiwanaku, whispering over the smooth, red stones of an empire that predated the Incas by centuries. It's the wet season, and this otherwise stark landscape is alive with blooming, purple thistles and yellow butterflies. A pair of seagulls float over the handful of tourists taking selfies in front of the Gate of the Sun, Bolivia's 'Eiffel Tower,' in the distance.

Standing before the Bennett Monolith – an imposing figure of red sandstone rising over 23ft into the sky – you feel the weight of an ancient civilization pressing down through time. Its blank stare seems fixed towards the past, towards a people who once ruled the highlands of Bolivia and many of the places associated with the Inca today.

Centuries after its decline, much of Tiwanaku's story remains a mystery. Where did its people go? Why did they leave?

The tourists shuffle between the stone walls, whispering theories about extraterrestrial landings and a return to far-off galaxies, but the truth of Tiwanaku's peak and decline lies less in science fiction theories and more in the foundation it laid for the Inca Empire that followed.

Tiwanaku was the cultural and spiritual heart of the Andean world long before the Incas expanded their rule, reaching its peak between 500 and 900 CE. The Inca wouldn't follow suit for another 600 years.

By the 15th century, the Inca commanded a vast stretch of South America reaching from Ecuador to Chile. After Francisco Pizzaro landed in Peru in 1526, monks chronicling Spanish expeditions assumed all of the advanced architecture they saw in the Andes was created by the Inca. But Tiwanaku's influence had already rippled across the Andes more than a millennium before the Spanish language ever reached these valleys. And the Inca had already incorporated many Tiwanku motifs into their own society.

Advanced Agriculture & Engineering

Unlike the Incas, who ruled through military conquest and rigid bureaucracy, the Tiwanaku thrived on trade, engineering and religious devotion. They weren't just warriors or conquerors; they were architects of one of the most advanced agricultural systems of the ancient world, taming the harsh climate of the Altiplano with raised-field farming, known as sukakollus, and harnessing a system of terraced fields that still surround Lake Titicaca.

The Tiwanaku knew about weather patterns such as El Niño and La Niña. They created microclimates on sukakollus to cultivate crops at a rate that is 20 times more efficient than many techniques today. And they freeze-dried potatoes cultivated in those fields on glacial peaks in the Royal Andean range, using them as insurance against drought and floods.

Even today, the Aymara descendants of Tiwanaku sow the same fields. And travelers can canter through many of them at places such as Isla Del Sol carefree.

The Tiwanaku were the original masters of monolithic construction in the Andes. Their masons quarried massive stones, some weighing more than 100 tons, and transported them across miles of unforgiving terrain to construct pyramids, courtyards and subterranean representations of the underworld that the Inca would later adopt.

The precision of their stonework – complete with interlocking blocks and intricate drainage systems – suggests a level of knowledge that rivaled, and perhaps even surpassed, that of their Incan successors. Tiwanaku's poured concrete is a match for that of ancient Rome.

Tiwanaku's Influence on the Inca

When the Incas expanded into Bolivia centuries later, they did not conquer Tiwanaku; they inherited its remnants, folding its legacy into their own grand narrative. It was from Isla del Sol that Manco Capac and Mama Ocllo emerged to found Cusco. And while the island's modern trek to its ancient temples is named for the Inca, the temples themselves trace their origins to Tiwanaku.

Beyond its engineering feats, Tiwanaku was also a spiritual epicenter, a place where religion and governance intertwined. The city itself was designed as a cosmological map, with the Kalasasaya temple aligning perfectly with the solstices and the Gateway of the Sun displaying celestial motifs that suggest a deep understanding of the heavens. These would later give rise to theories of extraterrestrial contact and an ancient space port at the Puma Punku complex, not far from the ceremonial center of Tiwanaku itself.

The Incas, for all their grandeur, borrowed heavily from this legacy. Their veneration of Inti, the sun god, echoes the solar reverence seen in Tiwanaku, and their sacred city of Cusco, designed in the shape of a puma, reflects a similar cosmic consciousness. But where the Incas consolidated power under the divine rule of the Sapa Inca, researchers believe Tiwanaku to have been more communal, its society built upon a network of regional elites rather than a single emperor's decree.

However, the starkest contrast between the two civilizations may lie in their declines.

The Incas fell swiftly, undone by Spanish steel, disease, and the internal fractures of civil war. Tiwanaku, however, faded over time. The empire's downfall came not from foreign invaders, but from a changing climate that finally outlasted their agricultural ingenuity – a lesson particularly relevant to travelers navigating a time of climate change today.

Prolonged drought strangled Tiwanaku's agricultural heart, forcing its people to disperse, leaving behind the silent stones that laid buried in the sand when archaeologists began to unravel their secrets in the early 20th century. Today, Tiwanaku remains a symbol of resilience and mystery, overshadowed by the more famous Incan sites of Peru, but no less significant.

Standing before the Bennett Monolith, staring into the face of a forgotten god, you can almost hear the echoes of a world that shaped the one to come in this place. Tiwanaku was not just a precursor to the Incas – it was the foundation upon which their empire was built.

INDEX

Map Pages **000**

M

Map Pages **000**

Map Pages **000**

Take in the 360-degree panoramic from Convento de San Felipe Neri's (p205) rooftop.

Explore a memento mori to civilizations past, and the nearest thing Bolivia has to Peru's Machu, at Incallajta (p198).

Mapping data sources:
© Lonely Planet
© OpenStreetMap http://openstreetmap.org/copyright

FROM LEFT: STREETFLASH/SHUTTERSTOCK, JANEK/ISTOCK/GETTY IMAGES PLUS

THIS BOOK

Destination Editor
Alicia Johnson

Production Editor
Ursula O'Sullivan-Dale

Image Editor
Clara Monitto

Cartographer
Julie Dodkins

Coordinating Editor
Michael MacKenzie

Assisting Editors
Kevin Ebbutt, Natalie Butler, Fionnuala Twomey, Melanie Dankel

Cover Researcher
Marc Blackwell

Thanks Fergal Condon, Karen Henderson, Gwen Cotter, Alison Killilea, María Virginia Moreno, Sofie Anderson, James Appleton, Ronan Abayawickrema, Saralinda Turner, Boris Alarcon, Ricardo Quintaza, Erika Palacios, Ernesto Vaca, Heidy Rivera Z., Carola Castro, Regis Viveros, Vane Pizarro

Paper in this book is certified against the Forest Stewardship Council™ standards. FSC™ promotes environmentally responsible, socially beneficial and economically viable management of the world's forests.

Published by Lonely Planet Global Limited
CRN 554153
11th edition – Oct 2025
ISBN 978 1 78868 426 2

10 9 8 7 6 5 4 3 2 1
Printed in China